How Children Think and Learn

Second Edition

Understanding Children's Worlds
Series Editor: Judy Dunn

The study of children's development can have a profound influence on how children are brought up, cared for and educated. Many psychologists argue that, even if our knowledge is incomplete, we have a responsibility to attempt to help those concerned with the care, education and study of children by making what we know available to them. The central aim of this series is to encourage developmental psychologists to set out the findings and the implications of their research for others - teachers, doctors, social workers, students and fellow researchers – whose work involves the care, education and study of young children and their families. The information and the ideas that have grown from recent research form an important resource which should be available to them. This series provides an opportunity for psychologists to present their work in a way that is interesting, intelligible and substantial, and to discuss what its consequences may be for those who care for, and teach children: not to offer simple prescriptive advice to other professionals, but to make important and innovative research accessible to them.

Children doing Mathematics
Terezhina Nunes and Peter Bryant

Children and Emotion
Paul L. Harris

Bullying at School
Dan Olweus

How Children Think and Learn, 2nd edition
David Wood

Making Decisions about Children, 2nd edition
H. Rudolph Schaffer

Children's Talk in Communities and Classrooms
Lynne Vernon-Feagans

Children and Political Violence
Ed Cairns

The Work of the Imagination
Paul Harris

Changing Families
Jan Pryor and Bryan Rodgers

How Children Think and Learn

The Social Contexts of Cognitive Development

SECOND EDITION

David Wood

Blackwell
Publishing

BLACKWELL PUBLISHING
350 Main Street, Malden, MA 02148-5020, USA
9600 Garsington Road, Oxford OX4 2DQ, UK
550 Swanston Street, Carlton, Victoria 3053, Australia

First published 1988
Second Edition 1998

10   2006

Library of Congress Cataloging-in-Publication Data

Wood, David J.
  How children think and learn : the social contexts of cognitive
development/David Wood.—2nd ed.
      p.   cm.—(Understanding children's worlds)
  Includes bibliographical references and index.
  ISBN 0-631-20007-X (pbk. : alk. paper)
    1. Cognition in children. 2. Learning, Psychology of. I. Title.
II. Series.
BF723.C5W66   1998
155.4'13—dc21   97–22303
                                                          CIP

ISBN-13: 978-0-631-20007-9 (pbk. : alk. paper)

A catalogue record for this title is available from the British Library.

Set in 10 on 12 pt Sabon
by Ace Filmsetting Ltd, Frome, Somerset
Printed and bound in Singapore by
Markono Print Media Pte Ltd

The publisher's policy is to use permanent paper from mills that operate a sustainable
forestry policy, and which has been manufactured from pulp processed using
acid-free and elementary chlorine-free practices. Furthermore, the publisher ensures
that the text paper and cover board used have met acceptable environmental
accreditation standards.

For further information on
Blackwell Publishing, visit our website:
www.blackwellpublishing.com

I dedicate this book, with greetings and gratitude, to Jerome S. Bruner

Contents

Series editor's preface   xi

Preface to the second edition   xii

Acknowledgements   xiv

Introduction: From Pavlov to Piaget . . . a round trip?   1

    Changing perspectives on learning and development   2
    Learning and instruction   8
    Uncertainty and information   11

1 Images of childhood and their reflection in teaching   15

    Learning and schooling   15
    From five to eleven   18
    Thought as internalized action   21
    Piaget's approach to language and cognition   24
    Vygotsky: instruction and intelligence   26
    Piaget and Vygotsky on talking and thinking   27
    Processing information: on becoming an expert   31
    Piaget, Vygotsky and Bruner: a brief comparison and summary 37

2 A decade of development (maturation and learning!)   40

    The impact of Vygotskian thinking   40
    Neo-Piagetian theory   43
    Information processing: mental models and expertise   44
    Mental modules and maturation   45
    Time to synthesize?   49

3 Are there stages of development?   51

Appearance and reality in the development of
understanding   52
Two key Piagetian terms: assimilation and accommodation   53
More technicalities: centration, disequilibrium and
de-centring   54
A critique of Piaget's theory   59
Part of Piaget's legacy   68
Discontinuities in development?   69
Drawing inferences from mental models   70
Summary   72

4 Learning how to think and learn   73

Attending, concentrating and remembering   74
A pause for review   80
Memory and schooling   80
Paying attention   82
Wholes and parts: theories of perception and understanding   89
Experience, expertise and explanation   91
Drawing inferences: logic and memory   93
What is effective instruction? First thoughts   97
The zone of proximal development   97
Learning and instruction as shared information processing   102
Rules of the mind   103
Learning and generalization: first thoughts on a thorny issue   108

5 Language and learning   110

Bernstein's analysis: restricted codes and elaborated codes   111
Bernstein's theory and educational politics   113
The Chomskian 'revolution'   115
Language acquisition and the LAD   120
Meaning and 'structure dependency'   122
Some examples of the early stages of language development   123
Language: discontinuity and change   124
Language learning: one process or many?   125
Deixis: words that 'point'   129
Teach yourself language?   131
Re-organization and representational re-description   136
Educability: some first thoughts   138
Summary   140

6 Making sense   144

Non-verbal and verbal communication   144
From home to school: conversation and narrative   150
Telling stories: four to ten   153
Representational re-description re-visited   157
Language and cognition (again!)   159
Pause for reflection   165
Information–giving   167
Classroom 'registers': means to ends   173
Summary   178

7 The literate mind   181

Logic, literacy and reasoning?   182
Thinking in childhood and adolescence   186
Logicism   190
Logic and reasoning   195
Language in talk and text   200
The written and the spoken word: learning to read   202
Writing, planning and self-regulation   208
The eleven to thirteen shift: a linguistic perspective   210
Becoming literate   213
Spelling and syntax   216
Self-regulation and reading comprehension   220
Conclusions   222

8 The mathematical mind   225

Part I: Theory and research into mathematics learning   226
Counting and one-to-one correspondence   229
Counting: out, on, up and down!   230
Cardinal knowledge   235
Derived number understanding   236
Addition and subtraction as models for situations   237
Pause for reflection and review   239
Multiplication and division: some beginnings   240
Sharing, splitting and dividing   242
Dividing and division: parts and wholes   245
New kinds of numbers   247
Understanding written numbers: base, place and space   250
Language variation: reading, writing and using numbers   254
Mathematics in school and community   255

Part 2: Theory and practice   257
Children's achievements and problems in mathematics   257
Mathematical abilities and mathematical misconceptions   258
Instruction, interview and dialogue   262
Learning and teaching mathematics: why is it all so hard?   265
Language, instruction and self-regulation   269
Maths and culture   272
Concluding comments   273

9 Education and educability   **276**

Theories of psychology and practices of education   277
One intelligence or many?   279
Effort and ability   282
Attending and concentrating   283
Effort, ability and motivation: the social dimension   286
Theory to practice: a hard road?   288
Theory, technology and teaching   291
Concluding comment   295

Bibliography   **296**

Index   **308**

Series Editor's Preface

In this new edition of his splendid book, David Wood takes us through the various images of childhood presented by the key developmental theorists and explores the new ideas, research and practical lessons for teachers that have emerged from these theories in the last decade. He steers us through the ideas of Vygotsky, the neo-Piagetians and 'neo-nativists' and brings these very different approaches together in a helpful synthesis. He highlights the challenges to cognitive theorists posed by recent research, emphasizing the ways in which children's thinking and learning are grounded in social situations. Within his social constructivist framework, he examines the most recent ideas on children's language acquisition, on the development of children's ability to make sense of others, on literacy and cultural context. And he gives us an extensive and timely consideration of the conceptual developments involved in children's understanding of the foundations of mathematics. In his important last chapter he tackles the key challenge of understanding *individual differences* in children's achievements and experiences at school. Why do some children struggle and fail at school? Why is it so hard to relate the encouraging findings of cognitive research to the world of the classroom? Throughout the book, the implications for educational practice of the most recent studies are drawn to our attention, and the central importance of understanding children's conceptual development if we are to help them learn is exposed.

Preface to the Second Edition

The first edition of this book appeared ten years ago. Anyone who has attempted to maintain a broad view of progress within developmental psychology will appreciate the vigour with which both theoretical and empirical issues have been pursued in the discipline during the intervening decade. We have seen both increasing theoretical divergence and some serious attempts at theoretical synthesis. The rise of 'neo-nativist' theories has motivated research which has led to a much greater appreciation of the inborn capacities of the human infant and the role of maturation in development. This, in turn, has created many challenges for 'classical' cognitive developmental theorists who seek to attribute to experience what nativist theories claim for inborn abilities. At the same time, research from a quite different theoretical tradition has also challenged cognitive theory on the grounds that learning and knowledge are much more 'situated' in everyday experience than such theories proposed. Cognitive theory, it is claimed, locates too much processing in the mind and too little in the physical and social situation within which learning takes place. Some psychologists within the cognitivist camp have responded to these challenges by extending their own theoretical frameworks in an attempt to encompass and integrate elements of maturation and socio-cultural considerations within a developmental account of psychological growth.

Thus, although the major 'images' of childhood around which I organized the first edition are still with us, they have undergone a number of important modifications and extensions. These will be a major focus of this new edition.

Anyone who has been in this field for any time will realize that it is impossible to do justice to all of the theory and research that is relevant to a book like this one. I have had to be selective and realize that I have left out much of merit. As I did in the first edition, I concentrate mainly on ideas and issues, using illustrative examples from research in an attempt to make these accessible to newcomers to the field.

Much of what I wrote in the first edition remains, though this book is about 20 per cent longer than its predecessor. I have left the historical sections of the book pretty well untouched since I found no reason to re-write my own view of the past. I have added a new, overview chapter (ch. 2) in which I try to outline some of the major developments that have occurred over the past decade. I have also amended the ensuing chapters to discuss these developments in relation to the substantive topics addressed in each. The chapter on mathematics is almost completely re-worked and much longer than that in the first edition. The main reason for this is my own sense of excitement about the advances that have been made in this area, both in our theoretical understanding and in our knowledge of children's understanding. These advances have also led to some important new ideas about how mathematics teaching might be improved. In the last chapter, which has also been revised considerably, I have included a short section on educational technology and its relation to the major theories of learning and development considered in the book.

I think this edition may be less easy to read and understand than the first one. I excuse myself by claiming that the thinking of researchers in the field has become conceptually more subtle. Further, attempts to create more integrative and over-arching theories also means that a wider and more varied literature has had to be consulted and summarized than was the case a decade ago. However, I hope that, though difficult, the ideas presented are accessible. Time will tell.

David Wood, Nottingham.

Acknowledgements

Peter Bryant, Judy Dunn,. Terezinha Nunes and Peter Robinson each read a draft of this edition and provided many constructive comments. I hope that my response to their input has led to a more informed and accessible book and am only sorry that I lacked the wit, time and space to respond constructively to all of their suggestions. I would also like to thank both Jane Hammond Foster and Heather Wood, each of whom read draft chapters and put a good deal of time and effort into framing detailed comments and suggestions for textual improvements. Finally, I am grateful to the staff at Blackwell for their guidance and support in the planning and preparation of this second Edition.

The author and publishers gratefully acknowledge the following for permission to reproduce copyright material: figure 2.4: from Margaret Donaldson (1978) *Children's Minds*, William Collins & Co. Ltd and W. W. Norton & Company, Inc; figures 3.1, 3.2, 3.5: from E. Vurpillot (1976) *The Visual World of the Child*, International Universities Press, Inc.: figure 4.1: from J. Bruner and A. Garton (eds) (1978) *Human Growth and Development*, Oxford University Press, based on Clark & Garnica (1974) *Journal of Verbal Learning and Verbal Behavior*, no 13; figure 4.2: from A. Karmiloff-Smith (1979) *A Functional Approach to Child Language*, Cambridge University Press; figure 7.4: from K. M. Hart (1981) *Children's Understanding of Mathematics*: 11–16, John Murray (Publishers) Ltd.

The publishers apologize for any errors or omissions in the above list and would be grateful to be notified of any corrections that should be incorporated in the next edition or reprint of this book.

Introduction

From Pavlov to Piaget . . . a round trip?

Theories about how children think and learn have been put forward and debated by philosophers, educators and psychologists for centuries. E. B. Castle in his book *The Teacher*, for example, explores the historical influences that have helped to shape modern views about children and their growth into adults and citizens. He traces back to Ancient Greece, Rome and Judea competing views on the nature of learning and education that are still debated today. He also discusses the way in which ideas about the nature of infancy and childhood dictate the ways in which we think about teaching and education. Our images of children-as-learners are reflected, inevitably, in our definition of what it means to teach.

In this book, I will be describing and discussing theories about learning and thinking that have been formulated and explored over the past twenty-five years or so. However, it is important to recognize the fact that contemporary thinking about education, learning and teaching is not 'brand new' or untouched by the work of previous generations of scholars and teachers. Their ideas and insights have been absorbed and transformed over time and translated into modern terms, not eradicated. Although I have chosen to focus on recent developments, mainly for reasons of space, I will try in this chapter to give a brief overview of how and why certain theories of human development, particularly that of Jean Piaget, became prominent and influential in the mid-1960s. I begin with what seem to me to be some of the more important 'landmark' discoveries and observations that have helped to shape contemporary theories of human nature.

Changing perspectives on learning and development

Throughout the 1960s and 1970s, our thinking about the nature of children's thinking and learning was dominated by the ideas of Jean Piaget. The seventies in particular were marked by an extensive international research effort designed to test out the implications of his theory. As we shall see in chapter 1 and indeed throughout the book, this revealed the main strengths and weaknesses of his ideas and laid the foundations for a new generation of 'neo-Piagetian' theories which have emerged and, in turn, been tested over the past decade. It should come as no surprise, then, to find frequent references to his theory in this book. Although not an educationalist, nor primarily a psychologist, Piaget's astute observations of children and his extensive theorizing about what these have to tell us about the growth of mind can hardly be ignored in a book about children's learning and thinking. And yet, and this is perhaps surprising, Piaget's theory was neglected for many years, at least by English-speaking psychologists. Although his first works were translated into English in the 1940s, it was not until the mid-1960s that they were given serious consideration by the majority of American and British psychologists.

The rise of learning theory

In a book that he edited in 1964, *Theories of Learning and Instruction*, the American psychologist E. Hilgard predicted that Piaget's views, neglected for twenty years or so, were destined to achieve prominence thereafter. How right he was. But why was the theory neglected for so long, and what was happening in the 1960s that brought it onto centre stage? Well, the major theories and debates that figured in Hilgard's book and had dominated the psychology of learning for several decades were of such a nature that they effectively ruled out any serious consideration of the ideas that Piaget was putting forward. For example, a great deal of thought, time and study had been given to analysing the nature of 'reinforcement' and its role in learning and instruction. Ivan Pavlov, a Russian physiologist and psychologist, had demonstrated in 1927 that it was possible, using quite simple experimental techniques, to teach an animal to make novel 'responses' to new 'stimuli'. For example, given sight of food, a hungry dog will, naturally, salivate. Normally, a 'neutral' stimulus, say the sound of a bell ringing, will have no such effect on the beast. However, if on a number of occasions the bell is made to ring just *before* food is presented to an animal, its sound alone will come, eventually, to evoke the salivation response. From this apparently simple observation grew several different theories of learning.

Psychologists in many parts of the world attempted to discover general *laws* that would lead eventually to a scientific theory of learning. Such theories, and there are several, are usually referred to as 'S–R' ('Stimulus–Response') or 'learning theory'. Pavlov's experimental demonstrations of animal learning were replicated many thousands of times with different species, focusing on a wide variety of behavioural responses that were conditioned to many types of stimuli and 'reinforced' in a multitude of different ways. Although several alternatives to Pavlov's theory arose out of this research, most shared the same quest: to formulate laws whereby, irrespective of the species, stimuli, responses or reinforcer used, the relations between the *conditions* of learning (e.g. when and how often a response to a given stimulus was reinforced) and the learning *outcomes* could be predicted. To give but one example, one of the most influential American psychologists, B. F. Skinner (e.g. 1938) demonstrated in many experiments that the best way to guarantee that an animal learns how to make a particular response to a stimulus is *not* to give it reinforcement every time it performs the response. The secret to rapid and enduring learning is what Skinner termed an intermittent *schedule* of reinforcement. His experiments showed that the key to effective teaching (a process that he referred to as 'shaping behaviour') involves only the occasional reinforcement of the desired response. So, for instance, if a hungry rat is being taught to press a lever, only some of the presses should deliver a pellet of food. The experimenter's aim should also be to withdraw reinforcement as quickly as possible.

Basically, what Skinner has shown is that shaping an animal's behaviour to ensure that it maintains the response (that is, it continues to make the response whenever it meets the appropriate stimulus) involves a specific and rather complex relationship between response and reinforcement. It is not simply a case of rewarding behaviour every time it occurs. When Skinner applied his findings on animal learning to the teaching of children, it led him to criticize teachers for not employing effective 'schedules of reinforcement' in the classroom. In 'Why teachers fail', a chapter of his 1968 book, he argued that formal education is usually based on 'aversive control'. Teaching rests on punishment and ridicule for inappropriate behaviour, rather than showing a concern for the shaping and reinforcement of responses to be learned. He also claimed that lessons and examinations are designed to reveal what pupils do not know and cannot do, rather than to expose and build upon what they do know and are able to learn. Thus, he argued, teachers fail to 'shape' their children's behaviour effectively, leading to inappropriate learning or to learned responses that are quickly forgotten. Skinner went on to design the first 'learning programs' for use on teaching machines in an attempt to apply his theory to education.

Skinner's observations led to a vast technology of experimental studies of learning. Many different reinforcement schedules were designed, and their effects on the speed of learning and on the retention of what was learned were tested out. Such investigations of learning and arguments about the nature of reinforcement – e.g. what *constitutes* a reinforcer for a given species – were at the heart of theory and research in the period between Pavlov's pioneering work and Hilgard's review of the field in the mid-1960s.

The decline of learning theory

Part of the appeal of these approaches to the study of learning was the promise they offered of formulating theories that dealt only with directly *observable* and *manipulable* phenomena. By creating accounts concerned exclusively with 'objective' relationships between conditions of learning and observable responses it was hoped that a science of behaviour could be constructed that needed to make no appeal to 'subjective' mental states such as 'interest' or 'curiosity'.

Many of the contributors to Hilgard's volume had come to the conclusion that this general approach to the study of learning and the many seemingly intractable problems that it was facing was ceasing to be productive or profitable. The reasons for the rise in scepticism and a search for new concepts and methods were many, varied and complicated. We will not explore them in detail here. However, I will give a few examples to help to explain why the psychological territory of the time proved fertile to Piaget's ideas.

In one of the chapters in Hilgard's book, Pribram, an American psychologist, makes favourable reference to Piaget's theory and attempts to integrate some of its insights with his own ideas. Pribram had undertaken a number of research studies into animal learning. He cites observations which helped to convince him that external reinforcement was *not* a necessary condition for learning, thus questioning the very foundations of the then dominant theories of learning and instruction.

In one study, for instance, a monkey was being conditioned to operate a bit of machinery that, when a lever was pulled, delivered a reinforcing peanut on an intermittent basis. The animal was left free to operate the lever for as long as it so 'desired'. When a reinforcer appeared, the monkey would often 'store' it in its food pouch (located inside the mouth). It did not, then, always consume the peanut after a 'reinforced' response. Occasionally, when no peanut appeared after a pull on the lever, the animal would take a peanut from its pouch and eat it. In so doing, it reinforced itself after a supposedly non-reinforcing trial (thus somewhat defeating the psychologist's attempt to put it on a specific, pre-determined schedule!). As the experiment continued, there came a point at which the animal's food pouch was fully stuffed and its cheeks bulged to capacity. Despite being satiated and, hence, unlikely to profit from further 'reinforcement', it continued to operate the lever. Hands and feet stuffed with peanuts, the monkey began to chuck nuts out of the cage but still operated the lever to gain more.

Such observations led Pribram and many other psychologists of his time to question the assumption that external reinforcement of the sort implicated in some theories of learning was a necessary condition for learning to take place. One could speculate about Pribram's monkey in several ways. Perhaps the animal continued to operate the equipment not for nutritional gains but more for the 'pleasure' of playing with it. Was it trying to 'outwit' the schedule, like a gambler, by attempting to work out the 'rules' governing payoff? Whatever the reason, it seemed to Pribram that the *activity* itself held some *intrinsic* interest for the animal.

Piaget's theory, as we shall see, places *action* and self-directed problem-solving at the heart of learning and development. By acting on the world, the learner comes to discover how to control it. In human beings, learning how to act on the world and discovering the consequences of action form the bedrock of thinking itself. As psychologists studying learning began to entertain (or, more accurately, to re-entertain) ideas about intrinsic motivation and the importance of activity and mastery for its 'own sake', Piaget's theory provided a compatible and already well-developed approach to the study of learning and development. The time was right for the theory to be taken seriously.

Piaget's theory also seemed to provide answers to several other difficult problems. For instance, many references are found in Hilgard to the phenomenon of 'critical periods' for learning. Whilst animals and humans are able to learn some things with little effort at certain points in their life cycle, they seem incapable of learning the same things at other times. So, for example, learning to walk and, as we shall see, learning to talk, seem to follow a natural time-scale. Attempts to teach very young children to talk, for instance, will fail. Once 'ready', however, they seem to learn how to talk 'naturally' and without any deliberate or conscious teaching by adults. If exposure to a language is left late, say into puberty, the nature of any learning that takes place is of a different kind. Learning a second language involves psychologically different processes from those which make mother-tongue acquisition possible. Piaget's theory, as we shall see, offers a detailed and specific account of universal *stages* in human development which provide a possible explanation as to when and how a child is ready to learn or develop specific forms of knowledge and understanding. Attempts to teach the products of a 'later' stage before previous stages have been passed through cannot facilitate development, nor can it foster understanding. So, Piaget's theory offered a 'ready made' explanation for critical periods in the development of human intelligence: its time had arrived.

Although Hilgard anticipated the surge of interest in Piaget's theory, he was not in a position to envisage the directions that debates and arguments about it would take. Indeed, many of the specific issues that have grown up around the theory find no mention in Hilgard's bibliography or index. One central theme that you will find running through the chapters of my book concerns the nature of the relationship between talking and thinking. Although 'verbal behavior' is listed in Hilgard's index, the term 'language', and related words like 'talking' and 'listening', are not mentioned. This was a sign of the times. Psychologists interested in learning had, it seems, yet to read or to digest the early works of Noam Chomsky, an American linguist. These started to appear in print in the late 1950s. They were to inflict a serious, some would say lethal, blow to learning-theory accounts of how children learn their 'verbal behaviour'. Indeed, Chomsky's theory led some students of language development to reject the idea that children are *taught* how to talk at all, as we will see in chapter 5.

Piaget and Chomsky were united in their opposition to the view that human learning can be understood in terms of the reinforcement of connections between stimuli and responses, but offer very different perspectives on the nature of language and its development. Briefly, for we will look at the issue at greater length in later chapters, Piaget's theory leads to the claim that a child's ability to understand what is said to him and, in turn, his ability to use language informatively, depends upon his stage of intellectual development. This view leads to a number of *explicit* predictions about when children *can* learn how to talk and, when they do so, what they will understand by what they say and hear. Young children's understanding of terms like 'if . . . then', 'as much as', 'the same as', 'more than' and 'because', for example, differ from the meaning put upon them by older children and adults. At a deeper level, the theory also predicts that young children at certain stages of development are theoretically incapable of *expressing* ideas that involve the ability to understand the world from another person's point of view. What they are able to say is constrained by their stage of development. Chomskian theorists, on the other hand, argue that the course of specifically *linguistic* development, like the child's use and understanding of *grammar*, cannot be understood simply in terms of stages of intellectual development, nor in terms of communication skills. The child, in this view, possesses a natural capacity to discover how language is structured. Language development is a 'special' affair and cannot be explained in terms of the child's general knowledge of the world. This seemingly remote and academic argument, as I hope to demonstrate later in the book, has important implications for the way in which we view children's abilities to think, learn and understand.

Another important series of questions and issues that received no mention in Hilgard's book, but which have since achieved great significance, also revolve around arguments about the nature of language and its role in learning and education. In the 1960s, the USA was, as it remains today, a multi-cultural and multi-lingual society. However, students of learning had yet to address the many important questions this state of affairs raises for education and teaching. In the UK, Basil Bernstein (1960), a sociologist, was about to announce what was to become an influential and controversial thesis about the relations between socio-economic class and language. He put forward the view that differences in the average levels of academic achievement attained by children from different home backgrounds can be understood and explained in terms of the ways in which language is used and structured in different social groups. Children from diverse social groups learn how to use and understand language in different ways. Such linguistic differences affect adjustment to, communication in, and learning at, school. Seizing upon these ideas, educational theorists and researchers in the USA extended them to provide 'explanations' as to why American black children fared less well in school, on average, than their white peers. This, as we will see in chapter 5, was to have a dramatic effect on political action in both the USA and the UK as both societies attempted to ensure greater equality of opportunity for less well-off children by state action designed, amongst other things, to overcome 'linguistic deprivation'. Here too, academic debate about the relation between language and thought, largely ignored until the late 1960s, spilled over into heated educational and political debate. Bernstein's ideas were also destined to come into conflict with those expressed by Chomsky and other linguists. Is it really the case that some children fail to 'learn' language as some American theorists seemed to suppose? If children acquire language naturally, as Chomskians argue, is it theoretically sound to assume that some families 'deprive' their children of language? Such assertions, from a Chomskian perspective, are literally nonsensical. We consider the arguments, and their educational implications, in chapters 5 and 9.

Learning and instruction

Piaget wrote very little about the educational implications of his theory. However, the idea that children pass through stages of development, and the assertion that they cannot learn or be taught how to function at 'higher' levels before they have passed through the lower ones, were taken up widely and formed the basis for a new theory of learning *readiness*. Many psychologists and educators (e.g. Schwebel and Raph, 1974) explored the educational ramifications of Piaget's theory and transformed it into curricula, approaches to teaching and a whole philosophy of education. Developmental theory was *en route* to educational practice. J. S. Bruner, one of the American psychologists who contributed to Hilgard's book, was also beginning to formulate a theory of instruction which, though similar in some respects to Piaget's views, differed radically from them in a number of other ways, particularly in relation to the notion of developmental stages. Perhaps the different perspectives are best introduced with a very brief account of the intellectual background and motivation of these two theorists.

Piaget and Bruner

Piaget's academic roots lay in biology. As a teenager, for instance, he had undertaken and published the results of experiments on mollusc growth which gained him international acclaim (Boden, 1979) and an invitation to become curator of a museum in Switzerland! His main quest, which motivated his studies of children, was to create an integrated theory of biology and philosophy of mind. For reasons we explore later, he went on to explain the evolution of mind and intelligence in terms of the development and realization of *logic*. He also sought common principles that would establish a theoretical continuity between biological and mental evolution and would help us to understand the origins and development of logical, mathematical and scientific thought. Though he studied the thinking and understanding of children and adolescents in breadth and depth, he did not, as far as I know, conduct any extensive or systematic studies of adult thinking. What he did do, however, was to provide explanations to mathematicians and natural scientists about the genetic and developmental foundations of their theories. For example, he lectured to physicists on the relation between time, velocity and distance and suggested that by looking at the formation of these concepts in children, they might understand how their own formal concepts of time and space evolved and discover their 'primitive' intellectual foundations. His views on concepts of time and space motivated Einstein to ask him if the origins of the theory of relativity could be understood in developmental terms. This question, according to Boden, led to theoretical work by Piaget's physicist colleagues who provided such an account.

Some of Bruner's early research was concerned with the study and analysis of adult reasoning. Working with others (Bruner, Goodnow and Austin, 1956) he undertook a series of experimental studies which convinced him that people do not utilize a single 'method' or 'logic' in reasoning and problem-solving: instead they adopt one of a number of *strategies* that differ in scope, power and efficiency. Whereas Piaget was interested primarily in the *structure* of mature thinking, Bruner sought to describe the different *processes* that are implicated in creative problem-solving. Such processes, in Bruner's view, vary from individual to individual and from discipline to discipline (e.g. Bruner, 1966a, 1971).

The similarities between the two theories are, however, of equal interest. Both place emphasis on the importance of *action* and problem-solving in learning. They also adopt a similar position with regard to the different ways in which knowledge can be 'represented' or embodied, as we will see in chapter 8. Abstract thinking, in both accounts, should grow out of, be abstracted *from*, material actions. From both perspectives, teaching that teaches children only how to manipulate abstract procedures (e.g. learning how to solve equations) without first establishing the deep connections between such procedures and the activities involved in the solution of practical, concrete problems (which the procedures serve to represent at a more abstract level) is bound to fail. Children will only *understand* and generalize lessons about abstract mathematics, for example, if these are grounded in practical problem-solving. Where the two theories part company is in relation to the value of formal *logic* as a description of the ultimate 'destination' of intellectual development. Bruner argues that logic is not the basis for mature, adaptive thinking; rather, it is one of several 'special' ways of thinking. The rejection of logic as a framework for understanding the nature and development of thinking leads on to many other points of disagreement.

Another aspect of Bruner's psychology, in comparison to Piaget's, is a greater emphasis on the role of language, communication and instruction in the development of knowledge and understanding. For Bruner, the *processes* that underlie intelligent and adaptive thinking are not exclusive inventions of the child. Rather, they are *communicated*, albeit in subtle ways, from the more mature to the immature. Whilst Piaget does provide a role for social interaction and communication in his theory, it plays a far less important part in the development of intelligence than it does in Bruner's account. Another major theme, perhaps the main one, that permeates this book is a discussion of these proposed relations between instruction, communication, learning and thinking. Different theories about the character of these relationships lead to radically different views on the nature and the importance of teaching in development, as we shall see.

Vygotsky and Bruner

Two years before Hilgard's book was published, Bruner had written an introduction to a book entitled *Thought and Language,* a translation of a work first written in 1934 by a Soviet psychologist, L. S. Vygotsky. Like Bruner and quite unlike Piaget, Vygotsky also placed *instruction* at the very heart of human development. Indeed, he defined intelligence itself as the capacity to *learn* through instruction. Vygotsky's views received no mention in Hilgard. Indeed, the assimilation of his thinking into Western psychology has been slow. With a few exceptions, like Bruner (and Piaget), students of human learning and thinking made little reference to his ideas. During the past decade, however, his influence on psychological thinking worldwide has been considerable. One 'landmark' event in the introduction of his ideas to the West was the publication in 1984 of a book edited by James Wertsch. This was dedicated to the exploration of Vygotsky's perspectives on human development and included chapters by American, European and Soviet contributors. I will refer to some of its content later in the book.

Vygotsky's thinking on development is difficult to summarize in a few words. Let me make a few preliminary comments here to provide some sense of the directions in which his approach points us. Like Bruner, who was influenced by him, Vygotsky puts language and communication (and, hence, instruction) at the core of intellectual and personal development. What is unique about Vygotsky's account is its scope and its philosophical foundations. Unlike Piaget, with a background in biology and natural sciences, Vygotsky's primary concern lay in understanding the nature, evolution and transmission of human culture. His early work included the study and analysis of 'representation' in art and literature. His perspective on psychology reflected his views on the *historical* and *cultural* origins of the way in which people in different societies come to act upon, construe and represent their world. So, where Piaget sought to unify biology, natural science and psychology, Vygotsky's quest was to integrate psychology with an analysis of history, art, literature, cultural activity and sociology. He sought nothing less than a coherent theory of the humanities and social sciences. As we shall see, these very different theoretical orientations lead to different images of childhood and schooling.

Uncertainty and information

The invention of Morse, radio, radar and other electronic means of communication has had, and continues to have, a profound effect on psychological theory. The development and perfection of electronic communication systems was made possible not only by the creation of new gadgets and hardware but also by the development of communications theory. As we will see in the next four chapters, some psychologists drew upon these theoretical developments in electronics to create new analogies for thinking about and constructing mathematical 'models' of human abilities. The conception of people as 'limited information-processing systems' developed apace during the Second World War when a generation of psychologists put their knowledge and skills to work in a number of areas, such as the construction of tests for personnel selection and the development of training techniques. They also helped to design the machines of war and instruments of defence, detection and communication to take account of what has become known as 'human factors'.

Effective 'communication' between humans and machines and the skilful control of complex systems demands designs that do not overtax or exceed people's abilities to attend to, monitor and react to the behaviour of the system under control. We are able to attend to just so much information at any one moment and the assimilation of information and adaptive responses to it demand time. Any system that provides too much critical information at any one moment or which leaves the human operator with too little time to interpret and react to it makes inhuman demands and cannot be controlled. So, for instance, the design of instrument panels in aircraft and the layout of aircraft runway lights incorporate results from psychological analyses of human information-processing abilities (e.g. Gibson, 1950). These helped to maximize the probability of effective pilot reactions and to minimize the possibility of pilot error.

Information processing

During the 1950s and 1960s, the use of mathematical models to try to provide explicit, formal theories of human abilities became a major area of research in psychology. Although attempts to generate very precise models failed for a number of interesting (but currently irrelevant) reasons, the view of man as an information processor remains a powerful metaphor in the discipline. For many years, the information-processing approach in psychology provided a *language* for constructing 'models' of specific areas of human activity (for instance, to describe how we go about solving mathematics problems). With the advent of fast, powerful and cheap computers, we have seen, over the past decade, a proliferation of 'computational models of the mind' and terms such as 'cognitive architecture' have entered the psychological dictionary as a means of expressing information-processing theories of mental processes. Don't worry if this seems rather abstract and vague at the moment: we will be exploring specific examples in later chapters.

The information-processing approach in psychology provided a new language and an 'image' of man to rival S–R approaches. To illustrate the difference between the two perspectives, imagine the following. As I am writing this section, I have a cup of coffee by the side of my computer terminal. Every so often, I reach out to grasp the cup and take a swallow. Usually, I begin to reach out for the cup whilst reading what I have just written. Just before my hand reaches the cup, I glance towards it to make sure that I am poised in a suitable position to pick it up and lift it to my lips. One could describe my behaviour as a series of responses, each triggered by a specific stimulus. The language of information processing, however, provides a very different account. Were my movements to be filmed, on several different occasions, each episode of picking up and drinking from the cup would be unique in some fine detail. My 'responses' may be similar in effect, but they are not identical in form. In what sense can they be called the 'same' response?

My *goal*, each time I reach for the cup, is the same and the achievement of that goal rests upon the same consequence (i.e. ingestion of coffee). However, the *means* to obtain the goal differ in detail on each occasion. The precise position of my body as I begin to reach, the exact location of the cup and the trajectory of my hand and arm towards it vary each time. My cup-lifting behaviour, unlike that, say, of a two-year-old child, is usually extremely *skilful*, so much so that, again unlike a two-year-old, I do not need to pay much *attention* to the act of picking it up. Given that each action is unique, it is reasonable to assume that I must be exerting some continuous *control* over my movement. Should I, for example, overreach and brush the cup with my sleeve, I am likely to switch my attention to take more 'care' over what I am doing. Although I do not appear to be attending to what I am doing, when things begin to go wrong my swift shift of attention betrays the fact that somehow I was monitoring my own activity whilst the main focus of my attention lay elsewhere.

Changing the description of human activity from one couched in terms of responses to stimuli to accounts which talk about more-or-less skilled actions aimed at goals represents a major shift in theoretical orientation. The language of information processing, couched in terms like 'goals', 'attention' and 'control', invites one to think about behaviour in *purposive* terms. The 'same' goal may be achieved by different *means*. So, for instance, should my right hand be occupied when I want a drink, I may reach with my left, or ask someone to pick up the cup for me, and so on. I adapt *means* to *ends* in ways that reflect my interpretation of the current situation and this demands continuous control, even though I am not necessarily aware of being in control all the time.

Information-processing theory led to the development of concepts like 'plans', 'skills' and 'strategies', and to a particular way of thinking about 'expertise', a term I will be using a good deal throughout the book. I use this word in preference to the term 'skill' for reasons that are perhaps best outlined here and now. In everyday talk, the word 'skill' is usually applied to describe the quality of overt behaviour. We talk, for instance, about football skills, skilled back-hands in tennis or skilfully executed cover drives in cricket. However, the use of this term in psychology, at least since two influential books by Sir F. Bartlett (1932, 1958), also refers to *mental* activity. Bartlett argued that the identification of similarities between skilled physical and mental activities involves more than metaphor. Both involve common elements to do with timing, self-control, error detection and organization.

I use the term *expertise* to draw attention to the fact that *knowledge* and *action*, or concepts and procedures, are two aspects of a single process. Comparisons of expert performance with that of a novice, for example, reveal differences not only in the speed, smoothness and accuracy of their actions but also in the structure of their perception, memory and mental operations. Throughout the book, I will be exploring the notion that the differences between adults and children, in the ability to attend, concentrate, study, reason, talk and solve problems, can profitably be viewed as reflections of different levels of *expertise*. Looked at from this perspective, learning how to learn, think and communicate are described in terms of the acquisition of various kinds of expertise. How this might come about is a major question explored in later chapters.

Throughout the history of psychology and, before it, in philosophy, great theories about how the mind develops and works have been seemingly 'overturned' only to return as a new generation of intellects re-visits old ideas with new perspectives, tools and methods (and, typically, with a different vocabulary). This is true of behaviourist theory. As we shall see in the chapters that follow, the idea that human psychology can and should be understood without reference to minds and mental processes is still with us and continues to hold out a challenge to those who put cognitive theory at the heart of our thinking about human development.

In this brief opening chapter, I have tried to provide a short and selective overview of some of the perspectives and issues that have arisen during the past century in the field of child development. I have also used my opening pages to introduce most of the main characters and themes that pervade the rest of the book, on the assumption that even a little background knowledge about where different theorists 'came from', and some insight into the source of their interest in children and education, help one to understand and to evaluate what they have to say. In the next chapter, we look in more depth at some of the 'images of childhood' implicit in the main theories introduced here and begin to explore their educational implications.

1

Images of childhood and their reflection in teaching

In this chapter, I describe, in outline, four ways of thinking about the nature of learning and thinking. I try to present and discuss these views in terms of the way in which they invite us to think about the nature of the intellectual abilities of five- to eleven-year-old children. Theories that offer very different accounts of the way in which children think and learn also lead to alternative views on what is involved in teaching them. So, this chapter also revolves around a discussion of what roles the three images of childhood etch out for teachers.

The chapter is also designed to provide a guide to the rest of the book. Some of the ideas involved are difficult and they are often expressed in unfamiliar language. I have tried to keep jargon to a minimum. Where I have felt obliged to introduce uncommon terms, I have provided concrete examples and illustrations to try to convey their meaning. The main themes explored are discussed several times in later chapters, so it is not necessary to grasp or to remember all that is said here. I suggest a quick read to obtain a general sense of what is to come later in the book, rather than a close study of the contents of this chapter. Details come later.

Learning and schooling

About thirty years ago, I read my first book on psychology and education. It was Bruner's (1966b) influential *Toward a Theory of Instruction*. One of the observations he made in that book was that schools and the social roles they have created (such as 'teacher' and 'pupil') are relatively modern inventions. There are non-technological cultures in which schools do not exist. Indeed, a number of languages have no verb meaning 'to teach' in their vocabulary. The notion that children must be taught in order to learn, let alone the expectation that they will do so in classrooms, is by no means a universal one. Rather, it seems to have been an invention of technological, schooled and literate societies. Another of Bruner's arguments is that the widespread availability of schooling involves far more than a change in the place where (some) learning and development take place. Rather, schools engender new and distinct *forms* of learning and lead to new *ways* of thinking. These contentions will be a major focus of the present book. We will be exploring the impact of formal education and, more specifically, teaching, on the development of children's powers of attention, concentration, memory, thinking, learning and language. I hope to show how a consideration of these topics bears directly on a range of practical issues having to do with children's adjustment to and, for some, problems in school. These concerns, in turn, will lead us to discussions about 'readiness' for learning, 'relevance' in the curriculum, 'discovery' methods in learning and factors that help to shape children's capacities for disciplined, self-directed learning and sustained, rational thinking.

Although I do not subscribe to the view that children are, in any simple sense, directly taught how to learn and think, I do believe that the development of certain ways of reasoning and learning about things is a direct product of both spontaneous and contrived social interactions between the developing child and more mature members of his or her community. By 'contrived encounters' I mean social interactions that come about as a result of *explicit* educational goals. Many interactions in school are, of course, of this nature. However, learning is obviously not synonymous with schooling. A great deal of what children learn occurs spontaneously outside the school walls as they play, observe, ask questions, experiment and make sense of the world around them. Similarly, many spontaneous encounters between children and their parents, relatives and peers involve an element of *informal* teaching. Suggestions, hints and warnings, conversation, practical tasks shared, family reminiscences and the like, all provide contexts within which the developing child's learning and understanding are orchestrated and extended through social interaction. Often, as we shall see, the formative influences of such interactions on the child's mentality are not *intentional* outcomes of what we seek to communicate to the child. Rather, they are products of implicit features of the social *practices* within which communication and attempts to teach take place. We are usually unaware of such things. They are, so to speak, like water to the fish, 'transparent' to the participants.

The child is not a passive nor always a compliant partner in such encounters. I share with Piaget and most contemporary theorists of child development the view that children actively 'construct' their knowledge of the world. I will discuss and illustrate this proposition in some detail. But I will depart from Piagetian theory in a number of important directions. I believe that adults, social interaction and communication play a far more formative role in the development of children's thinking and learning than his theory allows. Although Piaget accepts that social experiences and inter-personal behaviour are an important part of development, they play a rather limited and secondary role in his theory. The child's intercourse with the physical world provides the main constraints on and contributions to intelligence. Children construct their own knowledge by acting upon objects in space and time. Social interactions (particularly those which take place between children themselves) may facilitate the course of development by exposing a child to other points of view and to conflicting ideas which may encourage him to re-think or review his ideas. However, for Piaget, any social facilitation of development only works when the child's own understanding, based on his commerce with nature, is in an appropriate state of readiness for change. I will be arguing that social interaction plays a more important role than this view permits. Children's knowledge, I suggest, is often a product of the 'joint construction' of understanding by the child and more expert members of his culture.

I will also examine alternatives to Piaget's concept of knowledge, of what it is the child is learning about. These alternative views, we will find, question his account of young school children's ability to learn and think. Bruner and the Soviet psychologists, such as Vygotsky and his colleague, Luria, place far more emphasis than Piaget does on the role played by culture and its systems of symbols (e.g. its languages, sciences, books, diagrams, pictures and other artefacts) in forming the child's intelligence. Such systems have a dynamic, structuring effect on learning and development. They are not to be viewed as the mere 'content' of thinking but seen as part of its structure and its activity. When the child learns a language, for example, he does not simply discover labels to describe and remember significant objects or features of his social and physical environment but ways of *construing* and *constructing* the world. When he watches television or examines pictures in books, he is not merely experiencing another way of depicting things but is involved in medium-specific activities which, in time, generate mental 'operations' that become part of the fabric of his intellect. But I move on too fast.

From five to eleven

Theories of development and the evidence they have generated provide the framework for this book. The main *subject* explored is the study of learning and thinking in children aged between five and eleven years. It is not an easy topic. What we mean by 'thinking' and what is entailed by the term 'learning' are not easily expressed. Indeed, the meaning of such terms varies, often radically so, across theories of development. Similarly, our everyday usage of such terms also betrays a multitude of different attitudes towards, and implicit theories about, what thinking and learning involve and how they are fostered or nurtured. I do not think it would be useful to try here to outline and discuss definitions of thinking, learning and related aspects of our intellect. This, I suggest, is best achieved through a detailed consideration of concrete examples and illustrations. When we begin to weigh up the various interpretations offered to explain why, for instance, seven-year-olds are able to do many things that five-year-olds cannot do, we will, I hope, see how different theories offer us several ways of viewing and thinking about our own intelligence and its development.

Debates about the nature of development are inescapably and necessarily bound up with concepts of teaching. A book about the development of children's cognitive abilities, their powers of perception, attention, learning, memory, thinking and language, is also a book about teachers and teaching. Some theories afford only a supporting role for adults in the drama of development whilst others cast them into starring parts. What it means to be a 'teacher' rests, amongst other considerations, on how we construe children-as-learners. And how should we go about the task of creating the conditions under which teachers and learners are enabled to fulfil their roles? Do schools provide contexts within which anything approaching 'optimum' conditions for teaching and learning arise? What 'optimum' means depends upon how we choose to view the developmental process. At one level, then, it is impossible to divorce the academic study of children's thinking and learning from moral, political and economic issues concerning the resources we allocate to education and the way in which we train our teachers. Although it is not my intention to bring such issues to the forefront of attention, they will, inescapably, lurk in the background of many discussions.

Metaphors of mind: how do we talk about how we think?

When we think about what goes on in our minds and try to describe what takes place there, what terms do we use? How do we try to capture and describe the content and structure of thought? Well, we resort to metaphor; to phrases like 'in our minds'. If we are asked to describe what we are doing as we try to remember something, for instance, we often talk about 'searching', as though our memory is a 'place' or a 'store'. What we are 'looking' for is in a 'location', 'somewhere'. By talking about searching our memories, we invite comparisons with the processes involved in physical activities like searching a room, looking for a mislaid object. As we search our memories, we may know that something that we can't yet recall, but that we know we know, is 'at the back of our mind' and that we will recognize it when we 'find' it. Meanwhile, perhaps, another place or word that we have already thought about and rejected keeps coming to the 'forefront' of our thinking and, despite all our rejections, will not 'go away'.

When we talk about our reasoning, we often use expressions like 'imagining what would happen if. . .', 'picturing', or, particularly if one is a cognitive psychologist, 'making a mental model of . . .'. We may on other occasions be aware of a process that resembles 'talking to oneself' or hearing an imaginary other talking to us. If during the course of our imaginings we think about a serious mistake, we might 'cringe' at its effect and feel the ghost of whatever feeling it would entail if we 'really did' what we 'thought to do'. As we reason, we reach decisions and make judgements, deciding, perhaps, that something 'will not work','doesn't fit', leads to a 'dead end' or that it takes us a 'step forward' and a 'stage further on'. We may chide ourselves for stupidity or praise our own ingenuity. If we are lucky, we may decide that we have 'made a discovery', 'got there', 'thought it out', 'found out' or 'done it'. Often, as many innovative thinkers have commented, following the feeling that an insight or solution has been 'grasped', 'seen' or 'felt' comes another period of often hard and protracted work as one sets out to *prove* or *explain* or *demonstrate* the fact that a solution has been 'worked out'. Reasoning, then, is often described in terms also used to talk about physical activity, discussion and inter-personal evaluations.

But we are not always 'in control' of our mental activity. When we are supposed to be thinking about one thing we may suddenly 'find ourselves' considering something else that we should not be thinking about and, probably, be unsure or mystified as to why and how we found ourselves doing so, or when we 'went off course'. Our concentration may lapse or we might 'lose hold' of what we were supposed to be 'working on'. On the other hand, a sudden idea, insight or solution may seem to 'come to us' in a 'flash of insight'.

The metaphors that we employ to talk about, describe and explain the invisible, often fleeting, processes that go on as we think are, not surprisingly perhaps, derived from the visible, talked-about aspects of our directed *physical* activities and our experiences in the real world. But are our descriptions and explanations anything *more* than metaphorical? Are they an adequate starting place for a psychological analysis of mind? Are there any fundamental and demonstrable connections between the spatial, temporal and corporeal aspects of practical activities and mental processes that we often describe in similar terms? One theory of human development which suggests that there are more than metaphorical relationships between the language used to describe mental processes and that used to talk about activities in the physical world is that of Vygotsky. Although, as we shall see, he did not claim that mental activities are direct 'enactments', 'copies' or 'recordings' of external activities, he did argue that their *nature and their structure* are derived from them. He explored the theory that activity in what he termed the external, social plane is gradually 'internalized' by the child as he develops until it *forms* his intellectual processes. When we speak, say, of creating a 'mental model', there is a real sense in which the 'imaged' actions that we perform and their 'imagined' consequences are derived from physical actions that have previously been done to real objects and whose consequences have been directly felt or observed.

Of course, we often make errors and misjudgements in reasoning. Our models of the world are never perfect replicas. We may find, when we try to 'really' act out what we previously thought of doing, that the world resists the enactment of our imagined actions, or that the result of our actions surprises us. Thought, thus viewed, is a *substitute* for overt action and permits 'trials' whose 'errors' are only imagined. Viewed in evolutionary terms, thought (up to now at least) has proved its survival value. Though not immune to error, it has, on balance, conferred evolutionary advantage. Thinking before acting must have proved sufficiently reliable and valid to enable energy to be saved (mental activity consumes less time and food than overt action) and dangers to be avoided. Perhaps, then, the use of words to refer to mental actions *as though* they are related to similar or analogous physical actions involves more than metaphor. However, as I have already warned and will argue later, establishing the *nature* of the relations between actions and thoughts is no simple matter.

Thought as internalized action

Piaget shared with Vygotsky a similar conception of the relations between action and thought. He also argued that the foundations of mental processes lie in action-in-the-world. His often cited, deceptively simple, statement that 'Thought is internalized action' declares his view that the analysis of human knowledge and intelligence must begin with a consideration of motor activity and practical problem-solving. It also alerts us to one of his important educational messages, which is that children have to be active and constructive in order to develop their understanding of the world.

Although this book is focused on the development of children aged between five and eleven years, I think it is important when trying to grasp the significance of Piaget's analysis of the relation between acting and thinking to consider, albeit briefly, his observations of infants in the first year of their lives. The many examples he gave of babies' activities, play, imitation and problem-solving provide a concrete sense of the way in which he charted the beginnings of a transition from physical to mental activity.

Initially, the newborn's movements are reflex responses to internal and external stimulation. The infant may grasp a finger placed in his palm, respond to a light touch on the cheek by 'rooting' around, or blink in response to a puff of air. At first babies do not *anticipate* the impact of such stimulations, even when, so to speak, they can 'see them coming'. Things just happen to them. With experience, however, the infant starts to discover some of the *predictable* patterns in his experience. For instance, if a baby notices that a mobile placed over his cot moves when he happens to strike the cot side, he may well repeat the movement in order to maintain the interesting sight of the mobile in motion. At this stage, however, the infant is not aware of the fact that it is 'his' hand that has produced the effects on an object (i.e. the mobile). Both his actions and their consequences are part of a continuous flow; an undifferentiated experience or 'scheme'. However, this soon changes. When the infant starts to show evidence that he is *intending* to produce *anticipated* end results through his own actions, then true 'practical intelligence' has emerged. The infant's activity displays such intelligence when he begins to use different *means* towards a common *goal*. So, for example, an infant, having failed to reach up and touch the mobile, might push his mother's hand towards it, which is most likely to happen if both the mobile and her hand are in view at the same time. It is when the infant exhibits a *sequence* of different actions to achieve the same purpose that Piaget endows him with the beginnings of a practical intelligence. This intelligence takes the form of *anticipating* or desiring a state of affairs, being able to hold or represent what is sought 'in mind' and trying out various actions that, *in the past* have accomplished desired ends. Eventually, the child will come to 'reject' certain actions on the basis of mental activity alone as he imagines their consequences and mentally evaluates their desirability without actually performing them. Thus, interiorized or internalized *mental actions* start to substitute for (represent) physical actions; action is being internalized to form thought.

Several other theories of learning also offer explanations for such phenomena, and some of these (explicitly) proceed without making any reference to 'minds', infantile or otherwise. What is distinctive and original about Piaget's analysis is the fact that such 'elementary' learning is only one aspect of a much more elaborate theory of development. Sensory–motor schemes, the learned co-ordinations between actions and their sensory consequences, provide the bedrock of all knowledge, but the biology of human beings dictates that such sensory–motor learning is *structured* in the infant to form not only 'internalized actions' but, ultimately, *mental operations*.

I do not intend to go into detail here about Piaget's account of the operations of mind since this is best achieved after we have looked at some of the other observations that he used to illustrate the nature of children's thinking. These, I hope, will help to make his ideas more graspable. However, I do need to say a little about the distinction between mental actions and mental operations, both to explore Piaget's hypothesis that thought is internalized action and to help to show how his theory leads to a very different view of intellectual development from those provided by theories of learning that predated his.

Some actions in the world have rather special properties in that, for instance, their effects can be reversed (and observed). Imagine a child playing with a set of bricks. He has five of them, say. Each time he moves one, he changes the configuration and, hence, the *appearance* of the set of blocks. He may pile them so that they get higher. He may then take the pile down and lay the bricks side by side so that they cover a larger surface area. Each of these actions leads to a perceptible change. To an adult eye, of course, whilst the appearance of the set of blocks changes, their *number* remains invariant. The adult appreciates the fact that any action can be 'reversed' to recreate an earlier configuration, for instance. Configurations are interchangeable and appearances are ephemeral but number is an invariant *property* of the set of blocks. Only if blocks are added or taken away, we realize, is their number changed. As we shall see in chapters 3 and 8, Piaget argues that young children (aged below seven years or so) do not appreciate the fact that actions which change the appearance of things do not also affect their number, because they can't grasp the concept of invariance itself. Recognizing the fact that certain actions are also *operations* which form logical groups and can be *reversed* or which may be 'offset' by other actions is a prerequisite for the ability to *understand* invariant properties like number. Whilst such mental operations are 'abstracted' from physical and mental actions, they have a special status. Although they are derived from practical experience, they are not a direct product of 'learning' (or teaching) in any simple sense. One may observe an action but not an operation. Operations are 'mental constructions' which the child creates to make sense of his or her experience of the world. The transition in human development from an intelligence restricted to a capacity to perform single mental actions to one structured as systems of mental operations marks an intellectual *revolution* that occurs at about seven years of age (although Piaget himself was not over-concerned with 'dating' his stages). How and why the development of operations takes place is considered in chapter 3.

Piaget's analysis of the stages of human intellectual development emerged from a more over-arching endeavour, which was to understand the nature, structure and evolution of knowledge. Piaget was a 'genetic epistemologist', one who studies the origins and evolution of knowledge. He based his analysis of knowledge and his observations and interpretations of children's knowing and understanding on a theoretical framework derived from logic and mathematics (hence, he employed a 'logical-mathematical' approach). This framework led him to analyse and interpret children's development in terms of systems of logical operations that are taken to be the basis for rational understanding of the physical world and of mathematical systems for representing reality. Although it makes life difficult, we have to bear Piaget's main quest and his theoretical approach in mind. It is not possible to separate either an evaluation of his theory of development or its educational implications from a consideration of the value of using logic as a framework for thinking about thinking and learning. One consequence of Piaget's theory is the prediction that logical reasoning, described in terms of operations of mind, represents the culmination of intellectual development. As we shall see, the implication that mature thinking is adequately or even properly described in terms of logic has aroused a great deal of debate. If we decide that Piaget's view of logic does *not* offer an appropriate description of mature thinking, then we must question his interpretations of young children's abilities and, with them, the educational implications of his theory. Such questions are part of the agenda for this book.

Piaget's approach to language and cognition

Perception and thought

If Piaget places action at the foundation of thought, where do perceptual 'images' and verbal thinking come on the scene? Although there has been and continues to be much debate about the role of 'imagery' in thinking, many people report that they 'use' images when they think in order to represent or 'picture' a situation, object or event. How does Piaget's theory tackle the notion of mental images and what implications does his view have for teaching and learning?

Part of the answer is that Piaget 'relegates' perception to action. For instance, when the infant sees an object, what he perceives, recognizes and knows about it depends upon his past actions. An object is, so to speak, defined by the past actions that have been done to it. The 'sensory' aspects of experiences, such as what an object looked, smelled, felt, tasted and sounded like, are consequences of what was *done* to that object. Thus, the sensory aspects of experience are 'classified' in terms of actions. Some objects can be sucked and others cannot. Some can be grasped and picked up whilst others resist such actions. Some materials can be stretched, others are not so malleable, and so on. A child's intuitive knowledge of the world is based on the actions that he performs on it, and an object is 'known' in terms of the repertoire of actions to which it can and cannot be 'assimilated'. This is one sense in which (past) actions dictate how children perceive the world.

Perception, for Piaget, also involves *activity*. One example of such activity is the movement of the eyes as a situation is inspected and observed. What we see is determined, in part, by where we look. What we remember is largely dictated by what we attend to. As we shall see in chapter 4, Piaget argues that a child's ability to *control* where and how he looks at things is itself determined by his stage of development. Pre-operational children, he argues (those who have yet to develop mental operations), cannot inspect situations *logically*. Thus, what they perceive is more unreliable and idiosyncratic than what is perceived by an 'operational' thinker, whose inspection of the world is guided by a logical understanding of it. The educational implications of this view of perception, as a process under the control of action and, eventually, mental operations, are profound and far-reaching. If Piaget's theory is sound, then it follows that young children are logically incapable of seeing the world as adults do. Any attempt to 'teach' them by demonstrating how things work is bound to fail if children do not possess the necessary mental operations to *make sense*, in logical terms, of what they are shown.

Language and thought

Piagetian views on the role of *language* in thinking are similar to those on visual perception. Language, for Piaget, is a system of symbols for *representing* the world, as distinct from actions and operations which form the *processes* of reasoning. So, for example, if we had asked the five-year-old child playing with the blocks 'How many?' he had, he would not have *understood* what we asked (at least, in our terms) because he lacks the operations that endow questions like 'How many?' with logical meaning. Suppose we *told* him that he had five blocks, taught him how to count them and managed to obtain from him the answer 'five' when we asked him how many blocks he had. Does the child understand what we said and did? Not according to Piaget – at least, not in the sense that the child shares our understanding of things. It is not the case that he now understands and has been 'taught' the *concept* of number. What the child has learned is simply a *procedure* (making certain sounds) in response to a question ('How many?'). He has not developed a *conceptual* understanding of number. Such an understanding demands that the child comes to the realization that many actions which change appearances have no effect on the abstract, invariant property that we call number. He will not understand such abstract concepts until he has reached operational thinking.

Thus, Piaget's theoretical arguments about the nature of thinking and of the relationships between what is seen, heard and understood have direct implications for teaching and its effectiveness (or lack of it). Attempts to question, show or explain things to children before they are mentally 'ready' cannot foster *development*, though the child may *learn* some 'empty' procedures. Indeed, premature teaching and questioning may demoralize or frustrate a child who can't begin to understand what he is being 'taught'.

A teacher can provide appropriate *materials* and contexts for development, and organize time and space so that children are free to act upon the world with objects and tasks that serve to foster the emergence of operations and an understanding of invariance. But the basis for such an understanding is constructed by the child through his own, self-selected problem-solving; not through any direct efforts of his teachers.

Vygotsky: instruction and intelligence

Children who are unable to perform tasks, solve problems, memorize things or recall experiences when they are left to their own devices often succeed when they are helped by an adult. Piaget, as we have just seen, takes a somewhat negative view of such apparent successes, claiming that they involve the teaching and learning of procedures and not the development of understanding. He views 'genuine' intellectual competence as a manifestation of a child's largely unassisted activities. Vygotsky, on the other hand, argues that the capacity to *learn through instruction* is itself a fundamental feature of human intelligence. When adults help children to accomplish things that they are unable to achieve alone, they are fostering the development of knowledge and ability. Without a natural ability for teaching, as well as learning, human *cultures* would never have developed since they can only be perpetuated if the immature learn and the mature teach (though not in the narrow sense of these terms, of course). From this perspective, which places instruction at the heart of development, a child's *potential* for learning is revealed and indeed is often *realized* in interactions with more knowledgeable others.

One of Vygotsky's main contributions to educational theory is a concept termed the 'zone of proximal development'. This he used to refer to the 'gap' that exists for an individual (child or adult) between what he is able to do alone and what he can achieve with help from one more knowledgeable or skilled than himself. This concept leads to a very different view of 'readiness' for learning from that offered by Piagetian theory. Readiness, in Vygotskian terms, involves not only the state of the child's existing knowledge but also his capacity to learn with help. Two children at nominally the 'same' level of (unassisted) performance in a given task or discipline may differ in how much they are able to learn given similar amounts of instruction. A child's current level of performance must be distinguished from his *aptitude* to learn with further instruction. Some children have larger zones of proximal development than others, even when their existing levels of performance are similar. Such children are able to learn more from instruction (though not necessarily in every domain of learning). Vygotsky's theory, then, offers a way of conceptualizing individual differences in 'educability' where Piaget's theory has little or nothing to say about the issue. Note, however, that this is not intended as a criticism of Piaget's theory. Piaget never set out to explore individual differences in rates of development so it is hardly surprising that he said little about the issue. Perhaps this explains why he wrote little about the educational implications of his theory, and even then apparently with some reluctance and late in life (Elkind, 1974). In chapter 4, we will see how Vygotsky's concept of differing zones of proximal development has led to important new techniques for diagnosing children's learning needs and for tailoring instructional methods to meet these.

For Vygotsky, then, *co-operatively achieved success* lies at the foundations of learning and development. Instruction – both formal and informal, in many social contexts, performed by more knowledgeable peers or siblings, parents, grandparents, friends, acquaintances and teachers – is the main vehicle for the cultural transmission of knowledge. Knowledge is embodied in the actions, work, play, technology, literature, art and talk of members of a society. Only through interaction with the living representatives of culture, what Bruner terms the 'vicars of culture', can a child come to acquire, embody and further develop that knowledge. Children's development thus reflects their *cultural* experiences and their opportunities for access to the more mature who already *practise* specific areas of knowledge.

In order to provide a flavour of Vygotsky's analysis of development and a sense of how it resembles Piaget's theory in some respects but differs from it in others, let me compare and contrast their views on the relation between language and thought.

Piaget and Vygotsky on talking and thinking

The most widely reported difference of opinion between Vygotsky and Piaget, about which they argued in print, concerns the nature of language and its effect on intellectual development. Piaget, as we have seen, argues that language exerts no formative effects on the structure of thinking. It is a 'medium', a method of representation, within which thought takes place. Mental actions and operations, the processes of thought, are derived from action, not talk.

Piaget's position is more subtle than this statement suggests, however. Although language does not create the structure of thinking, it does facilitate its *emergence*. He suggests, for example, that it is through talking to others, particularly other children, that the child's thinking becomes socialized. What another child says about some event or happening may provoke thought, discussion or argument. It may lead both children to re-view and re-think their points of view. But it is the structure of the child's intelligence, based on activity, that determines when such collaborative exchanges come about. When Piaget analysed conversations between young children, for example, he found no evidence that they were able to discuss things rationally. Piaget writes, 'if, before the age of 7 or 8, children have no conversation bearing upon logical or causal relations, the reason is that at that age they hardly understand one another when they approach these questions' (Piaget, 1967).

What can be talked *about* is determined by children's stages of development. The pre-school child's thinking (and talk) is largely 'egocentric', reflecting the child's own thinking, activity and point of view. At this stage, the child may respond to what another person says, but he cannot stand in their shoes nor understand what they are saying from *their* perspective. Piaget writes, 'Clearly . . . one must start from the child's activity in order to understand his thought; and his activity is unquestionably egocentric and egotistic. The social instinct in well-defined form develops late. The first critical period in this respect occurs towards the age of 7 or 8.'

One line of evidence that Piaget used to illustrate his views on language arose from observations of pre-school children at play. Although children talk as they play together, they do not, according to Piaget, really *converse*. The pre-operational child cannot think about what the world is like from another person's viewpoint. To do this, he must be capable of ignoring his own physical and mental position and be able to 'construct' situations as they appear from other perspectives. For various reasons discussed later, children can only perform such constructions when they have developed mental operations. Before this stage is reached, they assimilate what is said by another person, adult or child, to their own point of view, often 'distorting' the meaning of much that is said to them. The impact of language on the child, then, is limited to what he can assimilate, and this is determined by the structure of the child's thinking. True 'reciprocity' and attempts at mutual understanding only emerge with the development of concrete operations, at around age seven. This is why young children playing and talking in each other's company are usually involved in 'collective monologues' rather than true dialogue.

Vygotsky's theory shares a number of similarities with Piaget's but differs radically in its treatment of language and its influence on thinking. He agreed with Piaget's view that children do not think like adults and applauded the fact that, unlike most child psychologists before him, Piaget did not simply set out to discover what children could *not* do in comparison with adults, but sought to find out what they could do and what they actually did. However, childhood speech, in Vygotsky's view, is not a personal, egocentric affair but the reverse: it is *social* and communicative in both origin and intent. Vygotsky also observed what Piaget termed 'collective monologues' by young children but he gave them a different interpretation. For Vygotsky, they represent an important stage of transition between two quite different *functions* of language. In the beginning, speech serves a regulative, communicative function. Later, it also serves other functions and transforms the way in which children learn, think and understand. It becomes an instrument or *tool* of thought, not only providing a 'code' or system for representing the world but also the means by which *self-regulation* comes about. The initial motivation for gesture and speech is to control the world through the agency of other people. The infant is weak and cannot sustain himself. Consequently, many of the things he wants or needs have to be met with the help of others. Gestures and speech serve this role, giving the infant a way of influencing the course of his immediate future which he could not achieve otherwise. Speech, like any system of movement, is a physical *activity*, a way of controlling one's own body in order to achieve goals and avoid discomfort. The overt activity of speaking provides the basis for 'inner speech', that rather mysterious covert activity that often forms the process of thinking. For Vygotsky, then, not only do physical actions that serve to manipulate and organize the world get internalized to become (non-verbal) thinking: the physical activity of speaking, which serves to regulate the actions of others, also becomes internalized to create verbal thinking. All forms of thought, then, are *activities*.

The 'monologues' produced by pre-school children, such as those observed by Piaget, lie midway between the social and intellectual functions of speech. For Vygotsky, the child who is talking to himself is *regulating* and planning his own activities in ways that foreshadow verbal thinking. As the child discovers how to control the actions of others through speech, his developing knowledge of language 'acts back' on him in that others can also regulate his actions through speech. As he discovers how to gain people's attention by speaking and learns how to direct their attention to features of the shared physical world – to solicit specific actions and services, inhibit, refuse and so forth – he becomes subject to the same regulative forces through the speech of others. They can begin to control and direct his attention, solicit his services and inhibit his activities. Alongside 'other-control' by verbal means comes verbal 'self-control-by-others'.

As such developments are taking place on the linguistic front, the child is also developing his non-verbal knowledge of the world through his own activities. In relation to this aspect of early development, the Soviet emphasis on activity is similar to Piaget's concept of sensory–motor development. At around three years of age, a merging and integration of the two streams of development, non-verbal and verbal, begins. The pre-school child's verbal commentaries on his own activities are evidence of the emergence of *linguistic control* over his own non-verbal activities. In 'talking to himself' the child is playing two roles: the regulated and the regulator. In the past, other people played one of these roles. Sometimes the child regulated their actions; at other times they regulated his. The pre-school child is beginning to play both parts before 'internalizing' the process to become a verbal thinker.

Children's monologues, for Piaget, reflect the egocentric nature of their thinking. When, at around age seven or eight, genuine discourse is made possible by the development of logical operations, language starts to become rational and social (though egocentric thinking does not disappear entirely). Egocentric speech disappears from the scene because the child is now aware of the need to make what he says accessible to his listener and has the intellectual competence to start to learn how to make himself intelligible.

Vygotsky argues, however, that egocentric speech serves an intellectual purpose for children and does not 'disappear' at age seven but is internalized to form 'inner speech' and verbal thinking. When Vygotsky and his colleagues observed pre-school children, they also found evidence of egocentric speech, but noted that this was most likely to occur when some *frustration* or difficulty arose. For example, when a child discovered that he did not have a blue pencil to colour a drawing he said 'Where's the pencil? I need a blue pencil. Never mind, I'll draw with the red one and wet it with water; it will become dark and look blue' (Vygotsky, 1962, p. 17). So, egocentric speech often serves a *planning* and *self-regulating* function and is stimulated by problems and frustrations.

In this way, speech comes to form what Vygotsky referred to as the higher mental processes. These include the ability to plan, evaluate, memorize and reason. Note that these processes are *culturally* formed in social interaction. Looked at in this way, language does not simply *reflect* or represent concepts already formed on a non-verbal level. Rather, it structures and directs the processes of thinking and concept formation themselves. Where Piaget views young children's play and talk as a manifestation of a natural desire to manipulate and assimilate the physical world, laying down the sensory–motor and intuitive foundations for mathematical and logical operations, Vygotsky sees it as a product of social experience and evidence for the emergence of intellectual self-control.

Processing information: on becoming an expert

One of the influences that helped to shape the development of Piaget's theory was a discipline called 'cybernetics'. This arose in the 1940s, fathered by a mathematician, Norbert Wiener, and a physician, Arturo Rosenbluth. It is defined, in modern terms, as 'the science of effective organization' (Beer, 1977). The initial aim of cyberneticians (the term is derived from the Greek word for 'steersman') was to identify the fundamental and universal principles governing the development and functioning of all complex systems, be they organic, physical or mechanical. Are there universal laws which govern how such systems must be organized and structured in order to work effectively in any environment?

The concepts of *information* and information *control* are employed by cyberneticians to analyse the workings of natural systems such as the human brain, and to design efficient and workable manufactured systems such as computers, large industrial organizations and so on. How should information be distributed, processed and controlled in order for such systems to work? In company with another set of concepts, derived initially from electronic engineering and called information theory, the ideas and terminology of cybernetics have been absorbed into psychology to provide a theoretical *language* for the study and analysis of human intelligence.

Piaget's interest in cybernetics stemmed from his desire to create a field of study, genetic epistemology, that would cross the traditional boundaries separating several disciplines (biology, psychology, philosophy, the natural sciences, mathematics and logic). Like the cyberneticians, he wanted to discover general principles of *organization* that applied to all living systems and which would establish theoretical connections between biology and knowledge: how has the evolution and structure of biological systems led to the emergence of rational intelligence? The study of 'self-organizing systems' that develop towards stable and efficient functioning, governed by universal principles of structure and function, was of central relevance to his endeavour, so it is no surprise that he should have been attracted to the ideas of cybernetics.

Other psychologists also adopted the concepts and the language of cybernetics and information theory. Although, as we shall see, they put them to uses that are different from Piaget's, their main motivation was also to explore the nature of human cognition viewed as a system organized to process information in order to adapt, learn and understand.

In engineering, information theory has been used to study, design and evaluate ways of transmitting information between two points without distortion, loss or degradation. No information-processing system, be it telephone, radio, television or whatever, is perfect. Information may be lost during the encoding phase (consider, for example, how a voice over a telephone compares with the 'real thing'), or it may 'leak' or be distorted by noise (like the 'crackle' on a telephone line). The role of the information theorist is to provide the means to measure and improve the performance of systems that transmit, process and store information and the engineer's task is to design and make systems that minimize distortion, loss and noise and which work fast.

The term 'information' used in this sense has a more precise, technical meaning than that implied by its use in everyday talk. Imagine, for instance, that I have drawn a single card from a normal deck of playing cards. I ask you to discover what card I am holding. You ask if it is a red card. I inform you that it is not. You have been given an item of information that rules out one-half of the set that the card was drawn from. More formally, I have given you one 'bit' of information (short for 'binary digit'). You next ask if the card is a club. I say that it is not. You can now rule out from the set of candidates for the card I am holding a further 50 per cent of the possibilities (i.e. you now know it must be one of the thirteen spades). I have now given you two bits of information overall. In short, any item of information that reduces uncertainty about an event by a half conveys one bit of information. Of course, when an electronics engineer calculates the amount of information being conveyed in a complex system, the maths become somewhat difficult!

What has all this got to do with the psychology of learning and thinking? Well, do we discover anything by thinking about human beings as 'information processors'? Is it useful, for example, to look at human speech as a system for transmitting information? Can the workings of the brain be analysed usefully as an information processing device like a computer? Do children become better at 'processing information' as they develop? Can learning usefully be viewed as information processing, memory as information storage and knowledge as information structures?

These are, in fact, controversial questions in psychology and I will not attempt to answer them in detail here. I list them to provide some sense of how and why information processing theory has been embraced by many psychologists. An important paper, written by George Miller in 1956, paved the way for many insights into the nature of human intelligence based on the image of 'man the information processor'. Let me say a little about the background to and content of this paper before discussing what it might have to tell us about the nature of learning and thinking.

If adults are asked to remember random strings of digits (i.e. to transmit information about them from one moment in time to another) they usually manage to handle sets of six or seven items without making many errors. Increase the number of digits and they begin to make mistakes (they lose information and introduce 'noise'). Imagine tasting two drinks which vary in saltiness. You are presented with each in turn and asked to describe them to someone or, perhaps, to press one of two keys to signal which you have just sampled. Adults find this task easy. Increase the number of drinks to three (high, middle and low in saltiness). Then move on to four, five, six, seven, and so on. Here too, we find that adults can usually 'transmit information' without error in situations where they are exposed to six or seven different degrees of saltiness, but once the set exceeds seven then errors, information loss and noise creep in. Miller, who drew attention to these and many similar phenomena, suggested that whatever the nature of the stimuli used in such situations (they may be sounds, tastes, degrees of brightness, colour saturation and so on), provided that they are 'random' and that the sequences used have no meaning (e.g. tones that do not form a recognized tune), we find that mature people can 'transmit', without loss or distortion, information about sets of stimuli that number somewhere between five and nine. The title of his paper was 'The magical number seven, plus or minus two'.

Why is this interesting? Well, described in the language of information theory, it demonstrates that adults have a limited and relatively fixed *channel capacity*. We are only able to transmit information, without loss or distortion, about a specific number of (unstructured) items. It follows that if people are put into unfamiliar situations and expected to take note of and react to (i.e. to process) more than a relatively small number of elements, they will be overwhelmed by information and uncertainty ('What do I attend to next?', 'What should I do about it?'). They will make mistakes. In such situations, *training* and/or *experience* will be needed before anything approaching error-free performance can be achieved.

The analysis becomes more interesting when we consider the answers to two questions. The first asks if children have the *same* channel capacity and information-processing limits as adults. The second concerns the nature of *expertise*. What happens with training or experience that enables people to *overcome* their information-processing limitations? Why is it, for example, that a concert pianist may be able to sight-read a piece of music that involves, say, sequences of eight-note chords in a novel combination? The pianist is transmitting far more information than subjects in the experiments just outlined, but how? How is practice and experience translated into expert performance? What is being *learned* and how is it remembered?

First consider the question about children. If three-year-olds are asked to remember strings of digits, they begin to falter when the set exceeds three items. By five, children can handle about five items. By age eight or so, mature levels of performance are reached. There is debate about exactly what happens during development to explain this phenomenon, and I will discuss both the arguments and their educational implications in chapter 3 when I explore the view that children have to learn *how* to memorize such things. For the moment, the important point is that children have a smaller 'channel capacity' than adults do. Consequently, in unfamiliar, uncertain situations, they are less able than the mature person is to attend to, memorize and respond to events. Perhaps we should explore the view that five-year-olds (but not seven-year-olds) fail to solve many problems because they lack the *information-processing capacities* needed to do such tasks. This I also do in chapter 3.

In thinking about the nature of expertise and how it is learned or acquired, consider an example. We find a chess Grand Master willing to take part in an experiment. We show him or her a chess board on which pieces are arranged in a 'state of play'. We show them the board for a few moments and then ask them to turn away and then to recall the positions of the pieces they were shown. They are likely to perform this feat without error even when the board has on it most or all of the pieces. Ask a novice at chess to do the same task and he or she is unlikely to remember more than a handful of pieces (De Groot, 1965). Does the chess Grand Master have a phenomenal memory? Is this why he or she was able to achieve Grand Mastership? No: outside their area of special expertise, the Grand Master suffers from the same information-processing limitations as the rest of us. Their feats of perception and memory are *specific* to chess boards and pieces.

More detailed studies of how they manage this feat illustrate the important and far-reaching connections between what may appear to be 'fixed' or 'natural' capacities – like the ability to see and memorize – and 'higher mental processes'– such as learning and thinking. What the expert, but not the novice, 'sees' when he or she inspects the chess board are *configurations* of pieces, or in Miller's term, 'chunks'. These configurations, in turn, represent familiar, recurrent patterns that occur as an outcome of particular strategies of play, or some pattern that shows an 'interesting' departure from such prototypical configurations. Experiments designed to analyse the way in which experts perceive the structure of chess games (Chase and Simon, 1973) show that they have memorized a huge repertoire of such configurations. In other words, the chess Grand Master can recognize a very large number of different patterns that are typical or interpretable states of play. Whereas the novice 'perceives' isolated pieces which, perhaps, he or she can barely recognize or identify, the Master recognizes individual pieces as parts of larger configurations. Put in information-processing terms, the expert and novice share the same channel capacity, but the six or seven chunks that the expert encodes are meaningful configurations, not isolated chess pieces. Through playing chess, and the observation of others at play, the expert has not only discovered clever strategies and good tactics of play but also developed an *organized memory* which enables them to assimilate much more of what they see than the novice. This also means that they are better able to *plan* and think ahead because their representation or model of the chess board is robust, accurate and enduring. So they are also able to think more clearly and in greater depth.

The differences exposed in such studies between experts and novices are found in many other contexts. Indeed, there is a fair case to be made for the assertion that they are typical of differences found between experts and novices in *any* field. The expert reader, for example, perceives and processes larger units of text than the beginning reader. An adult can look at an array of objects and 'subitize' them – perceive them in groups of a certain size (e.g. as sets of three) – whilst a young child cannot. Thus, the speed with which we are able to 'encode' what we see, the *organization* of what we see and the amount of information that we can memorize are related to and symptomatic of the *structure* of our knowledge.

Children are novices at life in general and find many of the tasks and demands they face in school novel and full of uncertainty. They are more limited than adults in how much they can attend to and memorize in unfamiliar situations. Perhaps, then, it should not be surprising to find differences between the mature and immature in the ability to profit by a specific experience or to solve an unfamiliar problem. It may be that what is at stake in such situations is not young children's inability to perform *logical operations* but their general lack of *expertise* which leads them to perceive situations in different ways from the adult.

An informal, but telling, finding that emerged from studies of chess players was their inability to identify, describe or articulate how they were 'seeing' chess boards. Surely, much of our expertise is like this. Our knowledge is 'tacit', locked into the way we act and perform and not easily articulated or described to others. Experts may find the problems of the novice puzzling or even infuriating if they do not recognize that novices do not perceive situations in the same way as they themselves do. It should come as no surprise, for example, to find that even when the expert *points out* things to be attended to, the novice may not be able to 'take in' what they are shown because they lack the prerequisite *knowledge* which would enable them to perceive and memorize configurations. If so, it is also not surprising that the expert's ability to *act* and *think* is surer, smoother and more accurate than that of the novice.

Viewing children as limited information processors who have yet to learn or acquire expertise offers a third image of the child as learner and thinker. This makes no recourse to 'large-scale' concepts like logical operations, but suggests that knowing how and what we are about is far more *domain-* or task-specific. Children's ability in one area, be it chess, arithmetic, reading or whatever, may not reflect their abilities in others if their *expertise* in different subjects and activities varies. This view makes no use of concepts of *stages* of development: however, it does agree with Piaget's view that perception, memory, knowledge and understanding are all deeply related and change with learning and development.

Piaget, Vygotsky and Bruner: a brief comparison and summary

Before moving on to the next chapter, I will summarize some of the main ideas we have just considered. Rather than simply repeat myself, I will try to re-examine these ideas whilst exploring a little more of the biography of the three main characters I have introduced.

I have outlined three main perspectives on the development of learning and thinking. These will be explored in more detail in the following pages. One view, which stems from Piaget's theory, holds that all children pass through a series of stages before they construct the ability to perceive, reason and understand in mature, rational terms. In this view, teaching, whether through demonstration, explanation or asking questions, can only influence the course of intellectual development if the child is able to assimilate what is said and done. Assimilation, in turn, is constrained by the child's stage of development. This leads to a specific concept of learning 'readiness' and, as we shall see, holds out many implications for the design of curricula and the timing of formal instruction.

A second perspective, introduced by Vygotsky, shares some important areas of agreement with Piagetian theory, particularly an emphasis on *activity* as the basis for learning and for the development of thinking. However, it involves different assumptions about the relationship between talking and thinking. It entails a far greater emphasis on the role of communication, social interaction and instruction in determining the path of development. Vygotsky died in his late thirties in 1934. His death came after ten years of illness from tuberculosis. In that ten-year period, Vygotsky wrote about a hundred books and papers, many of which have only recently been published and translated into English. Many psychologists, including some of his own former students and colleagues, recognize that much of what he wrote was speculative and, in places, self-contradicting. Unlike Piaget, who worked on into his eighties and lived to see a dramatic expansion in the field of developmental psychology, Vygotsky did not have access to what has become a vast literature on child development. Consequently, whilst many of the ideas we will explore later in this book are consistent with his general position and were sometimes stimulated directly by it, we are left to guess at what Vygotsky himself might have had to say about them.

Bruner, influenced as I have already said by Vygotsky, was constructing the foundations of his theory of instruction in the 1960s when the assimilation of information theory into psychology was under way. Unlike both Vygotsky and Piaget, Bruner came to the study of child development after extensive research into adult thinking and problem-solving. Although sharing with Vygotsky a stress on the importance of culture and cultural history in the formation of mind, his background provided him with a more detailed sense of the *processes* involved in mature, socialized cognition. His theory, unlike either Piaget's or Vygotsky's, is grounded in the language of information theory. For instance, he entitled one of his early papers 'Going beyond the information given' (Bruner, 1957). In this, he explored the nature of creative thinking and originality in terms of our ability not only to acquire information but also to 'go beyond' it by inventing codes and rules. Learning involves the search for pattern, regularity and predictability. Instruction serves to assist children in the formation and discovery of such patterns and rules. We return to a fuller discussion of these ideas in chapter 8.

Like Vygotsky, Bruner was convinced that social experience plays a major part in mental development, though his theory of the way in which social experience is involved in development differs from Vygotsky's account in a number of ways (not least by being informed by research findings that Vygotsky did not live to study). For example, throughout his writings on human development, Bruner laid considerable stress on the importance of acknowledging not only the role of culture and social interaction but also the influences of biology and evolution. He often drew parallels between the abilities of humans and other species when he theorized about the formation of mind: 'I take it as a working premise that growth cannot be understood without reference to human culture and primate evolution' (1968, p. 2). Vygotsky also acknowledged the importance of biological study in the creation of psychological theory. He distinguished between what he called the 'natural line' and the 'cultural line' in development. But he did not live to provide a synthesis of the two streams of growth. Indeed, unlike Bruner, he largely 'ignored' the natural, biological line in his desire to establish the importance of historical, social and cultural influences on human development (Wertsch, 1985, p. 8). You will find that discussions of the interplay between biology and social experience pervade this book. As we shall see, the last decade has seen a dramatic upsurge of interest in, and knowledge about, the innate capacities of the human infant and this has led to far more emphasis on the role of biological influences on human growth and development in recent theorizing about how children think and learn.

Looked at in one way, Bruner's theory stands between those of Piaget and Vygotsky. Like Piaget, Bruner emphasized the importance of biological and evolutionary constraints on human intelligence. At the same time, and more in sympathy with Vygotsky, he laid stress on the way in which culture forms and transforms the child's development, and he gave a more central role than Piaget did to social interaction, language and instruction in the formation of mind. Bruner employed the language of information processing in formulating his ideas and, in so doing, offered us an opportunity to integrate the findings from work on adult cognition with those arising from the study of children. All too often, cognitive psychologists who study adult intelligence ignore the process of development and education. They often leave one with the impression that mental activity springs, fully formed, out of a developmental vacuum. Bruner, however, sought to ground his account of the 'processes of mind' in a theory of culture and growth, often drawing and building upon insights delivered by both Piaget and Vygotsky.

Piaget's theory, with its emphasis on the active, constructive nature of human development, is often referred to as a 'constructivist' approach. Whilst Bruner also accepted the image of children as active architects of their own understanding he, in company with Vygotsky, stressed the role of social interaction and cultural practices in shaping the course of human development. Their approach is often referred to as 'social constructivism'. As we shall see in the next chapter, both of these theoretical perspectives have been extended and modified over the past decade. They have also come under critical scrutiny from those who hold that nature and biology play a far more crucial role in shaping human destiny than either of these approaches allow.

2

A decade of development (maturation and learning!)

It is ten years since the brief historical overview presented in the last chapter was written. The major theoretical issues addressed in the first edition are, unsurprisingly, still with us and the main 'images' of childhood around which I organized my introduction to the field are still being explored and articulated. Indeed, one aim of this edition is to examine new ideas that have arisen out of the various theories outlined in terms of the impact that they have exerted on research into child development. Another aim is to explore the implications of this research for the practice of education. In this, rather short, chapter, I will try to anticipate and illustrate the major developments that have shaped the theoretical landscape over the past decade and erect a few signposts to the contents of later chapters. Although short, this chapter is not easy because it introduces a wide range of new terms and concepts. Fear not, however, for we will return to the ideas introduced again . . . and again.

The impact of Vygotskian thinking

One of the most dramatic changes that has taken place in the intellectual climate of developmental psychology and educational theory has come from the impact of Vygotsky's thinking within the field. In relation to the present volume, this influence surfaces in a number of places. Because, as we have seen, his conception of human development places interactions between children and more mature members of their culture at the heart of psychological growth, considerable research effort has gone into the analysis of adult–child interactions in an attempt to isolate and describe the processes which serve to mediate the proposed cultural transmission of knowledge and competence. These efforts have spawned a variety of new concepts and terms in an effort to elaborate Vygotsky's theory about how the social construction of mind might come about. Such new ideas will surface in just about every chapter of the book.

Vygotsky's theorizing about the influence of culture on mind was not limited to claims about the role of social interaction. Cultural 'tools' or, in Bruner's terms, cultural 'amplifiers' also exert a formative influence on human cognition. Furthermore, access to, and skills in using, such tools is made possible for the developing child through observations of and interactions with those who are masters of their use.

There are many accounts of the impact of inventions such as the wheel, steam power and the internal combustion engine on social practices and a society's means of production. It also seems self-evident that, as such innovations permeate a society, new skills must be developed and disseminated to exploit them. Innovative cultural tools demand the perfection and transmission of the knowledge and skills needed to realize their potential. However, less commonplace are accounts of the effects on the human mind due to the invention and spread of new systems of representation and new symbolic notations. For instance, what effects did the invention of written forms of language, or the spread of the Hindu-Arabic notation system for representing numbers, have on human knowledge?

According to Vygotsky and Luria, such systems for representing and communicating knowledge generate important transformations in the minds of those who master them. So when children learn how to read, and how to make use of mathematical symbols, they acquire new ways of thinking as they master and internalize activities needed to work upon and exploit these new mental tools. If all this proves to be correct, then systems for representing the world are not just things that we think *about*; they determine *how* we think. We will return to a critical evaluation of these bold claims in the chapters on literacy and mathematics.

In presenting and discussing the impact of Vygotsky-inspired theorizing, I also want to emphasize the diversity of interpretations and views that have been derived from his writings and those of his colleagues. As I suggested in the last chapter, Vygotsky's perspective on human development can hardly be called a fully fledged theory. Although his writings display an impressive and exciting breadth of vision and serve to point the way as to how, in general terms, it is *possible* to think about how we might integrate our theorizing about history, social practices, systems of signs and the formation and development of mind, he was not able to articulate this vision in any great detail. Consequently, there are many ways of 'reading' and interpreting his work. As a result, the impact of his thinking on psychological research and theorizing has been neither straightforward nor unequivocal. Indeed, as we shall see, it is probably fair to say that there are as many grounds for disagreement amongst those who count themselves as 'neo-Vygotskians' as there are, say, between Vygotskians and those who derive theoretical inspiration from Piaget.

Given that one of Vygotsky's ambitions was to integrate psychological theory with that of the humanities and the other social sciences, it is also unsurprising to find that members of other disciplines, including sociologists, anthropologists and linguists, have also embraced his approach. Coming from such diverse intellectual traditions, motivated by somewhat different theoretical concerns, these various 'readers' of his work have often arrived at different and conflicting positions about how a 'socio-cultural', 'socio-historical' or 'social constructivist' perspective might be theoretically developed and about its implications for education.

In relation to our concerns in this book, such conflicts of interpretation will become most urgent when we consider 'situated action theory'. Briefly, for we will explore this and related ideas more fully later on, the concepts of situated action and 'situated learning' arise out of the view that the physical and social contexts within which learning takes place remain an integral part of that which is learned. For example, it has been argued that many of the skills and much of the knowledge that children acquire in the course of their everyday activities outside school fail to 'transfer' to the classroom. Children who seem to have difficulties in learning 'school mathematics' may appear competent in solving everyday problems outside of the classroom which demand mathematical reasoning, as we shall see in chapter 8. One explanation for such phenomena is that teachers fail to make school learning 'relevant' to children's everyday lives and, by such failure, do not succeed in exploiting the child's mathematical competence in school. From the perspective of situated learning theory, however, this account is unsound. Learning in school is different from learning on the streets because it serves different purposes and is embedded in different activities and practices. Any 'mental processes' associated with the two situations are different because what is learned actually *embodies* those very purposes, activities and social practices: they remain an integral part of learned experience. The psychologist, or teacher, who believes that the 'same' mental processes are implicated in such different learning activities is thus misguided. He or she is guilty of inventing abstract or 'reified' mental entities (cognitive processes) which have no reality in human nature. On a radical interpretation, situated learning theory leads, like behaviourism, to a rejection of cognitive psychology. Mind, the argument proceeds, is 'situated' in activity, not in the head.

Such ideas are difficult to assimilate in one pass. But fear not because they will be explored and illustrated in more detail later. For the moment, the main point to grasp is the fact that Vygotskian thinking has created a range of new debates, and rekindled some old ones, on theories about what and how children learn. These are on the agenda for this new edition.

Neo-Piagetian theory

During the 1960s and1970s, as I said in the Introduction, a major research effort in developmental psychology revolved around the critical evaluation of Piaget's theory. This research generated a range of conceptual and methodological issues about how we should investigate and interpret children's mental abilities which are as important today as they were then. Although Piaget died in 1980, his theoretical legacy remains and many important extensions of his general position have been carried through by his followers.

For example, Karmiloff-Smith (1992) has proposed a new theory of cognitive development. Although her theory retains a strong Piagetian flavour, it stands distinct from it in a number of ways. First, she places much greater emphasis than Piaget did on innate mechanisms which underpin development. Like Piaget, she believes that children experience developmental change (not just learning). But hers is not a general stage theory. Unlike Piaget, Karmiloff-Smith (and many others) argue that knowledge is organized into distinct and somewhat independent systems. For instance, the development of children's linguistic knowledge is independent in some important ways from their developing knowledge of how the physical world works which, in turn, is distinct from their understanding of other people. This more 'modular' view of mind allows for the fact that a child's understanding of some domains of knowledge may be more advanced or sophisticated than it is in relation to others. Consequently, whilst the child's ways of thinking exhibit structural changes throughout development, these changes are not of the global nature envisaged in Piaget's account of stages. Piaget's view invites us to think about the child as a scientist with one all-embracing theory about life. But modular accounts, like Karmiloff-Smith's, and Carey's (1986), suggest that the child develops several distinct theories to make sense of different realms of experience. Such 'modular' views of mental development will be explored further in a later section of this chapter. In the next chapter, we will look in detail at some of the reasons why Karmiloff-Smith, like most neo-Piagetians, has dispensed with the concept of general stages of development.

Information processing: mental models and expertise

In introducing the information-processing perspective on development in the last chapter, I argued that 'All too often, cognitive psychologists who study adult intelligence ignore the process of development and education. They often leave one with the impression that mental activity springs, fully formed, out of a developmental vacuum.' This complaint is less valid now than it was ten years ago. Not only have there been several notable attempts to integrate findings from developmental psychology within a more general theory of human cognition, but there are also examples of the application of such theories to education and instructional theory. Happy though one has to be about this trend, it makes the task of writing a book such as this rather more difficult because it obliges us to refer to relevant theory and research in contemporary cognitive science. And this is going to confront us with a range of new concepts and terminology.

An important theme which pervaded the chapters I wrote ten years ago was the concept of 'expertise' and the 'expert–novice' distinction. In the last decade, this distinction has provided a bridge between theories of adult cognition and developmental theory. One interpretation of this work (e.g. Chi, Glaser and Rees, 1982) is that the source of differences in performance between adults and children should not be attributed directly to age or stage of development but to differences in the extent of relevant experience and task-specific or local *knowledge*. This work, as we shall see in chapter 4, makes theoretical contact with Vygotsky's theory of inner-speech and its role in the development of self-regulation. However, as we shall see, particularly in chapter 8, there are grounds for the belief that the concept of expertise might not, in fact, be enough to explain the facts of human intellectual growth. As Piaget argued, children not only learn, they also develop.

Another integrating theme in research into adult and child cognition is the concept of 'mental models'. I discussed this notion briefly in the first edition but it has achieved much greater prominence in the past decade. The idea that reasoning involves the construction and manipulation of imagined models of the world has been around for many years in psychology. However, two books, both using the title '*Mental Models*', appeared in 1983 (one by Gentner and Stevens, the other by Johnson-Laird). These lent new meaning and direction to the concept. Indeed, the term is now so widely used that it has taken on a variety of meanings.

According to Halford (1992), one of the reasons why the concept of mental models has proved so influential is a general disillusionment with the idea that human reasoning can be described and understood in terms of a 'psycho-logic or mental logic'. Since Piaget's theory sees the achievement of logic as the driving force behind human conceptual development, it is not surprising, as we shall also see in chapter 7, that theories such as that formulated by Johnson-Laird came into conflict with Piaget's in interpreting the nature of adult thinking. And since a central concern of developmental theory is all about how and when children come to think like adults, this conflict created a forum within which debates about theories of adult and child cognition met.

Mental modules and maturation

We talk about children learning to reach, walk and speak. We use the same verb – to learn – when we talk about their learning to read, write and do sums. But are we to assume that the same psychological processes are involved in every case where we employ the verb 'to learn'? Reaching, walking and talking are universal achievements for non-impaired human beings. They are a 'species characteristic' and, although infants vary in the precise age at which they start to reach, walk and talk, they follow similar paths of development. Once 'learned', these abilities are never forgotten. Only if we suffer damage to particular parts of our anatomy or nervous system do we ever lose these capacities. Should we not conclude, then, that, like breathing and digesting, these are innate abilities; abilities which simply mature and 'unfold' as we age?

Conceptualizing intellectual competence as the sole product of learning, or as the acquisition of expertise and skill, lays stress on the role of empirical experience in human development. Such views are the modern versions of a long-standing philosophical tradition termed 'empiricism'. Traditionally, 'nativist' theories, which stress innate mechanisms over experience in explaining human nature, have opposed the empiricist position. Modern neo-nativist theories regard development as a process of maturation and the 'unfolding' of capacities driven by a genetic 'blueprint', not learning. Where, historically, terms such as 'instincts' and 'faculties' were coined to provide a vocabulary with which to talk about the proposed innate bases of human psychology, today, terms and phrases such as 'mental modules' and 'frames of mind' do the same job.

Since the formulation and propagation of Darwin's theory of evolution, the general idea that the physical structure of an organism is a product of adaptive evolution to fit an ecological niche has passed into common sense. But could *ideas, rules* and *mental structures* also be the fruits of evolution and be transmitted genetically as neo-nativism claims? Piaget's theory is that they cannot; they must be *constructed* on the basis of experience. Learning theorists argue that all knowledge and expertise has to be learned. Neo-nativist theorists disagree with both positions. Why?

As we shall see in chapter 5, Chomsky argues that children are not taught how to understand and use their language. The process of language acquisition has to be viewed as a natural one in which genetically transmitted 'mental organs' or brain mechanisms automatically extract and use the rules and structures of language. This is why all normally intact babies eventually start talking. Exposure to speech sounds 'triggers' the nervous system into action and provides all that is needed to explain how children learn the structure of their language. If one accepts the idea that mental processes, such as those which underpin language, are the outcomes of the working of physical systems in the brain, then it is but a short (though difficult) step to the idea that mental processes (or, better, the physical brain processes which realize them) could also have emerged out of evolution and be passed on genetically. But if language is innate, why can't newborns talk?

The structure of the body undergoes continual change with age. For example, the biological changes which herald the onset of puberty are natural phenomena which obviously do not have to be learned. Their onset can, of course, be influenced by social factors such as diet and living conditions, but their eventual emergence is genetically predetermined. Thus, a process or state of being does not have to be present at birth to be counted as the product of genetic pre-programming. Similarly, although children cannot talk, walk or reach at birth, it does not necessarily follow that they have to learn how to do such things. Provided that they receive the necessary environmental inputs, maturation of the body and nervous system will ensure that these capacities emerge. Just as the body naturally processes food and drink to ensure digestion and growth, so innate structures in the nervous system process speech to ensure the extraction and use of rules and structures.

If this is true for a complex process like language acquisition, why could it not hold true of other psychological capacities, such as logical reasoning? If reasoning, like language, is made possible by structures in the brain and if those structures emerge along genetically pre-determined lines, then reasoning is innate, not learned or developed. Perhaps, as Fodor (1982) argues, all human concepts rest on the workings of innate brain processes.

Common experience tells us that people vary in how fast and far they develop and that achievement relates to effort and experience. So the fruits of development can't all be put down to maturation. But what if psychological processes such as interest, effort and motivation are also innately determined? Suppose, for instance, that interest arises, not from systems of external rewards and punishments, but from a search for stimulation and information. Perhaps individual differences in interest are just external, behavioural signs of innate preferences for certain kinds of stimulation and information over others. If the brain processes which direct the search for external stimulation are genetically driven, then motivation, interest etc. are not the *cause* of individual differences in development but simply the products of them. Looked at in this way, the study and explanation of individual differences in human growth takes on a major significance. To what extent should we be prepared to accept such differences as bi-products of genetic variation as opposed to the specific products of differential experience and opportunity? The ways in which we seek to understand, explain and, in education, respond to such questions betray the stance we adopt in relation to fundamental issues about the nature of the interactions between maturation, development and learning. Consequently, the issue of individual differences and their origins forms another theoretical theme which pervades this volume.

For example, some children are good at sums but can't dance very well. Others seem to show a natural aptitude for music and learn how to play a musical instrument early in life to achieve levels of excellence which many of us struggle to gain but never attain. But these children may not make friends easily, whereas other children might possess a natural empathy for others and make friends without effort. Are learning and achievement in all these activities rooted in different natural abilities? Over the past decade or so, neo-nativist theories have held that there are, indeed, separate 'modules of mind' (Fodor, 1982) or multiple intelligences underlying different 'frames of mind' (Gardner, 1983). If all this is true, then effective education might have less to do with instruction and learning and more with selecting children on the basis of their aptitudes and guiding them towards activities which enable them to exercise those aptitudes.

Research into the psychological abilities of young infants (which lies outside the remit of this volume) has provided strong evidence in support of neo-nativist, modular theories. Infants do not enter the world as psychological blank slates, nor can their early development and achievements be understood without recourse to explanations involving the maturation of both the body and the nervous system. This all provides grist for the neo-nativist mill. Another source of grist is less obvious: it comes from the achievements of computational approaches to developing models of the mind.

With the advent of modern computers and demonstrations of so-called 'artificial intelligence', the long-standing idea that mental processes are but products of physical structures in the brain has taken on a new look. It is common now to liken the brain to a computer, or a set of computers, and to regard psychological processes as the results of 'neural computation'. Neural or 'brain computers' are physical entities and, hence, candidates for evolution and genetic transmission. The computer metaphor provides concrete 'models' of how the mind might be structured, what are often referred to as models of our 'mental architecture'. Similarly, the idea of the mind 'running a program' provides a way of thinking about how mental processes and computational structures in the brain might be related. The unlikely combination of computer models of mind, genetics and empirical studies of the innate psychological capacities of babies hence provides a new (or, better, a revitalized) theoretical approach to trying to understand psychological growth and structure.

However, as we move away from infancy and further along the life cycle and consider how human development differs within and across cultures, the idea that the maturation and the 'triggering' of brain mechanisms can provide an adequate account of human psychology looks increasingly less convincing. If, for example, the development of written language and mathematical sign systems helps to structure intellectual processes, then we will not be able to dispense with theories of development and learning. Written language may be built upon an auditory 'language module' or 'mental organ', but it is also processed by the visual system (or, in the case of Braille, the fingers). The processes involved must be, at least, 'cross-modular'. And, if Vygotsky and Luria are to be believed, systems of signs like written words and written numbers also lead to the development of historically and culturally relative psychological processes, in which case they can't be carried directly by the genes.

Some modularity theorists accept that cultural tools and inventions can lead to the re-structuring of knowledge and understanding (e.g. Carey, 1990). However, as you might anticipate, explanations about how the processes of maturation, development and learning interact in the course of psychological growth vary from theory to theory, as we shall see.

Time to synthesize?

Contemporary learning theory accounts of cognitive development are, perhaps, the closest to everyday common sense. As children gain experience, they develop expertise. If we can motivate them to keep on task, confront them with learning tasks that they can master and with curricula that develop their knowledge and understanding, then we can provide them with an effective and worthwhile education.

But both neo-Piagetians and neo-nativists reject this position as, at best, inadequate. Children not only learn but also develop and mature. Their stage of cognitive development, or of maturation, places constraints on what we can expect them to learn or hope to teach. I have already said that some neo-Piagetian theorists, including Karmiloff-Smith (1992), Halford (1992), and Case (1991), accept that the concept of mental modules needs to be integrated and accommodated within a model of development and each has proposed his or her theory which attempts to do just this. There is also widespread agreement that development and maturation take place in a cultural milieu and that, particularly in relation to theories about the later stages of development, the impact of the tools, systems of signs and means of instruction that a culture makes available has also to be acknowledged and explained in an adequate theory of intellectual growth. Although attempts to relate theories of maturation, development and learning might seem to be mere academic enterprises, they promise profound implications for the way in which we are likely to view the processes of socialization and education.

Both developmental and modularity approaches stress the internal or 'endogenous' aspects of cognitive growth. The process of achieving understanding is personal, active, selective and constructive. Motivation, attention and interpretation are largely driven by internal processes, rather than by external incentives or instruction.

Social constructivist theories of development, like learning theory accounts of expertise, stress external or 'exogenous' influences on development. The social constructivists also argue for the cultural relativity of learning processes and attribute to both social practices and sign systems a causal role in cognitive development. The means by which a culture inducts its children into its values and practices is of crucial significance within such an approach and the role of education is likely to be seen as central to our understanding of the human mind. The nature and origins of individual differences in the pathways of human development are also a major concern of this approach. Since its main theoretical tenets lead to the expectation that variations in patterns of cultural and social activities will be reflected in differences on the psychological plane, the investigation of differences in cultural and sub-cultural ways of life provide a natural source of data in exploring the explanatory power of the paradigm. Thus, the study of psychological variation associated with differences in social context, task, and inter-personal relationships forms a major concern of students of this school of thought.

If it does prove possible to achieve even a partial theoretical synthesis of the competing 'images' of childhood derived from learning theory, constructivism, nativism and social constructivism, then our grasp of what we might expect of education and what we must leave to nature will prove much firmer than hitherto. In the following chapters, we will consider a number of attempts to achieve some degree of theoretical synthesis. For example, as already indicated, we will consider recent attempts to integrate theories of cognitive development with a 'modular' view of the mind. We will also examine attempts to explore how the formation of relationships within the family and children's emotional experiences within the home are reflected in their cognitive development, and efforts to integrate an analysis of cultural values, practices and systems of signs with the development of children's understanding and use of mathematics in different contexts.

To the extent that any or all of these attempts to integrate different perspectives are judged successful, the better placed will we be to evaluate the promise of the hitherto competing theories about how children think and learn.

3

Are there stages of development?

This relatively brief chapter includes a more detailed consideration of some of the issues raised in the Introduction (I promised to be repetitive!). More specifically, we examine Piaget's proposition that a major change occurs in children's thinking and in their readiness for certain types of learning at about seven years of age. The aim of the chapter is not simply to provide a more detailed and extensive account of Piaget's theory of stages. It also considers and illustrates some of the major criticisms that have been levelled against his views, and examines alternative descriptions of the nature of development and learning during the first years of schooling. By looking in detail at the demands placed on children in experiments that are designed to study their thinking and analyse their understanding, we can gain some insights into the complexities of adult–child communication in formal, contrived encounters. These suggest a number of ways in which children may misunderstand what adults ask them to do which may have nothing to do with their possession, or lack of possession, of logical competence. If one accepts these alternative explanations, then one may reject the notion of stages of development and accept a more central role for language, communication and instruction in the development of children's thinking and learning than that portrayed in Piagetian theory. Alternatively, as several students of Piaget's approach have done, one can seek to modify the theory in ways that overcome the empirical challenges levelled against it by his critics.

Appearance and reality in the development of understanding

A central aspect of Piaget's theory is the proposition that children's thinking is different *in kind* from that of more mature individuals. All children develop through the same sequence of stages before achieving mature, rational thought. The structure of children's thinking at each stage is distinctive, the same for all children at that stage, and different from that of children and adults at other stages. Development, for Piaget, is not simply the continuous accumulation of things learned step by step. Rather, it involves a number of intellectual 'revolutions' at specific junctures in the life cycle, each one of which involves important changes in the structure of intelligence. Each stage yields a different way of thinking about and understanding the world from that which it grows out of and replaces.

Several important arguments about children's ability to learn flow from the theory. The effects of a particular learning experience on a child's knowledge and understanding vary according to his or her stage. Whilst a young child might learn or be taught how to solve a given problem, to provide what sounds like an appropriate answer to a difficult question, or to execute a particular routine (counting or adding numbers, say), the impact of such experiences on the child will be different in kind from that experienced by one at a later stage of development. The status and significance of what children learn is a direct function of their stage of development.

It follows from this view that the impact of lessons taught by parents or teachers also varies as a function of a child's developmental stage. Indeed, a major implication of the theory is that the effects and effectiveness of teaching are fundamentally constrained by the structure of the child's intelligence. Recall the example given in chapter 1. It may be possible to teach a five-year-old child to recite the words one to five, but it does not follow that he or she understands numbers. Learning routines by rote (repetition and drill), and discovering how some properties of sets of objects remain invariant despite changes in their appearance – one of the preconditions for achieving numeracy – are worlds apart. When we teach the young child to recite numbers and, later, attribute her eventual numeracy to our own instruction, we are, in Piaget's view, falling into the trap of 'magical thinking'. We have done things to and with the child. In time, the child changes and learns. Therefore our actions 'caused' the child's development. No, says Piaget:

the child's understanding arises out of her self-directed *actions* upon the physical world.

The question we must turn to now is how self-directed activity leads the child to *construct* his or her own understanding of natural phenomena. We also consider how they come to question and reject the assumption that changes in the appearance of things entail a change in their nature or substance. To address these questions, I need to introduce and explain some of Piaget's theoretical terminology.

Two key Piagetian terms: assimilation and accommodation

In the last chapter, I outlined the way in which an infant might perceive objects in terms of the past actions that she has exerted on them. Objects become 'known' and 'recognized' in terms of the actions that serve to *assimilate* them to the fulfilment of intentions. So, for example, a bottle may be known and perceived in terms of activities like grasping, bringing it to the mouth, sucking and swallowing. To the extent that any new 'container' can be assimilated successfully to these schemes in order to fulfil the desire to drink, then it too will be 'known' in terms of 'bottle-related' actions.

At one level, of course, every action we perform is unique. When the infant grasps, lifts and drinks from a particular bottle, containing a certain amount in it, from a specific surface, in a given context, her actual performance will vary in minor detail from other, similar performances. Put in Piagetian terms, every act of assimilation involves an element of *accommodation*. Piaget uses this term to refer to the changes, often minor ones, that have to be made to pre-existing schemes of activity in order to make possible the assimilation of a new experience. Imagine, for example, the infant trying, for the first time, to pick up and drink from a full, pint-sized container. She tries to assimilate this new object to her existing schemes of grasping and drinking but finds that the object *resists* her efforts and begins to tilt and spill. She will eventually come to know that some things are too heavy for her to lift. Indeed, this experience is laying the developmental foundations for the concept of weight itself. She is learning that some things cannot be picked up unaided. The child cries out or in some way requests assistance. Her father helps her to lift the container until it is in a position that enables her to fulfil her intention to drink (to assimilate the object). She has now *accommodated* her activities to this new experience. The realm of objects that can be assimilated to the activity of drinking is now split into those that can be assimilated by the original schemes of grasping and drinking, and others that require other means (e.g. a call for help) to enable assimilation. The child would probably centre on size as the perceptual cue which discriminates one sub-class of things that afford drinks from others that only do so with help.

Some accommodations require dramatic changes in the structure of the child's understanding of the world, particularly those which herald a change in stage. To understand how and when these revolutionary changes come about, we need to delve deeper into the theory.

More technicalities: centration, disequilibrium and de-centring

When a child is trying to do something, whether her intention arises as a consequence of her own activities or is stimulated by a request or question from another person, what she *attends* to in the situation will be dictated by the *actions* that, in the past, have served to achieve similar intentions. So, the child's past activities dictate what is perceptually salient to her.

Suppose we show a five-year-old child two lines of coins laid out as shown in figure 3.1a. We ask her if one set contains more coins than the other. The child is likely to say that they have the same number. Since the sets of coins are essentially similar in all respects, whatever the child looks at in comparing one set with the other will probably lead her to a judgement of equality. We now rearrange the coins so that one set is longer than the other (figure 3.1b). Are they still the same? The child will, in all probability, decide that the longer set contains more coins. Presumably, length is taken as an index of 'amount' or 'number' because, in the past, this dimension proved a reliable guide to relative amount. What the child does not *notice* is the fact that whilst the length of one line has been changed, this change was, so to speak, 'offset' or 'compensated for' by an equal and opposite change in the relative *density* of objects in the two sets. What seems salient to the child is the change that occurs in length or extent. Relative length can be estimated by comparing or centring on the end points of the two sets. Estimating relative density, on the other hand, demands more intense and systematic scrutiny of the objects in the two sets.

What the child is unable to do, then, is to take account of and 'co-ordinate' two or more changes that occur *simultaneously* as the coins

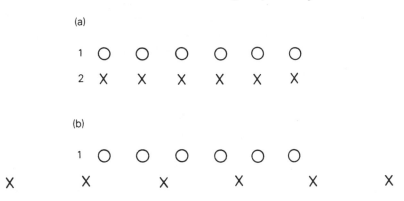

Figure 3.1 Conservation of number: (a) prior to transformation; (b) after transformation

are moved about. Similarly, she cannot co-ordinate her initial judgement (the sets have the same number) with the final one (one has more). She does not sense any discrepancy or 'illogicality' in her two judgements because the act that changed appearance also changed the 'number' of objects. Her judgements, from her own perspective, are not inconsistent since appearances *have* changed. Similarly, if we put the pennies back into line again the child will say that both sets are the same again, but not appreciate any inconsistency. Each judgement that the child makes involves only *one* centration; a single act of observation and comparison. Thus, any change in appearance of necessity involves a change in amount. Asking questions, shuffling pennies, drawing the child's attention to the relative 'density' of the two sets, will not teach her otherwise because she cannot *co-ordinate* her judgements or her observations in order to detect any discrepancy or conflict.

Nature, however, will not 'tolerate' the assumption that any obvious change in appearance always entails a change in the 'nature' of things. As the child plays with sets of objects, be these blocks, beads, coins, animals, marbles, people or whatever, and rearranges or sees them rearranged, she will eventually and inevitably encounter a situation in which her tacit assumption about the nature of change will be violated by events. This could happen in an indeterminate number of ways. Perhaps she *discovers* the fact that two sets of objects which looked different actually fulfil some common purpose (e.g. filling a small container). Or her joy at increasing her wealth by enlarging the area of floor covered by her savings might be dashed when she finds they can only buy the same amount, however she lays her money out. Who knows? The argument is that, nature being what it is, the child must discover some situation that will challenge her assumptions. She then enters a state of *disequilibrium*. She is confused as her assumption is brought into question by the reality of events. This mental state is intolerable and motivates thought and action. Eventually, the child will discover a more embracing or 'over-arching' idea or mental scheme which will restore equilibrium. She might realize, for example, that if she takes account of *both* linear extent and density, her confusion begins to lift. She is *de-centring* herself and moving away from an *intuitive* understanding of number, involving centration on only one thing, to judgements based on the *co-ordination* of several acts of centration.

Now mental *operations* appear on the scene. Mental actions involve single action–consequence relations (e.g. when pennies are moved, a line gets longer or shorter). Mental operations are *classes* of actions that are integrated with other (logically related) operations. In other words, they appear as *systems,* not, like actions, as isolated entities. Perhaps I can help to explain this difficult notion. The ability to 'see' that changes in length are offset by changes in density (co-ordination and compensation) is part and parcel of understanding that the effects of an action (e.g. extending the line of coins) can be *reversed* by an equal and opposite act (aligning them again). Actions *become* operations when they are embedded in systems of thought that are co-ordinated and reversible. Thus, the ability to *conserve* abstract properties, like number, emerges as a part of a new system of understanding that involves operations. Once the child's thinking becomes co-ordinated and reversible, for instance, she 'knows' that changes in appearance may be deceptive and realizes that, in any situation, number *must* remain invariant (i.e. two sets remain equivalent) if nothing is added or taken away. Indeed, by a similar line of argument, the *concept* of adding and taking away is now *understood* in relation to invariance. All these aspects of understanding co-emerge as part of a system of thinking: concrete operational intelligence has been constructed. Learning arithmetical concepts can begin.

Piaget's theory (and evidence) suggests that the ability to co-ordinate, compensate, reverse and appreciate the nature of invariance (to conserve) emerges in relation to several areas of knowledge at about the same time in development (usually around age seven). Piaget suggests that the ability to conserve (grasp invariance and equivalence) involves similar intellectual abilities (e.g. co-ordination) whether we are dealing with concepts of number, area, volume, weight, quantity or whatever.

This explains why a child who lacks such abilities cannot grasp any of these abstract notions. A child who displays understanding in one area, however, possesses the necessary competence to develop an understanding of other 'invariances'. She has entered the stage of 'concrete operations' and begun her career as a 'conserver'.

Not all conservations appear at the same time. Some, like conservation of weight (realizing, for example, that changing the shape of a lump of clay does not also change its weight) come later than others (e.g. conservation of quantity). Piaget's argument is that the same logical abilities are involved: some things are more difficult to learn (for reasons that are not always clear) and are assimilated to concrete operational thinking later than other things, but they are nonetheless assimilated to the same system of understanding. The notion that intelligence can be analysed in terms of such 'general purpose' mental abilities is, as we shall see, one of the most controversial features of Piaget's theory.

Before moving on to consider the educational implications of Piaget's theory and alternative explanations for children's learning and understanding, let me discuss another example of the transition from pre-operational to operational thinking. This should help to show how Piaget identifies the same intellectual abilities at work in superficially quite different domains of knowledge to give credibility to the notion of stages of development.

Suppose we show our five-year-old two identical beakers filled with liquid and she judges that they contain the same amount to drink. Then, in full view of the child, we pour the contents of one into another vessel with a different shape. Imagine that it is thinner and taller. We ask the child to judge whether the new container holds the same amount of liquid as that contained in the beaker left untouched (are the two quantities equivalent?). The child is likely to say that the thinner one, in which the liquid rises to a greater relative height, contains more. Why does the child make this judgement? Why can't she 'see' that the two vessels must contain equivalent amounts?

As we have seen, the child's thinking, intuitive at this stage, is perceptually dominated and limited to judgements based on a single point of comparison across the two objects. She sees and appreciates the fact that the action of pouring leads to a change in appearance, in relative height, but what she does not (and, of course, cannot) appreciate is that several changes in appearance occur simultaneously. Consequently, her judgement of quantity is based on only one of the simultaneous changes that occur. When the two vessels are identical, a judgement based on any coupled centrations (i.e. on an inspection of two similar aspects of the two vessels) will result in the 'correct' answer. When the vessels are different, however, attention to only one dimension gives the 'wrong' answer. The child does not understand the notion of quantity, nor can she appreciate the fact that this remains invariant when pouring occurs.

The child's thinking and understanding are the same here as in the number conservation study. Whilst pouring is taking place, she can only attend to one dimension of change. When pouring is finished and the child is asked to compare the two quantities, she also fails to appreciate the equivalence of the two quantities because her visual inspection is limited to a single act of comparison. Reminding her of her previous judgement is also ineffective because, lacking the capacity to co-ordinate her answers and believing that changes in appearance entail changes of substance, the child does not experience any sense of conflict or discrepancy in her answers. When the child achieves *operativity*, she can 'perceive' the fact that pouring leads to simultaneous changes in several aspects of a phenomenon and discover the fact that one change offsets, or is compensated by, another. When she has constructed systems of operations, her perception of the world is, quite literally, transformed.

Conflict, instruction and accommodation

Imagine a child who has entered the stage of concrete operations presented with the quantity conservation task. Although she has not seen this phenomenon before and has never been confronted with the problem of conserving continuous quantity, she is able to perceive and co-ordinate simultaneous changes in appearance. She also knows that changes in the way things look do not necessarily mean that they cannot be equivalent. She is able to co-ordinate her answers to questions posed before and after pouring and, being logical, will not tolerate any inconsistencies between them. She also knows that if liquid is poured back, any changes in appearance can be reversed to retrieve the initial state of affairs. In consequence, while the problem is just as novel for her as for the five-year-old, the intelligence she brings to bear on it and what she 'sees' are different in kind.

If she has only recently achieved operational competence, the solution to the problem may not be immediately apparent to her, but she is intellectually ready to *discover* its solution. At this stage, a teacher (or another child) may say and do things which *conflict* with our child's interpretation of events. For instance, if one child suggests that quantity has changed because liquid in one glass is higher, then the other person, drawing her attention to opposing differences in another dimension (e.g. the other glass is wider) or reminding her of her previous judgement (that both held the same amount), may activate a sense of conflict. Since she is beginning to perceive things that, hitherto, she was unaware of and realizes that more is going on than used to meet her eyes, it is possible that this conflict will set her thinking and trying to solve the puzzle facing her. She sets out to resolve any contradiction and achieve some degree of coherence in her theory of what is going on. The way out, the way to accommodate the conflict, is for her to restructure the way she thinks.

Restructuring

Social experience, then, may help a child to restructure her thinking by inducing disagreement and cognitive *conflict* that mobilize thought and help to bring about the next stage of development. But children have to be in an appropriate state of intellectual readiness for such social facilitation to take place. They can only experience conflict when their intuitive view of the world is beginning to break down. Even here, the restoration of equilibrium, and the restructuring of knowledge that makes it possible, are products of the child's own thinking. Illustration, explanation and interrogation might help to mobilize the child's problem-solving, but only she can discover the solution.

A critique of Piaget's theory

The great power of Piaget's theory stems from his identification of structurally different, pre-operational and operational, structures of mind. The *universal* nature of a stage, the fact that it structures everything the child perceives and thinks, provides a general explanation for the fact that, in many different situations, seven-year-olds are likely to think quite differently from their younger peers and are 'ready' for a different stage of learning. The promise of *generality* is what makes Piaget's theory so attractive and important.

However, there are many people who do not accept Piaget's theory. As early as 1936, for instance, Susan Isaacs reported many observations of children in her nursery school at Maltinghouse in Cambridge. Her pre-schoolers, she argued, displayed clear evidence of rational thinking.

Her observations and her interpretations of what these implied for Piaget's theory anticipated many contemporary arguments in child development. There is now a significant body of opinion which holds that Piaget's methods and demonstrations led him to underestimate or misconstrue the nature of children's thinking. Let us consider some alternative explanations for children's 'failures' in tasks demanding 'operational' thinking.

Did Piaget underestimate the importance of language?

Think again about the demands being placed on the young child in Piaget's task situations. The experimenter obviously has to *communicate* the nature of the problem being set to the child, and we can analyse the process of communication into a number of levels. A *breakdown* in mutual understanding between adult and child at any of these levels might account for children's apparent illogicality.

First, we obviously need to consider the actual words and grammar involved in what the adult says to the child. In the quantity conservation task, for instance, we find expressions like 'as much as', 'same amount to drink', and so forth. Do children actually *understand* these words and expressions in the way that the adult intends? Young children may appear to understand and use them in familiar situations, but are the meanings that they carry in everyday talk between adults and young children the same as those involved in contrived, experimental tasks? If we examine and analyse children's linguistic development, will we discover that they do not, in fact, really understand the language involved in experimental tests?

Let me provide an illustrative example. Another of the intellectual structures that Piaget analysed to reveal marked differences in the thinking of five- and seven-year-old children involves concepts of 'classes' and 'class inclusion'. To the mature mind, a given object (e.g. a chair) or a class of objects (e.g. animals) can, at one and the same time, be members of any number of more inclusive categories. So, a chair is also a member of the class 'furniture' or of 'manufactured artefacts' and so on. Categories like 'animals' can be subsumed under more inclusive labels (e.g. living beings) and decomposed into more exclusive ones (e.g. canine, feline). For an adult, such classifications exist as enduring, organized structures of knowledge. Saying that a dog is an animal or a member of the canine family does not change the *thing* being referred to. The same concept can belong to any number of classes at the same time.

Figure 3.2 'Are there more flowers or more tulips?'

But pre-operational children cannot co-ordinate different judge-ments or acts of centration. So, for example, a tulip cannot be conceived of as both a tulip and a flower at one and the same time. This demands co-ordination which, as we have seen, pre-operational children cannot do. So, if we show the pre-operational child the set-up illustrated in figure 3.2 and ask her 'Are there more flowers or more tulips?', the child will probably say 'More tulips'. 'More' is interpreted as a reference to the largest available sub-class (of flowers). Since there are more tulips than daisies, there are more tulips. Piaget's interpretation of this phenomenon is that the child cannot 'see' or, rather, cannot *organize* what she sees, so that the same entities (the tulips) are *simultaneously* both tulips and flowers.

Questions like 'Are there more flowers or more tulips?' sound distinctly odd! However, before we look into rather murky linguistic depths to analyse the nature and consequences of their strangeness, let me consider the issue of class inclusion with what looks like a much simpler example. A child (one of Piaget's own), aged two-and-a-half, is often taken for a walk by her father along a particular road. This road is often infested with slugs. The child sometimes points to a slug saying (in French), 'There's the slug again.' Her father asks (since she had pointed out another slug earlier), 'But isn't it another?' The child goes back to the first slug encountered and is asked, 'Is it the same?' 'Yes.' 'Another slug?' 'Yes.' 'Another or the same?'. . .The questions, Piaget concluded, 'obviously had no meaning' for the child.

What does 'the' mean? When the child says 'There's the slug again', is she, perhaps, using the word 'the' as part of the act of pointing to and talking about an object in the situation? But when Piaget asks if it is 'the' same slug (i.e. as a previous slug), he is using the word to refer *back* to a previous experience. These two uses of words like 'the' are quite different and children develop an understanding of the first 'the', as something being pointed at, a long time before they learn how to use and understand the second 'the', which is used to refer back to an earlier utterance or experience. Even if the child is aware of the fact that a slug is both itself and a member of the class 'all slugs', she would not understand the question because she does not and cannot understand the *language* involved. Are we, then, dealing with absence of *logic* or a failure of communication based on the child's stage of language development, or both? Piaget's observation does not allow us to answer this question.

Suppose we find, in general, that specific problems in understanding language can explain why children fail to answer Piaget's questions. Would this mean that we have sufficient evidence to reject Piaget's explanation for their 'errors' of reasoning? Well, not really. It might still be argued, for example, that understanding a word like 'the' in all its meanings demands concrete operational competence. Part of the elegance and power of Piaget's theory is the way in which it integrates many aspects of development, including the relationship between intellectual and linguistic understanding. One might argue, for example, that understanding the second form of the word 'the', to refer back to previous experiences, demands an ability to co-ordinate judgements, which explains why young children cannot understand it when it is used in this way (although this explanation is hard to sustain, as we will see in chapter 6).

Piaget's theory also leads directly to the prediction that pre-operational children will *not* understand phrases like 'as much as' used in conservation tests in the same way as adults do. Mature understanding of what such expressions mean demands the capacity to co-ordinate different judgements, so of course the child doesn't understand the words involved. If we are to reject Piaget's account, we must provide an alternative and equally robust theory of how the child comes to understand language, and provide evidence that it is *language* or communication abilities as such that create problems for the child, not his or her inability to reason logically. We have to find some way of distinguishing linguistic problems from intellectual problems. Perhaps we could try to provide evidence that when linguistic problems are avoided, the young child can reason rationally. Or we might try to demonstrate that the acquisition of linguistic knowledge involves 'special' features that are not simply reflections of the difficulties a child faces in understanding the concepts or ideas embodied in language. Put another way, does the development of thinking dictate the development of language, or are some features of language development independent of intellectual growth? Or is the capacity to use language itself the basis for understanding and grasping concepts like equivalence and classification?

To investigate the theory of stages and all its educational implications, we must, then, examine alternative accounts of linguistic development, and of the relationships between language and thought, to those espoused by Piaget. This we do in chapters 6 and 7.

Can children make sense of Piaget's questions?

I have already drawn attention to the fact that communication between adult and child in Piagetian tests of class inclusion sound, to say the least, rather strange. Even if the child, in one sense, understands the *words* and the grammar involved in such questions, there is still a question mark over what they think the questioner intends to *mean*. What does the child think is going on in the experimental situation? How does she *interpret* the performance of the experimenter? How do the 'social practices' that govern interactions between adults and children in the world at large influence how the child *interprets* what the experimenter expects of her?

First, note that the child is often asked a similar question at least twice in such experiments. In the test of conservation of continuous quantity, for instance, the child is usually asked something like 'Are they the same or different?' at least twice: once before the liquid is poured into the new container and once after pouring has taken place. What *function* does the repetition of a question usually serve in everyday encounters between adults and children? Blank, Rose and Berlin (1978) suggest that a repeated question is usually a signal that the *first* answer given was wrong, inaccurate or inappropriate. If so, perhaps the child in conservation experiments is thrown, not by the 'logical' demands of the task, but by her interpretation of what she assumes the adult is *implicitly* communicating. There are now several experiments which have shown that changes in the way such problems are presented to children which ensure that only one question is asked (e.g. the second of the two questions mentioned above, asked after pouring has taken place) lead to a greater chance of 'correct' or conserving answers from young children. So, perhaps breakdown of mutual understanding, rather than logical incompetence, explains the child's apparent 'errors' of reasoning.

The issue of questioning draws our attention to 'pragmatic' features of communication about which I will have a good deal to say in this book. 'Pragmatic', in this sense, refers to the way in which the meaning of an utterance is influenced by its social context and by the relationship between the speaker and hearer. For example, if a teacher asks a child 'Can you close the door?', he or she is unlikely to be enquiring about the child's physical prowess in the practice of door-shutting (unless, of course, there is some reason to doubt that the child can do such things and the teacher really wants to know if he or she can do so). Many utterances involve 'indirect' acts of communication. The example above, for instance, is probably a request or order 'disguised' as a question. If a child fails to comply with or fails to understand a request or question from an adult, we must ask whether any 'indirect' or 'hidden' meanings are implicated. The meanings associated with utterances in everyday interactions may differ from those implied in experimental tasks, leading to confusion for the child and a breakdown of communication. Such features of communication are complex and of immense importance in evaluating what a child knows and understands, as we shall see.

Thus, when we begin to explore the interaction between experimenter and child as a *social encounter*, and one that displays some 'special' and, from the child's perspective, unfamiliar properties, a number of questions arise. Until we consider and resolve these, we would be unwise to draw inferences about children's intellectual ability and logical competence.

Another concrete example illustrates how pragmatic aspects of everyday social practices influence children's interpretation of experimental or 'contrived' situations. In a quantity conservation study, Light, Buckingham and Roberts (1979) performed the usual transfer of the contents of one container to another, but they incorporated an important modification to Piaget's method. One of the two identical beakers had a broken, razor-sharp rim. The children's attention was drawn to this flaw, and the potential danger it presented was given as a reason for transferring its contents to another (differently shaped) container. Asked to compare quantities after pouring in this context, children were more likely to be successful than they were when no such reason for the experimenter's actions was given. One interpretation of this finding is that the explanation for changing glasses made the experimenter's actions *sensible* to the child. Put another way, the child's everyday social experiences render what the experimenter does intelligible. She sees no reason to assume that he is showing her something unusual that demands an explanation. When no such reason is given, perhaps the child (erroneously) believes that there must be some hidden reason that she does not understand. Adults usually appear to know more than children do. When children cannot infer a sensible reason for the adult's behaviour, they may think that there is more to the problem than 'meets the eye', perhaps assuming that there is something they do not understand and need to learn.

Finally, here is a rather different illustration of the way in which children's interpretations of what an experimenter is getting at can influence their apparent competence. If ten-year-old children are asked to compare two sets of ten objects (these are arranged in two haphazard sets) in order to find out if they comprise the same number, they usually perform the task accurately. However, if the experimenter asks 'Why are there more in this set than that set?', many ten-year-olds, like younger children, will give an explanation based on appearances, even when the sets are equal. That is, they will choose the set that *looks* more numerous. But when the experimenter says 'I *think* there are more in this set than that one', most children count the set and disagree (Hundeide, 1985). Consequently, it is not the case that children are not prepared to challenge an adult's judgement or opinion. Rather, when they are asked to *explain* something by a question like 'Why are there ... ?', they take *on trust* the fact that there is a difference to be explained. The experimenter's question does not reveal a lack of logic in children's judgements. Rather, it illustrates how people's *interpretation* of what others mean by what they say involves more than the words or questions used: mutual understanding rests on a range of conventions and expectations which are often violated in experiments. As we will find in chapter 7, they are also frequently violated in classrooms.

Do *children understand Piaget's tasks?*

Another criticism that has often been levelled against Piaget's studies is that many involve tasks that are 'artificial' and unfamiliar to children, and that this explains why they make errors. For example, one of the predictions that arises from Piaget's theory is that pre-operational children are psychologically 'egocentric'. He argues that they are incapable of conceptualizing a situation from any perspective other than the one they themselves are occupying. Their thinking is domi-

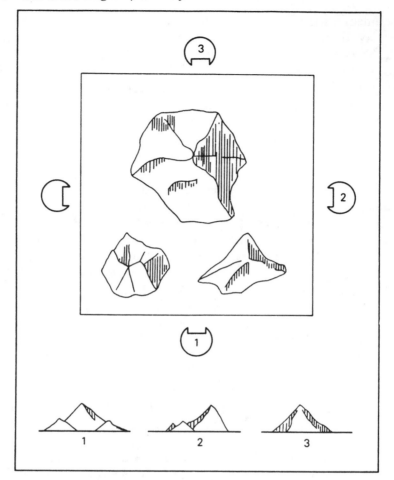

Figure 3.3   The three mountains problem. A child is positioned at location 1. She is asked to select from a group of drawings the view of the mountains that would be seen by persons at locations 1, 2 and 3

nated by their perceptions and, since they are unable to co-ordinate judgements based on different observations, when they move from one position to another they can't integrate judgements made at different times to achieve an 'objective' view of situations. They are always dominated by their own perceptions and hence cannot construct a view of things as seen from another point of view.

One experiment designed to test and display this feature of pre-operational children's thinking involves the situation illustrated in figure 3.3. Children are shown a model of three mountains together with a

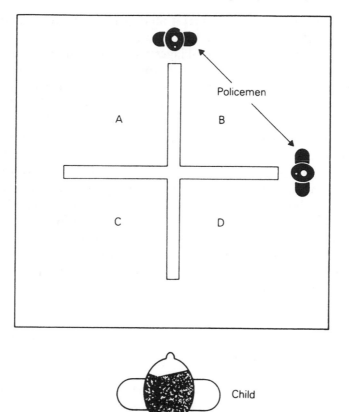

Policemen

A   B

C   D

Child

Figure 3.4 The child is asked to show where a doll might hide so as not to be seen by the two policemen

number of pictures that depict how the mountain scene appears from different positions of observation. Imagine that a child is looking at the model from position 1. She is asked to pick out the picture that represents what another person would see if they were to look at the same model from position 2 or 3. Children below the age of seven years or so, who have yet to develop operational thinking (pre-operational children), are unlikely to succeed in this situation and will probably choose the drawing that represents what they themselves see of the three mountains. They are unable to conceptualize or form a mental representation of what the model looks like from other than their own point of view. This task, for Piaget, illustrates pre-operational children's egocentrism and demonstrates that their concept of space is subjective and centred on their own body. Unlike adults, they cannot conceive of space in 'objective' terms:

they cannot construct an interpretation of what 'their' space might look like from another perspective, for example.

Although, as with most of Piaget's demonstrations, many other experimenters have reaffirmed his findings with children from several different cultures, other researchers have shown that so-called, pre-operational children can conceptualize viewpoints other than their own when the problem makes more 'sense' to them. Figure 3.4 illustrates a task used by a group of psychologists working with Donaldson (1978) in Edinburgh. The child's task here is to decide where to place a doll in the set-up so that it can 'hide' from the two policemen. To solve this problem, the child has to relate the points of view of the two police dolls to discover the region of space that neither can see and in which the other doll can hide. Many pre-operational children succeed in solving this task. Donaldson's interpretation is that where the actions of the characters in the problem are interpretable to the child, where they refer to experiences that are relatively familiar and involve actions that the child can make sense of, then the child is not egocentric or limited to a subjective concept of space.

Part of Piaget's legacy

As I have already said, most of the observations and demonstrations that Piaget made have been replicated many times by researchers in different parts of the world. The main issue concerns their interpretation. The promise of generality held out by the theory has been questioned. As we shall see in later chapters, and as Donaldson argued, his theory was too insensitive to the nature of tasks and neglected the social and cultural meanings of the materials used to test children. When we come to study mathematics learning we will see that this is a general and crucial problem for the theory.

The generation of research that was stimulated by Piaget has served to reveal the complexity and difficulty of designing experiments, tests and observational methods to reach any compelling evidence to show how children think and learn. As we shall see, such methodological problems are still a cause for debate in attempts to test and interpret more contemporary ideas about growth and development. Testing good theories is hard work.

Part of Piaget's legacy is also a set of questions which are still the subject of research and debate. Does logic provide an appropriate framework for understanding the development of children's understanding and reasoning? We consider this question further in chapters 7 and 8. Are any failures of communication that arise between adults and children due simply to the child's stage of language development? Or might they be due to differences in levels of expertise? Perhaps failures of communication between adult and child arise out of differences in their relative abilities to perceive, remember and think about situations in which one, but not the other, is an expert. We take this issue up in the next chapter. Or, as Piaget contended, are there still real *discontinuities* in development? Whilst disagreeing with Piaget's emphasis on the role of logic in intellectual development, there are several contemporary theorists who still insist that there are, indeed, discontinuities and that children's thinking changes with age. We obviously need to explore such issues further.

In the preceding chapter, I mentioned several 'neo-Piagetian' theories. Here, I will begin to explore these in order to provide a basis for challenging 'non-developmental' theories which rely on the concept of expertise to explain cognitive growth. We will be exploring such theories further in the pages that follow.

Discontinuities in development?

Although the various developmental theories that have arisen to replace Piaget's differ in important details in their accounts of what changes during development, there are some central areas of agreement shared by most if not all of them.

First, by definition, they argue that we cannot dispense with a theory of development. There is general agreement that learning processes must be integrated within an adequate theory, and contemporary theories are more explicit than Piaget was about the nature and role of learning in intellectual growth. But they all agree that learning alone cannot explain the nature of children's understanding as they grow to adulthood. Logical operations do not, however, play any explanatory role in most neo-Piagetian theories. Thus, the contention that we can understand how children come to understand their world by interpreting their thinking in relation to a 'psycho-logic' has been abandoned by most. There also seems to be a general acceptance of the fact that development has to be conceptualized relative to its social context and that culture-specific knowledge and skills must be identified and explained in order to construct an adequate explanatory theory. For example, as we saw in the last chapter, both Case and Halford explicitly acknowledge the role of culture and its systems of symbols in their theories.

Why, then, have such models of development not converged on a single explanatory theory? The main reason, as one might anticipate, has to do with the proposed mechanisms which underpin and explain developmental discontinuities. Let me try to illustrate some of the main points of contention here. We will explore them in more detail later.

As children mature, their 'speed of mental processing' increases (Case, 1985). For example, the rate at which they can 'encode' and produce speech and retrieve information from memory gets faster with age. Thus, whether they are taking information from the world or recalling it from memory, their minds work more slowly than those of adults.

Because of their slower speed of processing, children cannot hold so much in mind as adults can when they think. They have more limited 'working memories'. Consequently, the representations (Case, 1991; Fischer, 1980) or mental models (Halford, 1992) that they can construct and reason with are less complex than those which adults can entertain. Herein lies one source of discontinuity in development and an explanation as to why adults can solve problems which children cannot yet manage. Halford, accepting the evidence that children's speed of processing increases with age, also contends that children and adults have different processing capacities. Adults, he argues, can process more information simultaneously (i.e. in parallel) and this enables them to solve problems that children do not have the mental capacity to get a mental 'hold' on. Perhaps an example will help to illustrate these issues. They will also be followed through in later chapters.

Drawing inferences from mental models

Consider the following, seemingly simple problem. You are asked to decide 'who is tallest if John is taller than Peter and Peter is taller than Alan'. Children below the age of about five years are usually unable to combine such pairs of propositions in order to draw inferences. Why?

In order to solve the problem, it is necessary to remember the first premise (John is taller than Peter) whilst taking in or encoding the second (Peter is taller than Alan). Then the two mentally represented relations have to be combined in some way. Now, if the speed at which a child can encode and mentally integrate information is so slow that whilst taking in the second premise they forget the first, then they will not possess the necessary information-processing resources needed to draw such inferences. Their inability to do so, on a speed-of-processing account, is not because they lack logical operations but because they cannot yet process information fast enough to hold onto and integrate mentally represented information.

Halford's treatment of the same experimental evidence is somewhat different. Adults usually solve such problems by constructing a 'mental model' that corresponds to the situation or state of the world being described (we elaborate on this point in chapter 7). Most would construct a model representing an ordered list or image in which John is placed at the top, Alan at the bottom and Peter in the middle. Thus, we use a spatially ordered list as an *analogy* for the situation being described. Having constructed our mental model, we can, so to speak, directly 'read off' from it the inference that John is taller than Alan.

Halford suggests that to be able to solve the problem, the child must have the resources to hold both premises in mind at the same time: i.e. to process them in parallel. In Halford's view, children under five can only process *one* relation at a time (e.g. that between John and Peter). Beyond five, they can process two relations in parallel. At this point, they are then able to draw the necessary inference. So, it is not simply speed of processing but also changes in processing capacity which limit the number of relations that can be held in mind at one and the same time. Changes in both speed and capacity help to explain the discontinuities in children's powers of thinking with age.

On first sight, Halford's theory may appear to be the same as Piaget's in that, on both accounts, children are unable to see, at one and the same time, that Peter is shorter than John but taller than Alan and that this results in a failure to co-ordinate the two premises. However, Halford differs from Piaget in that he does not appeal to logic as an explanation. He does not, for example, claim that children pass from a pre-operational to a concrete operational stage. Such operations play no role in the theory. The basis for development is attributed to changes in processing speed and the capacity to process information in parallel, and to the nature of the analogues that children (and adults) use in constructing mental models in order to reason about the world.

The issue of developmental discontinuity has not, then, been ruled out by post-Piagetian research. Theories of how children think and what they are able to learn, based on proposed changes in mental powers with age, are still with us.

Summary

The examples and illustrations I have just discussed identify a number of factors that we need to consider and evaluate in trying to make a decision about how children conceptualize the world and reason about it at different ages. If children do not understand the words and expressions involved in attempts to test their understanding; if they are so unfamiliar with the task they are asked to perform that they do not know what is relevant to the questions asked and, hence, cannot analyse and grasp what they need to take into account; if they are unsure of the experimenter's motives or misled by the way in which the interaction is conducted; if they assume that there is more to the problem than meets the eye; then they may appear logically incompetent.

Piagetian theory did provide explanations for some of these phenomena. Children cannot understand many things that adults say because they lack the necessary intellectual structures to make sense of what they mean. They may well misunderstand an experimenter's intentions because they are 'egocentric' and cannot diagnose those intentions. They are unable to analyse tasks into their important elements because they cannot 'de-centre' from their own viewpoint. If we accept these explanations, then we also accept the stringent notion of readiness for learning and the relative unimportance of language, communication and instruction.

If we reject these explanations, then we must find others. Vygotsky's theory invites us to consider the possibility that children understand those things that are common features of their social experience. Learning *how* to think about and learn about things that are relatively *unfamiliar* are not 'natural' achievements that occur with time, but special forms of 'self-regulation' which rest on *relevant* experiences. However, if we accept that children's mental powers do develop with age because their ability to construct mental representations changes, then the influence of socio-cultural factors may be less crucial than Vygotsky and others claim. Attempts to help and teach children will still be constrained by their stage of development. We will take this issue further in the next chapter.

We have seen that most neo-Piagetian theorists now reject logic as a useful basis for understanding cognitive development. But if intelligent, adaptive thinking is not based in logical operations, what *does* it involve? How does it develop? To what extent is it a product of communication and teaching?

4

Learning how to think and learn

Piaget's analysis of pre-operational thinking suggests that young children tend to form their judgements about the nature of things on the basis of single acts of centration. He argues that their perception is thus 'dominated' by what they happen to attend to. They cannot 'de-centre' their thinking or co-ordinate their mental actions to achieve stable, logical judgements. Only later, when they have constructed logical operations, do they develop the capacity for sustained and systematic perceptual analysis and rational thought.

Whilst the changes in children's ability to perceive, analyse and remember events that Piaget identified are consistent with the results of many other experimental studies, interpretations of how such changes come about vary. Research in the 'information processing' tradition, introduced in chapter 1, provides a different account of the mental activities involved in development which are viewed as evidence of growing expertise. Research in the Vygotskian tradition offers yet another view of the origins and nature of children's abilities. Vygotsky argued that mature mental activity involves adaptive 'self-regulation' which develops through social interaction. In this view, instruction and schooling play a central role in helping children to discover how to pay attention, concentrate and learn effectively. These ideas, and some of the research they have motivated, are the focus of this chapter. We also begin to explore the relationships between the child's perception of the world and his understanding of it.

Attending, concentrating and remembering

When teachers are asked to evaluate a child's likely potential in a particular subject or discipline, their answer is likely to relate to a specific feature of the child's classroom behaviour: the child's willingness or capacity to *concentrate* on tasks relevant to that subject. Those children who spend most time 'on task' in the classroom are most likely to be judged capable of doing well in the subject or discipline being taught. More importantly, if we monitor the children's progress we will find that teacher predictions are, more often than not, borne out. Concentration is a good indicator of interest and potential (Keough, 1982). There are several reasons why teacher judgements, children's powers of concentration and school achievement might be related in this way. One possibility, considered in more detail later in the book, is that teachers are in the business of fulfilling their own prophecies. Perhaps they treat children they perceive as more likely to succeed differently from those they think are less likely to do so and, in so doing, foster the expected patterns of achievement. While we may not rule this factor out entirely, I will be arguing later that such an explanation is far too general and even simple-minded to be convincing. As I will try to show in this chapter, many factors influence children's powers of concentration and thereby exert a marked influence on how much and how readily they learn.

It will come as no surprise to find that, on average, children's concentration span increases with age. But why does it? Well, anyone who has worked with children might observe that younger children are usually more 'distractable' than older ones. Again we ask, why? What is it about young children that leaves them relatively open to distraction? To answer this question, we need to look at the general nature of young children's powers of perception, attention and memory and at their knowledge and 'planning' abilities. The ability to keep on task and to ignore distractions is, in fact, a symptom of the structure of the child's intellect, and changes in concentration span are related to intellectual development. Consider some experimental evidence which illustrates and supports this proposition (see Kail, 1990, for a more detailed and very readable account).

Learning to remember: rehearsal and organization

If five-year-old children are shown a set of twenty pictures and asked to predict how many of them they will be able to remember, they are likely to grossly overestimate their own capacities and may claim that they will remember them all. If we ask eleven-year-olds the same question, their assessments will probably prove accurate. Again, perhaps unsurprisingly, older children will remember more than younger ones. Thus, changes in the ability to memorize go hand-in-hand with more accurate and realistic assessments of one's own mental abilities. Deliberate attempts to commit information to memory are not the product of a 'natural ability' but involve learned *activity*. In fact, they involve a series of activities. The skill in undertaking each of these increases with age throughout the early years of school and beyond.

I think we often mislead ourselves by describing our own psychology using nouns like memory, perception and attention when we should be thinking in terms of verbs such as memorizing, perceiving and attending. Intellectual processes take time to execute and, like manual skills, can be organized and executed more or less effectively. Deliberate memorization involves such skills. It does not emerge full blown at some point in life, but involves a series of interlocking activities which eventually become automatic and often seemingly effortless, but which in reality take years of learning and practice to develop and acquire.

The five-year-olds' unrealistic estimates of their own powers of memory are reflected in their concentration or habits of study. Whereas older children distribute their attention carefully between the different things they are trying to memorize, and spend time in so doing, the younger ones are likely to make a cursory and non-exhaustive inspection before deciding that they are able to remember. As they gain in proficiency, children not only learn how to commit things to memory, but also become more aware of and accurate in their assessments of their own memorial powers. They also become aware of what they do and do not know and this leads to the development of more effective concentration and study skills. For example, if we ask a five- or six-year-old to commit a series of familiar objects to memory we will find that they will recall, on average, about four. Suppose we then ask the child to have another go. Will he pay more attention to the ones he failed to recall the first time round? No: he will probably be *non-selective*, and just as likely to attend to those he remembered the first time around as to those that he did not memorize. The eleven-year-old will be reasonably selective and proficient in such circumstances, and hence will further outstrip the performance of his younger peers.

Two of the most well-established principles of human memory are that 'rehearsal' is a powerful aid to deliberate memorization and that the imposition of some structure or meaning on what we seek to memorize also determines the likelihood of successful recall. Rehearsal refers to the continuous repetition, out loud or under the breath, of what one is trying to hold in mind (obvious examples are the repetition of a shopping list or an unfamiliar telephone number whilst dialling). Five- or six-year-olds asked to remember a set of things that can be named and, hence, rehearsed will probably not rehearse them. It is possible to help them to use a rehearsal strategy and this increases their chances of success, particularly if they are asked to say words out loud so that they can be corrected if they miss one or more things out. However, even after being taught how to rehearse and having experienced evidence of its success, children will *not* usually rehearse spontaneously when they are asked to memorize other material. The use of rehearsal as an aid to memorization might appear to be a simple, self-evident and obvious way to aid learning. But children learn how to do it gradually, throughout the early years of school.

Even adults, to whom such tactics may seem obvious, often fail to use rehearsal when it would aid their attempts to learn. Investigations into the study techniques of undergraduates, for example, suggest that they often do not rehearse what they have been taught. Listening to a lecture or reading a text, understanding what is heard or read and believing that understanding implies learning, students fail to rehearse and then pay the penalty later. In one study, groups of students were asked to recall a lesson. Some were asked after a day, others after several days and some several weeks following the event. The amount recalled 'decayed' sharply over the first few days, but more interesting was the finding that students who, early on, were asked to recall and recount the lesson showed very little subsequent forgetting over a period of several weeks. Going over notes, thinking and rehearsing what has been heard or read, greatly facilitates how much is memorized. This may seem like common sense, but experience and evidence suggest that even people who are able to use rehearsal strategies fail to do so.

Imposing some *structure* or organization on what we are trying to learn is another seemingly obvious strategy for improving performance, and one that seems to come naturally. But it does not. Imagine giving a number of objects to be remembered to an eleven-year-old. These can be grouped into a set of categories. Suppose, for example, the child is presented with a number of toy animals, toys which represent various forms of transportation and some toy pieces of fruit. The child is likely to recall them in organized sets: he may, say, give first a set of animal names, then a set of transport names, followed by fruit. Similarly, if we allow the child to move the objects around, he or she is likely to group them physically into categories as an aid to improved memorization. So the eleven-year-old exploits the fact that organizing material to be learned into well-established groups or categories increases the chances of successful recall. Five-year-olds, on the other hand, are unlikely to exploit this kind of categorical organization even when they can, when requested, arrange the objects into categories. Although they know how to group objects, and can be helped to improve their learning by instructions to arrange the objects into groups before trying to learn them, as with rehearsal they will not exploit the strategy spontaneously when they are presented with another set of objects.

Memorizing: one activity or many?

But, you might ask, are we really dealing here with changes in memory skills? Might it not be the case that children simply don't understand the instructions given? Perhaps the five-year-old child does not understand the meaning of words like 'remember'? Well, the evidence suggests that we are dealing with changes in the child's cognitive skills and not simply with linguistic development. There are situations, for instance, in which pre-school children show that they understand what an instruction to remember entails (at least in one sense). Imagine placing a sweet beneath one of a set of upturned cups that are identical in appearance. We ask a two-year-old to remember which cup the sweet is placed under. Then we tell the child that we have to go and fetch something from another room and that they must remember where the sweet is until we get back. Surreptitiously, we arrange for someone to observe the child while we are away. What we are likely to find is that our pre-schooler will keep touching the appropriate cup from time to time. The child uses his digits to 'keep hold' of the information he has to remember, literally 're-mind-ing' himself of it by physical means (i.e. putting his finger on it, hitting it on the head – the source of many a metaphor). Young children do, in some senses at least, understand what it means to remember. What they learn with age are more powerful and efficient strategies for memorizing and learning; they learn *how* to control or regulate their own performance more effectively.

Let us consider another example of the pre-schooler's powers of memory which helps to illustrate other aspects of the 'natural history' of memory development. Imagine a playground with a series of fence posts around its perimeter. An adult is going to walk with a group of pre-schoolers from one post to another attaching coloured pieces of paper to each post. When they reach, say, the third post, the children are told that when they have attached paper to all the posts they will have their photograph taken. They are shown the camera to be used which is removed from a bag held by the adult. The adult then hides the camera when the children are not looking. When they reach the last post, the adult laments that the camera has been lost. Now, what do the children suggest and do? Do they simply begin to search at random for the camera or, perhaps, go back to the first post? Or do they remember the fact that the camera was last seen at post number three? They are more likely to return to the scene of the event, post three. They remembered where they last saw the camera and also *infer* that this is the best place for a search to commence. They are making intelligent use of past experience to formulate a plan of action – evidence of both memory and reasoning.

Why, when pre-school children seem so competent in such situations, do five-year-olds seem to perform so poorly in the experiments I outlined earlier? Well, such differences in children's apparent competence are symptomatic of important features of human memory and cognition. They also help to illustrate the *multiplicity* of intellectual activities that we commonly (and mistakenly) lump together under headings like 'memory'. The abilities deployed by pre-schoolers in the situations just outlined are different in kind from those demanded in the first experiments presented, which demanded 'deliberate' memorization. Basically, what young children learn and remember are things that arise as a 'natural' and often *incidental* consequence of their activities. No one needed to alert the pre-schoolers in the playgroup to the fact that they would be expected to remember the location of an object. Setting out deliberately to commit a body of information to memory is a quite different affair from such examples of natural or spontaneous remembering, where what is subsequently recalled is something one literally handled, attended to or in some way had to take cognizance of in the course of doing a practical activity. Perhaps another example will illustrate the distinction I am attempting to draw.

Recall that earlier in the chapter I outlined the five-year-old's relative incompetence when asked to make judgements about his or her own memory ability, and the resulting poor performance. Suppose instead of *asking* the child to remember objects we ask him to *do* something with them. We might, for example, ask him to point to and label every animal in the set of toys. Subsequently, we ask him to recall what he has seen (and touched). We will find that the number of items recalled by the child is superior to that achieved when we simply *ask* him to memorize. The task of pointing and labelling encouraged the child to attend systematically to the objects, and led to activities or *interactions* with the material destined to be remembered. The child's active involvement with the material and his concentration on the task at hand helped him to 'encode' or become consciously aware of the objects handled. In such circumstances, memorization usually takes place quite spontaneously. Similarly, in the playground experiment, children were actively involved in tasks (e.g. putting paper on posts, searching for a misplaced object) that made sense to them and were comprehensible. Furthermore, as in the cup experiment with the pre-schooler, the object to be remembered was *external and spatial*. Such tasks both provide concrete external cues that prompt recall (which help to remind the child) and involve practical demands in their performance which lead the child to act upon the material to be remembered. Young children's spatial memory is, in such circum-stances, good. Contrast such situations with the task of deliberately committing to memory discrete sets of objects through rehearsal when there are no simple, physical locational cues to aid memorization or recall, and there is no purpose, other than memorization itself, being served.

So, in tasks where *memorization* is an end in itself, rather than an incidental product of activities that are instrumental in achieving some practical end or objective, young children do not know how to proceed. Special skills in rehearsal and some form of (self-induced) interaction with the material in order to 'make sense' of it (e.g. grouping it, or forming the elements into a story or some other pattern) take time to learn and perfect.

It follows that if we help the young child to make sense of a task by asking him to group objects together into appropriate sets, or by embodying the objects to be remembered into a story or pattern for him, then we may facilitate his performance of the task. However, as with rehearsal, simply exposing children to such strategies does not lead to their immediate adoption and generalization. If we want children to learn and remember things, we must often 'scaffold' the process for them by setting tasks, arranging materials, reminding and prompting them. Eventually, they will come to do such things for themselves (at least, on occasion) and will discover how to re-hearse and so on. Put another way, the teacher's role in facilitating learning and memory will change as a function of the child's age and capacities.

A pause for review

Before moving on, let us rehearse some of the arguments I have been putting forward. Attending, concentrating and memorizing are *activities*. Simply asking a child aged five or six to pay attention, concentrate, study, learn or remember is unlikely to bear fruit. Unless we embody the material to be learned and remembered in a task that makes sense to the child, one that involves objectives he can realize and that draws his attention 'naturally' to the elements we wish him to take in, our imperatives to concentrate, memorize or learn are almost bound to fail. Young children can and will concentrate and remember but will often need the support of a more knowledgeable and intellectually skilled assistant. Such assistants in a real sense act as external aids to memorization, as 're-mind-ers'. At the same time, they provide living illustrations of the processes involved in memorization which eventually the child comes to 'internalize' and exploit himself. Looked at in this way, the processes involved in deliberate memorization and contrived or formal learning situations take place first in external, observable and social terms before being internalized by the child to become personal, mental activities. More mature individuals or adults who are involved with children in shared projects and activities provide children with the means to become autonomous and self-regulating. The importance of such shared social activities as a basis for mental development is, as you will find when you read on, a recurrent theme of this book.

Memory and schooling

If the assertion that certain powers of concentration and memory are fostered in social interaction has any value, then it should follow that the development of such powers will vary from one culture to another to the extent that the social practices which help to create them are different in those cultures. There is evidence to support this case. It comes from comparing the memorizing activities of adults in our own society with those of adults from non-schooled/non-literate cultures. I will refer several times to such comparisons at various places in the book where they both help to illustrate the *social* origins of mental life and assist us in our search for the specific features of social practices that influence the development of mental abilities.

In a number of studies of non-schooled, non-literate societies (Cole and Scribner, 1974) some marked differences (and important similarities that we consider later) have been revealed between the characteristic ways of memorizing found there and in Western technological cultures. There is a growing body of evidence, for example, to show that rehearsal is *not* a feature of deliberate attempts at memorization by people in non-technological societies and, further, that strategies like grouping familiar objects into categories to aid memory are also the product of schooled, literate cultures. In the past, such differences between the mature people of different societies, and what appear to be similarities in performance between young children in our kind of society and adults in 'traditional' cultures, were regarded as evidence that characteristic modes of thinking in these other cultures are 'childlike', 'non-rational' or in some other way less developed than in our own. Such views, at least in informed circles, have been revised of late as more sophisticated ways of studying and theorizing about culture and cognition have been developed. What I think we may conclude from such observations is that deliberate attempts to memorize 'arbitrarily' sets of information, i.e. memorization for its own sake, is a product of technological societies and more specifically of schooling and/or literacy. Perhaps if we ask ourselves a different set of questions, these rather puzzling differences and their implications will become clearer.

First, we must ask ourselves what possible *need* an individual in a traditional society would have for deliberate memorization of the sort we have been discussing. Certainly, they need to remember places, routes, seasons and those practical skills and knowledge that enable them to survive in their own environment. Studies of the navigational powers of people in fishing and trading cultures, for example, reveal extremely complex and intricate systems of mapping and navigation which demand considerable powers of memory and planning. As children go about daily life in these cultures they 'naturally' or 'incidentally' acquire such knowledge as they observe, imitate or are helped to perform necessary tasks by the more knowledgeable and mature. But they do not sit down in a specially constructed building with teachers to be shown about and told about things outside their common cultural experience. Sitting, attending, listening carefully or diligently watching a performance by an adult, in relation to a task that the adult has set, leads to demands on concentration, memory and thinking that are not a feature of incidental learning. As I pointed out in the Introduction, the notion that children learn by being deliberately 'taught' by adults is by no means universally shared.

Indeed, as Newson and Newson (1974) have pointed out, contemporary Western concerns with issues like the psychological well-being and educational potential of children are of historically recent origin. Compulsory schooling for all is a relatively modern cultural invention and with it has come a new range of questions and concerns. In the eighteenth century, for instance, parents were understandably more concerned with the physical well-being and survival chances of their offspring, since life then, by modern standards, was far more hazardous, particularly for young children. Only with good medical and nutritional care and all the other achievements of modern societies have we come to worry more about the mental welfare of children. The invention of schooling and the creation of roles such as 'teacher' and 'pupil' has led to new demands on adults, as they try consciously and deliberately to 'transmit' their knowledge and culture. It has also created special demands on children as they attempt deliberately to learn, memorize and think in specially constructed buildings, away from and out of contact with adult activity. In non-schooled societies, children are gradually acculturated, socialized and 'educated' by becoming progressively more involved in adult economic activity until they eventually learn and inherit their social roles. Our own children, meanwhile, are effectively excluded from centres of adult activity and learn, not by doing the things that their parents are involved in, but by listening, reading, experimenting and solving problems set for them by a 'specialist' teacher. Since members of non-schooled cultures have no need to develop skills such as those involved in deliberate memorization, it is perhaps unsurprising that, when confronted by a strange Western person with his odd questions and peculiar demands, they are unable to perform what are culture-specific and culturally transmitted skills that take children in our own society years to master.

We are used to thinking about bits of machinery, architecture and technology as special, cultural inventions. We accept that each upcoming generation of our society will need to learn about new things, and develop new skills in order to operate and work new instruments of production. It is strange, perhaps, to think of what seem to be 'natural' aspects of our mental life as cultural inventions in the same vein. Strange though it may seem, I suggest that it is nonetheless the case.

Paying attention

One reason why older children are likely to be able to sustain longer periods of study and concentration than younger children is that they have discovered how to exploit strategies such as rehearsal and organi-

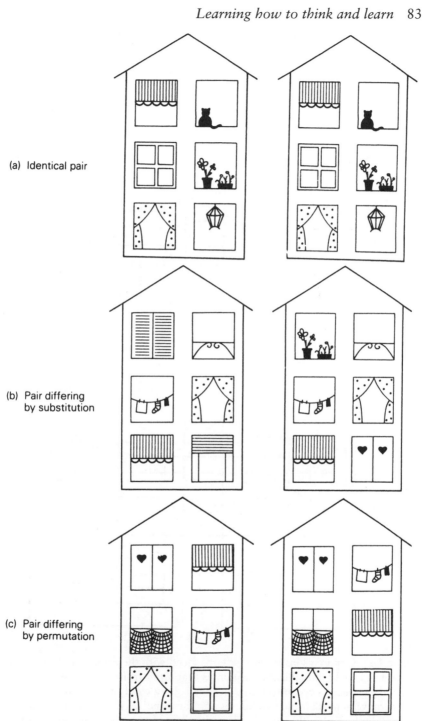

Figure 4.1 Children are asked to compare each pair of drawings to say whether they look the same or different: (a) identical pair; (b) pair differing by substitution; (c) pair differing by permutation

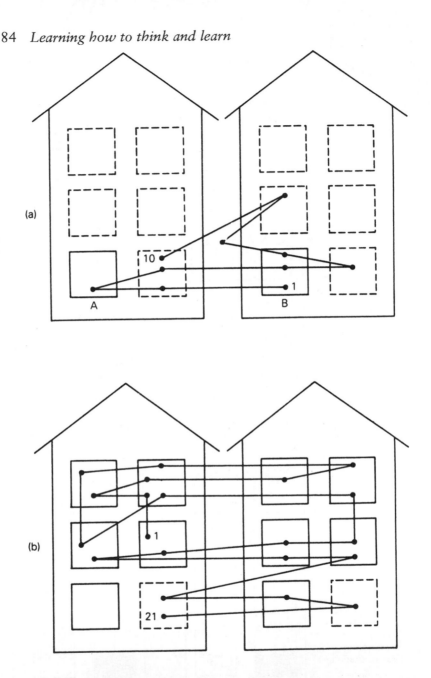

Figure 4.2 Children's inspection patterns faced with the drawings illustrated in figure 4.1. Dotted lines illustrate windows that *differ* from one house to the other; the children's eye movements start at 1: (a) a child of 4yrs 4m judges in 10 eye movements that the two houses are 'the same' on the basis that windows A and B look similar; (b) a child 8yrs makes 21 eye movements before deciding that the pair differ

zation of material for learning. Lacking such skills, the child below age eight or so is often likely to appear more impulsive and capricious than the older child whose attempts to regulate his or her own learning or memorizing take time to execute.

If we look in more detail at how children distribute their attention – to examine, for instance, what they look at when they are trying to solve a problem or answer a question – we find other important differences between the performances of children who have just entered school and those aged around seven to eight. Where the older child's patterns of attention are becoming systematic and exhaustive and reflect a sensitivity to the demands of the task facing them, the five- to six-year-old's attention seems impulsive and brief. Why? Before discussing possible answers, let us consider a few examples which illustrate how children's powers of attention emerge and develop through the years of schooling.

Inspect the three pairs of drawings shown in figure 4.1 and spot any differences between each pair. When children aged between three and six years are asked to do this, we find that they are unlikely to be very accurate. If we observe their eye movements as they compare pairs of figures, we discover that they tend to compare only one or two features of the drawings before reaching a decision. If they happen to compare two points which reveal a difference, then they make a correct decision (showing that they understand what the experimenter means by 'different'). However, since their inspection is brief and not exhaustive, they are unlikely to 'see' differences and instead judge that pairs which are different look identical. Figure 4.2 illustrates the inspection pattern of a four-year-old and compares it with that shown for an eight-year-old child. Older children are more careful, analytic and exhaustive in their inspection of the figures. Not surprisingly, their judgements are more accurate. When they say that two drawings are identical, it is on the basis of a more thorough search. Performance on this task keeps on improving up to age eight or nine years, as children become increasingly cautious and careful in their perceptual activity (Vurpillot, 1976).

As we observed for tests that require deliberate memorization, children below the age of seven or so often appear impulsive when asked to undertake unfamiliar tasks. As children grow through the early years, we find increasing evidence that they are learning or discovering how to control their own attention, learning and problem-solving in situations where other people set them tasks to perform. Paying attention, like deliberate memorization, is an *activity* that can be executed more or less skilfully. There is an implicit *plan* in the eight-

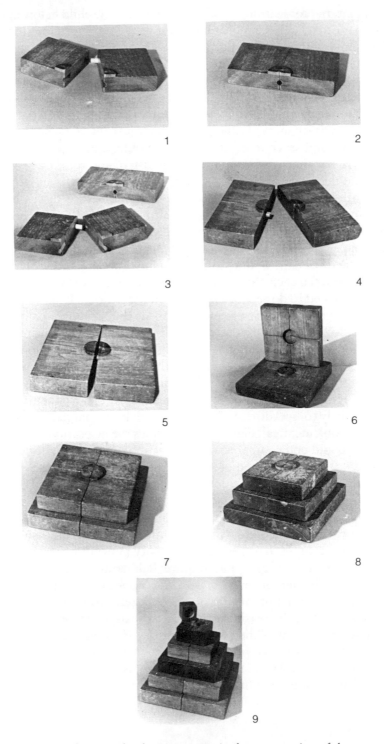

Figure 4.3   Photographs showing stages in the construction of the pyramid

year-old's inspection of the figures that is lacking in the five-year-old's attempts to do the task. What might appear at first sight to be a simple issue of perception, of 'seeing' a solution, turns out on closer inspection to involve intelligence, knowledge and skill in self-regulation.

When we ask young children to look at a situation and, say, ask them a question about what they are 'seeing', we cannot assume, simply because they move their heads and eyes to look at what we are showing them, that they will perceive the situation in the same way as ourselves. The relationships between requests, questions and other utterances, and the systematic search for information that these utterances are designed to stimulate in the other, change with age towards increasing degrees of accuracy, or what Bruner terms greater 'analytical competence'. Understanding the demands of a question, such as 'Are these the same?', and undertaking a systematic search for information to answer it are two interlocking aspects of knowledge.

But, you might ask, aren't children younger than eight years of age capable of using pictorial aids to instruction in some situations? What about jigsaws, model-making or following Lego instructions? Surely children are able to guide their own activities in such tasks before age eight? Yes, they are. Indeed, in a series of studies, we have found that children as young as four years of age are reasonably adept at using pictorial aids to help them put together quite complex construction toys (Murphy and Wood, 1982). We gave them a series of nine photographs (figure 4.3) and asked them to make the model depicted. Although four-year-olds almost never completed the task successfully, when we looked at their eye movements to see how they 'interrogated' the pictures, we found that they did usually look at a picture that was relevant to what they were trying to do with the blocks.

The differences between model-building tasks and the 'inspection' tasks discussed earlier are similar in some respects to those between 'natural' and 'deliberate' processes of memorization. Tasks like assembling models and making use of pictures to put together jigsaws are relatively common activities for many children in our society. So when they were asked to make up the model in our experiment, they had some intuitive sense of what we meant and relevant past experiences to draw upon. They came equipped with enough experience to make sense of what we asked them to do. The photographs were used as an aid to their own practical activity. In the comparison and questioning tasks, there were no external guides to provide children with feedback about the success or otherwise of their efforts (unless, of course, an adult were to help them by pointing out relevant features that they had overlooked).

Unlike the model-building tasks, where the results of their activities were visible and could be compared with the photographs, the inspection problem demands that the child make a judgement about how and when he has satisfied the requirements of the questioner. The ability to make such decisions, coupled with the more 'abstract' nature of the inspection tasks, is what marks off the performance of eight-year-olds from that of younger children.

I will explore ways in which others help children to overcome their limited knowledge and inexperience in analysing, planning and regulating their own activities later. For the moment, I want to return to consider cross-cultural studies which reinforce the argument that understanding and using media like photographs involve knowledge of conventions and learned skills of analysis and planning. To the trained user of such artefacts, perception and recognition of what is illustrated in a photograph or picture might seem automatic and hence 'natural'. But this is not the case. When people from non-pictorial cultures, who have never seen or used paper to represent or depict objects, are asked to identify drawings or photographs of familiar objects or animals, they cannot do so. Pictures are two-dimensional representations of things that, in the real world, occupy three dimensions. Real objects are solid and have depth. When we look at a picture we have to *infer* solidity and depth from cues like the relative size of different things in the picture or from differences in texture, perspective cues, overlap of parts of one object by another and so forth. Perception of such things is neither 'natural' nor automatic. Rather, the implicit conventions governing the interpretation of drawings and photographs have to be learned. When children in our society use pictures to help them make things, look at family snaps, watch television or are involved in the many experiences in which pictorial materials intrude into their lives, they are learning how to interpret what is being depicted. Lacking such experiences, people from non-pictorial cultures cannot 'make sense' of such representations and only after a period of training can they learn to 'see' what we see (Serpell, 1976). Next time you visit a good art gallery, compare the way in which, say, geometric perspective has been represented by painters across the centuries. Conventions for trying to capture the three-dimensional world on two-dimensional canvas have undergone several revolutions over time and, following each revolution, people have had to 'learn to see' paintings in the new ways intended by the artist.

Perceptual/attentional activities take time, demand guided selection, memory and interpretation. Perhaps it becomes less surprising, then, to find that young children in the first years of schooling still have much to learn about how to attend to and interpret their world in the same way as more mature members of their culture do. When we ask a young child to 'pay attention', we should recognize that any failure to comply might not result from boredom, wilfulness or 'distractability' but from the fact that he or she lacks the necessary knowledge and skill to bring to bear on the task or topic at hand. This is not to say that young children (like all of us) might not concentrate or attend because they are uninterested in what is going on, or because they prefer to do other things. However, we have to recognize that when we ask children to pay attention and concentrate on tasks that we have set and which provide little by way of concrete, perceptual support, they may find it impossible to comply with our demands.

Wholes and parts: theories of perception and understanding

In this section, I want to discuss another dimension of what is involved in learning how to attend and understand, which brings us back to the study of children's thinking and reasoning and to arguments about the relationship between perception and knowledge. So far, my discussion of children's development has been largely descriptive and has avoided theorizing. Now we must start to consider explanations for the nature of young children's abilities and discuss some of the factors that different theorists believe influence and promote development and learning. Different theories, as we shall see, have quite different implications for teaching.

Suppose we show a young child the picture illustrated in figure 4.4 and ask him to describe what he sees. If the child is aged below five years, he will probably identify the various objects (such as the light bulbs) in the display but will not 'see' the larger figure that these suggest. He seems unable to 'synthesize' the objects into a larger configuration. When the individual elements are meaningful, have an identity of their own, the child is likely to focus on each in turn and cannot 'stand back' in order to see the more all-embracing figure. A small number of five-year-olds, however, may report seeing the larger configuration and will not be able to 'see' or identify the smaller objects. Briefly, children aged below seven tend to 'centre' upon either the overall configuration or its parts. What they cannot do is attend to or perceive both at the same time. It's a case of one thing or the other.

In other situations, children of this age seem unable to break down a

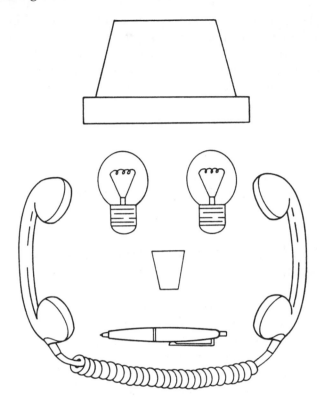

Figure 4.4   Children under the age of 7yrs are unlikely to see the figure as a face

larger figure into its constituents or to perceive a part of a figure as 'belonging' to two or more larger units. Examine the diagrams illustrated in figure 4.5, for example. Such illustrations, called 'embedded figures', are used in some tests of intellectual maturity. A child aged below seven is unlikely to be able to trace the contour of the figures shown in set A when they are 'embedded' in the complex line drawings of set B, even though four-year-olds are able to trace the outlines of the simple shape shown in sets C and D. Such simple forms, or *Gestalten* (well-formed, regular shapes), seem to have a 'natural' identity. Young children can perceive such shapes when they are hidden by other lines but, unlike older children, are incapable of analysing more complex figures.

In some situations, then, the young child cannot *synthesize* meaning-ful elements into larger units. In the 'embedded figures' problem, he fails to break down or *analyse* complex forms into their elements. In both situations, the child seems incapable of perceiving a given element

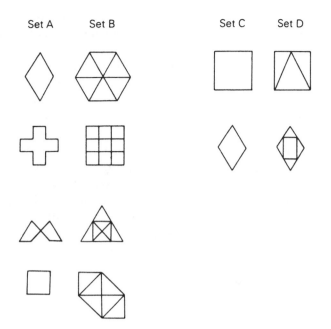

Figure 4.5 The child is asked to outline, in sets B and D, the figure that matches the shape in sets A and C respectively

as a constituent of two or more configurations at one and the same time. Once the child perceives something in a particular way, he seems unable to 're-view' it from a different perspective. After the age of seven or so, children not only become more systematic and accurate in their perceptual judgements but also display greater flexibility. They are, in Piaget's terms, able to de-centre themselves to view a task from more than one point of view. Such experimental findings are consistent with Piaget's prediction that pre-operational children *cannot* entertain the idea that an element of any task or situation, whatever its nature, can belong at the same time to two or more categories or classes. What the child 'sees' is determined by how he thinks.

Experience, expertise and explanation

If children are more limited than their elders in their ability to attend, memorize and generally regulate their own learning, problem-solving and thinking, then it may be that they often fail where older people succeed, not because they lack 'logic' or are have more limited processing capacities, but because they do not possess the relevant experience and expertise.

Experts in a discipline, game, sport, craft or whatever are able to perceive and memorize more accurately and fully than a non-expert any phenomenon that is relevant to their area of expertise. I have already discussed chess as a paradigm case. An expert's knowledge endows them with the ability to perceive *organization* and structure where the novice's perception is piecemeal and fragmented. What we perceive in a situation is *motivated* by our immediate purposes or interests. What we consider salient and worthy of attention is dictated by what we are trying to do. To the extent that we are expert at fulfilling our intentions in a situation which 'lends itself' to the fulfilment of our goals, we usually perform well. We are able to think and act relatively quickly, smoothly and accurately. Because of this, we are also more likely than the novice to notice any *departures* from our expectations. Imagine, for instance, watching a game of American football with an American fan. Then think about watching a game of cricket. Who responds to the novel and unusual? The person who already knows the rules and existing *practices* of play. Unlike the novice, whose concentration is likely to be fully engaged in monitoring and making sense of immediate events, the expert can appreciate what is currently happening in a wider context; he is likely to appreciate strategies of play and clever tactics. He is also more likely to spot any mistakes or unusual happenings and will detect any departures from the rules of the game more readily. He will probably remember more about what takes place and be better able to give an accurate account of the proceedings after the game. Expertise structures the process of perception and memorization. This makes thinking and acting fast, smooth, accurate and sensitive to error, novelty and unusual events.

The range of experimental evidence in support of these informal generalizations about the effects of knowledge and experience on performance is impressive (Chi, Glaser and Rees, 1982). Studies of expert performance in several domains of knowledge (e.g. chess, maths and physics) have revealed that experts (a) take in more information faster and with greater accuracy than novices; (b) recall relevant information from memory more readily; and (c) perceive and interpret what they see in terms of rules and principles whilst the novice only perceives the surface features of the situation. Further, asked to explain their problem-solving activities, expert performers are more likely to be able to provide a coherent and comprehensive account of what they are doing – the so-called 'self-explanation effect', about which I will have more to say later.

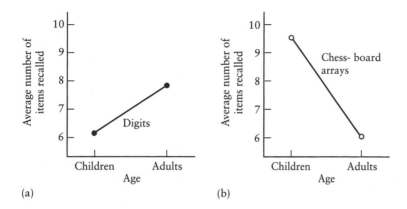

Figure 4.6 Average recall of digits and chessboard peices by same groups of adults and children

Since children are novices at life in general, perhaps we need only consider such differences in experience and expertise to explain why adults and children vary in what they know and understand. If we could find a task on which young children are more practised and expert than adults, then it might be possible to test the idea that it is not age (i.e. not development or maturation) but simply experience that explains differences in performance and understanding. One investigation which did just this was performed by Chi (1976).

First examine figure 4.6a. This illustrates a well-established finding about the relations between age and the ability to recall random lists of numbers. Adults outperform children. In figure 4.6b, however, this pattern is reversed even though the same group of adults and children were involved in performing both memory tasks. The data in 4.6b refer to the abilities of the two groups to remember the positions of chess pieces on a chess board. The children involved were all good chess players. The adults were not. Thus, where the usual relations between age and experience are reversed, children outperform adults. Experience and expertise, not age-related changes in cognitive capacities, explain how and why the performance of the two groups changes from task to task.

Drawing inferences: logic and memory

If children fail to master a task, not because their thinking is different in kind from that of adults, but simply because they lack the necessary experience and expertise, then it may be possible to help them to learn and understand situations which, left alone, they cannot master. A more experienced partner can help by augmenting their limited expertise and trying to teach them how to regulate their own activities in the face of uncertainty. If this is possible, then we might, with Vygotsky and Bruner, claim far more importance for teaching in development and a greater potential for learning through instruction in young children than Piagetian theory suggests. Let us consider some examples to see if this is the case.

One of the many tasks that Piaget invented to study the transition from pre-operational to operational thinking involves the ability to place objects of different sizes into order from small to large – so-called 'seriation' tasks. Imagine, for example, five sticks, each of a different colour and length. We show a child aged five an arrangement of these sticks in serial order and ask him to reproduce the configuration with another, similar set of sticks. The child cannot do it. He may produce the odd pair of sticks, one small and one large, but he cannot, for example, insert a third stick *between* these to produce a longer series. Piaget's explanation for this phenomenon is consistent with those given for children's failures in conservation experiments. To insert a stick between two others in the appropriate sequence, for example, demands the ability to view it *at one and the same time* as a stick that is longer than one of the pair and smaller than the other. It has to be viewed simultaneously in two ways. This demands intellectual *co-ordination* of perceptual judgements which, as we have seen, pre-operational children cannot achieve. Similarly, if we tell the child that one stick is longer than another which in turn is longer than a third one, he cannot draw the *logical inference* that the first must be longer than the third, because such inferences also demand co-ordination of the statements given.

Bryant (1974), however, suggests that young children's inability to draw such inferences and solve seriation problems is not due to the fact that they are pre-logical. Rather, their failure is due to the fact that these sorts of problems overload their mental capacities. To solve such problems, the child has to examine carefully, compare and *memorize* the relations between the five sticks in order to draw any inferences. We have just seen that each of these demands creates difficulties for children and that they are unlikely to rehearse spontaneously, so they will probably spend little time on the task, be unsystematic in their inspection of the sticks, and lack the powers of rehearsal needed to solve the problem. If we help them to do these things, will we discover that they are more likely to draw inferences? Yes. To demonstrate this, Bryant showed three- to four-year-old children five sticks of different colours and sizes, but only as ordered pairs. So, for instance, the child might have been shown a red and a blue stick where the red was longer. He was then shown the blue stick compared to a smaller green one, followed by the green paired with yellow and then the yellow with the shortest stick, say orange. Bryant repeatedly showed the pairs of sticks to children until they could tell him (before seeing each pair) which was longer. Having thus ensured that the child had *memorized* the information needed to solve the problem, he asked them which was longer, the blue stick or the yellow stick. Many children were able to give the right answer.

Thus, where the experimenter helps the child to pay attention to, rehearse and memorize the 'propositions' from which he will be asked to draw inferences, the child succeeds.

This experiment demonstrates the fact that children can be helped to perform tasks that they find hard or impossible to do alone, but the implications that the findings have in relation to establishing the age at which children can draw transitive inferences have proved more controversial. Halford, as we saw in the last chapter, argues that solving such problems involves two main steps. First, the child has to construct a mental model of the set of elements and then they must know how to 'read off' from this model the relationship asked for. Bryant's study shows that children seem able to 'read off' an answer from information that they have commited to memory, but does it demonstrate conclusively that children can also integrate information to construct a series? Halford suggests not.

The fact that Bryant and his colleagues trained the children by always giving the 'premises' in the appropriate order (i.e. from longest stick to shortest, or vice versa) means that the child could simply have remembered this order without ever mentally integrating the premises into a model. What happens if the children are trained to remember each pair of relations but these are given in an order (e.g. blue and green followed by red and blue) that is different from the size-ordered series? Young children fail.

Halford argues that the ability to make transitive inferences demands the mental integration of information in parallel, and that such demands cannot be met by children aged below about five years because they lack the mental capacity and speed of processing required. Whilst he does not appeal to logic as an explanation for age-related changes, he argues that pre-school children cannot draw inferences.

This argument illustrates a number of points, some of which I will develop in later chapters. First, it shows that there is usually more than one way to solve a problem and this makes it difficult to arrive at firm conclusions about the age at which certain intellectual capacities are developed. As Piaget argued, the ability to perform a task is not necessarily a reliable indicator of the methods or cognitive resources used to solve it. It also demonstrates another major tenet of Piagetian theory, which is that assisted performance does not have the same developmental status as spontaneous success by the unaided child. Finally, if Halford is correct, then accounts of cognitive growth which rest entirely on explanations in terms of experience and expertise cannot be complete. Thus, arguments which divided Piagetian theory from those of Vygotksy and Bruner are still with us.

Many other attempts have been made to 'train' young children in ways of performing Piagetian tasks. The argument motivating many of these studies was that children do not pass through a pre-operational stage of development in which they are unable to learn or be taught how to reason 'logically'. Rather, the argument proceeds, the tasks used are so unfamiliar to children and make such (for them) unusual demands that failure is attributable to a lack of relevant *experience*, not to intellectual incompetence.

Some attempts to teach children how to solve Piagetian-style problems have produced positive effects, others have not. Deciding whether such results confirm or disconfirm the notion of a pre-operational stage of development is not a straightforward affair for reasons I have just explored. Other difficulties of interpretation stem from the fact that what we mean by 'teaching' is problematic. Do some attempts to teach children (e.g. as in Halford's study) fail because the teaching techniques used were weak? How can we evaluate the quality of the teaching styles used by experimenters? What criteria do we set up to evaluate success? Is it simply enough to show, like Bryant did, that children can be helped to do things that they cannot do on their own, or do we demand that children so taught must show that they can *transfer* or *generalize* what they have been taught to another situation before we say that they 'really' have learned a lesson?

Trying to answer one difficult question (can children make transitive inferences?) thus confronts us with three other issues. How do we define effective instruction? How and when do children *generalize* what they are taught to new problems? If adults do not reason logically in the manner implied by Piagetian theory, how do they think? Let us start with the first question.

What is effective instruction? First thoughts

Any theory that presents a view of how children learn or develop implies a theory of instruction. Although Piaget did not attempt to explicate in detail the implications of his analysis of development for a theory of instruction, several of his followers have attempted so to do (e.g. Schwebel and Raph, 1974). Other learning/developmental theorists (e.g. Skinner, Gagne, Sheffield, Vygotsky/Luria and Bruner, to name but a few) have worked out in some detail the educational ramifications of their ideas. It is not my intention here to review and evaluate all these points of view, although in later chapters I will discuss some of the research they have inspired. Instead I have decided to concentrate on three approaches, trying to synthesize the insights they have generated. The three in question are Bruner's steps towards a theory of instruction, Soviet developmental theory (inspired by Vygotsky's writings), and research that has grown out of the information-processing paradigm outlined in chapter 1.

The zone of proximal development

When we help a child to solve a problem, we are providing conditions in which he can begin to perceive regularities and structure in his experience. Where, left alone, the child is overcome by uncertainty and does not know what to attend to or what to do, instruction can help in a number of ways. When we point things out to the child, we help to highlight what he should attend to. By *reminding* children we are helping them to bring to mind and exploit those aspects of their past experience that we (as experts) but not they (as novices) know to be *relevant* to what they are currently trying to do. If the task involves a number of steps, the child, whilst concentrating on how to execute one, may forget about things he has already done. He may also lose his sense of 'direction' and, whilst working on a part of the task, lose sight of the whole problem. By drawing his attention back to what he did earlier and reminding him of what the ultimate goal is, we help to maintain his 'place' in the task and prevent him from total submersion in his immediate activity. When the child performs some activity that takes him closer to success, he may not recognize the significance of what he has done, particularly if he has lost sight of the overall goal. Here, praise and reassurance confirm the relevance of what he has done and act as a signal that he should move on.

Looked at in this way, many of the seemingly simple and even trivial things that the more mature do as they help children in everyday activities take on an important significance. Pointing out, reminding, suggesting and praising all serve to orchestrate and structure the child's activities under the guidance of one who is more expert. By helping the child to structure his activities, we are helping him to perform things he cannot do alone until such time as he becomes familiar enough with the demands of the task at hand to develop local expertise and to try things alone. By breaking complex tasks down into manageable, smaller problems, we help the child to detect regularities and patterns in his activity that he is unlikely to discover alone. We are also providing living examples of the way in which more expert people go about the task of regulating and managing activity in conditions of high uncertainty. When we suggest, remind, prompt or whatever, we are providing insights into processes that usually take place 'in our head'.

Vygotsky, as we have already seen, argues that such *external* and *social* activities are gradually internalized by the child as he comes to regulate his own intellectual activity. Such encounters are the source of experiences which eventually create the 'inner dialogues' that form the processes of mental self-regulation. Viewed in this way, learning is taking place on at least two levels: the child is learning about the task, developing 'local expertise'; and he is also learning how to structure his own learning and reasoning. Piagetians are likely to see direct instruction and attempts to help children who are not ready to do things alone as premature, misguided efforts that result in rote learning or the acquisition of empty, 'procedural' knowledge; but Vygotsky (and Bruner) see them as the 'raw material' of learning and development. In such encounters, the child is developing expertise and is inheriting culturally developed ways of thinking and learning.

Vygotsky, as we have seen, coined the term 'zone of proximal development' to refer to these 'gaps' between unassisted and assisted competence. How can we determine whether or not instruction is *sensitive* to a child's zone of development? When does it make demands beyond his potential level of comprehension? How can we be sure that instruction does not underestimate his ability?

Such questions motivated much of the early research into adult–child interaction in tutoring and learning situations. One of the first series of studies, undertaken by Wood, Bruner and colleagues, illustrates this early phase (Wood, Bruner and Ross, 1976; Wood, Wood and Middleton, 1978). One of their investigations involved an analysis of the teaching techniques used by mothers with their three- to four-year-old children. The task was designed to incorporate demands that, according to Piaget's theory, pre-operational children would not be able to master. The question addressed was whether, with help, pre-school children could be taught how to do so. The task facing mother and child was to assemble a construction toy made up of twenty-one wooden blocks and an arrangement of pegs and holes to create a pyramid (see figure 4.3). To learn how to do the task alone, the child had to co-ordinate three different features of the wooden blocks (their size, type of peg or hole, and orientation of pieces) in order to fit them together. To complete the task, the child also had to pile levels into a size-ordered series.

Children younger than about seven could not do the task without help (a finding which is in line with Piagetian theory). However, some children as young as three succeeded in doing it alone after they had been taught by their mothers. In an attempt to characterize what the adult did to support the child's learning, we coined the metaphor of 'scaffolding' to describe their activities. Young children succeeded with help, where alone they failed, because the tutor performed a number of functions which kept the child on task whilst they learned. For example, tutors lured the child into task activity by a variety of tactics, such as showing them how pegs fitted into holes. They often simplified problems facing the child by helping them to select pieces, by showing them how to 're-view' objects by turning them around, and so on. By removing all but the pieces that the child was working on to one side, the tutors removed potential sources of distraction, leaving the child to concentrate on the next step. Where a child overlooked or ignored a feature that needed to be taken into account, the tutor could highlight it by pointing it out or naming it. By such seemingly simple tactics, tutors could keep the child involved in task activity long enough for them to figure out how to do it for themselves.

Not all attempts at scaffolding succeeded, however. Some teaching strategies were more effective than others. For example, some tutors attempted first to show the child how to do the task before allowing them to have a go for themselves. This strategy over-loaded the child's powers of concentration and often led to complaints, to appeals to have a turn and attempts to leave the situation. Other tutoring strategies relied almost exclusively on verbal instructions such as 'put the little blocks on top of the big ones' which the child could not understand without first being shown what actions such instructions entailed in practice.

The approach to teaching which helped children to learn most about how to do the task involved two main 'rules'. First, when a child was struggling, the tutor immediately offered more help. Conversely, when, having been given help, the child succeeded, the tutor attempted to 'fade' or to 'up the ante': they gave less help with the next steps until, eventually, the child was managing the task alone. We termed this aspect of tutoring 'contingent' instruction. Such contingent support helps to ensure that the child is never left alone when he is in difficulty, nor is he 'held back' by teaching that is too directive and intrusive.

Throughout the 1970s and 1980s, investigations into patterns of interactions between parents and children in such 'contrived' encounters proliferated. These typically focused on tasks which a child could not perform alone and situations where adults (usually mothers) were asked to help their child to do such things as maths homework (Pratt et al, 1988), picture-book reading (DeLoache, 1984) and classifying objects (Rogoff, Ellis and Gardner, 1984) whilst an experimenter recorded their interactions. There have also been important extensions of the scaffolding concept to analyse the nature of individualized instruction in reading and writing which I will consider in a later chapter.

The main limitations of this style of research were also etched out during this period. In everyday, naturalistic interactions between adults and young children, it is usually the child, rather than the adult, who initiates interactions and sets the shared agenda. For example, both Carew (1980) observing US homes and Wells (1981) in the UK reported that more than 75 per cent of interactions in the home are child initiated. So, the issue of 'task induction', where the adult takes responsibility for maintaining the child's involvement in task-relevant activity, is less of an issue in natural interactions than it is in ones contrived for experimental purposes. In everyday life, children are often in social contact with more than a single adult. Both mothers and fathers, as well as siblings, grandparents and other significant figures, may be involved in frequent interactions with the child. An emphasis on adult–child tutoring situations should not blind us to the fact that the child obviously learns through his contacts with more than one adult and also learns through watching and listening to interactions between other people (a topic taken up in chapter 6).

The early research into scaffolding and similar notions was also concentrated on Euro-American cultures. In other societies, adult–

child interaction may be relatively infrequent and older siblings or a child's peer group may be important agents of socialization. Similarly, styles of interaction found in cultures vary in ways that reflect values and attitudes towards child development. The practice of questioning children, for instance, varies from society to society (Heath (1982), cited in Rogoff, 1990).

In an extensive review of this 'generation' of research, Rogoff (1990) suggests adopting 'guided participation' as a more inclusive concept than terms like 'scaffolding'.

> In the concept of guided participation, I mean to include not just parent – child relationships, but also the other social relationships inherent in families and communities, such as those involving children, parents, teachers, classmates and neighbors, organized not as dyads but as rich configurations of mutual involvement . . . In guided participation, children are involved with multiple companions and caregivers in organized, flexible webs of relationships that focus on shared cultural activities . . . [which] provides children with opportunities to participate in diverse roles' (pp. 97–8).

Despite the proliferation of different ways of conceptualizing adult –child interaction, Rogoff suggests that guided participation does exhibit a number of general characteristics:

(1) Tutors serve to provide a bridge between a learner's existing knowledge and skills and the demands of the new task. Left alone, a novice might not appreciate the relations between what the task demands and what they already know or can do that is relevant and, hence, fail where, with help, they can succeed.

(2) By providing instructions and help in the context of the learner's activity, tutors provide a structure to support their tutee's problem-solving. For example, while focused on their immediate actions, learners, left alone, might lose sight of the overall goal of the activity. A tutor can offer timely reminders.

(3) Although the learner is involved in what is initially, for them, 'out of reach' problem-solving, guided participation ensures that they play an active role in learning and that they contribute to the successful solution of problems.

(4) Effective guidance involves the transfer of responsibility from tutor to learner.

Not all guided participation involves deliberate or explicit attempts to teach and learn. Interactions with the four characteristics just listed may occur when, for example, children set out to 'help' their parents, or as they participate in everyday activities or in playful encounters with siblings and peers.

Learning and instruction as shared information processing

Although theory and research into the social construction of knowledge and skill has generated a number of different theoretical perspectives, they all share a common emphasis on the role of interactions between the developing child and significant others in everyday life. What remains obscure and controversial, as I have already said, is the nature of what it is that children learn, internalize or 'appropriate' in the course of such encounters. As we shall see in chapter 8, some situated action theorists go so far as to suggest that we should dispense with such 'cognitive' notions altogether.

Here, however, I want to consider proposals about what it is that gets learned during the course of tutor-assisted learning, which come from a very different tradition: learning theory and cognitive science. This begins a discussion of the value of modern learning theory as a framework for understanding how children think and learn that will be extended and developed in later chapters.

This is one of those areas, mentioned in chapter 2, in which a growing convergence of interest between developmental psychology and information-processing theories of adult cognition is taking place. As I also promised, this makes for some intellectual hardships since it is necessary to consider yet more theories, concepts and terms to be able to get some grasp of what is emerging as a new field of research: developmental cognitive science.

The most explicit theory of learning under instruction has been formulated by John Anderson and his colleagues (e.g. Anderson, 1993). Though coming from a different theoretical direction from that which stimulated research into adult–child interaction, this theory has, in fact, converged on principles of instruction which echo those suggested by such research in face-to-face tutoring.

Anderson's theory of human learning is expressed as a computer model or 'cognitive architecture'. He and his colleagues have used the theory to design, build and evaluate computer-based tutors called

Intelligent Tutoring Systems or ITS. Before discussing these, however, I have to say a little about some of the theoretical concepts on which these are based.

Rules of the mind

In the study of scaffolding outlined above, I cited an example where young children failed to learn how to perform a task if they were simply told what to do. Instructions such as 'put the little blocks on top of the big ones' lack meaning for the young child until this has been negotiated in interaction with the tutor. In Anderson's terminology, such a child does not possess knowledge of the *procedural* meaning of such 'declarative' instructions. Learning, for Anderson, involves discovering *rules* which relate declarative knowledge (e.g. verbal instructions, pictures, diagrams, mathematical symbols) to procedures in the service of goals. Such rules are called *productions* (they are also sometimes referred to as situation-action rules).

Perhaps some examples will help to clarify these ideas. In figure 4.7, a number of production rules are illustrated. These describe or 'model' how children at different ages understand how a simple beam balance works.

Model I expresses what a typical five-year-old knows. It is a theory of the child's understanding expressed as a set of production rules. These specify what a child will think and do as a consequence of what he sees. Thus, the THEN part of production rule P1 expresses what our five-year-old thinks will happen IF they put the same weight on each side of the balance. The second rule specifies what they think will occur IF they see a situation in which one side of the balance has more weights on it than the other.

Our typical five-year-old does not take any notice of how far any weights are from the centre or fulcrum of the balance beam. So, there are no rules in which distance serves as part of the condition for an action. The child has yet to appreciate the fact that judgements about distance (declarative knowledge based on perception of the task) must be taken into account to construct the conditions which rule how the beam balance works.

Model II, which represents what the average nine-year-old has learned, contains an additional rule which acknowledges that distance is important. Our nine-year-old recognizes that IF they put the same weight on each side *and* they place one further away from the fulcrum,

Model I

P1:   IF same *weight* on each side THEN
the beam is balanced

P2:   IF any side has more *weight* THEN
that side of the beam goes down

⎫ Age 5

Model II

P3:   IF same *weight* on each side and
one side has more *distance* THEN
the side with more distance goes down

⎫ Age 9

Model III

P4:   IF side X has more weight BUT that same side X
has less distance THEN muddle through

P5:   IF side X has more weight AND that same side X
has more distance THEN side X goes down

⎫ Age
13–17

Model IV

P4:   IF side X has more weight BUT that same side X
has less distance THEN get the torques

P5:   IF side X has more weight AND that same side X
has more distance THEN side X goes down

P6:   IF same *torque* on each side THEN
the beam is balanced

P7:   IF any side X has more *torque* THEN
that side X goes down

After Siegler and Klahr (1978)

Figure 4.7   Levels of understanding for the balance beam expressed as
production rules

THEN the side on which the weight is further away will go down. In
circumstances where both weights and distance are different, the child
might fall back on production rules 1 and 2, or simply guess.

Model III contains two additional rules which represent what most
thirteen- to seventeen-year-olds learn. Model IV represents the 'correct'
understanding of the forces involved.

In principle, it is possible to analyse and represent any procedural
knowledge in terms of sets of production rules. Anderson and his group,
for example, have produced complex rule systems to model knowledge

in areas such as school geometry and computer programming. An expert has rules to fit all situations. In problem-solving, they recognize what actions need to be taken in response to any conditions they are likely to meet. Like chess Grand Masters or expert mathematicians, they can encode situations quickly and accurately and these serve to 'fire' the relevant production rules. A novice, on the other hand, may not recognize the conditions which demand action (like the five-year-old who ignores distance on the beam balance) or may know some rules which sometimes, but not always, give correct answers (like those shown in Model II) or which lead to errors of overgeneralization.

Now, suppose we wanted to try to help a child who knows rules 1 and 2 to progress to Model II. We would need to draw the child's attention to and highlight the dimension that they are currently ignoring (i.e. distance). We might, for instance, select a series of problem situations in which weight was held constant whilst distance was changed, thus encouraging the child to attend to distance and, hence, to start learning new rules, like P3, in which both dimensions are taken into account.

Intelligent Tutoring Systems (ITS)

Production rules of the kind just illustrated can be programmed into a computer and used as a basis for a teaching machine. The machine is programmed with a set of rules that are to be taught (called the 'ideal student model'). By setting the learner problems, the ITS can discover which rules the learner already knows and those they do not yet know by comparing their performance with that of the student model. This reveals 'gaps' in their knowledge or rules which are wrong or only partially correct. Once the system identifies inaccurate rules or rules that the learner does not yet know, these help to create tutorial goals for the ITS. It selects problems to give to the learner which demand use of the rules in question, and it supports them in learning those rules. In this way, the system can create a tutorial programme which is individually tailored to the needs of each learner.

Principles of instruction

We have known for a long time that individual teaching by an expert human tutor leads to faster learning and better performance on academic tests than classroom teaching in groups. Anderson argues that research into the use and effects of ITS helps to explain why this is the case.

One of the central features of an ITS, like face-to-face tutoring, is that it can provide individualized instruction contingently in the context of a learner's real-time activity. In Anderson's terms, it honours the principle (1) *provide instruction in the problem-solving context.*

In group teaching situations where pupils might, say, be talked through a maths problem or see a demonstration proof worked out on a blackboard, this principle is not met. When the pupils are asked to work on problems themselves, they not only have to recall the teacher's advice, but also to recognize the specific problem contexts to which it relates. In face-to-face teaching, however, the timing of any help or hint can be offered by the tutor at relevant junctures, i.e. contingently. Here the expert, not the novice, takes responsibility for relating any help given to the contexts to which that help applies.

With individual support, the learner can be saved from spending time and prevented from losing motivation by expending large amounts of effort in confused and fruitless activity. To avoid such confusion, the theory advocates (2) *immediate response to learner errors.* Within the theory, nothing is learned from errors; they only waste time. Thus, the tutor should provide contexts in which the incidence of errors is minimized (e.g. by not setting problems that involve too many productions that the pupil does not yet know) and should give immediate feedback on errors when they happen to occur.

Since learners have a limited working memory capacity, they may overlook important features of the task at hand or lose sight of what they are trying to achieve. The system can support learning by (3) *providing reminders of the learning goal.* It can also remind the learner about what they have already achieved, helping them to focus their efforts on what remains to be done. Opportunities for such individualized support are minimal in large group teaching contexts.

Initially, with a learner who understands little of the lesson at hand (i.e. knows few relevant rules) the tutor may have to step in frequently to show the learner what to do. However, the overall aim of teaching is (4) *to support successive approximations to competent performance.* An effective tutor does as little of the task at hand as possible, leaving the learner with the responsibility for performing as much as possible for himself. The tutor only provides support for those aspects of the task that the learner cannot currently handle. Consequently, the learner and tutor, together, always solve any problems encountered, but the balance of responsibility passes from the tutor to the learner as new rules are acquired. As the learner learns, the system fades and eventually becomes silent.

Anderson's evaluations of his tutoring systems (in maths teaching, for example) show that pupils progress significantly faster than those taught in classroom groups.

A return to behaviourism?

As Anderson acknowledges, his theory has a strong behaviourist flavour. It is not, however, synonymous with S–R theory. In the first place, whilst behaviourism rests on a rejection of mentalistic concepts, Anderson's theory makes very explicit claims about what goes on in our minds as we think and learn. His analysis of knowledge into systems of production rules, and his characterization of learning as the acquisition of new productions, are not motivated simply by a desire to produce computer-based models. Rather, he argues that they are theoretical constructs which explain what happens in human cognition. Productions are offered as 'rules of the mind'.

Production system models (Anderson's is but one of a family) have been successful in producing computer simulations which mimic many aspects of human cognition. They provide explanations for a range of phenomena, such as the effects of practice on learning and memory. Of particular importance to our concerns here, however, is recent work which provides a new perspective on the role of language and 'inner dialogue' in intellectual activity.

VanLehn, Jones and Chi (1991) have constructed computer models which simulate differences in problem-solving by (relative) experts and novices. When experts are asked to explain how they solve problems, they are usually able to give clear and intelligible accounts of what they are doing. Their accounts demonstrate evidence of a search for underlying principles, planning, self-monitoring and self-correction. In other words, they show effective and efficient self-regulation. This is termed the 'self-explanation effect'. Novices, as one might expect, do not. They find it hard to describe or explain what they are trying to do. Chi and VanLehn constructed production system models of expert problem-solving in which they modelled both task knowledge (i.e. sets of rules which specify what to do in response to specific conditions) and rules which simulate self-explanation. Their model was designed in such a way that they could 'switch off' the sets of rules which model self-explanation. When they did so, they found that the model lost flexibility and some of its powers of generalization. This is important to us because it implies that when experts 'talk' themselves through problems – either aloud or 'in their heads' – they are able to solve problems that they could not otherwise solve even though they know the actual rules or task knowledge needed to do so. Their 'inner dialogue' serves to make connections to, and draw analogies from, previous experience, which would not otherwise be possible. If this result proves to be a general one, as VanLehn and Chi acknowledge, then it provides strong evidence in support of Vygotsky's views on the role of language in self-regulation. Language is not simply *what* we think about but part of the thinking process itself.

I will return to this issue in later chapters where we consider in more detail issues surrounding the complex topic of language and cognition.

Learning and generalization: first thoughts on a thorny issue

Piaget provided us with an explicit account of 'readiness for learning' based on the claim that how children learn and what they can understand is constrained by their stage of development. I have already explored evidence against the notion of stages in the last chapter. In the first part of the chapter, I explored the view, compatible with Vygotsky's theory, that children have to discover how to regulate their own activities in order to learn – a species of what used to be called 'learning how to learn'. I have also examined, albeit briefly, evidence which shows that differences in the abilities of adults and children can often be understood in terms of differences in experience and expertise, not variations due to stage of development or changes in intellectual capacity.

Research in both developmental psychology and cognitive science has also revealed aspects of the process of one-to-one teaching and identified principles of instruction which are compatible with a theory of procedural learning. This research demonstrates that instruction can play a vital role in learning, as envisaged in Bruner's theory. There is also emerging evidence which helps us to understand the role of explanation in learning to which I will return in chapter 6.

So, can we disregard those theories which argue that children not only learn but also undergo cognitive change with age that arises from development or maturation? I fear not. Let me end this chapter by exploring some reasons why such a conclusion is premature.

First, as Halford argues, we do not have enough evidence either way to rule out the possibility that children's basic cognitive capacities change with age. Whilst he accepts that changes in knowledge and in strategic self-regulation account for many observed differences in how adults and children think and learn, this does not warrant the conclusion that there are no differences due to developmental change. For example, as we have seen, changes in speed of processing occur as a result of experience and underpin changes in expertise. However, speed of processing also changes with age. It is by no means certain that one phenomenon explains the other. By this I mean that change due *both* to experience and to development may be implicated in cognitive growth. Nature may imitate itself.

The second reason for not yet ruling out developmental explanations will be explored in chapter 8. There I will go into some detail in describing various conceptual changes in children's understanding of number that take place during the period of schooling. Such discontinuities in conceptual development may eventually be explained by a theory of learning but there is, as yet, no convincing evidence that they can. Re-examine, for example, the production rules that I used in figure 4.7. The age gap between Models I and III (most of us don't get to IV) extends from around five to at least age 13. There is, as yet, no satisfactory explanation as to how changes between the different models come about. It is possible that learning theory can be extended to account for the changes indicated but, to the best of my knowledge, no such extension has yet been made. This example, coupled with more that I will consider later, leaves open the possibility that we will need a theory of conceptual change, not just learning, to explain the course of development.

The third and final reason for not rejecting developmental accounts of cognitive growth also has to do with the scope of current models of learning and with their educational applications. I have already refered to the fact that both Piaget and Bruner were critical of purely procedural approaches to teaching on the grounds that children can learn how to perform such activities with little or no conceptual grasp of what they mean. The same criticisms have been levelled against models of instruction like Anderson's. Since we will need a number of concrete examples to explore this debate, it will be developed further in chapter 8.

5

Language and learning

This chapter addresses a range of difficult and controversial topics that revolve around competing views of the relationship between language, learning and educational achievement. You might find it hard going in places. I have already identified some of the theoretical issues surrounding theories of language and thought. I have asked, for example, if the problems that children face when we attempt to test their ability to reason logically stem, wholly or in part, from misunderstandings created by problems of communication and language. Do children, as some students of development believe, have to develop special ways of communicating and thinking in order to learn in school? If they do not learn, are their problems of an intellectual kind or do they arise from poor communication skills? If so, where are the roots of such problems to be found: in the home, or in school, or both?

Children enter school speaking a range of different accents and dialects. These are often associated with variations in social background and parental occupation. As we shall see, some educational theorists believe that important and far-reaching effects on educational performance result from variations in the way that children from different backgrounds use language. Opposed to such views is the argument that such linguistic variations need exert no direct effects, positive or negative, on children's ability to learn and think. Rather, the argument proceeds, any connection between variations in language and school performance are caused by differences in the effectiveness of schools and teachers in their ability to reach and teach children from some social and ethnic backgrounds. Advocates of this second point of view have often appealed to linguistic theory to support their case. Consequently, we must consider, albeit briefly and selectively, ideas from linguistics that are central to arguments about the basis of educational success and failure. The inclusion of this aspect of development contributes to the difficulty of some parts of this chapter.

Bernstein's analysis: restricted codes and elaborated codes

Churchill once suggested that Britain and America are two countries divided by a common language. Basil Bernstein, a less well-known student of the English-speaking peoples, went further. He argued that the people of Britain themselves are divided by language, at least in relation to educational achievement and vocational opportunity. Others have argued that the same holds true of people in other societies.

Bernstein, a sociologist, attempted to explain the well-known and widely documented relationship between children's school performance and their socio-economic background in terms of variations in the uses and forms of language found in different social classes (e.g. Bernstein, 1960, 1961, 1970). He argued that children from middle-class homes are likely to be socialized, controlled and talked to in different ways from working-class children. These variations in language lead children to different 'world views', aspirations, attitudes and aptitudes for learning and, eventually, to different levels of school performance. The vocational opportunities open to the two groups of children are constrained by their academic qualifications, so they tend to gravitate towards different forms of employment. Middle-class youngsters are likely to find themselves in white-collar managerial roles while the working-class child is probably destined to follow her parents into manual occupations. Thus, generations move in cycles through time. Social classes tend to perpetuate themselves by means of differences in language and child-rearing practices.

Bernstein's views, first expressed in the 1960s, were met with both enthusiasm and hostility. On the one hand, his theory offered a degree of hope for those striving to create fairer schools and a more egalitarian society. His explanation for differences in school performance suggested that they are a product of social experience, not attributable to biological differences in native intelligence – the explanation favoured by some students of human nature. If social class differences in school performance did rest on problems associated with language and communication, then it might be possible to overcome them to ensure greater equality of opportunity and achievement. Perhaps the 'cycle of disadvantage' could be broken and hitherto self-perpetuating patterns of social class differences eradicated. His theory gave some educators grounds for hope and inspired enthusiasm.

On the other hand, intentionally or not, Bernstein's thesis implied that the seeds and causes of educational success or failure were to be found in the home. Whilst education might provide a means to help children overcome disadvantage, the implication was that schooling for children from some social backgrounds was to contain an element of remediation and repair. Whilst denying variation in educability due to biological differences, his theory still implied explanation by 'deficit'. The roots of disadvantage were to be found, not in the genes, but in the family and local community. Herein were the sources of hostile reactions from some people.

For reasons I will come to later, many linguists, sociologists and educationalists rejected Bernstein's apparent attempt to explain patterns of achievement in terms of factors located 'in' the child. There are, of course, audible differences in the accents and dialects that children bring into school. These reflect language variation across different regions and communities and are likely to *identify* a child's socio-economic background. Some ways of talking, revealed in pronunciation, vocabulary and the use of certain grammatical devices (such as 'Ain't got none'), announce regional and perhaps socio-economic origins.

Bernstein's theory went beyond such surface differences in speech, however, to suggest more fundamental and far-reaching variations in the way language is *used* and *structured* in different social groups. He suggested, for example, that children from better-off homes, whose parents are likely to have had a relatively extensive education and hold white-collar jobs, are exposed to what he termed an 'elaborated code' of the English language. Working-class children, on the other hand, are more likely to experience and learn to use a 'restricted code'. These codes are supposedly revealed by a number of characteristic differences in ways of talking.

A restricted code user is likely to frame what she says in such a way that her listener must be aware of or share her physical situation in order to understand what she means. The use of 'non-determinate' ways of referring to things (for example, 'this', 'that', 'those' and 'them') are typical of restricted code language. To understand what is being referred to, a listener must know what the speaker is thinking about, looking at, touching or in some way indicating non-verbally. The elaborated code also uses such terms, but in such a way that the thing they refer to is first established *verbally*. For instance, if one heard something like 'John brought his new bike to school. "Look at this", he said proudly' one might reasonably assume that 'this' refers back to (is a 'pro-form' for) the object 'bike'. The elaborated code user, the argument proceeds, speaks in such a way that her listener need not share her physical *context* in order to understand what she says. In this and other respects, elaborated code language is more similar to written text than is restricted code language.

Because the elaborated code is more verbally specific, precise and less physically 'context dependent', it forms a much more effective mode of communication in situations where speakers cannot resort to non-verbal communication or to common shared experience in order to make what they say mutually understandable. Since school teaching confronts children with speech that is often, even usually, independent of the immediate physical context, children who are fluent in elaborated code language will find communication and learning relatively easy in comparison to those whose major experiences of language are confined to a restricted code. Consequently, children from different social backgrounds come to school more or less prepared for the communicative and linguistic demands they will encounter. This is one reason why a child from a middle-class background is likely to learn more readily in school than her working-class peers.

There are many more facets to Bernstein's description of language codes than their different relationships to context and non-verbal communication, and I will consider some of these later. The important thing for the moment is to understand in general terms how the theory predicts that differences associated with accent and dialect coincide with more important differences in language *use*. These differences, in turn, arise from the linguistic and personal demands associated with different roles and occupations within society.

Bernstein's theory and educational politics

Although Bernstein's theory was developed to explain some of the differences in the educational achievement of British children, it was also embraced by educators and politicians in the USA, where it was extended to explain differences in the educational achievements of black and white children. There has been considerable controversy about the extent to which Bernstein's ideas were misunderstood and exaggerated by educationalists who made use of them to explain educational inequalities. Beyond noting the fact that some people did seem to adopt a far more radical stance about the linguistic abilities of black children than his theory implies, however, we will not be concerned with the details of this argument.

Bernstein's theory appeared at a time of Government affluence and public optimism in both the USA and the UK. In the United States, the poverty amongst many black Americans was a subject for heated political debate. Action through education seemed to some politicians the most direct way to tackle the problems of inequality and poverty. Similarly, in the United Kingdom, 'Educational Priority Areas' were identified and targeted for additional financial help and action designed to assist children from economically poor homes.

The political will to act coincided with, and was no doubt partly shaped by, theories and findings emerging from several disciplines, sociology and psychology in particular. These suggested that differences in intelligence and educability were not innate but direct products of early social experiences. Poverty, it was claimed, depresses children's health, motivation, intelligence and language. Bernstein's views on language, coupled with psychological studies of intelligence (including Piaget's), provided a theoretical rationale and, perhaps, a stimulus for political action to wage a 'war on poverty'.

In 1965, President Johnson announced the launch of 'Project Head Start' in the USA. This was a federally funded venture designed to provide educational opportunities for pre-school children from poor homes. It also financed improvements in medical, social and family support systems. Johnson was reported by Mohr (1965) in the *New York Times* as follows:

> 5- and 6-year old children are inheritors of poverty's curse and not its creators . . . Unless we act, these children will pass it on to the next generation, like a family birthmark . . . We have taken up the challenge of poverty and we don't intend to lose generations of our children to this enemy of the human race . . . Before this summer, they were on the road to despair . . . But today . . . children who have never spoken learned to talk. Parents who were suspicious of school authorities came to see the centres and they stayed on to help the teachers. Teachers tried new approaches and learned new techniques.

This speech was made less than three months after the Head Start programme had been initiated! The quote is important in the present context because it betrays some of the attitudes and theories that shaped educational policy. Note the assertion that 'children who have never spoken learned to talk' (in three months?). The belief that many poor children, particularly black ones, were not only exposed to a different dialect but were in fact *mute* clearly went far beyond Bernstein's views on class and codes. Where did such an opinion come from? Well, there were a number of empirical studies which seemed to suggest that pre-school black children could not talk or were able to understand and say very little. In 1966, Bereiter and Englemann, for example, concluded, on the basis of experimental investigations, that

> the speech of severely deprived children seems to consist not of distinct words, as does the speech of middle-class children of the same age, but rather of whole phrases or sentences that function like giant words . . . these 'giant word' units cannot be taken apart by the child and recombined; they cannot be transformed from statements to questions, from imperatives to declaratives, and so on. Instead of saying 'He's a big dog', the deprived child says 'He bih daw'. . . . Instead of saying 'That is a red truck', he says 'Da-re-truh' . . . the listener . . . may believe that the child is using words like *it, is, if* and *in*, when in fact he is using the same sound for all of them – something on the order of 'ih'. (Reported in Brown et al., 1984, p. 29)

The Chomskian 'revolution'

Such sweeping generalizations about the linguistic abilities of black American children and children from economically impoverished homes provoked many strong reactions. They were also totally at variance with what was, in the 1960s, fast becoming the dominant theory of language and its acquisition. This theory, developed by the American linguist Noam Chomsky (e.g. 1957, 1965), was destined to change radically and, I suspect, irrevocably our views on language and learning.

From Chomsky's theory there came the argument that children are not *taught* to speak at all, nor, in any simple sense, do they *learn* language, by imitation, say. Rather, children *acquire* their mother tongue(s). Furthermore, although children obviously develop different accents and dialects depending upon the social group within which they live, there is no theoretical justification for the view that such differences are in any sense for 'better' or 'worse'.

Why then did experimentalists conclude that some children are deprived of language; that they come to school mute or, at best, inarticulate? Perhaps because such children did not want to talk to them. For example, black American children, when addressed by a white middle-class academic in formal laboratory settings, said little and appeared monosyllabic, but were found to be loquacious, witty and capable of rational argument when observed on their own territory in the local community. Labov (1969), who pioneered such observations, concluded that whilst their speech might sound different from that of white middle-class people, these children's command of language was no less articulate, rule-governed, complex or rational. Labov's argument, which he extended against Bernstein's thesis, was that the way in which people talk, and what they do or do not say to each other, is fundamentally affected by the *social and institutional* context in which they are observed. The 'register' of language used – say, by a black child talking to white middle-class representatives of authority – is a socio-political phenomenon. In this last case, the child, he would argue, is well advised to say little and hold her peace. She is in a 'no win' situation in which anything she says and does is likely to appear 'wrong' or incompetent. However, in situations where the child feels relaxed and in control, her 'register' of speech changes to reveal her linguistic and intellectual competence.

Extensions of this argument into the classroom lead to a very different interpretation of the relationships between language, learning and educational achievement from those entailed by theories of linguistic deprivation. Before considering these, let me outline, briefly, some of the main elements of Chomsky's early theory of language and give some sense of the impact that his ideas had on the study of child language. We can then return to reconsider and extend our discussion of the relationships between language, learning, intelligence and school achievement.

Our thinking about the nature of language and its acquisition, as I have already said, has been revolutionized since the formulation of Chomsky's theory, aspects of which were first published in the late 1950s. Although, as a theoretical linguist, he was involved in a rather different quest from those that concern psychologists and educators, it soon became clear that his views on the nature of language could not be ignored by those who were interested in the study or cultivation of human abilities.

Like Piaget, Chomsky rejected as inadequate those psychological theories of learning that had become prominent and dominant by the 1960s. Both theorists argued that exclusive attention to the 'stimuli' that children experience and the 'responses' these evoke provides an inadequate conceptual framework for the study or analysis of intellectual abilities. Piaget, as we have seen, argued that children not only learn responses or actions but construct operations. Chomsky, theorizing about language, argued that language cannot profitably be viewed as vocal 'responses' to 'stimuli'. Rather, language involves a system of grammatical *rules*. These enable a user of language to *generate* novel utterances that they may never have heard or produced before. He argued that the study of language must concern itself with discovering the grammatical rules that we use when we speak and listen. What kinds of rules do children acquire when they discover how to understand and produce speech? How and when are these rules acquired? These were the kinds of questions that Chomsky's theory stimulated.

Where Piagetians and Chomskians seem to differ radically is in their views on the relations between language and thought, and the way in which the development of one influences that of the other. Piaget's theory predicts that the use and understanding of language is constrained by stages of intellectual development. Chomsky, on the other hand, argued that language has a 'special structure' that involves systems of specifically *linguistic* rules that cannot be 'reduced' to cognition. More about this later.

These extremely complex theoretical arguments about the nature of language and its development are of central importance to our discussions of the relationships between language and learning. Though very academic and abstract in nature, they are of relevance to urgent educational arguments about the reasons why children from some social groups generally do less well in school than those from other backgrounds. The two theories also invite us to explore different explanations for the finding that children of different ages may appear more or less logical and able to learn things. For if language acquisition *is* partially or wholly independent of cognitive development, then it follows, as I have already argued, that children may fail to solve a problem being set by an adult or misunderstand something being taught or explained to them, not because they lack certain intellectual abilities, but because they don't understand what is being said to them. Furthermore, if language acquisition is a natural and largely automatic process, as some students of Chomsky have suggested, then it follows that differences in language, dialect and the like are unlikely to be primary causes of communication and learning problems, as linguistic 'deficit' theories imply. No language is more or less 'efficient' than any other. A child's ability to learn and understand should be quite independent of the particular language or dialect that he or she happens to speak.

Here, Piagetians and Chomskians are likely to be in agreement in their opposition to deficit theory, though for somewhat different reasons.

It is not my intention to explore Chomskian theory in detail, but we do need to consider some of the arguments favouring the view that language acquisition cannot be explained either in terms of teaching and learning or by stages of cognitive development.

Ambiguity and paraphrase: evidence of structure

The relationships between an idea to be communicated and vocal sounds that we make in order to achieve communication are complex and rule-governed. The same idea can be expressed in many different ways. Even what may seem to be a description of a simple scene can be said in many different ways (e.g. 'A cat sat on a mat by the bed', or 'By the bed was a mat that a cat was sitting on', and so on). So there is no single or direct relationship between a 'stimulus' (e.g. an object, event or happening) and the 'response' (a particular pattern of vocal movements) that is made to represent or refer to it. The fact that *paraphrase* is a central and general feature of language demonstrates that the relationship between an intended *meaning* and the *sounds* used to *express* it are too complex to be explained in terms of learned connections between words and things. Rules are involved in both producing and analysing language. By the same token, the same string of words (a famous example is 'They were flying kites') may express several *different* meanings depending upon the interpretation put upon it or, in other terms, upon how the listener 'parses' the utterance. 'They' might refer to people involved in the activity of kite-flying or to kites in flight. Thus, the same sound, 'flying', may be understood as a verb or adjective respectively, depending upon the overall meaning put upon the utterance.

Paraphrase and ambiguity are two pervasive and universal features of speech that must be acknowledged and explained by any theory that promises to provide an adequate analysis of language. Learning theory, Chomsky argued, is incapable of accommodating such creative, 'generative' aspects of language. Any theory that sets out with the assumption that the meaning of speech can be explained by patterns of associations between objects and sounds put together into a learned sequence (e.g. phrases, sentences) cannot, he argued, begin to provide a useful account of the nature of language. Such theories begin with an incorrect conceptualization of what language *is*.

A competent user of a language may produce an utterance that has never been spoken before and a competent listener is able to understand what is said. Any language enables its users to 'generate' a theoretically infinite number of (structured and rule-governed) utterances. Any number of sentences in this book, for instance, may never have been generated before, but a competent (and literate) user of English is able to understand their meaning (at least, I hope so). Such abilities also imply that language competence involves sets of rules. These rules are sensitive to the *structure* of language and enable us, for example, to understand which word or words in an utterance serve as the subject and the predicate, which act as verb and which as object.

This is not to say, of course, that we are consciously aware of working out verbs, objects and the like when we communicate. We, like the child acquiring language, may not even understand what such terms mean. However, our natural language abilities enable us to analyse utterances into their grammatical constituents 'automatically' and unconsciously. Linguists, in this view, have invented terms like 'grammatical subject' to refer to and develop theories about the natural processes that make the production and analysis of language possible.

Chomsky's theory thus puts generativity and creativity at the very heart of language ability and, as we shall see, at the heart of language development too. What the structural linguist attempts to do is to construct a working theory or 'model grammar' of a language which can produce and 'parse' (analyse) a potentially infinite number of utterances. This model grammar should only produce utterances that a native speaker of that language will accept as being 'well formed' (grammatical), and should not itself accept as grammatical an utterance that would not be accepted as such by a native speaker. To the extent that these conditions are met, the model represents a theory of what goes on in the human mind in the production and analysis of the grammar.

Chomsky and many structural linguists (though not all) are not concerned with 'real' speech. By this, I mean that they are not studying things like the way in which people hesitate, pause, make false starts and correct themselves when they talk. Nor are they concerned with the way in which gestures, pointing and other non-verbal aspects of communication aid mutual understanding. There are many such features of language *performance* that are not of direct interest to theoretical linguists who are trying to construct 'ideal models' of grammar. The different objectives being pursued by these linguists and by people who are interested in 'real life' discourse have led to many arguments and misunderstandings. I will not be concerned with these in this book, but I think it is important to keep in mind the fact that Chomsky's quest is somewhat *different* from that of most educators. Put another way, whilst it is useful and informative to see how far theories of grammatical structure help us to understand everyday uses of language, we should not be too ready to criticize such theories for being inadequate to fulfil our needs. They are not *intended* to do so.

Let us ask, then, what impact structural linguists have had on our knowledge of children's language development, keeping in mind the rather different nature of their goal and our current concerns.

Language acquisition and the LAD

Chomsky's analysis offered not only a dynamic new view of language but also changed attitudes towards and research into language acquisition. His theory displaced the image of the child language 'learner' who develops language by being taught and reinforced, and substituted it with the theory of a language 'acquirer' who discovers and makes creative, generative use of *rules* from the very start of language development. These rules, even before language is 'fully' mastered, enable the child to produce and analyse a theoretically infinite number of utterances. Child language study was thus transformed into a search for the 'rules' that children acquire and involved attempts to write 'child grammars'. More about this later.

In rejecting the theory that the capacity to learn how to speak and understand speech is in any sense taught, Chomsky leads us to a view of the language acquisition capacity that is rather like a 'mental organ' (Chomsky, 1980, p. 188). The way in which the eye and the nervous system respond to light of different wavelengths to produce the sensations of colour vision, for example, is a property of the way in which the visual system is structured. This sensory system is genetically determined and a fruit of evolution. Speech sounds stimulating the auditory nerves are 'processed' naturally to uncover (eventually) the rules by which that speech is structured. Although languages obviously differ in the word sounds they use and the grammatical rules they embody, Chomsky believed that they all share certain universal properties, which an innate system – what has been termed the Language Acquisition Device or LAD (McNeill, 1970) – has evolved to produce and acquire. The automatic workings of the LAD are such that a child 'knows' that the speech signal is the product of another similar system which generates sentences, words, and so on. Thus, the child does not have to 'learn' that speech is built out of words and sentences that possess components like subjects and predicates or verbs and objects. The LAD ensures that she perceives speech sounds in this way (though she still has to discover the specific rules underlying her 'host' language and learn the relations between words and the things to which they refer).

In recent years, the phrase Language Acquisition Device has largely dropped out of academic discourse. However, Chomsky's insistence that language acquisition is an automatic affair realized by innate mechanisms has been accepted and developed by many other students of language (e.g. Pinker, 1989). One particularly influential theoretical extension of his line of thinking was that undertaken by Fodor, who could be called the 'father' of modern modularity theory, in his book *The Modularity of Mind* (1982). In this, he proposes a theory of mind which endows innate mechanisms and maturation with a central role in human psychology, as we saw in chapter 2.

The perception of such things as human speech and human faces is, according to neo-nativist theory, a natural consequence of the way in which any normally functioning perceptual system works in everyday situations. Infants respond naturally and selectively to the human voice and to the human face. They do not need to learn that the speech sounds made by their mother and father belong to the same category and exhibit similar structural properties, nor do they need experience in order to discover the fact that different faces are examples of the same class of objects in the world. Their nervous system is 'hard wired' to extract the defining features of both. Recognition is part of their genetic endowment. Even for adults, according to Fodor, knowledge, experience and values cannot influence how they perceive the world. What they perceive is fully determined by the way in which the nervous system is structured and that structure is genetically determined.

Of course, the perceiver might choose, say, to avert their eyes from something they do not wish to see or to avoid listening to a voice they do not wish to hear. But what they perceive once their sense organs (transducers in Fodor's terms) and the modules these serve receive stimulation is determined by the nature of the stimulus and the way in which modules process it. Thus, we have no control over the output from a module once it is stimulated. For Fodor, this demonstrates that the processing undertaken by a module is 'cognitively impenetrable'. Values, desires, knowledge and needs cannot influence how a module operates nor govern its output. And if this is true, then we don't need learning (or, of course, teaching) to account for developmental change in relation either to language or to any other modular system. Other students of the mind, as we shall see, disagree and argue that the concepts of modularity and maturation are not sufficient to explain the facts of development.

Meaning and 'structure dependency'

In the 'flying kites' example already introduced, recall how the same word (flying) changed its grammatical category and hence its meaning according to the chosen meaning of the *sentence* as a whole. This is symptomatic of another universal feature of languages. Meaning involves much more than simply stringing words together: it is *not* simply the sum of word parts. Rather, the meaning of words themselves is constrained by the overall structure of the utterance in which they are embedded. Put another way, meaning is 'structure dependent'. This is one reason why a Chomskian view of language leads to the assertion that children are innately equipped to 'parse' utterances naturally into linguistic units. Only a system that is sensitive to such higher-order structures, the argument proceeds, could ever discover what speech means.

In this way, Chomsky turns the behaviourist analysis on its head. Language development does not proceed from learning isolated words to the discovery of progressively longer word combinations. Instead, the child 'expects' to hear units of meaning which are structured by rules. Similarly, when the child produces her first words and word combinations, these should not be viewed as simple responses attached to isolated things but more like embryonic sentences. The child is communicating ideas, albeit, in the early stages, through single words. Any theory which holds that utterances are learned by building up or stringing together single word units cannot capture such structural, rule-governed features of language.

Perhaps a final example will help to underline this point. Compare 'Green ideas sleep furiously' with 'Furiously green sleep ideas'. Although both strings of words are meaningless, are you prepared to accept that the first sounds more 'grammatical' than the latter? If so, it follows that knowledge of grammatical structure is independent of meaningfulness. We recognize grammatical structure *itself* even though we are not able to describe the rules that create such structures. We can recognize and use the rules but cannot articulate them.

Chomsky's theory has kept linguists and psycholinguists in business for many years and it has been used to make a number of predictions about language use and its development.

Some examples of the early stages of language development

Having read Chomsky, researchers were obviously going to look at children's speech to ask if it displayed any evidence of rule acquisition or use. Motivated by notions of an innate Language Acquisition Device of the sort Chomsky seemed to envisage, they searched for common patterns, structures and stages in the linguistic development of all children. If, as the theory implies, children do their own language *acquisition*, researchers were bound to ask if it follows that adult talk to children is largely irrelevant to their development.

Given these concerns with the notion of 'innateness' and the rejection of teaching and learning in language acquisition, it is perhaps not surprising that the bulk of research into child language development has concentrated on the very early stages over the first three years of life. Many detailed observations have been made of children's first 'words' and their early word combinations (Crystal, 1976; Pine and Martindale, 1996). Basically, such attempts involve the formulation of rules that will 'predict' which categories of words children will put together and in what ways, and, at the same time, will never produce an utterance with a structure that they never utter. Although most of this work on early language development and child grammar is not directly relevant to our current educational concerns, some of the issues, findings and ideas that have emerged from it are.

There seems to be general agreement that young children do acquire 'rules' in learning to talk (although many would argue that these are not of the type predicted by Chomskian theory). One line of evidence for this assertion comes from the common finding that children often produce utterances that, though systematically related to their stage of language development, are extremely unlikely to be the result of imitating adult speech. For example, some children produce plural forms like 'mouses' and 'catses' even though earlier in life they may have used the correct forms, 'mice' and 'cats'. Studies of the way in which children come to master the rules involved in creating plural forms illustrate a *general* phenomenon that recurs time and time again in language development right through to adolescence. Children pass through a series of stages or phases as they encounter and master (learn?) how to use and understand many aspects of language structure. Let me outline the proposed stages involved.

Language: discontinuity and change

I have already said that children often use words like 'mice' and 'cats' appropriately before they begin to make 'errors' like 'mices'. In this early stage, children do not seem aware of the fact that plural forms like 'cats', 'bats', 'bikes' are composed of *two* elements. Rather, they seem to treat all word-like sounds as though they are *single* elements of meaning (Gleitman and Wanner, 1982). Many words contain two or more 'morphemes' (i.e. units of meaning), like 'cat-s', 'walk-ing', 'un-cover-ing' and so on. Some of these units (sometimes referred to as 'free morphemes') are free to stand alone, like 'cat', 'walk' and 'cover', but others (like '-s', 'un-' and '-ing') are bound to occur in combination with free morphemes (hence, so-called 'bound morphemes'). Children, though producing a few 'multi-morpheme' words at this stage, do not seem aware of the fact that these can be 'decomposed' to reveal two or more units. When they *do* discover the fact that such words can be broken down, they come to realize that prefixes like 'un-' and suffixes like '-s' and '-ing' have very *specific* meanings. Having, so to speak, 'detached' such morphemes and discovered what they mean, the child proceeds to *generalize* the 'rules' for using them to produce words like 'undress' and 'rats' but she may also combine them with other words to produce 'errors' of over-generalization. So she might add '-s' to 'mice' producing 'mices', 'un-' to 'wipe' producing 'unwipe', and '-ed' to 'went' giving 'wented'. Although the child is unlikely ever to have heard such words, the fact that so many (though not necessarily all) children produce them at the same *stage* of development suggests strongly that they are inferring and generalizing rules.

Stage 1, then, involves the limited use of a relatively small number of words in 'non-rule-governed' ways. Following the discovery of new features of speech (like a particular prefix or suffix) and their meaning, the child moves into a second stage which may be marked by errors of over-generalization. As the child discovers irregularities like 'mice' (which is already a plural form) and 'went' (which is already a 'perfected' verb form), such errors disappear and the child moves on to a stage where a more mature understanding of the various linguistic rules involved is perfected.

This process is not nearly so 'automatic' an affair as some early students of Chomsky seem to suggest. It certainly implies that the child has to *work* on the problems involved in achieving mature understanding of language and that *learning* is implicated (though not necessarily teaching – please read on). Though this form of learning (discovery of rules through problem-solving) is a very different affair from that implicated in 'response learning' theories, it is not, I suggest, very different from the learning processes described in the development of expertise. More about this later.

I have suggested that this pattern of stages (limited, non-productive mastery of a few forms followed by the discovery of new linguistic features and possible 'errors' of generalization prior to mastery and perfection of mature rule systems) is a general and recurrent feature of language development. Later, I will discuss recent theoretical accounts of such patterns in development. First, however, I will illustrate the suggestion with a few examples. These take us back to the study of school children.

Language learning: one process or many?

For a time, some developmental psycholinguists (psychologists and/or linguists who study language development) were sufficiently impressed by the linguistic achievements of pre-school children to suggest that the acquisition of grammar is all but completed before children start formal schooling. However, while they are impressive, the pre-school child's achievements fall far short of mature linguistic competence. The development of communication skills and grammatical knowledge continues at least into adolescence.

Because language is changing and developing over such a long period of time, it seems unreasonable to suppose that the process of language acquisition and/or language learning is a single, continuous one. It would be surprising if the processes involved in language development in children aged nine, say, were not to prove different in some important ways from those of children aged two. Establishing the nature of such differences and how they come about is not easy. But the issues involved are important. They will lead us, for example, to consider the importance of *literacy* as an influence on the development of 'clear speaking' and verbal reasoning. It has been suggested, for instance, that the ability to reason *rationally* about abstract phenomena is a direct product of literacy and the educational experiences that teach children how to read fluently. Thus, the issue of language development (acquisition and/or learning) is intimately involved with a range of important educational questions concerning both the teaching and consequences of literacy.

We have already met and discussed some of the evidence that points to changes in children's intellectual abilities between the ages of five and seven years. Now we examine other studies and observations which suggest that the same holds true of linguistic development. The nature of any discontinuities and the way in which they come about are a matter for debate. To what extent are developments after the age of five years attributable to school experience, say, or to changes in stage of intellectual development? Attempts to answer these questions will involve us in (at least) a three-cornered fight. Before entering battle, let us consider some of the changes in the child's understanding and use of language that occur during the first two to three years of schooling.

Listening and talking

Do children understand more than they can say? Put another way, are they able to comprehend utterances which they cannot form themselves? If they can, a number of things might follow. In the first place, it would imply that because a child cannot produce a particular type of utterance (for instance, a passive construction like 'The dog was scratched by the cat'), it does not necessarily follow that she will not understand it when she hears it spoken. If so, it may be important that we do not underestimate what children can be told and are able to grasp by assuming that they only understand language structures that they are able to say. More important, an ability to understand what they themselves cannot yet produce might provide children with a basis for the development of spoken language. Knowing what 'sounds right', a child is in a position to *evaluate* her own speech. She will know when she has said something that sounds 'odd', perhaps. If she is able to recognize whether or not what she is trying to say sounds right, she may not need anyone to *tell* her that some of the things she says are not linguistically well formed. She may school herself in the complexities of language use. This question is educationally interesting because it provides some measure of the importance of 'teaching' in language development. There are, in fact, several lines of evidence to support the view that children *are* able to understand more than they can say in this sense. Their *receptive* language ability (ability to listen and understand) is often in advance of their *productive* language (speech). Let me illustrate the argument.

I have already drawn attention to the fact that infants take some time to discover the fact that many words which sound like single units of meaning actually encapsulate more than one element. It seems unlikely that anyone in any simple or direct sense 'teaches' them this fact. Rather, what seems to happen is far more a matter of the child's biology, how the hearing system works, than a case for instruction. Studies of the *sequence* in which infants master different systems of prefixes and suffixes, for example, help to illustrate this claim. Consider the suffixes '-ing' and '-ed'. These are used to 'mark' the fact that a particular activity (walk, watch) is in progress (walking, watching) or has been perfected (walked, watched). Children usually master the progressive form before they crack the perfective. Why? Is it because they find it easier to relate a sound ('ing') to an *ongoing* event than they do to relate one ('ed') to an activity that has *stopped* and hence has to be remembered? Or does the answer lie in the way that adults talk to children? Perhaps we speak to infants more about events in progress than those that have been completed. If so, the order of acquisition would reflect frequency of exposure and might be an example of 'indirect' instruction. It seems, however, that the sequence of acquisition is not determined by the relative difficulty of the *ideas* involved in different verb forms, nor by frequency of exposure. Rather, because 'ing' is usually more acoustically *stressed* in speech than is 'ed', infants find it more *salient*. In other words, they become aware of the progressive use of verbs first and begin to use them in their own speech before they master the 'ed' form because the suffix involved is more 'audible'. Studies of language development in children acquiring other languages (e.g. Serbo-Croatian and Turkish) offer further evidence for this conclusion (Gleitman and Wanner, 1982).

On the basis of this evidence, one might conclude that infants acquire language 'naturally'. The fact that many children show a similar sequence of development which seems to rest on the way in which speech is structured (for example, where stress is found) is evidence favouring a Chomskian interpretation of language *acquisition*. Children's acquisition of language is paced by the way in which they hear – a biological phenomenon that has little to do with instruction, informal or otherwise.

Now let us consider some examples of language development in older children. When do children understand what the words 'this' and 'that' mean? Well, first consider how we might express the meaning of 'this' and 'that'. We might define 'here' as 'The region of space occupied by the current speaker ("I")' and 'there' as 'The region of space occupied by the current listener(s) ("you")'. Of course, when the speaker in a conversational exchange 'hands over' to her listener, 'here' becomes 'there' and 'there' becomes 'here'. Similarly, we might define 'this' as 'an object in the "here" of the current "I" and 'that' as 'an object in the "there" of the current "you". When 'I' becomes 'you', 'this' becomes 'that'. The use of such terms, of course, is not restricted to situations involving only two people. For example, if 'we' are talking about 'him', then 'there' may be where 'he' is along with 'that'. However, should 'he' start to address 'us' ('he' becoming 'I'), then both 'this' and 'here' are where 'he' (who, recall, is currently 'I') is located. If 'we' are in the same room as 'him', then 'there' is likely to be a region of space nearer to 'him' than 'us', when one of 'us' is currently 'I', that is. However, should 'he' be talking to 'us' over the telephone, say, then 'this' may well be something far removed, since 'here', when 'he' is 'I', is likely to be at the other end of the phone – in another country, perhaps.

Answering the question 'When do children understand 'here' and 'there' or 'this' and 'that'?' is not easy. In some situations, understanding and the use of such words comes very early in life. For example, a three-year-old says, 'Give me that' or 'I don't want to go there'. A father says to his infant daughter 'Come to me', and she complies. The pre-school child, in some contexts, seems both to understand and to use such words. However, when confronted with an experimenter across a table who says 'Will you give me this pencil' (as opposed to one located near the child), some children aged five years are likely to offer the pencil located nearest to 'them', apparently assuming that 'this' is located near where they themselves are. Reliable understanding of 'this' and 'that' in such circumstances appears at around five to six years (Clark, 1978).

On several occasions, I have drawn attention to similar discrepancies between the ages at which children use and understand utterances and solve problems in 'natural' everyday contexts as opposed to formal experimental situations. I have suggested that everyday interactions between adults and children are different in developmentally important ways from those in formal teaching and testing encounters. In everyday discourse, but not in such experiments, the *situation* shared by speakers and hearers provides several avenues for the achievement of mutual understanding. When we talk about 'this' and 'that' in spontaneous encounters, for example, we are likely to *look* at the thing being referred to. A child asked 'Will you give me that, please?' and presented with an outstretched hand, is likely to understand what 'that' is for a number of possible reasons. Non-verbal 'cues' to meaning plus the fact that she may, say, have something that does not belong to her, or which is in some way taboo, probably leave little room for doubt about what the speaker is referring to. 'Will you hand me this, please' is a little more unusual. Perhaps the person making the request is unable to move for some reason or has their hands full. The utterance also seems to imply that some other objects (other possible 'thats') exist and 'this' is something closer to the speaker than any potential 'that'. It also suggests that 'this' is closer to the speaker than the child being asked to hand it over. Put another way, there is likely to be some interpretable explanation or *reason* for the speaker's request and there may well be other cues (nods, points, eye movements) which indicate what 'this' is.

In the experimental situation, however, such reasons and cues are deliberately avoided to test the child's understanding of 'language' itself. The reason why children seem to understand the 'same' words in some situations but not in others is not, then, all that straightforward. I am suggesting, as I did in discussing tests of children's 'logic', that experimental encounters devoid of interpretable *reasons* or obvious *justifications* and which are stripped of many cues that normally make meaning and communication relatively 'transparent', confront young children with unusual demands. Although 'similar' forms of *words* are being used, the marked differences in available clues to meaning and the presence or absence of intelligible reasons for utterances show that such apparent similarities are misleading. Logical tasks, and utterances which look and sound 'identical', often differ in *kind*.

Deixis: words that 'point'

A psycholinguist, Eve Clark, has undertaken a range of experiments to investigate children's understanding of terms like 'here' and 'there','this' and 'that' and 'come' and 'go'. Such terms are referred to as 'deictic' forms. Deixis, from the Greek verb meaning 'to point', refers to words and to non-verbal features of communication like nods and gestures, which serve to point to or in some way to identify people, times, places and objects in the course of discourse. Pronouns like 'I' and 'you', for instance, unlike nouns, do not refer to members of specific categories of things like 'cat', 'dog' or 'chair'. Their meaning, who or what they refer to, is determined in *use*, so 'I' might be defined as 'the current speaker' and 'you' as 'the current listener'. As we have seen, 'here' can be defined with reference to who is speaking. 'This' and 'that' 'point to' things that are 'here' or 'there', and so on. Clark's experimental studies reveal a developmental *sequence* that children pass through in mastering such terms (again, in formal contexts lacking many 'natural' clues to mean-

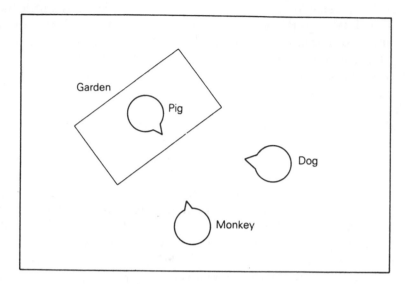

Figure 5.1 Testing deictic contrasts: positions of the three animals, all facing each other, with one inside a specific location and the other two facing in

ing). 'I' and 'you' are mastered before 'here' and 'there', followed by 'this' and 'that'. 'Come' and 'go' come later. 'Come' in a given encounter might imply 'you cease being an object in the "there" of the current "you" and become an object closer to the 'here' of the current "I".' Alternatively, if 'I' is talking about 'us' it might imply 'let "us" cease to be objects in the "here" of the current "we" to take up residence over "there".' Children's understanding of verbs like 'come' and 'go' and 'bring' and 'take' develops up to the age of about nine years. When we consider the complexity of some of the ways in which these verbs are used, we can see in a reasonably concrete way how the *learning* of language (I use the term deliberately) shades into verbal *reasoning*.

By way of illustration, examine the task shown in figure 5.1. When eight-year-old children are asked to work out problems like 'The monkey says "Go into the garden". Which animal is he talking to?', few children below the age of eight years six months were likely to give 'adult' answers. Although children are using the verb 'to go' quite early in life (e.g. 'Can I go out to play?'), their use and understanding of this and many other linguistic terms develops through into adolescence. While the 'same' verb is employed in many different circumstances, the nature of its *meaning* and the intellectual demands involved in working this out vary enormously from one context to another. This is why it is difficult, if not impossible, to give a simple, general answer to questions like 'When do children understand the verb "to go"?' The answer depends upon the *use* to which the verb is being put and upon the *situation* in which communication is taking place.

The evidence suggesting that language *acquisition* in infancy is strongly constrained by natural features of speech, such as acoustic stress, is persuasive. Infants, as many Chomskians have argued, seem to acquire their understanding of language 'naturally' without any teaching or instruction from the more mature. However, when we consider language development in later years, it becomes difficult if not impossible to disentangle language from reasoning and problem-solving. Children have to think about and to *work* at language in order to fathom its meaning. What may seem at first sight to be an issue of language learning turns out on more detailed consideration to involve *intellectual* development generally. Learning how to put ideas into words (or print) and working out what others mean by what they say (and write) is not a single, *continuous* process but one that changes with age and, perhaps, stage of development.

Teach yourself language?

Clark's experimental studies illustrate and chart the long developmental history involved in children's acquisition and mastery of deictic uses of language. She also observes, however, that outside contrived experimental situations, it is extremely difficult to detect any 'errors' in children's use of words like 'this', 'that', 'come' and 'go'. This observation raises some important issues. For example, if children do not make errors, or if any errors they make are hard to detect, it seems unlikely that they are 'taught' how to understand and use such linguistic devices by 'correction'. If adults trained in linguistics who have looked specifically for examples of children's errors in everyday talk cannot find them, it seems unlikely that parents are responsible for teaching their children about these aspects of language by correcting their speech.

A similar conclusion emerges from the findings of Karmiloff-Smith (1979), whose studies of children's use and understanding of determiners (e.g. 'a' and 'the') I referred to in chapter 3. Let me say a little more about her findings. Some of her experiments involved young French-speaking children. The structure of the determiner system in French differs in some respects from that of English. For instance, reference to *singula*r and *plural* objects in French involves not only the use of bound morphemes

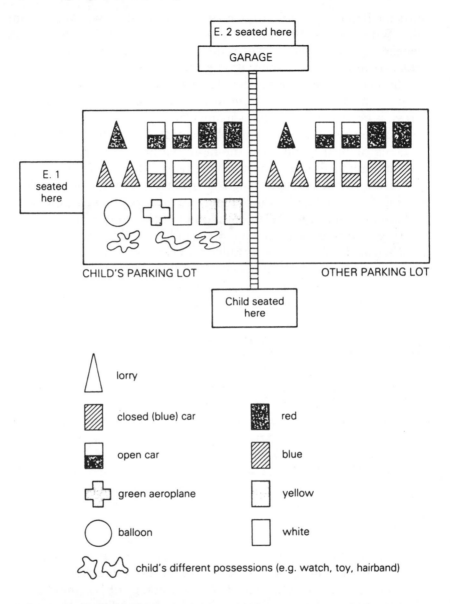

Figure 5.2   The child is asked by E1 to tell E2 to put, say, all the child's lorries in the garage

(e.g. '-s') to mark plurality (e.g. 'voiture', 'voitures') but also modifications to the determiner as well (e.g. 'la voiture', 'les voitures'). Indeed, as Karmiloff-Smith points out, the '-s' marker in French is often impossible to 'hear', i.e. it is often non-articulated or unstressed, unlike its counterpart in English (e.g. cat/cats). French children must, then, learn to use and understand plural *determiners* to make and comprehend distinctions between singular and plural references.

As with English children's grasp of words like 'come' and 'go', young French children use and understand singular and plural determiners in everyday discourse without obvious problems. Yet they experience significant difficulties with them in experiments. Part of the explanation for this now familiar (apparent) discrepancy between performance in natural and contrived interactions stems from the fact that words like 'le' and 'les' have several related but *different* meanings in French depending upon the circumstances of their use. They are, in Karmiloff-Smith's terms, 'pluri-functional'. For instance, four-year-old children face no problems in either saying or understanding the different meanings of expressions like 'Observez le chien' and 'Observez les chiens'. Pre-school children appreciate that the first makes reference to a single dog and the second to more than one. Compare this with the quite different though related meaning of 'les' when, in the experimental set-up illustrated in figure 5.2, the child is asked to tell another person that they must take *all* the cars shown and put them somewhere else (in the garage, say). In French, the expression 'Mettez au garage *les* voitures' would be a perfectly adequate instruction. 'Les', used in this context, does not simply mean 'more than one car' but *all* of the cars. Put another way, it refers not only to *plurality* but at the same time to *totality*, to the whole *set* of relevant objects (cars).

The use of 'les' by French children to refer to plurality and totality *simultaneously* emerges at somewhere around eight years of age (again, in this type of situation). Younger children who have not yet mastered the dual function of 'les' manage to get their message across to their listener by saying things like 'toutes les voitures' ('all of the cars'). By 'adding' words which to the mature French ear are 'redundant', the child manages to convey the appropriate meaning. Consequently, it cannot be the case that the child fails to grasp the communication needs of her listener, nor is it the case that she does not understand the concept of 'totality'. Her 'problem' is a *linguistic* one.

When I discussed the infant's understanding of 'multi-morpheme' words like 'walking' and 'walked', I suggested that they pass through a stage when such words are understood as *single* elements of meaning. Karmiloff-Smith's studies suggest an analogous state of affairs in relation to words that serve several *functions*. Thus, French children below the age of eight understand and use 'les' to refer to two or more objects but do *not* realize that in some circumstances it can serve *two* functions at the same time. Consider other examples. When children (still in the situation illustrated in figure 5.2) are asked to tell someone to place all the lorries in the garage, a child aged ten years eleven months said, 'Tous les camions . . . ou bien on peut dire *les* camions' which translates as, 'All the lorries . . . or you can say *the* lorries' (the child stressed the word 'les'). Faced with the same task, a child aged four years seven months said 'Mettez au garage les camions . . . les camions bleus, le camion rouge et les camions bleus' ('Put into the garage the lorries . . . the blue lorries, the red lorry and the blue lorries'). This child attempted to *describe* or list all the relevant objects. What he or she did not say, however, was where the lorries were to be found. The child also overlooked one of the red lorries (recall what was said about children's powers of attention in chapter 4). This child used 'les' to refer to 'more than one' but did not appreciate that the single expression 'les camions' can be used to refer to the total *set* of objects he or she was attempting to describe.

A child aged five years two months managed to get the message across saying 'Tous mes camions, un camion rouge à moi, deux camions bleus à moi et tous vos camions, deux camions bleus à vous. . .' ('All my lorries, one red lorry of mine, two blue lorries of mine and all your lorries, two blue lorries of yours. . .'). Note how this child, by employing *personal* pronouns, conveyed information about the *location* of the objects being described. But, as with the plural form 'les', he or she adds 'tous' to mark the fact that *all* the lorries are implicated (although 'mes' alone would suffice for a mature speaker). The child then proceeds to *list* the groups of objects which make up the *total* set. Eventually, he or she will learn how to refer to this set using the 'simple' utterance, 'les camions'.

I have gone into some detail about this experiment in an attempt to illustrate a number of important aspects of language development. In fact, there are at least eight points worth underlining, some of which we have already met in relation to other studies:

1 Single, seemingly simple, grammatical morphemes serve more than one function. Thus, words like 'mine', say, may simply refer to an object or objects that one possesses ('my watch', 'my toys' etc.), or at one and the same time to *totalities* of objects, like 'my cars' or 'my vehicles'. In figure 5.2, for example, the word 'my' can serve both to specify *which* set of objects is being referred to and to signal the fact that all members of this set are involved.

2 Children first employ such words for limited, uni-functional purposes and only after a considerable number of years do they acquire

the *system* of interrelated functions that these words also serve. Ten-year-olds may still be grappling with the task of achieving clear, efficient and 'mature' ways of referring to things.

3   The problems that children face in such situations cannot be explained in terms of an inadequate grasp of concepts to do with sets and subsets or by an insensitivity to their listeners' needs. The fact that children find other means of expressing their intended meaning some years before they master 'adult' conventions for making reference shows that they appreciate *what* they need to do. In such situations, development consists in working out the *linguistic* means to achieve efficient communication of their intended meaning. Language acquisition, then, cannot be explained simply in terms of cognitive development, nor can communication problems be attributed entirely to a child's insensitivity to other people's communicative needs. Whilst cognition and communicative competence do constrain what a child can understand and communicate, there are specifically linguistic problems that the child must also solve. It follows that we should be cautious when trying to explain a child's communication 'problems'. We cannot assume that all features of communication or every misunderstanding are a product of intellectual or social factors. Language development itself takes time and effort and may result in unexpected failures of mutual comprehension.

4   Experimental studies of the kind I have been discussing help to reveal aspects of language use which present challenges for children. These are not made obvious in everyday talk. Such problems are not trivial, nor are they simple 'artefacts' of experiments. Children have to learn how to talk in certain ways in order to make sense of many tasks they will face in formal learning situations. I take this issue up in the next two chapters.

5   So far as we can tell, children learn how to make themselves understood without frequent 'error correction' by adults. Indeed, in everyday situations, errors may not often arise to be corrected. The young child's limited understanding of adult talk is not revealed by casual observation: its discovery may demand careful and detailed study of the child in 'artificial' situations. If the child's linguistic limitations are not obvious to the naked ear, it seems highly unlikely that we would know *what* to teach the child in everyday interactions. Children do not often 'reveal' their limited grasp of language features that they have yet to master.

6   Before children achieve mastery of mature ways of expressing themselves, they appear to pass through a stage or phase of *self-correction*. I have provided a number of examples. The finding, so common, that children correct themselves yet seem seldom to be

corrected by others, suggests that they 'teach themselves' how to use and understand complex aspects of language structure. If social and educational experiences play any important role in helping children to teach themselves, that role must have little to do with overt correction or direct instruction.

7   Children are usually taught how to read some years before the learning processes that we have been discussing have run their course. This raises a number of questions. First, do children face unrecognized language problems in learning to read and write because, while they seem to 'know' and understand things like determiners, pronouns and 'deictic' words, they only use them for a limited range of purposes? Perhaps learning to read and write, like experiments and tests, confronts children with novel intellectual, communicative and linguistic demands. How far does the experience of learning to read and write itself help children to discover and master aspects of their mother tongue? We will take up these issues in the next two chapters.

8   Finally, Karmiloff-Smith notes how children who showed signs of self-correction often *improved* their performance in her experiments. Their instructions became more economical and 'mature' in form as they took part in tasks.

Re-organization and representational re-description

Karmiloff-Smith, a past student of Piaget's, has proposed a theory of linguistic and cognitive development in which such patterns of change are seen as evidence of discontinuity and re-organization in development. As I said in chapter 2, the proposed discontinuities in development are not seen by Karmiloff-Smith as evidence for global, stage-like changes in general intellectual functioning. Her view of cognition is more 'modular' in that, for example, some of the changes that occur in aspects of language function are specific to language, rather than symptoms of general changes in cognitive abilities. Unlike Fodor, however, Karmiloff-Smith argues that we need to go 'beyond' modularity to explain the facts of development. She agrees that there are innate mechanisms that underpin language acquisition and that the nervous system exhibits a natural capacity to extract regularities and patterns that are the basis of language structure. But, she argues, there is more to development than the modularity thesis allows.

Her theory offers an integration of the various changes with age in children's use of language that we have been exploring. It seeks to explain why, for instance, we often find examples in development where young children use words like 'feet' in a way that resembles (but is not the same as) mature usage only to produce 'footses' some time later in life before they return to using 'feet' again. As I have already argued, the child's first use of words like 'feet' is symptomatic of a very different command of language from that implicated in the use of the 'same' word later in development. Such early uses of the word occur before children have reflected upon and analysed the processes used in their language to mark features such as plurality. The period of time during which a child shows over-generalization of rules involving the use of markers of plurality is taken as evidence of the fact that they are becoming aware of how the 'one–many', or singular–plural, distinction is used in language and figuring out how to use linguistic rules or conventions to make their own meaning clear when they communicate. Once they have worked out the intricacies of the rule system, then such over-generalizations disappear.

Karmiloff-Smith argues that such phenomena are common in both linguistic and cognitive development and serve as indicators of conceptual change and re-organization – what she terms representational re-description theory.

The same theoretical model is also used to explain what happens as children move from uni-functional to pluri-functional uses of terms like 'les', 'mine' and 'yours'. Here phenomena such as the children's use of 'redundant' linguistic markers (as in 'toutes les voitures' met earlier) signals the fact that they are beginning to work out how to use language to serve several purposes within a single utterance. Before this stage, children may use single words like 'les' as do children who have figured out how to use the same word pluri-functionally. But the use of that word at the two different ages and stages is embedded in a different knowledge of language. Here too, Karmiloff-Smith argues, we must accept that the child's language is mentally re-represented in order to make possible the discovery of the 'higher order' structures in which initially separate or distinct uses of the same sound in different contexts can be integrated.

Evidence of re-description and re-organization is symptomatic of the fact that conceptual change is a universal feature of human cognition. As I have said, because Karmiloff-Smith's approach is more 'modular' than Piaget's, evidence of re-organization is not taken as an indicator of stage changes in his sense. However, because she shares Piaget's views that language and cognition clearly do interact in development and the child's conscious reflections on language play a central role in her account, she also goes 'beyond modularity'.

Educability: some first thoughts

The concept of early linguistic deprivation and the explanation for the connection between school achievement and social background that it offered have not withstood the test of time and observation. So the view, echoed in President Johnson's speech quoted earlier, that children are 'taught' how to speak, and the related assertion that some fail to learn how to talk at home because they do not receive appropriate instruction, seem untenable. Children may come to school speaking different dialects or regional accents but such linguistic variations are not to be taken as evidence that some exhibit 'defective' language. Yet, the fact remains that social background and, as we see in the next chapter, communication skills, are still reliable predictors of a child's likely performance in school. If we reject a linguistic explanation for these relations, we must seek out others.

In fact, a number of alternative accounts have been offered as explanations. One, for example, places the responsibility for differences in children's levels of performance at the door of educationalists and their attitudes. Teachers, the argument proceeds, perceive children who do not talk using 'received pronunciation' and the 'standard' form of their language as less able or less well motivated than children whose talk corresponds more closely to that of the currently 'dominant' dialect. Making (perhaps implicit or unconscious) judgements about children's educational potential on the basis of how they talk, teachers set up self-fulfilling prophecies which lead to differences in levels of achievement. Crudely, because teachers expect less of children from some social backgrounds, these children are taught and learn less.

The view that teacher *expectations* influence the way in which they teach and the amount that children learn is often supported by appeals to studies performed some years ago by Rosenthal and Jacobson (1968). The basic design of these studies is as follows: teachers are told that they are to instruct groups of children who are either very able or somewhat slow. In reality, however, the groups of children involved are 'matched' on the basis of assessments of their learning abilities. Thus, while teachers are led to *believe* that they are to teach either able or less able pupils, they are actually given classes of similar levels of (estimated) ability. The performance of the two groups of children are monitored over time to see if their achievements differ.

The first studies of this type suggested that children whose teachers had been led to believe that they were relatively able learned more than those labelled less able. So the conclusion was drawn that teacher perceptions and *expectations* exert a direct, *causal* influence on how much children learn in school. Add to such conclusions the theory that teachers view some children as less able because of the way in which they talk, and an alternative explanation for the effects of social background on educational performance emerges: one based on teachers' differential expectations (or prejudices).

Early attempts to reproduce this so-called 'Rosenthal effect' failed to produce the same results (Pilling and Pringle, 1978) and controversy about the nature and effects of teacher expectations on performance still persists. Whilst it may still prove to be the case that teachers do have expectations of children that are based on social stereotypes and that these do lead to the achievement of self-fulfilling prophecies, the evidence to date is not compelling.

Among other explanations given to account for the effect of social background and language variation on educational performance is the view that different social groupings within modern societies have different values, attitudes and aspirations. Children from different backgrounds are socialized into, come to embody, and carry into schools different world views, to find that they coincide to a greater or less extent with those implicit in the value systems of formal education. To the extent that the values of home and school do coincide, children are likely to fare well. Where there are marked discrepancies between the two systems, however, children may become confused, bored or antagonistic. Such analyses lead on to a radically different perspective on 'relevance' in education from those we have explored so far. They ask educators to examine their own values and their own views on what education is *for* and to measure these against those held by children and their families.

Another possible line of explanation seeks its power in terms of the quality and ease of communication between teachers and children from different backgrounds. Where children share a dialect with their teachers, communication between them is likely to be relatively easy, but where marked differences exist, the establishment and maintenance of rapport and mutual comprehension may be more difficult to achieve, thus inhibiting the transmission of knowledge and understanding.

We will be exploring this and other points of view in the remaining chapters. Be forewarned, however, that the situation is more complex than the suggestion I have just outlined implies. We will find ourselves questioning the view that language in school is in any useful sense the 'same' for (some) children as that experienced at home or in the community. There are marked and important differences in the nature and purposes of communication at home and school and these result in children's exposure to new functions and structures of language that present challenges and special problems. While it may be true that some children are better prepared than others to meet and master these demands, it does not seem to be the case that children from some backgrounds experience *continuity* of linguistic experience when they go to school whilst others experience discontinuity. Rather, I suggest, it is a question of *degree* of continuity.

Language development continues throughout the years of schooling. Children must learn new ways of communicating if they are to learn what it is schools seek to teach. By the same token, teachers also face special linguistic and communicative demands in school which require resources and expertise that are special to the process of education. Perhaps when we have explored some of what we know about the character of communicative development in the first years of schooling, we will be in a better position to discuss and evaluate competing claims about the relationship between children's educability and their social backgrounds.

Summary

The experiments and observations I have just outlined represent only a tiny fraction of a vast literature on language development. However, the points I have just made are, I believe, consistent with the more general picture that has emerged from that literature. The assertion implicit in the quotation attributed to President Johnson, that children must be 'taught' how to speak, and that some children cannot *talk* because they have not been taught 'properly' if at all, is untenable. The allied notion that some dialects or creoles only permit relatively inarticulate, ill-formed and non-grammatical communication must also be laid to rest. While differences in dialect and social background are demonstrably correlated with school achievement, we cannot, I suggest, explain the relationship in terms of early linguistic deprivation.

Modularity theorists, following Chomsky, argue that children acquire language naturally and that they are born with neurological equipment which enables them to appreciate and analyse the structure of speech. This point of view has proved difficult both to describe and to evaluate. The achievements of infants – their seemingly inborn sensitivity to the human voice and the way in which they respond to features of speech such as acoustic stress and word-like elements in streams of speech sounds – are consistent with this general position.

If learning how to understand and use speech rests on such natural capacities, can we conclude that the more mature, whether parents, older peers or teachers, play an important role in *facilitating* the child's mastery of language? If we accept that children are able to teach themselves, developing and correcting their own 'theories' about the structure of language, can we divest ourselves of all responsibility for the course of a child's linguistic development and achievements? I think not. As Peter Robinson (1981) has pointed out, accepting the now compelling findings that children generate, test and refine their own hypotheses about language and its working does not entail the complete abdication by the more mature of any teaching or enabling roles. Simply because the child is active, constructive and generative in his or her re-creation of language (and knowledge generally) it does not follow that others cannot be more or less helpful and facilitative, or unhelpful and inhibiting, along the way. It is self-evident that children acquire the dialect(s) and the ways of talking and communicating to which they are exposed. Some students of child language seem to argue that mere 'exposure' to a language is all that is needed for its acquisition. We have examined studies which demonstrate that young infants are naturally equipped to learn language and which imply that children perfect certain features of language without frequent exposure to external correction or instruction. But, I suggest, such evidence does not provide sufficient grounds for a *general* conclusion that inter-personal experiences play no formative role in the development of language and communication.

Teaching can be construed in many ways, and instruction by explicit correction is only one potential candidate for a theory of what it involves. In the next chapter, we look in more detail and from a different perspective at the nature of social and linguistic interaction to construct a somewhat different view of what teaching is. Bear in mind, though, that this or any other theory of what teaching entails will have to accommodate a view of the child learner as an active, constructive and generative architect of her own language and her own understanding.

When I tried to characterize Chomsky's approach to the theoretical study of language, I pointed out that his aim was not to provide an account of how people *use* language. His is not a theory of *communication* but of an 'ideal' grammar. Some of the studies and experiments I have just outlined reveal the limitations of such a view when we try to use it as a framework for achieving an understanding of language development (in passing, however, recall that this was never Chomsky's intention). The importance of intonation, gesture, and a shared situation in the achievement of mutual understanding (and, as we shall see in the next chapter, in the acquisition of language itself), were underlined by differences found in children's use and understanding of language in natural and contrived situations. Robbed of such important bases for the achievement of mutual understanding, children find incomprehensible a variety of tasks and utterances when these are encountered in unfamiliar experimental or test situations. Chomskian theory is designed to reveal and describe the general *rules* that are implicit in a language, and different utterances are compared and classified in terms of systems of these rules. However, utterances that are classified as 'similar' in structure for a linguist, because they are generated by the 'same' rules, may be quite different for a child (or an adult for that matter). Put another way, language, as an instrument of communication and an inter-personal *activity*, involves more than such hypothetical underlying grammatical rules. To understand the nature of language development and the way in which children achieve comprehension in the absence of important clues to meaning such as intonation, stress and situational cues, we need to look beyond 'grammar'.

The studies undertaken by Clark and Karmiloff-Smith help to illustrate the complex connections between language and reasoning. Some early followers of Chomsky seemed to argue that the acquisition of language was a rather rapid, almost automatic affair, that was largely completed in the pre-school years. As we have seen, the process is not particularly rapid, nor does it end before schooling. Piaget provided one of the first and most explicit accounts of the way in which the structure of the child's thinking constrains and paces her understanding and use of language. Several of the studies I have described in this chapter, and others I will discuss in the next two, point to important changes in the child's use and comprehension of various aspects of language that coincide with the advent of schooling at around age six or seven. Karmiloff-Smith, however, whilst accepting Piaget's insistence on the interdependency of language and thought, provides several lines of evidence which show that learning language involves the child in the solution of problems that are *specific* to language. Five- and six-year-old children often manage to communicate complex instructions some years before they have mastered the detailed structure of their language. The fact that they know *how* to get their message across shows both that they understand the requirements of such tasks (are intellectually competent) and possess sufficient communicative competence to make what they say intelligible to their listener, *before* they have reached mature levels of language comprehension and production. Consequently, it cannot be the case that language learning rests only on non-verbal understanding. It presents many problems of its own, as studies of re-organizational processes in language development show.

From this, we can argue that language learning in the school years may be a source of problems, misunderstandings and apparent failures to learn. Oracy – a rather ungainly word used to refer to the expertise, skill and knowledge involved in effective verbal communication – should, then, be an important part of the school curriculum (Norman, 1992). Human nature may ensure that most children learn how to talk. Social experience and schooling, as we shall see, play a central role in determining both what they have to say and how they are able to express what they mean.

Chapter 6

Making sense

We now move on to look in more detail at the development of language and communication during the years of schooling. We look at research designed to identify the communicative demands that children face in school and to evaluate if, when and how children respond to these. We also study explanations as to why some children find it difficult to fulfil these demands and examine classroom research which offers some suggestions about how schools might better serve such children.

Non-verbal and verbal communication

When children first start to speak, what they talk about is almost invariably prompted by that which currently fills their senses. Their first acts of speech are single words. Later comes a stage of two words, followed by a three-word stage, then four, until, around three years of age, the child begins to use simple sentences. Listened to out of context, much of what infants say in the early stages of language acquisition is ambiguous and difficult to comprehend – 'mummy sock', 'more train' or 'my teddy' might be given several interpretations. Indeed, attempts by linguists to discover a set of rules which would enable them to predict the structure of infant talk in the first stages of language development (that is, to write a 'grammar' for early language) have, to date, failed (Crystal, 1976). Put another way, we do not have any theory which provides a valid, formal account of what infants mean by what they say.

And yet, for most of the time, parents and other people who are familiar with an infant seem to understand what he says. There may be an element of guess-work involved. Perhaps we fool ourselves into thinking that we understand what young children mean. However, by paying attention to features of the situation and circumstances surrounding infant talk, we can usually find additional clues, such as what they are looking at, their facial expression, tone of voice and bodily movements, to help us decide what they are trying to mean. Research over the past few years has revealed the complex nature of the relationship between grammatical aspects of speech and non-verbal 'cues' to meaning, an aspect of what is sometimes termed 'body language'. This research helps us to understand the role of non-verbal communication in the achievement of mutual understanding, as we shall see. We will also consider the nature and function of what linguists call 'paralinguistic' features of speech. This term refers to things like voice intonation, pauses during speaking and the way in which stress is distributed over utterances. Although a detailed exploration of these topics lies outside our current concerns, non-verbal communication and paralinguistic aspects of speech are worth a brief look, since these will help us to understand some of the challenges that face children when they begin to talk to relative strangers in 'public' situations, like school. I will be arguing that the relationships between verbal, non-verbal and paralinguistic dimensions of communication in school differ from those found on home ground. Language at school is not simply an extension of language used at home. It involves some rather 'special' and unique features with which young children (and their teachers) have to come to terms.

People from some cultures – Italians, for instance – are more facially expressive, ready to move and freer with gestures when they talk than are members of other cultures (e.g. the British). Although many gestures and expressive movements of the face are culture-specific and often recognizably so (mentally compare, say, a Japanese and an Italian speaker), there are important aspects of non-verbal communication which, as far as we can tell, are universal. High-speed film techniques make it possible to examine bodily movements in great detail using frame-by-frame analysis. The results of such analyses can be compared with the sound track on the film to study the relations between speech and movement. Using such methods, students of 'kinesics' (a term used to refer to the analysis of movement) have discovered common features in the organization of talk and bodily movements displayed by members of many different linguistic cultures (e.g. Condon, 1980).

One finding is that when a gesture accompanies an act of spontaneous speech, its 'peak' (this is difficult to define non-technically but perhaps you can imagine what I mean) tends to occur close in time to the stressed part of what is being said (think of someone saying 'I did *not*' and thumping a table at the same time). Now, the *start* of any such movement or gesture *never* occurs *after* the word that relates to it. It may occur at the same time or, more usually, precedes the word by about one-seventh of a second. The organization of the movements creating sounds and those creating gestures displays a tight temporal structure. This structure plays an important role in co-ordinating the act of communication. For example, if one compares the movements of a person speaking with those of someone listening to him, a remarkable degree of temporal synchronicity emerges. The listener appears to 'shadow' the movements of the talker and usually responds to the speaker's movements with one of his or her own no later than 20 msec later (Kempton, 1980). What is so remarkable about this rapid synchronization is the fact that no known response mechanism (for example, the speed at which we can react to a visual or auditory stimulus) is *fast enough* to make this feat possible. The only explanation (barring clairvoyance) is that the listener is *anticipating* where the speaker will make a movement before it actually commences. It is often the case that movements accompany those features of what is said that are likely to be *stressed*. In turn, stress signals where new and important information is to be conveyed. So the mutual timing of movements between listener and speaker imply that the listener is also anticipating the important parts of what the speaker is *going* to say. Synchronicity of movement and speech, then, is likely to play an important role in the achievement of mutual understanding.

In a near-literal sense, the speaker and hearer seem to be 'in tune'. Indeed, List (1963) argues that people move together in everyday interactions, exploiting the same ability that allows them to dance or to sing together. Each of these activities is based on shared *rhythmic* abilities. Although no one as yet has discovered all the verbal and/or visual signals which enable this synchronization to take place, it seems certain that some such system must exist. It also seems to be the case that tiny babies respond to the temporal organization of speech and movement in similar ways. Such findings imply that the 'tuning in' of speakers and listeners is rooted in some shared biological rhythmic system. By this I do not mean to imply that movements and gestures are 'mechanically' tied together. The precise form of a movement, its magnitude and duration, vary from speaker to speaker and from language culture to language culture. Nor do the movements of the listener usually imitate those of the speaker – they may be quite different. What seems to be universal is the *synchronization* of mutual movement.

From pre-verbal communication to speech

But why is this of interest to us here? There are a number of reasons. Later in the book, I will discuss the way in which such, usually unconscious, aspects of non-verbal communication may serve to create distrust and discomfort when people from different ethnic or linguistic backgrounds communicate with each other. Differences in the form, manner and magnitude of bodily movements found across diverse human groups may lead to a degree of 'mis-timing' or mis-matching of expectations when members of different cultures interact. Given that people are not usually aware of the relations between their verbal and non-verbal movements (whilst these play an important role in mutual adjustment), members of different cultures or cultural groups may experience a diffuse, unlocatable sense of mutual discomfort when together. These and other features of the way in which we interact with each other may, I shall be arguing, provide obstacles to the mutual trust and relaxation which, as we shall see, lie at the heart of effective and efficient communication.

Another reason for introducing the topic of non-verbal features of communication is to outline the important role they play in the achievement of mutual understanding between adults and young children. Let me give another example. Imagine an adult engaged in interaction with a four-month-old infant. At this age, infants are usually taking an active interest in events going on around them. They constantly move their heads, eyes and bodies (when supported) to orient towards and focus upon things and events in the environment. When they do so, it is likely that the adult will monitor where and what they are looking at, following their line of gaze and pattern of attention. If they speak to the baby, then more often than not it will be to talk about what he is looking at. They may say what it is, perhaps, or comment upon its behaviour or nature. More surprisingly, should the adult, looking into the infant's eyes, turn suddenly to look at something else, the infant may well turn to attend to what she is looking at (for more on this, see Butterworth and Cochran, 1980). How babies manage this feat and know *where* to turn their eyes we do not know. The important point for our present purposes, however, is the fact that many occasions are likely to arise on which infant and adult are attending to the *same* thing. What the adult says, therefore, is likely to relate to what fills the infant's attention. They may put his perceived intentions into words, 'Do you want ... ?', or they might warn, reassure, exclaim, comment, or whatever. In so doing, they are bringing together acts of communication with the infant's early investigations of the world about him, relating language to reality.

Now add a few more elements to the story. Infants, from birth, are attracted and react to the sound of the human voice. By the age of two months, their babbling begins to take on some of the 'shape' of the language around them (Menyuk, 1971). Their intonation patterns, even at this age, demonstrate that they have begun to acquire aspects of the sound pattern of speech (sometimes termed 'prosodic' features, which we return to later). Paralleling these developments is the emergence of distinctive *reactions* on the baby's part to different tones of voice. By eight months, for example, the infant's responses to a questioning intonation are visibly different from those to statements (Kaplan, 1969). Similarly, a sudden 'No!' addressed to an eight-month-old may cause him to stop what he is doing. Consequently, when the infant begins his visual exploration of the world, he is already becoming sensitive to the 'mood music' supplied by human vocalizations. Such sounds enable an adult, say, to warn or reassure the baby about something he is looking at well before he begins to understand and use the words they are speaking. By making what they say and do *contingent* upon the infant's own attentions and activities, then, adults help to ensure communication before the advent of speech. Such communication also provides the baby with the means to *discover* what utterances (and their emotional effects) imply and, ultimately, to discover what speech sounds themselves refer to (Bruner, 1983). Verbal communication is deeply rooted in patterns of pre-verbal communication. Whilst words and longer utterances are destined to emerge from this matrix, they are never, as we shall see, totally divorced from it. Although the 'distance' or 'gap' between the social, emotional, non-verbal and paralinguistic aspects of communication, on the one hand, and speech, on the other, may in some sense widen with development, the two never totally part company.

The linguist may be hard put to write a grammar for an infant, but one who knows that child may experience little difficulty or confusion in understanding him because what he says is embedded in a rich, supporting communicative system. Non-verbal and paralinguistic dimensions of interaction, coupled with a personal knowledge of the child (e.g. knowing the things he knows, those he has never seen before and those that interest, attract or frighten him), enrich anything he might say to enable others to work out what he (probably) intends to mean. In this way, more mature individuals take the major responsibility for working out what the young child intends to communicate. Attending to his attentions, gestures, facial expressions, bodily posture and so on, they interpret what the infant probably means by any sounds he makes. As the child develops and, literally, becomes more articulate, the balance of responsibility for the achievement of shared understanding gradually shifts towards more equal partnership as the child plays an increasingly intelligible role in communication and takes greater responsibility for making what he says comprehensible. By three or four years of age, many children are able to talk to relative strangers with a reasonable chance of being understood.

As I said at the beginning of this chapter, when infants are passing through the early stages of language acquisition, what they talk about is likely to be what fills their senses: what grasps their attention, reminds them of their past or provokes desires for the (immediate) future. Recordings of adult speech to infants in different countries suggest that what is *said* to infants in many different societies is very similar (although there are some cultures which adopt very different practices in communications with their infants). Not surprisingly, talk usually revolves around everyday events – what the parent is doing with the baby and what he may be feeling or thinking. Talk to young children tends to be stimulated by and contingent upon the child's perceived level of understanding and interest. At the same time, speech to young children has some special properties. In comparison with talk between adults, it tends to be slower, more repetitive, exaggerated in intonation, simpler in grammatical structure and limited in vocabulary. In this way, adults help to maximize the probability that what they *say* will be within the reach of the child's mind and ear. Indeed, should such adjustments not be made (say, when two adults talk together in the child's company), the child will soon 'tune out' (or demand attention). The child selects and attends to talk that is within reach of his comprehension and ignores that which is not. At home, such 'inattentiveness' may not be perceived as a problem, but in school it may well be attributed to idleness, lack of interest or boredom. To the extent that a child experiences communication problems in class, we must be aware of the possibility that any 'tuning out' and inattentiveness may be a natural and inevitable feature of such problems.

The pre-school child's experience of language, then, is often tailored to his needs. Other people take the major responsibility for ensuring mutual understanding both by working out what the child means and by making what they say comprehensible to him. Although we are not usually aware of the complex interplay between speech and our other bodily movements, there are occasions when our attention is drawn to them. Irony, sarcasm and teasing, for example, usually, perhaps invariably, involve some *disruption* or deliberate manipulation of the conventional relations between acts of speech and other movements of the body. When teasing an infant, for instance, the expression on our face or what we do with our body may communicate a very different message from that conveyed by what we say. If the baby does not observe or understand our playful use of such conflicting signals and takes what we say or do *seriously*, tears may result where laughter was sought. However, the very fact that we are often able to play teasing games with quite young children stands as testimony to the fact that even babies are sensitive to and knowledgeable about, and can *play* with, some of the relations between verbal and non-verbal dimensions of communication.

If a listener's movements, gestures or attentions are out of synchrony with our own attempts at communication (for instance, they keep looking at a door when we are talking to them about something quite different), it usually acts as a clear signal of distress, boredom or preoccupations elsewhere. The very fact that such observations and experiences are commonplace also provides evidence that the interplay between verbal and non-verbal aspects of communication continue, throughout life, to play a central role in the achievement and maintenance of mutual understanding.

From home to school: conversation and narrative

I have undertaken this very brief overview of the relations between verbal and non-verbal aspects of communication to establish a basis for identifying and discussing some of the problems that children face when they move out of 'private' domains, like their homes, into more 'public' ones, such as the school. In the early years of development, adults take the major responsibility for working out what a child means by what he says and does. In school, where eventually the child must come to function as part of a group, *sitting down* for much of the time, the nature of the process of communication changes in a number of ways to confront the child with many new challenges. Let us now move on to consider some of these before thinking about the influence such experiences exert on the child's social, linguistic and intellectual development.

When young children are involved in conversation with teachers, talk sometimes centres on things like past experiences and events, hopes and plans or other people. Observation of teacher–child discourse shows that, in such circumstances, children's contributions are usually brief. Teachers ask questions and children usually attempt to answer them. A child might tell the teacher something or react to something he or she has said, but long periods of sustained talk in which the child provides a longish *narrative* account of his experiences, say, are quite rare. Where such narratives do occur, however, they illustrate the demands and problems facing the child. Let me present and discuss one example to illustrate the intellectual, social and linguistic hurdles that confront the immature narrator.

This is an exchange between a rising five-year-old and an adult in an English playgroup (Wood, McMahon and Cranstoun, 1980). They are talking about 'ogres' and the topic reminds the child of an experience he had with his father in which they encountered someone dressed up as a 'monster' to advertise a children's cereal. The child produces a 'turn' in the conversation some forty-six words in length – a rare occurrence in classroom talk:

Adult Do you know anyone that big?
Child Well, once we . . . once we saw one, but he shouted at us.
Adult You saw an ogre once?
Child No, not a real one, a pretend one. He kept shouting at us.
Adult Where was that?
Child That was in Banbury.
Adult In Banbury there was a pretend one.
Child He kept shouting at us.
Adult What did he [chuckles] shout at you?
Child I've forgotten now.
Adult He had a big, loud voice, did he?
Child Hm . . . and . . . he said 'I shall eat him' . . . Daddy said . . . our Daddy said . . . hm . . . he . . . he . . . he. 'Oh, what him!' Daddy said . . . Daddy just said, he said, and the giant . . . I said 'Would the giant eat us?' and Daddy said, 'If you make a noise it will'.
Adult Do you think he would, love? [gently]
Child He might just bite us.

There are many features of this short episode worthy of comment. Consider, for example, the child's use of pronouns, as in 'we . . . once we saw one'. Who is 'we'? Later contributions from the child show that 'we' includes at least himself and his father. In 'mature' narrative, of course, we would expect the characters to be *identified* by name before pronominal reference is made 'back' to them. As it stands, the child's use of 'we' remains, throughout the episode, somewhat ambiguous.

The child *does* have some command of pronoun usage, however. He says, for instance, 'No, not a real one, a pretend one. He . . .'. But later, when he produces a longer, more narrational stretch of talk, we can literally hear him grappling with the task of making sensible use of pronouns. His difficulty stems from the fact that both his father and the ogre are each potential 'he's'. Who, for example, was in danger of being eaten? Who was the 'he' who said, 'Oh, what him!'? Which 'him'?

The child's difficulties go even deeper. Should he wish to refer to things said *between* the two other characters, or to refer to what one said about the other's likely behaviour towards the child *himself*, then 'he' can also serve to refer to the current 'me' (the speaker). In live encounters, of course, where speakers, hearers and bystanders have visible presence, one can see who says what to whom and is likely to have clear signals about the person being referred to. I suspect that, in such situations, this child would have no problems in working out or understanding what is happening. Providing an *account* of such events, on the other hand, creates many problems for the young child, effective and unambiguous use of pronouns being one. Understanding and remembering an event, and providing a clear, smooth, efficient and expert narrative account, may be years apart, developmentally speaking.

In one sense, this child clearly knows what 'he' means. But the *use* of 'he' as a word to refer, on different occasions, to different people creates problems of *planning* and *sequencing*. The pronoun must be 'located' in talk in such a way that it refers unambiguously to the intended referent. The fact that the child at this age (and this one is very articulate for his age) often fails to 'frame' appropriately what he is going to say – by first setting the scene and explicitly indicating *who* the involved characters are, where they are situated, and so on – also creates problems for him in using pronouns.

The frequent pauses, 'hm's', repetitions, backtracking and attempts at self-correction evidenced in the child's talk suggest both that he is aware of, and that he is *working on*, the many problems that he has yet to solve in order to make what he says sensible to another person.

Younger or less verbally mature children, as we shall see in more detail later, do not seem to be aware of such problems with pronouns and do not often try to self-correct, as in the following excerpt involving a three-year-old:

Adult   Who is Kerry?
Child   Kerry. He's a girl. She's my friend.

There are other aspects in the ogre episode that serve to illustrate features of the child's developing mastery of, and existing problems in, his use of language. For example, when the teacher says, 'Where was that?', the child responds, 'That was in . . . Banbury', rather than simply 'In Banbury'. This phenomenon, the use of 'full forms' before they are 'elided' (shortened) as they usually are in mature speech, is also a general and pervasive feature of language development. Children only employ economical, elliptical utterances *after* perfecting the una-bridged versions from which these develop, even though the shorter forms are presumably more common in what they hear adults say (Gleitman and Wanner, 1982).

Although, up to this point, I have concentrated mainly on one child's use of pronominal reference, I will argue that this illustrates some general and important features of children's intellectual and linguistic development. We turn next to more controlled and extensive analyses of children's powers and problems as narrators. These illustrate in more detail the sizeable gap that can exist for children between what they may *know*, *remember* or *understand* and their ability to *account* for what they know.

Telling stories: four to ten

In a series of studies, Hickman (1985) has examined in detail some of the changes that occur in children's narrational skills between the ages of four and ten years. Children were asked to do one of two things. Either they were shown a short film and then asked to tell an adult about it, or they were presented with a sequence of pictures, rather like a cartoon strip, and requested to tell a story about the events depicted. Hickman recorded and transcribed everything said by each child (and the adult) and then analysed the narratives to evaluate their clarity, coherence and comprehensibility.

Various details of the children's accounts, such as their use of pronouns and determiners (e.g. 'a', 'the' and 'these') were examined, rather along the lines of the way in which I have just commented on the rising five-year-old's story about his encounter with an ogre. By showing children of different ages the same films and pictures, Hickman was able not only to look at children's command of such linguistic devices but also to etch out age-related changes in their abilities to do so successfully. Although the analysis focused on verbal details like the use of pronouns, Hickman based it on a more general distinction that is worth introducing and discussing here. It will play an important role in our consideration of reading and its relation to spoken language in the next chapter. Drawing on *functional* approaches to the analysis of language (Halliday and Hasan, 1976), she distinguished between those usages of words (more technically 'signs') that involve 'deictic indexical relationships' and the use of the same words to establish 'intralinguistic indexical relationships'. Briefly, deictic indexical signs involve the connection or relationship between a word and its 'extralinguistic' context. So, for instance, the use of 'the' to refer or point to an object in the immediate environment (recall Karmiloff-Smith's work outlined in the last chapter) is deictic, whereas its use to refer *anaphorically*, to a person or thing already mentioned (e.g. 'A man . . . *the* man'), is an example of an intralinguistic indexical (i.e. used to 'index', or refer to) use of the word. Used in the second way, such terms generate 'textual cohesion', helping to relate and integrate utterances that occur at different times in discourse (or written text). Pronouns can be looked at in the same way. The use of 'I', 'you', 'him' or 'it' in the course of face-to-face conversation, when the people and objects being referred to are present, involves extralinguistic, deictic reference. The same words can also be employed for intralinguistic purposes, as when, for instance, the word 'he' is used to refer back to an (absent) individual who has already been mentioned by name.

Hickman, then, like Karmiloff-Smith, concentrated on the *pluri-functional* nature of these terms and examined their use by children to see how far, at different ages, they are able to exploit them successfully to fulfil their different purposes. More descriptively, a child who is able to use words like 'the' to refer both to objects in the world and to things mentioned in previous discourse will be able to tell a coherent story in which everything he refers to is clear and unambiguous. A child whose command of such words is limited to their context-dependent meanings will find it difficult or impossible to tell a clear and coherent story because, as he lacks effective ways of making explicit who or what he is referring to, what he says will be ambiguous and sound 'egocentric'.

Let us consider a few examples from Hickman's studies of American school children: first, two 'extreme' cases, one of a ten-year-old who is well on the way to expertise in the use of such words and the other a four-year-old whose use of them is still largely limited to their more 'primitive', deictic function. Note, however, even in the first story from the ten-year-old, how reference to one of the characters as 'she' creates a little confusion. The adult's contributions to the discourse are given in brackets.

The ten-year-old's story A donkey and a giraffe . . . came-out (uh-huh) And . . . the . . . giraffe said 'Hi! Would you like to play with me?' And . . . the donkey said, 'No! I'm mad.' (uh-huh) And . . . she said, 'What happened?'. . . . and . . . the donkey said, 'Well, I made a box to keep my things in.' (uh-huh) 'And I found a penny. And I put it in the blo-box but now I can't *find* the penny' (uh-huh) . . . and . . . and . . . the . . . . giraffe said, 'Well, maybe it's at school! Remember? You took it to school.'And the donkey said, '*How* do *you* know? I think *you're* the one that took the penny.' (uh-huh) And . . . the gi-giraffe said . . . um . . ., 'No I didn't.' And . . . oh . . . she said, 'How do *you* know?' He said, 'Well . . . you know, I remember you took it.' (uh-huh) And . . . then she thought about it for a while and she s-said . . . ,'Well, friends don't steal! I'm sorry I was mad at you! Now let's go play.'

The four-year-old's story Penny was in the box. (Excuse me?) The penny was in the box. (Oh really? Oh good.) . . . The next day it wasn't . . . He was mad at the giraffe . . . (uh-huh). . . .'cause he took the penny. (He was mad at the giraffe because he took the penny.) Yeah, but he di-bu- but he thought he was *tricking* him. . . (Oh!) see b-because . . . bec-be- he-he-he didn't know that he had the penny. (uh-huh) . . . (Very good) They go play. (Hm?) They went to go play.

In the light of our preceding discussions of Karmiloff-Smith's work and the examples outlined above, I hope that the nature of the differences between these two excerpts is now reasonably self-evident. Hickman classified each child's use of referring words and referring expressions (e.g. 'There was a donkey in this film') as 'effective', 'ineffective' or 'mixed'. The four-year-old's story is rich in 'ineffective' referring expressions. The very first utterance, 'Penny was in the box', for example, fails to make clear who or what 'Penny' is. The next utterance, 'The penny was in the box' suggests that she meant 'A penny' but note how 'the box' is introduced. If 'a box' had been mentioned earlier (which it had not), then this expression would have been deemed effective; as it stands, it is not. Recall Karmiloff-Smith's conclusion that young children's use of 'the' is reserved for and limited to deictic purposes. In Hickman's studies too, use of referring expressions by four-year-olds suggests that young children do not often use them to fulfil their other, intralinguistic functions.

Seven-year-olds' narratives provided evidence that they were working on the problem of mastering and using referential expressions for intralinguistic purposes. In consequence, the meaning of what they were trying to say was often easier to work out than was the case with four-year-olds. Here is an example from a seven-year-old: this is typical of the age group, in that it provides several examples of attempts by the child at *self-correction*. Once again, the adult's contributions are in brackets.

> *An example from a seven-year-old*   A dog . . . and the- and a frog were
> . . . were was- were um . . . a fr- a dog was there and looked sad. (uh-huh)
> An- and then a . . . dog came along and . . . (uh-huh) the frog came along
> and said, 'Hi, today's my birthday.'

Unlike the four-year-olds, who seldom attempted to correct their own ambiguous referring expressions, the seven-year-olds' stories contained many examples of pauses, hazes, false starts, reformulations and repetitions – evidence that the children knew that they had work to do in order to achieve coherent, intelligible narratives. Ten-year-olds also frequently paused, hesitated and attempted to correct what they said (indeed, one suspects that adults would too). Unlike the seven-year-olds, however, their attempts at self-correction usually resulted in *effective* utterances whereas, more often than not, the seven-year-olds' attempts resulted in ineffective or mixed cases, such as 'This story was about the elephant and a lion'. Here, the child uses a scene-setting clause successfully ('This story was about . . .') and also uses the non-determinate form to first mention 'a lion'. However, 'the elephant' had not been mentioned before and, to be judged effective, should have been 'an elephant'.

Such mixed cases are informative. They illustrate the complexity of the seven-year-old's task in that a single utterance often contains two or more sources of potential difficulty. Whereas an expert narrator smoothly and seemingly effortlessly manages to co-ordinate all the necessary references in a single utterance, the seven-year-old apprentice usually manages to get one or more parts right but, in so doing, may 'lose hold of' or introduce an error into some other referring expression. He seems unable to attend to and co-ordinate *two or more* demands simultaneously. However, as he works on and perfects his control of each sub-problem or each sub-system (e.g. pronouns and determiners) he is able to handle two or more simultaneously, and eventually integrates them into effective, complex referring expressions.

The examples I have just given were taken from the 'film' condition in which the child first saw and then talked about what he had seen. When the children were asked to describe sets of pictures that remained in view while they told their stories, the performances of the seven- and ten-year-olds were not markedly different from the film narratives. The four-year-olds, however, behaved differently. In the cartoon-strip situation, they made more frequent use of deictic expressions, such as 'This cat . . .', 'That dog . . .', 'Like him . . .', than they did when talking about the (absent) film. Looked at in one way, this increased use of such expressions when the person present can also *see* what one is talking about seems reasonable. However, the fact that only the four-year-olds, not older children, made more frequent use of such devices is an indication of important changes in both language and cognition.

Representational re-description re-visited

In the preceding chapter, I introduced Karmiloff-Smith's theory and attempted to illustrate it with reference to the development of children's use of pluri-functional words. Here, we see how the same theory can be extended to explain some of the changes that occur in children's construction of spoken narratives and what these imply for their linguistic and cognitive development.

When children aged four to seven are shown a picture like the one illustrated in figure 6.1c in isolation and asked to describe what they see, they are likely to say something like, 'The man is giving a balloon to a little boy', typically making 'The man' the agent or subject of their utterance. Imagine now that the same picture is embedded in the sequence of pictures shown in figure 6.1.

When children aged about four to five are shown the picture sequence and asked to make up a story around the pictures, they typically make the boy the subject or agent when describing the first two pictures (e.g. 'A boy was walking down the street. He saw a man with some balloons'). However, when they come to picture c, like children who see this picture in isolation, they usually make 'the man' its subject. Older children on the other hand, will make the boy the subject of this and all

Figure 6.1   Example of a 'thematic subject' task

the other pictures, saying something like, 'He got a balloon from the man'.

Why is this informative? Well, for Karmiloff-Smith it provides yet more evidence for a discontinuity in language development akin to that illustrated in the previous chapter. The young child, she argues, looks at each picture in turn and describes what they see – what she calls an 'utterance grammar'. Thus, irrespective of whether the picture is seen on its own or in the context of other pictures, it is described in the same way. Now, the older children, having established the boy as the 'thematic subject' of their story, *impose* an interpretation of the picture based on a theme that they have already established (i.e. the boy). Thus, when they look at the picture in the story context, they co-ordinate what they say about it with what they have already said. What they say thus relates not simply to what they see (as in an utterance grammar) but also to the theme that they have in mind. Just as children have to discover how to relate determiners like 'a' and 'the' and learn how to use pronouns intralinguistically in order to achieve a coherent narrative, so, in constructing thematically organized sequences of utterances, the use of language is brought under cognitive control.

In using language forms such as pronouns, the child has to be able to co-ordinate his use across utterances. Similarly, to grasp pluri-functional expressions, the child has to co-ordinate the different uni-functional uses of a given word. To maintain a thematic subject in telling a coherent narrative, the child must also co-ordinate the way in which they construct utterances to achieve coherence. As we have seen, in Karmiloff-Smith's account, each of these changes in how children talk involves the emergence of new representations which serve to relate and integrate forms of language found earlier in development.

Language and cognition (again!)

Piaget was one of the first students of child development to draw our attention to the young child's problems in providing verbal explanations and accounts. He suggested that children entering the concrete operational stage, around age seven, are able to appreciate and begin to anticipate their listeners' needs when they converse with and explain things to other people. This happens because they are able to de-centre and can begin to construe events from other people's points of view. Piaget, then, might not be surprised to find that younger children do not and cannot create coherent stories. They lack the *intellectual* ability to appreciate the fact that when they say things like 'Penny was in the box', their meaning is not self-apparent. Being egocentric, they assume that other people share their perceptions, thoughts and memories and that to speak is to be understood.

As we have seen, however, language itself confronts the child with a special 'problem space'. The transition from an utterance grammar to the capacity to use language intralinguistically makes specifically linguistic demands on children. The young child may simply lack the verbal means to express (from a mature perspective) clearly and unambiguously what he knows and understands.

Vygotsky's approach, which motivated Hickman's studies, differs from Piaget's in its emphasis on the *formative* nature of verbal interactions. In this view, it is through talking to and with others that the child is exposed to the communicative *functions* of language. By conversing with and informing others, he discovers how to realize different functions in his own speech. In listening to and telling narratives, the child also meets demands such as monitoring his own use of language, taking into account a listener's perspective and planning sequences of utterances which are coherent and comprehensible to others.

In the studies of narrative that we have just explored, and in the research into children's linguistic understanding outlined in the previous chapter, children were asked to tell stories or give information to a second person. The situations usually involved pairs or dyads. In the next section, we will look at contexts in which we ask children to interpret what other people think, say and do. Going 'beyond the dyad' in which the child is the performer or responder, to see how he acts in situations involving three or more people and in which he may also serve as an observer and interpreter of social life, gives us an important new perspective on the child's developing understanding of what goes on in other people's minds.

Making sense of others: 'theorizing about the mind'

Imagine the following situation. We take a three-year-old child and tell him a story. We also use props to act out the plot. First, one character (a little girl doll, say) enters a room and puts a toy into a box. She then leaves the room and cannot see what transpires thereafter. Next, another member of the cast (a boy doll) comes into the room, takes the toy out of the box and hides it in a cupboard. The girl doll comes back into the room.

We are going to ask our three-year-old spectator where he thinks the girl doll might look for the toy, or where the girl doll now thinks the toy is to be found. Before doing so, however, we take the precaution of making sure that the child can actually recall the plot. He can. When we ask him where the girl doll thinks the hidden toy is, or where she will look for it, our three-year-old says that the girl doll thinks it is in the cupboard. By age four, many children can solve this 'false belief' task. They realize that the girl doll had no reason not to have held on to her belief (now seen by the child to be at variance with reality) and that she will look in the box where she left her toy.

One interpretation of this finding is that our three-year-old lacks a 'theory of mind'. He cannot recognize that another person can hold a belief that is at variance with what he himself knows to be true. Put another way, he does not yet realize that people hold representations of the world in their heads and that these representations (which may include false beliefs) help to explain what people do, say and feel.

The experimental findings from the use of the false-belief paradigm are quite robust. The change in children's responses just illustrated usually occurs between ages three and four. However, some studies suggest that less than one in ten three-year-olds possess such a theory of mind, others that almost all do. As you might expect, differences in the nature of the task and how it is presented, together with the language used and the type of questions asked, can lead to variations in estimating when children can understand false beliefs. More interesting, however, is the finding, reported in a number of studies, that birth order affects the age at which children pass such tests. Would you expect children who have no brothers and sisters to perform any differently from those who have older siblings? First-born and only children tend to pass theory of mind tasks at a *later* age than children who have older brothers and sisters. Indeed, children who have two or more siblings may fare better still, passing the task at an earlier age than children who have only one older sibling. What makes such findings surprising is the fact that investigations of birth-order effects usually find that singletons and first-born children develop language and communication skills faster than their later-born siblings. This is usually attributed to the fact that mothers of first-borns spend more time in interaction with them and talk to them more than they do with their later-born children (see Rogoff, 1990, pp. 96–7 for an overview).

Judy Dunn and her colleagues have undertaken extensive observations of home life designed to explore family dynamics surrounding the arrival of a second child into families with a two-year-old first-born. They have followed the progress of these families for a number of years and looked at the development of the relationships within them, paying attention to interactions both between the mother and her children and between the siblings themselves. Their research into the social, emotional and intellectual impact of family dynamics (e.g. Dunn, 1996; Dunn and Kendrick, 1982) did much to stimulate interest into the 'sibling factor' in theory of mind tasks. Dunn suggests a number of reasons which, singly or in combination, might help to explain why children with older brothers and sisters should reach an earlier understanding of the way in which other people think, feel and act than their first-born siblings. Let me try, briefly, to outline her suggestions.

When a second, third or later-born child comes into a family, they enter a situation in which parent–child relationships and, if third-born or more, sibling relationships already exist. The first-born or only child clearly enters a very different social and emotional world. For the later-born children, talk about and between other people with whom they are destined to forge emotional ties (for good or ill) is likely to be frequent. They encounter discussions about why other people do the things that they do. They are likely to encounter conflict where explanations and justifications might be offered and evaluated. They play, joke and are often exposed to and, eventually, involved in talk about moral issues, rights and obligations. They are surrounded by drama in which issues of personal rights, responsibilities, needs and fault are common. Reference to 'third persons' in situations which are serious, engaging and important to the young child are also likely to be frequent. In short, the later-born, in their early years, are likely to enter a more complex socio-emotional world than that into which their older sibling was born.

The relative importance of such activities to theory of mind performance is not known. It is not clear to what extent interactions involving either a sibling, parents or the whole family exert an influence. Whatever the reason, the research demonstrates connections between everyday social life and the origins of the child's ability to reason about other people and their states of mind. In Bruner's (1990) terms, younger siblings have more opportunities than their older brothers and sisters to explore relations between 'the landscape of action and landscape of consciousness'.

Much more is at stake here than claims and counter-claims about the age at which children are able to reason about the mental and emotional states of other people. In studies of home life and the formation of relationships within the family, issues about emotion and effect come into prominence. Contemporary theories of cognition and intellectual growth have not been framed to explain if and, if so, how the nature of emotional experiences impacts on cognition and understanding. Such questions lie outside the remit of most modern theories. And yet, part of Dunn's argument is that children often display their most 'advanced' levels of reasoning in situations that matter to them and that arouse their attention and emotions (though strong emotions, of course, can also serve to cloud reason and provoke intellectual regression!). The establishment of connections between experimental investigations of children's understanding of mental states on the one hand, and studies of social interaction, emotional experience and the formation of relationships on the other, has created new opportunities for understanding the interactions between social and emotional dimensions of experience and the development of mind (Dunn, 1996).

I will return to consider conflicting theoretical interpretations of theory of mind research later, after I have outlined another line of research which explores links between experiences in the family and the child's understanding of others.

Children are often in situations where they can overhear conversations between other people. They are immersed in 'living soaps' (!) where they are offered constant opportunities to overhear, oversee and learn. It is extremely difficult to discover how and what children might make of such encounters and to find out what influences their understanding. Can they, for instance, judge whether or not what other people say to each other is mutually comprehensible or not? Can they put themselves in the shoes of a person who is being told what to do, for example, to decide whether or not what that person has been told is explicit enough to enable them to do what they are being asked to do?

One situation used to try to answer such questions is set up as follows. A child is asked to observe two people involved in a communication game. One person has been given the task of telling the other which picture to select from a set of alternatives. The pictures are designed in such a way that incomplete descriptions can be formulated. For instance, imagine that the pictures include examples of boys and girls, some with and some without hats. The hats are also of different shapes and colours. An adequate description of the picture the instructor has in mind demands attention to gender and to the shape and colour of any hats involved. Suppose an incomplete message is given; say the person giving the instructions fails to mention colour and, in so doing, leaves the listener with an ambiguous description that fits two or more of the pictures. What do four-year-olds make of such a situation? Do they realize that what is said is incomplete and therefore ambiguous? Or are they so egocentric that they cannot understand the nature of the listener's dilemma?

Many four-year-olds do not appreciate the listener's problems. In fact, they tend to 'blame' him or her for any failures of understanding. They seem to assume that 'to speak is to be understood' and that the person who is talking and who intends to *tell* the other person what to do does just that. They are 'listener blamers'.

However, some four-year-olds are able to appreciate the fact that people do not always say enough or say the right things to enable others to understand what they mean. In other words, they appreciate the listener's dilemma and realize that what the speaker says is not necessarily a complete or comprehensible account of what they want the other person to do.

These experimental findings were reported by Peter and Elizabeth Robinson. What is special about their investigations is that they had access to extensive recordings made in the children's homes prior to undertaking the experiment and were able to explore relations between communication experiences in the home and children's ability to assess message adequacy in the experimental set-up. They used the language samples collected by Gordon Wells and his colleagues in Bristol (summarized in Robinson, 1986).

Four-year-olds who could judge the adequacy of communication had different communicative experiences at home when talking to their parents. Let me illustrate with an example. A child says something to his mother which she finds ambiguous or unclear. How does she respond? Well, she might *ask* the child, 'Which one . . .?', or, 'Do you mean *x* or *y*?' In other words, she asks questions to try to clarify what the child has said. Or she might say, 'I don't understand. I don't know whether you want me to do *x* or *y*'. Those children who were most likely to be given an *explicit account* by their mothers of how and why they found what the child said unclear were most likely to appreciate the listener's dilemma in communication games. Children whose parents employed questions to clarify and 'repair' without telling the child what it was they found unclear were those most likely to blame the listener.

The discovery of relationships between the way in which parents talk to their children and aspects of those same children's linguistic development does not necessarily imply, of course, that one phenomenon *causes* the other. It is conceivable, for example, that children who are verbally precocious solicit ways of talking from their parents that differ from those solicited by other children. Further evidence, however, strengthens the view that parents do influence their children's communicative competence and demonstrates that it is possible to teach young children to improve their so-called 'metalinguistic awareness' (that is, their knowledge *about* language in contrast to their ability to *use* it).

The Robinsons involved nursery school children as participants in the kind of communication game outlined above. Different methods were employed in response to any ambiguous or incomplete description given by different groups of children. When the children in one of these groups gave such messages, the 'teacher' responded by explicitly *telling* the child about the nature of their uncertainty. In other words, she would say something like, 'I don't know what you mean. I don't know whether you mean *x* or *y*.' Other children were asked questions in an attempt to solicit any information they had left out.

After a few teaching sessions, children from each of the groups were asked to listen to two other people playing a similar communication game and to explain why a listener sometimes faced problems. Children from the group who, when they played the game, had been told explicitly about any inadequacies in their own messages were less likely than those in other groups to blame the listener. They were more often able to articulate the nature of the listener's dilemma. This evidence, taken in conjunction with that from the home observations, provides strong support for the view that young children can be given experiences which help them to learn how to make explicit judgements about the adequacy or otherwise of what people say (at least, in some contexts).

Vygotsky, recall, argued that intellectual and linguistic development proceed from the external, social plane to become personal, mental activity by a process of 'internalization'. Children's verbal reasoning, for example, represents 'inner speech' and 'inner dialogue'. Talking to others and being addressed by them are destined to become mental activity as the child 'takes on the role' of others and holds inner dialogues with himself. The *form* that this dialogue takes depends upon the characteristic ways in which the child talks to and controls others and, in turn, is talked to and controlled by them. Those of a Vygotskian persuasion could argue, then, that the findings from the Robinsons' studies support Vygotsky's view and demonstrate that social interaction and such experiences as talking to, informing, explaining, being talked to, being informed and having things explained structure not only the child's immediate activities but also help to form the *processes* of reasoning and learning themselves. The child inherits not only 'local knowledge' about given tasks but, gradually, internalizes the *instructional process* itself. Thus, he learns how to learn, reason and regulate his own physical and mental activities. More about this later.

Pause for reflection

Josef Perner and his colleagues (e.g. Perner, Leekam and Wimmer, 1987), who first introduced the false-belief paradigm into developmental psychology, suggest that a change in representational competence explains what develops during the fourth year of life in children's understanding of other minds. For neo-Piagetians, like Halford (1992) and Case (1991), such changes are symptomatic of a general increase in children's cognitive capacities. Halford, for example, draws parallels between the child's ability to solve theory of mind tasks and the ability to draw inferences (see chapter 3). Believing that general changes occur in the 'cognitive architecture' with age, they search for commonalities in the structural complexity of the tasks that children can handle at

different ages. Thus, for Halford, the representational change that
Perner and his colleagues propose is but an example of the kinds of
mental models that the four- to five-year-old, but not the average three-
year-old, can construct and reason with. Similarly, in the Robinsons'
investigation, the child has to be able to co-ordinate utterances made by
another with an interpretation of what the task facing the listener
demands before he is able to disabuse himself of the notion that any
blame for failures of communication necessarily rest with the listener.
This co-ordination also demands greater processing capacity.

In her many observations, Judy Dunn reports incidents between
children much younger than three and their older siblings which suggest
that, in 'real life' encounters, they can and do take the mental states of
others into account. For example, children may try to manoeuvre their
older brother or sister into doing something naughty and thus get
punished (e.g. by picking up the older sibling's favourite toy in order to
get them to snatch it back when an adult is likely to see them do so!).
Such machiavellian tactics suggest that much younger children are
capable, in contexts charged with motivation, emotion and meaning, to
reason about other people's desires and the actions likely to be taken on
the basis of these mental states. Perner, however, suggests that, without
experimental evidence, we cannot confidently interpret such observations. Hence, as we have found in much earlier studies of language and
cognition, the issue of context or situation and its relation to experimental evidence surfaces again.

Both Dunn and Bruner argue for a social constructivist, or 'apprenticeship', interpretation of the child's developing competence in theory
of mind tasks. But before outlining their views, let us consider some of
the achievements that mark later developments in the child's emerging
understanding of other minds.

Understanding the fact that people have beliefs about the world
which differ from one's own – beliefs which motivate their actions and
may be at odds with what appears to be the 'reality' of things – is
obviously a vital watershed in the child's understanding of other people
and how they tick. However, the connections between how people
think and what they do become predictably more complicated when we
introduce a 'third person' onto the scene. Consider, for instance,
situations in which the child can only make sense of the way in which
a second person behaves (mother, for the sake of the example) on the
basis of ideas she has about the beliefs of a third party (father, say).
Imagine situations involving mother, father and daughter in which the
mother disagrees with the father's treatment of the daughter on the

basis of what she takes to be a false belief held by the father about what the daughter thinks and does. Here, our child-as-mind-theorist must think about the mother's beliefs about the father's beliefs about the daughter's in order to make sense of how they all interact together. Whether this is a typical age or stage at which children master such 'higher order' reasoning about the mind is not clear, although we do know that some groups of children seem to have specific problems in learning how to think in this way (Harris, 1989). Controversy over the issue of stages in children's understanding of other minds still rages.

Dunn and Bruner argue that explanations for changes in children's competence in such tasks (like that put forward by Perner and his colleagues) which are based on assumptions about developmental shifts in cognitive architecture and representational competence are, like Piaget's theory of stages, misguided. They argue for a more gradual, piecemeal and socially mediated process of development in which exposure to everyday explanations and to narratives plays a central role in development. On this view, narratives, which serve to create 'possible worlds' that children can enter and explore, are a major vehicle for the transmission of a culture's theories of human nature. The term 'narrative' is not, of course, to be restricted to written stories. It also includes oral narratives which serve to relate personal histories, justifications, plans for the future and the like, together with the 'living narratives' encountered in family drama. As in Dunn's observations, interactions within the family, living soaps, often exhibit considerable complexity in terms of the number and variety of relationships involved. To participate in family life, or in peer groups, children come naturally to reason about their own and other people's ambitions, fears, thoughts and feelings and to construct theories about how and why others (and they themselves) act as they do. On a social constructivist account, then, it is to be expected both that children will display their greatest competence in reasoning about others in everyday situations and that we will find relations between factors such as family composition and the sense children try to make of psychological experiments designed to explore their theory of mind.

Information-giving

The finding, reported by Robinson and Robinson, that young children can be helped to increase their 'metalinguistic' understanding in reasoning about the process of communication also lends some weight to the argument that linguistic and intellectual development are, in part at least, facilitated by specific social experiences. This is not to say that children are usually taught how to talk and how to make what they say meaningful and informative in any direct or explicit way. We have encountered many examples of *self-correction* by children which provide strong evidence that self-instruction plays an important and central role in learning. Even so, this does not mean that others more expert than the child exert no influence upon his learning and development. The seven-year-olds in Hickman's studies, for example, were not explicitly *told* that their use of referring expressions was often ambiguous. They seemed to realize when what they were saying did not 'sound right', and themselves worked on the problem of finding the right way to make what they said comprehensible. We are obliged, I suggest, to assume that children often know a great deal about what they cannot yet do successfully. One way of expressing this is to say that they often *understand* and can *recognize* as correct what they cannot yet themselves *produce*. Given this state of affairs (which, as we shall see, is more widespread in development than the examples I have given to date), the child is in a position to *construct* and to *perfect* his own performance through problem-solving. Recognizing, for example, what 'sounds right', he has a goal or target against which he can measure and evaluate his own performance. He can assess when he has 'got it'.

The image of the child as a problem-solver and architect of his own knowledge and understanding is, of course, compatible with Piaget's views. It is also consistent with those implicit in several other theories of learning and development. Bruner, for example, describes the child as a problem-solver and views the process of instruction as one of helping the child to *discover* manageable problems. But accepting the child's 'natural' problem-solving and self-instructional abilities does not *necessarily* imply that his interactions and encounters with others exert no formative influence on what and how he learns. Before looking more analytically at the nature of such influences, let me discuss further evidence relating to the nature of children's capacities to make sense to others. This, from studies of adolescents, paints a far less rosy picture of children's 'natural' linguistic and intellectual abilities. It also suggests that educational experience can play an important role in determining how far and to what extent children are able to perfect their own expertise in using language as an instrument of explanation, instruction and 'other-regulation'.

In an extensive investigation of adolescent communication skills, Brown and her colleagues (1984) worked with 500 fourteen- to seventeen-year-old Scottish school children. Three hundred of these pupils were judged, by their schools, to represent the lower 'third' of their year in academic ability and were considered unlikely to leave school with any formal academic qualifications.

Underlying this research is a distinction between what Brown et al. term 'chat' and 'information-giving speech', the latter being the main subject of their investigations. Chat is what we have been referring to as conversation. It is a highly interactive affair in which all participants share the responsibility for ensuring mutual understanding and for developing topics of talk. Observed chatting to each other in pairs, the pupils were talkative, were often witty and seemed to suffer no problems of communication. Though a little more reticent with an unfamiliar adult interviewer, they were able to engage them in intelligible conversation. However, even relatively minor increases in demands on communication produced noticeable impairments in their performance. For example, simply asking a child to 'talk' to a friend into a tape recorder led to speech that was more hesitant, not so articulate and less coherent than that found in face-to-face conversation. Even such a relatively minor degree of 'disembedding' of the process of communication led to measurable deterioration in performance. The absence of a 'live' partner, and the non-verbal, paralinguistic and interactional support they would have offered, had marked effects on these pupils' ability to make what they tried to say accessible. When demands were further increased and children were asked to give detailed instructions and explanations, performance deteriorated to an even greater extent. Before discussing the studies of information-giving, however, let me pause to say a little more about the nature of conversation and the important differences that exist between, say, relaxed talk with a friend and more stressful interactions with teachers.

In a very readable and informative book, Wardhaugh (1985) considers in detail the many social practices and values that are implicated in conversation. He points out that conversation is, by its very nature, typically and literally mundane. It is about everyday experiences and events. It is important that one does not delve too deeply or react too analytically to the conversational talk of others. People have the right to remain silent if they wish and there are implicit conventions that inhibit us from going 'too far' in probing people's motives, proclivities, behaviour and beliefs. Privacy has to be respected and we must be aware of the bounds over which we should not pass. These bounds, of course, vary according to our relationship and degree of intimacy with the person with whom we are talking. Insistence upon 'the total truth', upon absolutely clear and unambiguous utterances and full disclosure, is threatening, disruptive and rude.

These seemingly self-evident observations take on an important significance when we consider the differences between the child's everyday experiences of conversation and the use of language in school. Schooling is about imparting, sharing, discussing, analysing and evaluating knowledge and skill, among other things. The 'search for truth', accuracy, clarity, for *evidence* of knowledge and understanding, are part and parcel of the process of education. Reflecting these differences in the underlying *purposes* of talk in the community and school are marked differences in the nature of the relationship between people involved in discourse and different aspects of their use of language. For example, in school it is quite legitimate (if not always desirable, as we shall find) for the teacher to ask all the questions. In everyday discourse, questions perform a variety of functions. Most obvious is the search for information. People usually ask questions of others in order to find out things that they do not know and need to know. Such questions are 'legitimate' if the person asked can understand *why* his questioner wants to know and if disclosure of the information asked for has no implied negative consequences for the answerer. Then the usual process is to *negotiate* the conditions under which an answer will be provided. Imagine, for instance, being asked a question about how much you earn by a stranger on your doorstep.

Questions are also used to frame requests, to ask for help or permission. Here too, gaining an answer is not only a *linguistic* issue but a moral one. Does the person have the *right* to make such requests? Have they taken proper account of what compliance would entail for the person asked? If, say, the loss of time, prestige or rights that will be experienced by the answerer is far greater than the relative benefit that will accrue to the questioner, then the request is likely to be deemed unreasonable at best. Questions are also used to display courtesy and interest and to cement relationships. They are a way of being polite (Goody, 1978). Showing concern about and interest in another person by asking them to tell you things is a commonplace but often delicate activity. As I said above, knowing how far it is permissible and polite to go in probing a person without causing offence involves knowledge of the cultural values of the person being asked. I will return to this point when we discuss interactions between people from very different social and cultural backgrounds.

Questions asked in school 'violate' many of these normal conventions. Teachers are licensed by our society (like police officers, doctors and lawyers) to ask questions with the expectation that they will receive answers, even though these often transgress everyday conventions.

There are, of course, still limits to what can legitimately be asked about, but teachers are allowed, even expected, to ask questions to which they know the answers. Although parents of pre-schoolers often address what Wells calls 'display' questions to their children, that are also designed to solicit known answers (often known to both parent and child), any failure to comply by a pre-schooler with a home audience is likely to have a very different significance from failure by a school-aged child in the classroom. Failure for the older child in school is likely to be more serious and personally threatening. Teachers may also ask children to justify, prove or in some way demonstrate the basis for, and rationality of, anything they say. Getting things 'right' in class may be at a premium in a way that it is not in informal chat. The child, on entering school, has to discover and comply with a range of conventions, rights and obligations that constitute the roles of pupil and teacher. Implicated in these conventions are important differences in the functions of language.

Chat between teachers and children, though founded in different conventions from those governing other social encounters, is still typified by shared responsibility for the achievement of mutual understanding (in which, as we shall see, teachers usually play the leading role). Information-giving acts of speech, as their label implies, are concerned with things like providing clear instructions, directions and explanations. When Brown et al. tested their academically less able pupils' ability to use speech for information-giving purposes, they discovered that these pupils were usually incapable of providing coherent, comprehensible, informative narratives. Even when asked to tell an interviewer about events or experiences that were familiar to the child, their performance was frequently uninformative and difficult to understand. The following extract, in which a pupil tries to tell the interviewer about the film *Jaws* (the child had also read the book), illustrates the listener's difficulties. Each plus sign indicates a pause of a few seconds.

Interviewer	Is the book like the film?
Pupil	+ + A wee bit.
Interviewer	Hmm + + What's different in the book?
Pupil	In the book + + + Hooper dies in the film but he never dies but he went in a cage down + to see if he could see the fish + and like + + + + and trying to get in + the fish + but he couldn't + + the fish turned er the cage over but then he went away and Hooper just went and

> swum out and hid behind a rock and + in the book he
> said that he died.

Did Hooper die in the book or the film? Brown and her colleagues went further than simple observation, however. They designed a range of co-operative tasks of varying levels of complexity and difficulty which they used with some of the pupils to help to foster their skills in giving information and instructions. Some were communication games in which one child had to tell another how to perform a task. Others involved creating narratives.

A variety of techniques were used to introduce these different activities into the classroom in co-operation with teachers. A detailed account of the study is not possible here, but a number of its main findings are worth noting. The researchers developed a range of assessment procedures that involved teachers in evaluating children's language. These included attention to things like the presence or absence of critical information and the extent to which information was provided in an appropriate rational sequence. Also examined was the child's use of referring expressions involving terms like determiners and pronouns to see if it was clear, from the child's narrative, who or what these referred to. The assessments revealed considerable progress as children participated in the activities. Later, follow-up studies demonstrated that the pupils *remembered* what they had learned and were able to *generalize* what they had learned in one task to improve their performances in others. Use of referring expressions also became more explicit, accurate and intelligible.

Another finding, one that I will elaborate upon in the next chapter, was that the children who first played the role of *listener* were significantly more articulate and informative when it came to their turn to play the role of speaker than were children who first acted as speakers. Brown suggests that the experience of trying to *comply* with instructions sensitizes the child to the problems of being on the receiving end of less than informative instruction. The children obviously learned how to solve some of these problems, how to make what they said less 'egocentric' and ambiguous, by playing the seemingly 'passive' role of listener. Provided, then, that the child has to act upon what he is told, *listening*, at least in some contexts, is a more powerful vehicle for learning how to *talk* informatively than is exclusive experience as a speaker.

Classroom 'registers': means to ends

These findings give rise to a number of implications and questions. They demonstrate, perhaps unsurprisingly, that the potential for the development of communicative competence (or what now seems to be referred to as 'oracy') extends throughout the years of schooling. In so doing, they pose a question and raise some issues: why were these children, many of whom were about to leave school, so inarticulate and poor at giving information, directions and explanations before participating in the study? The fact that they could be helped to improve these skills shows that they did not lack the necessary *competence* to learn. Why, then, had they not learned in the normal course of their education?

A number of very different explanations might be advanced in response to this question. We might argue that the development of such communication skills is not part of the business of schooling, but such an argument is difficult to sustain. Lacking the ability to plan, organize, regulate and express what they know in order to inform others, these children are surely likely to be handicapped in their vocational choices and in their personal lives. Even if the ability to inform and explain did not influence other aspects of the child's educational achievements (and I will argue in the next two chapters that it does), an inability to present oneself as articulate and informative must surely act as a barrier to competence in many situations – not least in interviews for jobs.

Note that what is at issue here is not whether a child speaks using the 'Standard English' dialect. Rather, it is his ability to *exploit* his own linguistic resources to achieve certain communicative ends: to use certain 'registers' of language. This research was not intended to 'remediate' speech or to 'teach' children to speak a dialect different from their own. Its goal was to help them to learn how to make sense and give a good *account* of themselves. If we can accept that the development of 'oracy' is a legitimate goal of education, as the UK's Bullock Report recommended (Department of Education and Science, 1975; Norman, 1992), why is its achievement seemingly so elusive for many children?

Brown and her colleagues suggest that at least part of the answer to this question lies in the typical 'registers' of classroom discourse: the way in which teachers typically talk to pupils. Let me outline (and elaborate upon) this line of argument. Many studies of classroom discourse in different parts of the world have found that the most dominant feature of teacher–pupil interaction is the question–answer –acknowledgement exchange. Teachers ask nearly all the questions. By way of illustration, in two studies, one of English pre-school children in playgroups and nursery schools and the other focused upon American high school students (aged seventeen), the frequency of teacher questions as a proportion of all their utterances was 47 per cent and 43 per cent respectively. For the pupils, the incidence of questions was 4 per cent and 8 per cent (Wood and Wood, 1988). The more questions the teachers asked, the less children had to say. The pupils were also less likely to elaborate on the topic being talked about, ask questions or talk to each other when teacher questions were frequent.

There is an extensive and argumentative literature on the topic of questions and their role in teaching. Here, I can do no more than select and discuss fragments of research that are most relevant to our present concerns. Some educationalists (e.g. Blank, Rose and Berlin, 1978) argue that teacher questions are powerful tools for encouraging pupils and students to *listen* and to *think*. To be effective, however, a teacher's questions must be of the appropriate kind and at the right 'level of demand' if pupils are to profit by them. Blank has developed an elaborate scheme for classifying questions that she offers as a way of analysing and evaluating teaching talk with pre-school and young school children. Some questions (for example, 'What do we call this?', asked in relation to a common object) are concerned with relatively 'low level' demands and permit a very restricted range of answers, perhaps only a single word. Others, e.g. 'Why did that happen?', may call for more thought and explanation. Yet others, e.g.'What do you think about . . .?', may have no obvious, correct answer but call for analytical reasoning and informed judgement.

Observations of teacher questions addressed to children of widely different ages and in a variety of disciplines have led to the conclusion that teacher questions are more often of the 'closed' type with known right answers. The responses to such questions by pupils are likely to be terse and simply correct or incorrect. When pupils have answered a teacher's questions, they usually say no more. Consequently, where such specific, closed questions are frequent, children will say little. Now, if the goal of asking questions is *only* to ascertain whether or not a child knows a particular fact or name, one can argue that such results are defensible. However, if other goals are also being sought – for example, encouraging children to reason out loud, to ask questions of their own, to state their own opinions, ideas and uncertainties, or to *narrate* – then the frequent use of specific, closed questions will not bring about the desired ends.

In one extensive study of teachers' use of questions in a number of disciplines, including natural history and physics lessons, Nuthall and Church (1973) investigated the impact of different types of questions on pupil performance. They compared lessons in which teachers used a preponderance of closed questions demanding specific factual answers with those in which they employed more open-ended questions designed to encourage reasoning, discussion and speculation. They found that the children taught through specific questions tended to do better when tested for retention of factual information. Those who were asked open-ended questions did indeed speculate, hypothesize and discuss more (though they did not learn so many specific facts per unit of teaching time). This finding may not seem surprising. It does, however, suggest that what and how children think and learn can be influenced by the way in which the teacher conducts his or her lesson!

Schools are expected to achieve a variety of different, often conflicting, goals with their children. Teachers may find some of these goals, say teaching a body of facts, to be in 'competition' with others, like fostering the development of skills in narration, self-presentation and informing others. The hope that each of these objectives can be met with the same 'register' and approach to teaching, typically the question–answer exchange in which the teacher asks almost all the questions, seems a vain one. It is not my task to try to define what the objectives of a school or teacher should be. However, the findings that have emerged from studies of classroom interaction offer teachers some practical suggestions as to how instructional means and learning outcomes might best be married. Frequent, specific questions tend to generate relatively silent children and to inhibit any discussion between them. Telling children things, giving an opinion, view, speculation or idea, stimulates more talk, questions and ideas from pupils and generates discussion between them.

If all this sounds obvious, then explain why so many studies have found that classroom talk is dominated by teacher questions.

Although Nuthall and Church found that teachers' use of specific questions led to more rapid learning of factual information by their pupils, an examination of longer-term effects of different questioning 'regimes' suggests that pupil achievement is higher when they encounter more demanding, open-ended questions (Redfield and Rousseau, 1981). Further support for this conclusion comes from a study of the questions that *parents* characteristically employ with their children. Here too, more demanding, open-ended questions from parents were found to be predictive of a number of measures of children's educational achievement (Sigel and McGillicuddy-Delisi, 1988). Sigel argues that such questions facilitate the development of educability in children because they invite them to 'distance' themselves from the immediate, short-term consequences of their experiences. In so doing, the child is enjoined to de-centre, think about and reflect upon his own activities and, in consequence, becomes more analytic and less impulsive and achieves more effective control of his own learning. As we shall see in the final chapter, the notion that children 'internalize' the processes of control to which they are exposed in order to regulate their own learning and thinking emerges from a variety of research studies.

Other studies have shown that teachers can be helped to modify their own teaching styles to adopt different questioning techniques. Some of these illustrate the difficulties involved and relate back to our previous discussion of the relationship between verbal and non-verbal dimensions of communication. When teachers ask pupils questions, they tend to leave about a second of silence, on average, before they resume talking (if the children have not responded). In a study of the effects of different teacher 'wait times' on children's responses, teachers were provided with a buzzer (which only they could hear) and were asked, having posed a question, to wait until this was sounded before going on. The buzzer was controlled by an observer, who waited for three seconds after each question before activating it (again, if no response was forthcoming from the class). The increased 'wait time' allowed to children resulted in more frequent, relevant, thoughtful and 'high level' responses to the teachers' questions (Rowe, 1974; Swift and Gooding, 1983).

In face-to-face conversation, as I have already said, the *synchronization* of communication is finely tuned. Perhaps, when a teacher is faced with a group of pupils, the cues that enable such synchronization to emerge are destroyed or in some way inhibited, so that a teacher's timing is out of synchrony and sympathy with the pupils' responses (which are likely to vary from child to child anyway). Perhaps increasing the time allowed after a question has been asked enables most or all of the pupils to formulate their thoughts. Such results illustrate how specific features of discourse exert an important influence on the process of classroom communication. One suspects that it would prove a difficult task for teachers to sustain control over such normally spontaneous features of their classroom talk as time waited after questions, however.

In the book by Wardhaugh (1985) mentioned earlier, he says (p. 71):

> Teaching is not only a special form of conversing with others – it is an especially difficult form, if for no other reason than that the teacher must 'converse' with a large heterogeneous group of listeners. Good teaching requires one to be good at a particular kind of conversation; it is a skill not easily acquired because of the special demands it makes, and it is not a skill one can readily practise outside the classroom, since it is very rarely appropriate to any other circumstance.

The studies we have just been discussing lend considerable weight to his argument.

Classroom discourse is typically controlled by teacher questions that often demand quick, terse, factual answers and leave little time for children to respond, elaborate or reason out loud. Perhaps this explains, in part at least, why some children do not learn how to express their ideas, formulate their thoughts or say what they know. Furthermore, if the teacher asks all the questions, then he or she dictates the course of events – what will be thought about and when. We have to ask ourselves whether this provides the *pupils* with opportunities to plan, regulate, reason and explain themselves.

The issue of questioning and its role in teaching is a deeply contentious one that has aroused much heat and debate in education. As Gordon Wells (1992) observes, even those who subscribe to a neo-Vygotskian perspective are divided in their attitude towards the topic. Newman, Griffin and Cole (1989), for example, argue that the three-part structure of the question exchange used by teachers to encourage children to display what they think and know is 'quite nicely designed' to fit this purpose. And yet, as we have seen, it can also be argued that, used to excess, this strategy can inhibit pupil participation. Wells suggests that this conflict of view is symptomatic of a tension in neo-Vygotksian thinking itself. The cultural reproduction of knowledge demands that teachers structure and direct interactions with pupils to ensure that they are helped to make sense of the tasks they are set and come to the 'right answers'. On the other hand, learning and teaching should 'not be concerned only with cultural reproduction . . . It is equally important that pupils gain confidence in their ability to find their own solutions to problems . . . As important as teacher input, therefore, is the opportunity for pupils to pose their own problems . . . and to ask questions to which they themselves wish to find answers' (pp. 296–7). The issue of teacher control and pupil initiative is, as one might expect, central to many arguments about the nature of the learning process. It will re-surface in this volume when we consider teaching and learning in mathematics.

This dispute aside, it seems clear, as Brown and her co-workers suggest, that many children need more involvement in activities designed to help them to learn how to listen to and use language informatively and thoughtfully. Their evidence demonstrates that children *can* improve their own levels of performance. What the longer-term effects on such children's educational performance might be we discuss in the final two chapters. The researchers provide examples of the kind of materials that can be used to make this possible and show how teachers can analyse and evaluate their children's performance to monitor progress. Offering more opportunities for linguistic initiative to the child is not an abdication of teacher responsibility if and when the activities are structured carefully, managed effectively and evaluated properly.

Summary

I have deliberately juxtaposed research into the early stages of children's communicative development – which paints a rather rosy and romantic picture – with investigations of how some children perform in the latter years of their school life which portray a situation closer to that described by Bernstein. I have used this device for two reasons, one theoretical and the other more practical. Research into the development of language in early childhood fits in well with nativist theories. The research into children's understanding of other people's minds also fits well into neo-Piagetian accounts such as those put forward by Karmiloff-Smith and Halford. Each of these approaches stresses the natural competence that children bring to bear on the task of making sense of and to others.

But why, if development is so naturally and internally regulated, do so many children appear to have problems in communication (at least in some situations) as they reach the end of schooling? Why are so many seemingly so restricted in their ability to use language informatively? One could, I suppose, extend Labov's criticism to argue that, by not exploring children's performance in out-of-school contexts, Brown and her colleagues obtained an underestimate of their competence. As far as I am aware, no such observations have been made. It could also be argued that the children had reached some natural ceiling of linguistic and cognitive achievement. But neither of these possible explanations is consistent with the findings which show that, even within a relatively short time and after modest amounts of experience, children showed measurable gains in performance.

An alternative view, following Vygotsky, Bruner, Wells and others, is that children need specific kinds of communicative experiences and some external support in order to develop uses of language beyond those demanded by everyday conversation. Throughout the years of schooling, children's use and expertise in various functions of language develop. These developments can be detected in fine-grained but important changes in the way in which they use a variety of linguistic processes that are involved in producing sustained, coherent narratives and in both giving and understanding information. We should expect to find that a child's ability to employ determiners, pronouns and a variety of linguistic devices improves through a stage of hesitant dysfluency and self-correction to smooth, well-organized and comprehensible creation of verbal text.

We have examined evidence which demonstrates that some, probably many, children do not achieve such fluency and, outside relaxed and relatively undemanding conversation, face considerable difficulties in trying to explain themselves or instruct others. Such findings rule out any supposition that these aspects of linguistic function come about 'naturally' or inevitably. They demand specific types of experience. The fact that a significant proportion of adolescents are poor at giving a good account of themselves when asked to inform and explain suggests that schools need to do more if they are not to see children leave their gates for the last time unable to exploit their communicative resources to the full. Classroom-based studies show that children and adolescents can be helped to become more articulate, fluent and confident in their powers of self-expression.

We have also considered the challenges that communication in the classroom creates for *teachers*. What appears to be the dominant teaching register, involving frequent teacher-directed questions, may be effective in achieving certain managerial and instructional ends, but it seems unlikely to provide good conditions for developing children's powers as narrators, informants and, perhaps, self-regulating learners. The challenges confronting the teacher are far from trivial and demand considerable expertise in what are very special forms of communication.

I have already drawn attention to the implications of special linguistic problems for our discussions of children's learning and thinking.

Language and cognition are fused in verbal reasoning. Comprehension problems, which arise because children have yet to master specific features of language use and structure, act as a barrier to learning and understanding. Lacking expertise in the processes of creating coherent, 'disembedded' or 'decontextualized' accounts of what they know and understand, children may appear intellectually incompetent when, in reality, they are still grappling with the problem of making sense to other people. This process takes time and creates many challenges for both pupils and teachers.

In the next chapter, we explore more fully the proposition that in 'learning how to mean' (to borrow a phrase from Halliday, 1975) children not only advance their expressive linguistic abilities but also discover how to regulate, plan, evaluate and monitor their own intellectual activities. If sound, this proposition implies that the nature and quality of classroom discourse plays a vital role in developing a child's ability to learn and to reason analytically. Our attention shifts from talking and listening to consider the development of reading and writing. Though obviously related, in that literacy is 'parasitic' on the spoken word, there are many important differences between these two modes of communication. Learning to read and write promises more benefits than access to new ways of learning, instruction and recreation – as we shall see.

7

The literate mind

In the UK, children usually move from primary into secondary schools at around eleven years of age. When they make the move, they begin their preparations for public examinations. The curriculum in secondary schools is usually quite different from that followed in the primary school. It is expected that most if not all children will have learned to read well enough in the primary school to begin reading to learn in the secondary years, for example. Facility with the written word becomes increasingly important as secondary schooling proceeds. Some children over the age of eleven still find writing and reading difficult, however. We explore some of the reasons why these children find the achievement of literacy difficult and what might be done to help them.

In order to understand how children learn to read and write and to identify the learning difficulties that some of them face, we will need to explore connections between spoken and written language. How does learning to read and write relate to what pre-literate children know and can do with their spoken language? As we saw in chapter 5, many students of child language have been impressed with the apparent ease and speed with which young children master their mother tongue. As we shall see here, however, we have to draw some distinctions between being able to use and comprehend spoken language on the one hand, and achieving a degree of conscious awareness of the structure and use of language on the other. Unless the child comes to understand, for example, how it is that words and longer utterances can be broken up and represented in terms of a common set of written elements, then she is likely to find the task of learning to read and write a daunting one. So, we need to examine what it is that children understand about the sounds and structures of spoken language as they embark on the task of learning to read.

In company with Vygotsky, some psychologists and anthropologists believe that the development of literacy leads to stage-like changes in linguistic and intellectual abilities. On this account, both our knowledge and use of language are transformed by learning how to read and write. Such a view motivates a search for differences between spoken and written language and to an exploration of the idea that writing is not simply speech written down. Rather, new 'theories' about the structure and function of language are made possible by the invention and acquisition of literacy, both in the child and in a culture. If this is true, then we should expect to find changes in ways in which language is structured and used that come about through literacy. We will also explore the idea that written language leads to important changes in thinking. Indeed, if we are to believe some theorists, it underpins the development of abstract, logical reasoning itself. All of this leads us on to discuss the effects of poor literary skills on children's thinking and academic prospects: hence the title, 'The literate mind'.

We begin the chapter with an exploration of Piaget's view that the onset of adolescence usually sees a change in the nature of children's intelligence. More specifically, we examine his theory and alternatives to it about the relation between logic and thinking. This topic, difficult though it is, provides us with a way of comparing and contrasting theories which argue that formal, logical reasoning is a product of literacy with the view that it emerges as a natural product of development. Even more fundamentally, we will find ourselves asking if the rules of logic, whatever their origins, provide a useful framework for thinking about the development of thinking at all. And all of this achieves practical significance when we come to consider the issue of if, how and when formal reasoning influences 'readiness' for learning in the later years of schooling.

Logic, literacy and reasoning?

Let us start with Piaget's views on the nature of mature, logical thinking. These are not easy to summarize or to evaluate. So why bother? Why should we concern ourselves with an issue, namely the relation between logic and everyday thinking, that has taxed the minds of philosophers and psychologists for many years yet still remains unresolved? Well, as I hope to show, it is not really possible to evaluate Piaget's theory or its educational implications without some sense of where, in Piaget's view, the developing structure of the mind *culminates*. In his theory, intellectual development has an ultimate destiny or destination. Cognitive structures are driven towards a specific, structural end point, a state of ultimate stability and *equilibrium*, which involves the achievement of a sense of logical necessity. The natural direction followed in intellectual development leads to the stages and structures that we have already considered. If we decide that Piaget's account of the nature of mature, logical thinking is unacceptable, then we must be prepared to reject or revise both his account of children's thinking and the constraints imposed by the proposed stages of intelligence upon the nature of learning and understanding, teaching and explaining.

Evaluation of the theory is difficult for a number of reasons. First, Piaget never suggested that adults *typically* reason in logical terms. A good deal of everyday thinking is practical and intuitive, not formal and logical. Consequently, as we see later, though there are several lines of evidence which show that even highly educated people (including those trained in logic) find it very *difficult* to think in formal logical terms, Piagetians might argue that this does not refute the theory. Piaget never implied that logical thought was easy, as far as I am aware.

A second source of problems comes from the fact that Piaget appeared to modify his own theory about the formal operational stage of development. He seems to have accepted that this stage, unlike the earlier ones, may not emerge from self-directed, everyday interactions in the world but from specific *educational* experiences. For instance, the study of mathematics and learning how to plan and conduct scientific *experiments* may provide the cognitive demands and intellectual problems that foster the emergence of formal, deductive reasoning. Therefore, evidence which shows that people from some parts of the world seem unable to solve problems involving hypothetical, propositional reasoning (I will give examples later) cannot be used to reject the theory (Piaget, 1971, pp. 94–6). Like several other major theorists, including Vygotsky, Bruner and Donaldson, Piaget accepted the importance of a fluent, articulate command of *language* to foster the transition from concrete to formal operational thinking. Although he argued that logic arises from action, not language, he accepted that verbal reasoning is a major *vehicle* or medium upon which logical *operations* operate. Thus, evidence demonstrating the importance of linguistic abilities (like the capacity to read and write fluently) in the development of logical reasoning also leaves the theory untouched.

There are relations between the ability to reason in hypothetical, logical terms and literacy. For example, those people from non-literate cultures who have been studied to date fail to give evidence of formal reasoning. Most very deaf children, those who are born deaf or become deaf before learning to talk, eventually solve concrete operational problems but not formal operational ones – that is, problems which involve abstract or hypothetical ideas. I will give some examples of such problems later. The vast majority of them also fail to achieve functional literacy (Wood et al. 1986).

Such empirical relations between literacy and logical reasoning have led some theorists, like David Olson (1977), to conclude that learning to read and write fluently is what makes possible the achievement of deductive logic, both in the individual and in a culture.

In learning to read, children have to *reflect upon* the structures of language. Their knowledge of words, syntax and the process of communication becomes more 'objective' as a result. They read about things that they have never experienced, which may be hypothetical, imaginary and abstract. To achieve this end, they must be able to use and understand language without many of the contextual bases for achieving mutual comprehension that exist in speech. Their attention, in short, is drawn to the *syntax* of language. Because the written word endures, and permits review, analysis and comparisons between ideas that may have been written down at very different times, any *inconsistencies* implicit in text – contradictions, for example – are more likely to come to light than they are from speech, which is fleeting and not memorized *literally*. The increased powers of memory and the greater opportunity for detailed *analysis* of language afforded by written text enables the literate culture to reflect upon and evaluate its competing ideas, histories, opportunities, experiences and so on.

So, an explicit awareness of the formal *structure* of language and an *analytic* attitude to communication, fostered by the written word, combine to produce a stage-like change in thinking. The tests, rules and practices implicit in practical logic, what Piagetians refer to as concrete operational thinking, may now be applied to (hypothetical) propositions found in text. Statements about events or things that have never been directly *experienced* can be tested for consistency or conflict with other statements. Statements thus become *propositions* and reasoning about them becomes more formal and logical.

Piagetians, I suppose, might counter that experiences gained in the course of doing science and mathematics are as important, if not more so, than literacy. Perhaps the achievement of logical thinking is what makes fluent reading and writing *possible*?

Finally, one source of my difficulty in writing this chapter stems from the status of the educational implications that we have been drawing from the theory. As I mentioned in the opening chapter, Piaget wrote little, and that reluctantly, about such educational implications. Many of the recommended applications of the theory have been left to others (e.g. Schwebel and Raph, 1974). I will be arguing in this chapter and the next that the competence, knowledge and skills that we seek to pass on to children through education have little or nothing to do with helping them to learn how to reason in formal, logical terms. Being a competent, intelligent, moral, creative and adaptive member of our culture does not rest on a capacity to think as a logician. But this may not be incompatible with Piaget's theory of mind. Perhaps he would agree that, in everyday social life, logical operations and a sense of logical necessity are not often brought into play. Many people in other cultures lead adaptive, competent lives even though they fail to solve problems involving formal logic. Perhaps the very limited scope of the theory, judged in relation to what is involved in competent everyday activity and reasoning, is why Piaget wrote so little about education. I don't know.

A detailed examination of research into adult reasoning (e.g. Johnson-Laird, 1983), coupled with recent theoretical analyses by philosophers concerning the relation between formal logic and reasoning (Boden, 1979), seem, to my mind, to demonstrate that Piaget's use of formal logic as a framework for analysing rational human thought is of limited value. Trying to describe, assess and foster intellectual competence in children, adolescents and adults has little or nothing to do with helping them to construct or discover general-purpose logical operations. Others, of course, are free to reach their own conclusions.

In the next few pages, we look at the issue of 'logicism' in two ways. We ask if, measured against the rules of (one variety of) formal logic, adults emerge as 'sloppy logicians'. More positively, we explore some reasons why our everyday talk and thought should not be measured against logic at all but studied and described in quite different terms.

Thinking in childhood and adolescence

In the UK, children move into secondary schools at eleven years of age and most begin 'serious' preparation for public examinations two years later. Is this timing purely arbitrary, or are the educational demands placed on children changed at this age because the child is in some way 'ready' to meet new intellectual challenges? As we have seen, children's powers of concentration, their ability to study, pay attention, memorize and think analytically, to talk informatively and listen critically, all develop throughout the early school years (and beyond). Most children in the UK leaving primary school should have achieved a grasp of the foundations of literacy and mathematics and will have developed some ability to listen, as members of a group, to sustained episodes of narrative and explanation. Perhaps, then, most children are prepared for the study of a wider, more formal curriculum.

There are several lines of evidence, which I will consider later, that point to some important 'discontinuities' in the linguistic, communicative and intellectual abilities of children between the ages of eleven and thirteen years. We have already explored evidence for and against the view that an important change in cognitive abilities occurs between the ages of five and seven years. Allied to this were discussions of the issue of 'readiness' for learning and different theoretical perspectives on it. The same set of questions emerges again in this chapter in relation to a proposed change in stage of development that usually occurs in early adolescence. If we decide that adolescents think in different ways from younger children, then it follows that the nature of the educational demands we make of them might quite properly be different in kind.

We must also explore the influences that might lead to the different levels of competence in the child at eleven and thirteen, and ask how far these are part and parcel of the general stream of development or a direct and specific product of education. This will bring us, eventually, to a consideration of the impact of literacy on intellectual abilities. Reading has served, traditionally, as a major avenue for gaining access to information – that is, we read in order to learn, to be informed and entertained. Perhaps the advent of other means of mass communication, like film and video-recordings, promises to obviate the need for text or to render literacy less educationally important than it has been in the past. Or does the ability to read help to foster intellectual abilities and ways of thinking that cannot readily be developed in other ways? That is the question we will consider later in this chapter. First, however, we explore the view that changes in the ability to learn, think and communicate occur as 'natural' developments accompanying the onset of puberty.

Another shift at age thirteen?

As I have tried to explain in earlier chapters, according to Piaget the patterns, regularities and implicit structures that are discovered by the child as she acts on the world lead to the construction of concrete operations. The infant and child, like all of us, are naturally intolerant of ambiguity and paradox. We cannot live comfortably with conflicting ideas about the same phenomenon, nor can we perform two mutually exclusive actions at the same time. Consequently, we are driven to create ever more all-embracing and internally consistent intellectual schemes. Thus, eventually, we construct and understand logic. The adolescent is in the business of constructing a more abstract logic than she entertained during the concrete operational stage – one founded in *formal* operations which permit the application of logic to *propositions* about the world and not simply to 'reality' itself. Thus, the thinking of the adolescent differs from that of the younger child in a number of important respects. Let me cite a few examples to illustrate the main differences between concrete and formal ways of thinking.

An often used example of a problem whose understanding demands the exercise of formal operational thinking involves the workings of the humble beam balance which we met in chapter 4. If children aged, say, nine or ten are asked to discover and formulate the principles which dictate the workings of such a balance, they will probably discover the fact that adding weights to one side of a balanced beam will cause it to tilt. They are also likely to discover, through experiment, that balance can be destroyed by moving a weight on one side further from the fulcrum or by moving one closer to it. When they achieve formal operational thinking, they may appreciate the fact that weight and distance *interact* in very specific ways (according to 'laws') to dictate the phenomenon of balance. They will discover how to calculate and comprehend *abstract* concepts that physicists have chosen to call 'moment' and 'torque'.

But concrete operationalists, though not devoid of intuitions and hypotheses about how beams balance, are not intellectually equipped to discover or grasp such abstract hypothetical concepts. They will appreciate, for example, that reversing a concrete operation annuls any change it brought about; so they are able to restore balance, say, by replacing a weight previously taken off or by moving one back to a position that previously ensured balance. What they *cannot* do, according to Piaget, is discover how to *co-ordinate* the effects of the two *systems* of concrete operations, i.e. one dictating the effects of weight and the other the effects of distance. Each of these systems has *observable* consequences on the behaviour of the balance. But to appreciate how they interact in order to grasp the abstract concept of a force requires a different *form* of reasoning.

Suppose we attempt to teach this concept to concrete operational children by using mathematical procedures. We might introduce them to the concept of 'commutativity'. So, we show them, say, that five units of weight (all objects used are of the same weight for the purposes of this experiment) on one side of the beam create a balance with one unit of weight which is five times as far from the fulcrum as that occupied by the five weights. Thus, we show them that 5(weight) x 1(distance) = 1(weight) x 5(distance). In essence, what we are trying to teach them is that the (constant) *units*, weight and distance, are commutative.

We then proceed to show them, using equations, that a numerical equivalence of the sums of products which represent the state of affairs on the two sides of the beam (e.g. (2 x 3) + (4 x 1) = (2 x 5)) always ensures balance, while any non-equivalence revealed will turn out not to balance. At this point, if they understand, children need not resort to further experiment. Having discovered the *principles* governing the phenomena in question, they realize that mathematics can be used, with certainty, to predict what *would* and *must* happen were they to test out any predicted outcomes. In so doing, they are also beginning to grasp the concept of an 'equation' and its relation to nature.

Understanding the concept of the 'moment' and the relation between the behaviour of the beam balance and mathematical equations demands *formal operational* thinking. A moment cannot be 'seen', it must be *constructed*. It is not a direct product of observation, nor the visible result of concrete actions (like adding weights or changing distances) but an intellectual construct which, when grasped, enables us to *understand* the 'deeper' or more abstract workings of nature. We are driven to create abstract concepts because we cannot make sense of natural phenomena without them. Nature 'obliges' us to construct abstract concepts and formal operations when we seek to understand and control it.

I will return to the issue of teaching and learning such abstract concepts in the next chapter. For the moment, I hope that this example serves to convey some sense of how and why Piaget distinguishes between concrete and formal operations. The former relate directly to perceived and tangible changes that occur as a product of specific actions, while the latter operate on and yield *abstract* concepts like the moment. This example also illustrates another general feature of Piaget's analysis of development. Intellectual demands that children have faced and mastered at one stage of development re-surface in a different form at the next stage. For instance, recall the example used in chapter 3 to illustrate the relation between concepts of number and the activity of counting. Numerical symbols and mathematical procedures only have meaning for a child when she has constructed the concepts to which they refer. Similarly, whilst we may be able to teach children under eleven years of age to manipulate equations to produce the 'right' answers, we should not assume that this means that they *understand* the phenomena that such procedures are designed to 'explain', model or predict. The child has to abstract, co-ordinate and construct in order to appreciate the ways in which such procedures serve to represent reality.

The intellectual divide between *procedural knowledge*, like knowing how to 'solve' equations, and *conceptual understanding*, such as that needed to grasp the connections between equations and physical phenomena, is surely real and important. How many times have we ourselves experienced the phenomenon of manipulating symbols without knowing what it is they really mean? Concepts of 'force', 'mass', 'acceleration', the quadratic function, differentiation and integration – how many children are 'taught' how to do sums and experiments which implicate such concepts without grasping what they mean on *earth*?

More is at stake, however, than agreement over the distinction between procedural skills and conceptual understanding. If one accepts Piaget's analysis, then it follows not only that the pre-adolescent cannot be schooled in the mathematics of physics but also that his or her stage of development militates against all forms of *hypothetical* formal reasoning. Consider, for instance, abstract concepts like 'money', 'profit', 'honesty', 'fairness', 'time', 'socialization', or 'rights' and 'obligations'. Some terms like these probably possess some meaning for primary school children. In some sense they know what it means to be 'honest' or 'fair'. They can grasp some sense of history and the fact that people in different countries live in different ways. But a *formal* and abstract understanding of such concepts, by definition, demands an ability to transcend 'common experience' and the construction of concepts that, while 'embodied' in everyday experiences, like a pound coin or sharing sweets, are not visibly *present* in them. An abstract understanding of economics, for example, involves the realization that our own notion of 'money' is part of only one system whereby people manage to co-ordinate and distribute the fruits, products and costs of their individual labour. Barter, cattle, members of one sex, may all serve the same 'purpose' in different economic systems. The notion that all societies encounter common needs and have to fulfil similar functions in order to survive and reproduce is an intellectual construction, not a 'visible' phenomenon. There may be little in common between the currencies of different lands, but their *equivalence*, in terms of the role they play in social organization, may be grasped if one can think abstractly in terms of certain *propositions* about how societies operate. What is at stake here is not simply whether one believes or subscribes to a particular theory of economics but the intellectual capacity to entertain abstract, hypothetical propositions about the subject which can be reasoned about in a disciplined and logical way.

If one accepts such views on the differences between adolescent and child thinking, it follows that many lessons, whether in economics, sociology, history, geography, psychology or whatever, will be closed to pre-adolescent children whenever they demand an ability to grasp formal notions of equivalence, such as an abstract concept of 'money' that embraces many different fiscal systems. The emergence of such concepts is made possible by the development of abstract, hypothetical and *formal* systems of reasoning.

Logicism

The elegance and power of Piaget's theory stem, in part, from his view that the structure of intelligence develops towards increasing levels of abstraction, generality and stability. Once a given phenomenon can be represented in formal, logical terms, its conclusions are irresistible and enduring. This does not mean, of course, that learning, creativity, new ideas and fresh insights terminate with the development of formal operations. Logic is, arguably at least, not the source of most of our insights. Further, an argument might well be logically compelling yet still prove wrong because the premises or assumptions upon which it is based, from which inferences are drawn, may be at variance with reality. A new discovery or observation, a novel way of looking at a phenomenon (like Newton's perception of the significance of the fact that apples fall from tree to ground, or Archimedes' supposed insight in his bath) may lead to changes in assumptions about the nature of the world and, eventually, to the displacement (sorry, Archimedes) of a previously held theory. That theory may have been logically compelling, but its explanatory power limited because it was based on an assumption or a set of assumptions that neglect what are discovered to be important aspects of the phenomena the theory seeks to explain.

Piaget's view of adolescent intelligence illustrates the divide between logic and reality. Although the adolescent's thinking is *structurally* completed with the achievement of formal operations, it does not follow that learning is at an end, nor does it mean that they understand the world in the same way as more mature members of their society. However, the *form* of adolescent learning is different in kind from that of younger children. The 'task' of the adolescent is, so to speak, to 'play' with logic, to deduce the conclusions that are implicit in her 'theories' of the world and to test these against reality. In this way, she comes to resemble the scientist, who tests the hypotheses and deductions that he draws, logically, from the structure of his theory. Piaget's portrayal of adolescents seems somewhat harsh. In 1940, for example, he wrote:

> Adolescent egocentricity is manifested by belief in the omnipotence of reflection, as though the world should submit itself to idealistic schemes rather than to systems of reality. It is the metaphysical age *par excellence*; the self is strong enough to reconstruct the universe and big enough to incorporate it.

I think this quotation illustrates a number of features of Piaget's thinking about the relation between formal reasoning and reality. In the first place, the fact that he suggests that 'the world should submit itself to idealistic systems of reality' demonstrates that while his view is that intelligence is pushed towards the construction of formal operations, it does not follow that it guarantees the discovery of real-world 'truth'. Logical proof (demonstrating that an argument is coherent and compelling) and the demonstration of empirical or real-world validity (does the same argument work in practice?) are not the same thing. However, formal operations endow the adolescent with the competence to *investigate* the implications and practical value of her ideas. The idealism of adolescents, in this view, is a natural consequence of intellectual development. The task of the adolescent is to recognize that a view of the world that might be true 'ideally' may turn out, on further reflection, observation and experiment, to be 'unrealistic' and unworkable. So Piaget offers us a particular 'image' of adolescents and, perhaps, helps us to understand why, to more mature minds, they often appear over-idealistic and hypercritical of the adult world.

If we accept Piaget's theory of development, one embraces not only his description of what children and adolescents can and cannot do, but also the very important argument that the course of intellectual development is constrained by the construction and emergence of logical operations. So, to evaluate the theory, we must question the view that children are developing towards logical competence and the implication that mature thinking can be analysed in terms of formal logical operations. Let me explore this very difficult question with a few examples.

One might accept the 'logic' of the following chain of reasoning yet know full well that the conclusion it entails does not make 'sense': 'All blue whales have pink feet. This is a blue whale. Therefore, it has pink feet.' To employ an argument analogous to that used by Chomsky when demonstrating the 'independence' of grammar from meaning, one could say that such examples show that 'logic' and a sense of logical necessity (i.e. given certain assumptions, certain inferences must follow) on the one hand, and what we might call 'common sense certainties' on the other, are different things. There are surely many good zoological and linguistic reasons why whales cannot have feet and still be called whales, and I doubt if any of us have ever seen a 'real' whale with pink feet. But this lack of 'sense' does not detract from the 'logic' of the argument. Logic, then, is not synonymous with making 'sense' and cannot be 'reduced' to it.

Other 'logical' conclusions are not, however, so easily evaluated (Wason and Johnson-Laird, 1972). For example, look at the four symbols in figure 7.1. You are shown four cards, displaying a red square, a blue triangle, a consonant and a vowel. You are also informed that each card shown has a geometric shape on one side and a letter on the other. You are told that if a card has a *red* square on one side, then it must have a *vowel* on the other. Which cards need to be turned over in order to test this rule? First, note in passing that in everyday problem situations one would probably find it much easier and more efficient to turn over the lot than to spend time thinking about the 'logic' of the problem!

Suppose I say that you must turn over the cards bearing the square and the vowel. Is that recommendation logically sound? No. Although most adults who have been tested with this problem say that this *is* the correct answer, they are, logically speaking, wrong. Why and how? Well, the rule does *not* imply that all vowels must bear a red square on

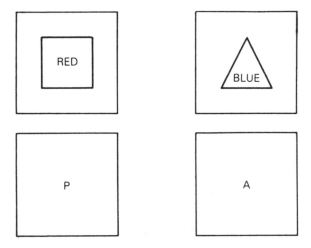

Figure 7.1 Wason's card-turning experiment

their obverse side. Consider, for example, the statement, 'If a man is a Texan then he is tall.' Does it follow that any tall man must be a Texan? No. Nor does it follow that if you are told that a red square has a vowel on the other side then it must be the case that a card bearing a vowel must bear a red square. However, if a red square *must* have a vowel on its obverse side, then it follows that a card bearing a consonant must *not* have a red square on its other side. If it did, we would have discovered a red square which did *not* accompany a vowel, and this would violate the rule. So, we must turn over both the card bearing a red square (no consonant on the other side) and the one bearing a consonant (no red square on the other side).

Given that the vast majority of adults (some of them trained logicians!) who have been tested with this problem get it wrong, does it follow that most of us are 'illogical', at least some of the time? Does it also mean that Piaget's analysis of the destination of intellectual development is indefensible? These, as I have already said, are hard questions.

First, let us not lose sight of the fact that adults not only get logical problems 'wrong' but that they usually give the *same* logically incorrect answers. If most of us agree in our conclusions, does it not seem plausible to suppose that our verbal reasoning is governed by certain 'rules' and that these are different from those implicated in formal logic? *Why* do we answer such questions in the way that we do? This is a difficult and controversial issue and I do not intend to spend a great deal of time on it. However, let me consider a few possibilities which suggest that we are not 'obliged' to assume that logic provides a good 'theory' of how people normally think. Let me illustrate this argument with evidence drawn from studies of formal reasoning undertaken with the help of people from non-schooled, non-literate societies.

In a very extensive study of the Kpelle, a Liberian tribe, Cole and his colleagues (Cole et al., 1971) posed verbal problems of the following type to adults.

Experimenter	At one time spider went to a feast. He was told to answer this question before he could eat any of the food. The question is: Spider and black deer always eat together. Spider is eating. Is black deer eating?
Subject	Were they in the bush?
E	Yes.
S	They were eating together?
E	Spider and black deer always eat together. Spider is eating. Is black deer eating?
S	But I was not there. How can I answer such a question?

(some time later, after the question had been repeated)

S	Oh, oh black deer was eating.
E	Black deer was eating?
S	Yes.
E	What is your reason for saying that black deer was eating?
S	The reason is that black deer always walks about all day eating green leaves in the bush. When it rests for a while it gets up again and goes to eat.

The answers given by the adult Kpelle to this and other 'logical' problems suggest that drawing 'logically compelling' conclusions, seemingly so 'obvious' to mature members of our sort of society, is not a common practice for the Kpelle. On first sight, one might argue that the Kpelle are 'illogical' or unable to reason rationally (indeed, many early anthropologists reached such conclusions about 'primitive' minds). However, a more serious analysis of what the Kpelle are doing in trying to 'make sense' of this, for them, curious social encounter with a foreigner, together with a consideration of our own 'failures of logic' such as those just illustrated, sheds a different light on the issue.

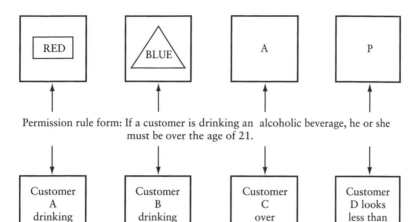

Figure 7.2 Wason's card-turning problem related to a pragmatic reasoning problem concerning legal permission to drink alcohol

First, as Cole and his colleagues point out, the Kpelle assess the plausibility of what is said and, eventually, agree to give an answer to the (repeated) questions by testing them against their 'common sense' knowledge. They do not see the problem in 'formal' terms, to be tested against some rules of logic, but as a description of an (implausible) event or situation whose *plausibility* is to be assessed. The conclusions reached reflect the *rationality* of what is said measured against what is likely to happen in Kpelle experience. Looked at in this way, the Kpelle way of reasoning is not totally dissimilar to our own.

Logic and reasoning

Such observations lead us to three main questions. Why and how do the 'rules' of logic and the practices of everyday reasoning diverge? If the rules of logic do not provide a valid model of mature, everyday reasoning, how do adults usually solve such problems? How, if at all, do children's powers of reasoning differ from adults'?

Let us start to consider the first two questions with another example. Consider the problem, given in figure 7.2. This has a 'similar' structure to that invented by Peter Wason. The lower problem in the figure has a similar structure to the upper one. However, people usually answer the two problems differently. In the lower one, they are unlikely to turn over the card B (no permission needed to drink tea) nor C (since someone of this age has permission to drink alcohol). They are likely to turn over D, because someone less than eighteen does not have permission to drink alcohol. The 'equivalent' cards in the Wason task are illustrated in the upper part of the figure.

People generally find this task much easier than Wason's version and appear to reason about it 'more logically'. Why? Well, this problem can be solved by assimilating it to everyday experience. It is an example of what Cheng and Holyoak (1985) term a 'pragmatic-reasoning schema': a set of rules or conventions which are socially prescribed to define the conditions under which certain goals or activities can legitimately be pursued. The particular problem illustrated relates to a 'permission schema', and its contents and structure are familiar to people whose cultures impose regulations on the consumption of alcohol. It provides a natural and familiar means for solving the problem.

Sometimes, assimilation of a problem to such rules yields inferences which are both pragmatically acceptable (i.e. consistent with social conventions) and logically true (i.e. similar to the inferences validly drawn when such statements are treated as propositions). However, it is not the case, say, that most of us reason 'illogically' when solving Wason's problems and 'logically' when we reason about Cheng and Holyoak's. Rather, in each case we assimilate the problem given to rules based on pragmatic, everyday reasoning; it is just that in one case these rules and schemas generate answers which happen to coincide with logic, whereas in the other they do not. When college students were given prior training in the rules of deductive logic, they did not show much improvement on Wason's problem. Even though, in some sense, they 'knew' the appropriate rules, they did not apply them, continuing to interpret the problem by assimilating it to schemas based on everyday reasoning.

So, the theory that we often assimilate 'logical' problems to pragmatic reasoning schemas helps to explain why, in some circumstances, everyday reasoning and logical thinking diverge. As we saw in Donaldson's studies of young children, and those undertaken by Cole and his colleagues of the Kpelle, performance on experimental tasks can also be explained by the way in which people, young and old, try to assimilate such problems to their everyday knowledge. They attempt to solve them by reference to analogous situations drawn from common experience.

Although such studies illustrate how and why everyday, pragmatic reasoning differs from logical rules and whilst they invite a rejection of

Problem: What conclusions can be drawn from the following premises:

No children are adults. Some adults are scientists.

No children are adults.

child
child
child

---

       adult
       adult
       adult

Some adults are scientists.

Model 1

child
child
child

---

       adult = scientist
       adult = scientist
       (adult)   (scientist)

Model 2

child
child
child   = scientist

---

       adult = scientist
       adult = scientist
       (adult)

Model 3

child   = scientist
child   = scientist
child   = scientist

---

       adult = scientist
       adult = scientist
       (adult)

Conclusion: Some scientists are not children.

In Model 1 an (arbitrary) number of children is imagined in a separate mental category from adults (since no children are adults). Model 1 is also consistent with the premise that some of the adults are scientists. However, Model 2 is also consistent with the premises since it is not said that no children are scientists. Model 3 , in which all children are represented as scientists, is also logically consistent with the premises. But, since some adults are scientists, it follows that some scientists are not children. A common type of error is to accept the first mental model as the only possible one and not to construct all possible models which are consistent with the premises.

Figure 7.3   Mental models and logical reasoning

'psycho-logic' as a basis for understanding how people think, there are still theoretical arguments about the nature and origins of 'formal' reasoning.

Johnson-Laird (1983) argues that adults tackle abstract logical problems such as that illustrated in figure 7.3 by constructing 'mental models' of the state of affairs they describe. On some problems, however, construction and consideration of only a single model will not suffice. Thus, asked to say what inferences might legitimately be drawn from the propositions that 'No children are adults' and 'Some adults are scientists', a model which is likely to spring to mind has the structure represented in Model 1 of figure 7.3. The model implies that we mentally 'separate' a set of tokens to represent children and a set representing adults. The use of brackets is a convention indicating that, in our mental model, we acknowledge that there are adults who may not be scientists and scientists who may not be adults. But this is not the only model that is consistent with the premises. A little reflection will reveal the fact that Models 2 and 3 are also consistent with them and support the conclusion that since some adults are scientists, there must be some scientists who are not children.

Johnson-Laird's theory of mental models helps to explain why some 'logical' problems are easy because they only demand the construction and interpretation of one model, whilst others, like that just illustrated, are difficult because we need to construct and evaluate several different models which are consistent with the information given.

Johnson-Laird's theory is 'domain independent' in the sense that such models can be constructed without any reference to the meaning or plausibility of the problem content. However, the kind of problems studied by Cheng and others demonstrate that we typically draw upon specific knowledge derived from everyday experience in reasoning and, hence, illustrate that the way in which adults typically think in such situations rests on the meaning of problem content. Herein lies the source of debate about the extent to which logical reasoning involves the achievement of domain-independent ways of thinking. The argument here is not about whether or not we use formal rules of deductive inference (all agree that we do not) but whether our mental models culminate in the discovery or construction of domain-independent, or 'decontextualized', ways of thinking.

Halford, as we have seen, builds upon the concept of mental models and upon the view that reasoning involves drawing analogies from everyday experience to construct a theory of how children think at different stages of development.

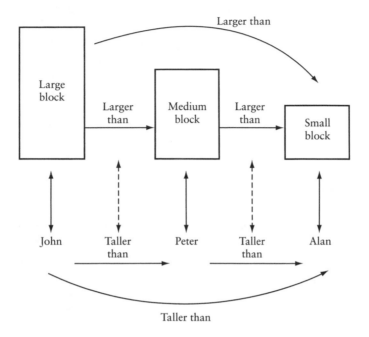

Figure 7.4   Transitive-inference problem: reasoning by analogy

Children may fail to solve problems which entail drawing inferences because they are too impulsive and accept the first model that comes to mind as the only possibility. They may also lack effective resources and/ or strategies for memorizing the results of their model-making. However, Halford, as we saw in chapter 3, argues that children are also able to process less information simultaneously than adults. Recall his argument that, like adults, children attempt to solve problems such as 'Who is tallest if John is taller than Peter and Peter is taller than Alan?' by constructing mental models and that these rest on analogues of previous experience. Thus, any concrete experience that a child has had which involves the construction of ordered sets or lists can be exploited as the basis for a model. For instance, if the child has had experience in sorting sets of three blocks into a size-ordered array, this can be used to solve the verbally stated problem by mapping each element of the verbal problem onto a mental model based on this analogue of everyday experience (see figure 7.4).

If, however, children are more limited than adults in how much information they can process, either because their speed of mental processing is slower (Chase) or because they have more restricted processing capability (Halford), then we should not expect them to solve logical problems like those in figure 7.3 because they do not possess the mental resources to build models which incorporate all the necessary relations. Thus, on this view, whilst both adults and children share the same ways of reasoning, *what* children can think about changes with age as the capacity to construct increasingly complex mental models develops. And if this general view is correct, then there are marked discontinuities in cognitive development.

Language in talk and text

Other students of child development, as we have seen in preceding chapters, emphasize the role of language and schooling in the formation of abstract reasoning. In chapter 1, we saw that Vygotsky argued that schooling and instruction involve the transmission of scientific ways of thinking and inculcate in children the development of 'self-regulation'. He also argued that learning to *read* leads to important and far-reaching changes in the *nature* of children's knowledge and use of language. In becoming literate, children do not simply learn 'another way' of communicating or a new 'code' for representing speech. Rather, writing and reading make novel demands on children and involve them in learning how to exploit new *functions* of language. Text is not simply speech written down, nor is writing merely the substitution of visible symbols for acoustic ones. Both reading and writing involve ways of communicating that transform the nature of children's knowledge of language and lead to more analytical ways of thinking.

Let me outline, briefly, the main aspects of Vygotsky's argument in the light of recent studies of children learning to read and write. In chapter 5 I introduced and tried to illustrate the way in which linguists traditionally analyse the nature of language. The term 'phoneme' refers to the theoretical 'units' of speech sounds which form the building blocks of languages. Morphemes are units of meaning comprising one or more phonemes. Some morphemes, recall, like 'dog', 'cat', 'green', are termed 'free' in that they can stand alone and still convey meaning, whilst others, like verb inflexions and markers of plurality, are only meaningful when combined with free morphemes.

The analysis of 'prosodic' features of speech drew our attention to phenomena, like stress, intonation patterns and pauses, that help to convey emotion and emphasis, to differentiate questions from statements, commands from requests, and to convey attitudes like sarcasm, irony and secrecy. The rules that govern how morphemes and words are structured to form grammatical utterances are labelled rules of syntax. Semantics and pragmatics refer to the analysis of linguistic meaning. They include, among other things, the study of how the meaning of utterances is influenced by factors like the relationship between the speaker and hearer and the social context.

Although, as far as I am aware, Vygotsky did not undertake his analysis of the differences between spoken and written language in this terminology, I don't think it will do any marked injustice to his views to reformulate them in such terms. This strategy also has the advantage of allowing me to relate his pioneering analysis to contemporary studies of literacy and its development.

Literacy and decontextualization

When two or more people are engaged in face-to-face conversation, communication between them rests on much more than the words they use and any grammatical rules they exploit, as we saw in the previous chapter. When children begin to write, they are likely to find the process difficult and demanding, not only because writing makes unusual demands on their bodily control, manual dexterity and powers of perception and attention – though such things in themselves are difficult enough. They also face a new range of *intellectual* challenges. Unlike face-to-face conversations, where responsibility for mutual understanding is *shared* between speakers and listeners, solitary writing requires children to bear all the burden of responsibility for making what they are trying to mean intelligible and accessible to their reader(s). When they talk with others, they know *who* it is that they must make sense to. If what they say is ambiguous, unclear or unintelligible, then the person or people they are talking to may ask questions, seek clarification or ask for elaboration. Writing on her own, however, the child must learn how to *anticipate* likely sources of misunderstanding and take them into account, when she may not know *who* it is she is writing to or for.

Looked at in this way, the effective writer must act both as the presenter and the receiver of communication. It should come as no surprise to find, then, that children who *modify and correct* what they write as they go along usually write more intelligibly and grammatically than children who do not edit their own work. Self-correction, as I have argued before, is evidence of the fact that children are involved in self-instruction towards the achievement of goals. They realize that what they write may not necessarily be comprehensible or readable. They do not assume that because *they* themselves know what they mean by what they write, other people will. They are 'de-centring' or 'disembedding' their ideas as they read what they write to evaluate its accuracy and accessibility.

Externalizing our ideas, imaginings, thoughts and feelings in such a way that they are put into a verbal context, sequenced in an understandable way and expressed unambiguously in a written medium is *not* a simple extension of what we do when we participate in conversations. In the last chapter, I outlined some of the problems that children face when they are asked to narrate their experiences and views. In these circumstances, children have to 'take on the role of the listener', de-centre or de-contextualize their thinking. We might expect, therefore, that such experiences provide a bridge into literacy. This idea has been put forward by a number of students of child language and literacy (e.g. Perera, 1984; Romaine, 1984). The work of Brown and her colleagues referred to at the end of the previous chapter also offers some indirect evidence for this view. Children who were poor at information-giving, a special and demanding form of narrative, were academically weak and, one suspects, not reading well. As far as I am aware, however, no strong evidence exists to prove that skill in producing and understanding coherent and intelligible narratives predicts levels of literacy. So the proposed connection between the two remains speculative.

Even in situations that demand giving and listening to extended narratives, however, the people involved are visible and audible to each other. A listener's reactions, both verbal and non-verbal, serve as feedback regarding his or her understanding of what is being said. Writing is a far more demanding occupation, since such feedback is non-existent. The absence of an audience, then, and the responsibilities this confers on the writer, make the task of learning how to write rather difficult for children. But the divide between spoken and written language is much deeper than differences in the nature of the audience involved.

The written and the spoken word: learning to read

Everything written in English can ultimately be 'de-composed' into the twenty-six letters of its alphabet. Analysing spoken English into its constituent phonemes, a more difficult and uncertain business, reveals forty-four elements (Perera, 1984), although estimates by different linguists vary between thirty-seven and forty-nine. Clearly, then, there can be no simple relationship between English as it is written and spoken. Consequently, when learning to read, children are not simply uncovering a simple code for translating speech into print. In fact, the relation between elements of speech (phonemes) and their 'correspond-ing' elements in written language (so-called 'graphemes') is consider-ably more complex than this suggests (see Underwood and Batt, 1996, pp. 15ff). Imagine the same word being spoken by a person with a Welsh, Yorkshire or Cockney accent, by a young girl or a grown man. When asked to write the word (given that they are literate enough), each will produce the same pattern of letters. But the nature of the sounds they make in producing the same word will differ considerably.

We do not normally speak in mechanical, clearly articulated words. The 'same' word in the context of different utterances, even when spoken by the same person, may *sound* quite different, yet it looks the same in print. Put another way, while the 'same' phoneme may sound very different when produced in different contexts by the same speaker or by different speakers saying the same thing, a corresponding *written* account of what they say may be 'identical'.

It is clear, then, that the task of reading and writing differs from speaking and listening in that literary forms are more uniform and less context-sensitive than speech. Indeed, as Perera points out, the 'neutral-ity' and the greater uniformity of the written word renders it less prone to 'prejudice'. Imagine the same words written by an Englishman, a Scotsman and an Irishman. Does their writing betray their dialect? Similarly, a thing written many years ago may still be readable today even if the way in which words are pronounced has changed. But from the child's point of view, learning to read may present many challenges and surprises since the uniformity of written text is bought at the cost of a rather poor 'fit' with speech. Although this is not an appropriate place to discuss how our 'commonplace' conceptions of things like words, sentences and language itself have come about, it is interesting to note that some linguists argue that modern 'theories' of language are based on experiences with *written* language and, as such, are *not* the proper place to start thinking about the nature and structure of *speech*. When we help children to learn to read, we are doing more than teaching a new and neutral 'code' for representing what they already do with and know about speech. Rather, we are introducing them to radically new ways of thinking about *language* itself.

Written English is 'irregular' in many respects. Put another way, how things said are written down does not always follow general rules: there are many exceptions, as Perera illustrates. So, for instance, the 'same' sounds may be written differently ('plain' and 'plane'; 'an ice cream', 'a nice cream'; 'attacks on buildings', 'a tax on buildings'). Words like 'the', which, as we have seen, serve several different linguistic functions, sound and are known to the mature, literate ear as the 'same' word that performs 'different' functions. Karmiloff-Smith suggests that for young children, the different uses of words such as 'the' may seem, like 'plane' and 'plain', to be two words that happen to *sound* similar but have different meanings. There are certainly enough 'homophones' in English (words that sound the same but are written differently) to reinforce such an assumption. It is possible, then, that children's discovery of the fact that the same word has several functions is *facilitated* by learning to read and write.

When one considers the way in which different accents and dialects treat many words, it also becomes apparent that speech sounds that are very similar in some dialects may be pronounced differently in others. Consequently, children who use different dialects may face a different set of 'puzzles' as they learn to read depending upon the nature of the 'matches' and 'mismatches' between their dialect and the written form (Perera, 1984, pp. 212–15).

Learning to write and read confronts children with challenges because they have to take greater responsibility than they do in conversation for making what they communicate intelligible and understandable outside a shared *context*. It also demands that they discover a range of often irregular relations between the nature of speech and the structure of written text. Literacy, Vygotsky argues, leads children to develop more explicit and objective 'theories' of language and helps to develop their self-regulatory abilities as they learn how to plan, monitor and evaluate their writing. Being able to write well demands the capacity to take other people's perspectives and states of mind into consideration and the ability to set up, in language, situations that, in conversational exchanges, may be 'given' and 'taken for granted'. The cost is a good deal of hard work.

The story does not end here. There are several other ways in which spoken and written language present quite different challenges to children. Let me consider some of these, briefly, before returning to the issue of the relation between literacy and intellectual development.

Prosody and punctuation

Written text provides a very poor and weak representation of features of spoken language such as intonation, stress and pause patterns which, as we saw in the last chapter, play an important role in verbal communication. Using written symbols like full-stops, commas and colons, writers can provide some guidance to their readers about how they intend their text to be organized and read. But the repertoire of symbols available to them is limited. Other punctuational tactics, like the use of underlining, italics or upper-case letters, can be used to give some sense of where the writer's intended *emphasis* lies and how she intends a sentence to be 'parsed' (analysed) and interpreted. Consider, for instance, the effect of 'simply' inserting a comma into 'I wasn't shopping seriously' to create 'I wasn't shopping, seriously'.

This example is illustrative of a general principle which, according to Frazier and Rayner (1982), governs the way in which expert readers process text. They suggest that, as each word is read, the natural tendency of the reader is to attach it to what has already been read if the result is grammatically acceptable. So, without the comma, this principle would dictate that the word 'seriously' is an adverb which refers to the manner in which shopping was undertaken. With the comma in place, it tends to 'block' this reading suggesting that 'seriously' is something of an aside. Thus, what seems like a simple piece of punctuation turns out to exert a marked effect on the most likely interpretation which is 'read into' the text by a good reader. The power of Frazier and Rayner's suggested principle and the important role of punctuation is also illustrated by the following sentences (Underwood and Batt, 1996, pp.154ff):

Because her sister loves to teach kids learn.
Because her sister loves to teach, kids learn.
While Pam was washing the baby started to cry.
While Pam was washing, the baby started to cry.

Thus, in constructing sentences in which two or more ideas or proposition are linked, the simple comma breaks up text in such a way that a writer can help the reader to avoid confusion and ambiguity. In the first sentence, the natural tendency is to read 'kids' as part of the clause 'her sister loves to teach'. Only when the reader comes to read 'learn' does it become apparent that this ''attachment' is not possible and that 'kids' is part of a new idea. Similarly, the presence of a comma inhibits the tendency to read Pam as 'washing the baby'.

Where, in speaking, the use of pauses and intonation would help to overcome any such potential ambiguities, in writing, rather tiny marks on paper carry crucial information to dictate how a sequence of words will be read. Becoming literate involves more than learning how to 'translate' written words into spoken ones. Reading demands *interpretation*. Similarly, a well-written text demands a sense of how the strategic use of words, grammar and punctuation is likely to affect a reader's interpretation of what is being written. As Perera points out, the fact that many features of tone of voice and manner of speaking cannot be conveyed by prosodic means in print has also led to the evolution, largely for literary purposes, of an enlarged vocabulary for describing and conveying manner of speech. When we hear talk, we know whether a person is shouting, whispering, insinuating, implying, hinting, or whatever. Even when we listen to verbal accounts of what other people have said in conversation and narrative, the speaker can convey *how* something was spoken by imitating the tone of voice used. In text, however, we must use special *words* (like 'whispered') to get such messages across. The reader must make inferences about how a written text should be analysed to reveal its structure and has to decide where stress and emphasis should be laid. Expert readers usually perform these functions 'automatically' and without conscious awareness of how they do so. But children have to learn *how* to 'interact' with text in order to interpret its writer's intended meaning.

As we delve more deeply into the nature of the expertise needed to read and write fluently, we will explore the view that it is by developing the ability to analyse and interpret written text that children acquire special linguistic and intellectual skills. These, I will argue, are often called upon in psychological tests of children's intellectual, linguistic and communicative abilities. They are also demanded by teachers when they confront children with lessons involving descriptions, explanations and questions about abstract, unfamiliar and hypothetical topics. First, however, we need to look in more detail at the different demands placed on children by the spoken and written word. What else, in addition to new vocabulary, skill in interpretation and a more 'objective' knowledge of their own language, do children learn in the process of becoming literate?

Consider what is involved in deciding on the meaning of what look like 'simple' written sentences such as 'John was washing the car'. As I will explain in more detail later, a reader, reading this sentence in isolation, is likely to 'sense' an emphasis on the 'clause-final' element (the car). However, imagine this sentence being *spoken* in a number of ways, with a different word being stressed in each case. Suppose, for instance, stress is laid on the word 'John'. Here, we could imagine the utterance serving as a *denial* of a previous utterance, such as 'Peter was washing the car'. Now suppose stress is laid on the word 'was'. This might imply the denial of another assertion – one which suggested that John was *not* washing the car. Emphasize 'washing' and we can imagine the utterance serving to deny yet another suggestion, perhaps that John was servicing it. Repeat the exercise with the addition of a single symbol, a question mark, 'John was washing the car?', and another range of possible meanings can be constructed.

As expert readers, we are able to construct or imagine a variety of spoken versions of what, in print, is an identical piece of text. In connected text, of course, such sentences would be embedded in longer sequences of written utterances which might lead one 'naturally' to a particular interpretation. An example might be: 'Mary had said that because Peter was washing the car, he couldn't help her with the dishes. But Alice said that she had been duped. Peter was sitting in the garden, sunning himself. John was washing the car.'

Hardly riveting narrative and, as we shall see, stylistically poor written text, but I hope it serves to illustrate a number of aspects of the reading process. Only when a reader is able to take in and memorize relatively long stretches of text does it become possible to estimate where any intended and important *stress* might lie. Expert readers seem to formulate such interpretations 'naturally' and, like the chess Grand Masters discussed in chapter 4, they are not usually aware of the processes that underlie their expertise.

When skilled readers encounter a particularly difficult text, they may resort to reading aloud or may start to talk themselves through the text. In so doing, they can try out various interpretations, perhaps experimenting with different prosodic possibilities to see what they 'sound like' and mean when location of stress is varied. Usually, however, skilled reading takes place at a rate of about 300 words per minute, approximately twice the speed of normal speech. It seems unlikely, then, that expert readers usually read by 'talking' to themselves. Precisely what they *do* do when they read is still not clear. It seems reasonably certain, however, that they do not convert visual symbols into sub-vocal speech (Underwood and Batt, 1996 pp. 124ff). Rather, their interpretation and understanding of what they read seems to involve so-called *direct* processes – that is, they seem to pass 'straight' from visual symbols to construct an interpretation of the meaning of what they are reading.

Writing, planning and self-regulation

I have just considered some of the problems and demands reading and writing create because the written word is a poor medium for representing prosodic information. However, the expert writer, by employing a number of techniques special to the creation of coherent written texts, can overcome these limitations. Similarly, an expert reader can, so to speak, 'reverse' these writing techniques and conventions to reconstruct a writer's intended meaning. Both the reader and the writer, as I have said, are usually unaware of the nature of their expertise. Systematic analysis and research are needed to help to articulate what it is that they *do* yet cannot describe. By making *explicit* what is implicit in their performance, we gain an objective understanding of the tasks, demands and problems that children have to face when we try to teach them to read and write fluently. Perhaps, following Vygotsky, such knowledge may also help to make us better teachers.

Competent speakers of English are strongly predisposed (without realizing it) to lay stress on the final element in a clause, what linguists refer to as 'end focus' (Perera, 1984, pp. 193–5). So in 'I went to the village on the *hill*' or 'I gave my daughter a *ball*' or 'Houses are so *expensive*', stress is normally placed on the words in italics. Of course, the 'rules' governing the distribution of stress, as we have seen, are waived or changed in some contexts. So, for instance, if the second statement was said in response to 'You gave your son a ball for his birthday', stress would probably fall on the word 'daughter'. Note, however, how stilted or pedantic such a response would seem. Far more likely, I suspect, would be something like 'No, not my son, my *daughter*'.

A writer, confronted with the task of 'communicating' a stress on adverbials, objects and complements, can capitalize on the fact that, in English, these parts of speech occur clause-finally. For example, 'I gave Daddy a sweet' (stress on the direct object) or 'I gave a sweet to Daddy' (stress on the indirect object), 'I went to town yesterday' (stress on an adverb of time), 'Flowers are so beautiful' (stress on a subject complement). The writer, wanting to stress such words, can 'rely' on the natural tendency of a reader to 'read in' stress at the appropriate places, and so needs no 'special' tactics to get her prosodic message across. But as Perera points out, when writers wish to stress other features – specifically words which form grammatical *subjects* or *verbs* – then they face problems (in English, that is: other languages have different rules and, no doubt, create a different set of literary problems).

When we speak, we can draw attention to nouns, pronouns, verbs or any word in an utterance by *stressing* them, making them relatively louder or longer, say: 'The *queen* gave him a pen', 'Someone really *ransacked* the house'. Underlining, bold type, italics can be used to convey the fact that the conventional foci of stress (i.e. the object 'pen' and the object 'house') are not the words to be stressed. However, there are also *syntactic* techniques for achieving the same ends. For example, if we write something like 'He was given a pen by the queen' or 'Last night, the house was really ransacked', the desired emphasis is achieved by ensuring that the final clause element is the word to be stressed.

Perera also demonstrates how, by including 'interrupting constructions' into a sentence, a writer can highlight a key word that might otherwise appear unstressed. For instance, if instead of writing 'The students' results were outstanding' we write 'The students' results, to their surprise and delight, were outstanding', we achieve stress on the word 'results' as well as on the final word 'outstanding'. So the way in which our 'habits' of speech lead us to place stress on a very specific element of the structure of utterances (i.e. clausal position) produces challenges to the writer and demands the 'invention' and fluent control over a variety of structural literary devices. These help to ensure that the organization of what is written corresponds to what the writer wishes to communicate. To appreciate and comprehend the message, of course, readers also have to have command of the 'conventions' involved.

Let us consider a specific example of a linguistic structure that is 'special' to the written medium. Some forms of the passive voice are very rare in speech and seldom addressed to children – utterances like 'Mary was kissed by John' or 'He was given a pen by the queen', for example. Mastery of such structures appears late in language development. When I was at school, I was told that one employs the passive voice in 'science' writing in order to depersonalize written narrative and to make it more 'objective' (e.g. 'A bunsen burner was placed under the retort'). However, linguistic constructions like the passive voice (there are many other examples) serve a much more general and important function than this. They enable a writer to make her reader's task easier. She can construct her sentences in such a way that her intended stress lies where her reader tacitly 'expects' to find it. In the examples just given, the use of a passive construction serves to highlight 'John' and 'the queen', enabling the writer to lay stress on words that, in 'active' sentences like 'The queen gave him a pen', would not be read as stressed. Thus, the use of a passive construction enables a writer to emphasize words that would not stand out if she were to use more common, spoken forms.

The phenomenon of 'end focus', the term given to our tendency to emphasize final clause elements, coupled with the absence of rich prosodic cues in written language, create a need for a range of grammatical devices in print that are not necessary in speech. The fact that young children do not often use or readily understand certain grammatical forms (like agented passives) should, then, come as no great surprise. Such constructions only become really *functional* when the child becomes *literate*.

Another general 'principle' governing the way in which we talk and write to good effect is the tendency to 'save the best until last'. The major 'theme' or most important or dramatic idea to be written should come as close to the end of what is said as possible. Contrast, for instance, 'The weary refugees dragged their precious burden onward towards the tiny light' with 'Onward, towards the tiny light, the weary refugees dragged their precious burden'. If the thing to be highlighted, the theme, is the precious burden, then the second version, where it appears at the end of the utterance, brings it into focus more dramatically than the first version, which better serves the purpose of highlighting the 'tiny light' towards which the refugees are moving. In speech, dramatic effect and highlights can be achieved by many verbal and non-verbal means. The listener, moving in rhythm with the speaker, can be caught up in the flow of words and actions to anticipate and share any drama. The writer, however, often needs to employ grammatical structures, punctuation and ways of sequencing ideas which, though rare in speech, offer the means for the achievement of her literary ends. If you are anything like me, you will now start to analyse this text to discover that some of your problems of comprehension can be attributed to my writing. (I think that's where I intended to place the stress.)

The eleven to thirteen shift: a linguistic perspective

By the time they reach their thirteenth birthday, many children are using grammatical forms in writing that are structurally more complex than those typically found in their speech. For the majority of younger children, the opposite holds true: their speech is grammatically more complex than what they write. As children develop and learn through adolescence, the efficiency and accuracy with which they can absorb information from the written word progressively exceeds what they can take in from listening to speech. For example, shown a video-tape of a discussion between two students and verbatim written accounts of the same events, sixteen-year-olds recall more if they read than if they watch. More interesting, perhaps, is the finding that the written word was superior for all the children tested, regardless of their reading ability (Walker, in Perera, 1984, p. 163).

Studies of the development of spoken language reveal the emergence, during the years of schooling, of a range of complex grammatical constructions that are also involved in the creation of effective and dramatic writing. As she learns to read and write, the child's speech begins to 'inherit' structures encountered in written text. Consider, by way of an illustration, four 'stages' that have been discovered in children's attempts to utter complex sentences. I have taken this example from Romaine (1984).

This guy he owns the hotel he went to B.
This guy that he owns the hotel he went to B.
This guy that owns the hotel he went to B.
This guy that owns the hotel went to B.

Note too, as Karmiloff-Smith discovered with children's emerging command of determiners, how children again pass through a period of dysfluency and 'over-marking' (in this case, with the 'redundant' use of pronouns) before they perfect the mature form of words.

In the preceding chapter, we considered various lines of evidence which suggested that children's developing skills as narrators and informants emerge through the years of schooling. The child who is fortunate enough to achieve fluent levels of literacy has at her disposal a whole new range of words, linguistic structures and skills in planning which enable her to create interesting, informative, dramatic and *coherent* narrative. Such a child may draw upon and exploit two powerful bodies of expertise. On the one hand, she has her *voice*, perhaps the most versatile of musical instruments, rich in prosodic melody and embedded in bodily movements that help to orchestrate her interactions with her listeners. On the other, she has command over a range of literacy devices and structures that can be exploited in speech to make what she says dramatic, flexible, variable, versatile and, should she so wish, fast and efficient.

No matter what accent or dialect a child happens to speak, the achievement of fluent literacy, powers of narration and the ability to use language informatively offer her the same rewards. Speech that is, so to speak, parasitic on written language should not be dismissed as merely 'posh'. It provides children with a range of skills to help make what they say clear, interesting and informative.

Once functional levels of literacy are achieved, a reader is able to read text at a much faster rate than she normally hears speech. The grammatical structures in written language tend to be more 'compressed' (and, therefore, structurally more complex) and more varied than those of speech. The amount of 'redundancy' in written text (such as the frequency with which the same idea is repeated or paraphrased, for example) is usually lower than it is in speech. Unlike a listener, who is likely to be subjected to the frequent pauses, hesitations and false starts in verbal communication that provide the *time* that she needs to comprehend, the expert reader may proceed at her own pace. She may review, anticipate and skip, consulting, if she chooses, paragraphs, pages or chapters in advance of where she has read to in order to get some sense of where the writer is 'going' (in academic texts, I always read the index and bibliography first). All these features of reading provide opportunities for greater efficiency and autonomy for a reader than a listener.

But what of children who do not reach levels of literacy that are deemed functional? Surveys of the levels of literacy in the USA suggest that around eighteen million American adults have reading ages below nine years. The Bullock Report (commissioned by the UK Government) estimated that two million people in England and Wales are unable to read beyond this level. In practical terms, these figures give some measure of functional illiteracy – of adults who are unable, for example, to read tabloid newspapers, recipes and other everyday aids to communication and social adjustment. People who leave school with reading ages of eleven years or less have not made the 'shift' we have just been discussing. It would be interesting to know what consequences this has on their language and communication skills. Are they, like the children in Brown's studies, likely to face problems in narration and in information-giving situations? I don't believe we have the necessary evidence to reach such a conclusion, but it seems a fair bet.

The reasons for this state of affairs, for illiteracy, are, of course, the subject of heated debate. I do not intend to consider the issues involved in detail here. Many articles and books have been dedicated to the subject (Perera, 1984, provides an excellent source of information) and there is not sufficient space to rehearse all the evidence and arguments here. However, I hope that the studies of language, communication and literacy that we have considered in this book will help to provide a psychological perspective on, and a framework for thinking about, such issues. Let me point out briefly how the ideas and findings we have been discussing can be used as a guide to help evaluate various theories of reading difficulties.

Becoming literate

We have just been considering a number of linguistic, social-communicative and intellectual demands that we might expect a child to encounter in reading and writing. It seems reasonable to suppose that difficulty in meeting one or all of these might explain why some children have problems in achieving literacy. In view of the fact that the written code relates to speech, albeit by a complex set of rules, we would predict that children who have problems either in hearing or in analysing the sound patterns of speech will face reading problems because they lack the necessary basis for learning how to 'encode' written symbols into speech sounds. Because written language does not map onto speech in any simple or direct way, we might also expect that these children will find it hard to use the written form in order to 'learn' about the structure of speech and language because the relations between the two forms of communication are too complex. Deaf children, as I have already said, face enormous problems in learning to read and only a tiny minority reach the eleven-year-old level when they leave school.

We have to remind ourselves that 'analysing' our own speech into the 'elements' that make possible the creation of a readable visual code is an intellectual achievement, not just a natural product of the ability to talk. Speech is an activity which fulfils purposes and needs, like informing, asking, refusing, explaining, negotiating and so on. The activity of speaking is, for most people most of the time, an automatic affair. In learning to read, language becomes an *object of attention or study* and, I have suggested, becoming literate affects the nature of our language and our conceptions of it. In learning how to write and read, children have to think 'objectively' about speech and learn how to analyse and, in writing, to represent it.

By this, I do not mean to imply that pre-literate children or non-literate peoples lack an explicit knowledge of their own language! Children's intuitive sense of the nature of language, though no doubt influenced and made more explicit by learning to read, probably comes about by quite different developmental routes, such as nursery rhymes, stories, word play and language games. For example, as part of a wide-ranging study of British children's play and folklore, the Opies (1959) documented a variety of children's play on words. Participation in these activities demands a subtle sense of the structure, functions and ambiguities present in language at a number of levels. Consider the following examples and reflect on what they imply about young children's implicit knowledge of language.

> Masculine, Feminine, Neuter,
> I went for a ride on my scooter.
> I bumped into the Queen
> And said, Sorry old bean,
> I forgot to toot-toot on my tooter.

> Sir is kind and sir is gentle.
> Sir is strong and sir is mental.

> Adam and Eve and Nipmewell
> Went in a boat to sea.
> Adam and Eve fell out,
> Who was left?

Although I have been stressing the role of literacy in the development of children's awareness of language, such widespread and often ingenious word games demonstrate that children's knowledge of the sounds, structures and functions of language is made evident in playful, everyday activity. Reading may help to sharpen, extend, develop and discipline their knowledge and use of language, but such word games, puns and the like suggest that most children are aware of the music of sound and the many possibilities (usually somewhat vindictive in intent) afforded by the rich ambiguity inherent in language and communication. Anthropologists have observed children in non-literate cultures playing games which also derive their fun and their sting from a play on words or from 'abuses' of language's more 'serious' functions (e.g. Schwartzman, 1978, p. 383). These observations, coupled with studies of word and sound play in babies and pre-school children, suggest that becoming aware of and exploiting the possibilities offered by the ambiguous and metaphorical nature of speech is not simply a product of learning to read. Rather, an awareness of the various 'levels' and functions of language revealed in children's word play may be an important preparation for the achievement of literacy itself, as we shall see in the next section.

Rhyming, alliteration, reading and spelling

The central importance of the quality of young children's awareness of the sound structure of speech in learning to read and write is now firmly established by research. If children lack what has been termed 'phonological awareness' (Hulme and Snowling, 1994) or fail to make the 'phonological connection' (Bryant et al., 1990) then they are destined to find learning to read and write difficult.

In a series of investigations, Peter Bryant and his colleagues (e.g. Bryant and Bradley, 1985; Goswami and Bryant, 1990) have shown that children whose phonological awareness is less acute than is usual for their age lag behind their peers in learning to read. If, for example, a school child has difficulty in detecting simple rhyming patterns in words, she is unlikely to progress in reading and writing. On rhyming tasks where they are asked to identify the 'odd one out', like 'man' in sets of words such as 'bun, fun, man', poor readers struggle. Similarly, these children will also find alliteration tasks difficult, not being able to detect similarities and differences between sets of words like 'pin, pun, pan and ban' on the basis of the features of speech which form the initial word sounds.

Such tasks can be used not only to demonstrate that children with poor phonological awareness are likely to become backward readers but also to provide a basis for remedial instruction in reading. Bryant and Bradley gave children with poor levels of phonological awareness extensive and intensive experience in activities which encouraged them to pay attention to rhyme and alliteration and to the connections between such speech sounds and their written counterparts. Their interventions showed both that children with poor phonological awareness can be helped to improve their sensitivity to the structure of speech sounds and that, when this occurs, their reading and spelling also improve.

Other intervention studies reinforce this conclusion. They, too, have demonstrated that where children can be helped to sharpen their phonological awareness, improvements in reading and writing follow (e.g. Lundeberg, Frost and Petersen, 1988; Cunningham, 1990). It seems clear from research in this area, then, that reading builds upon the child's intuitive knowledge of the structure of speech. Whilst there is evidence to show that learning to read helps children to articulate (!)

and extend that knowledge, phonological awareness developed before the child starts learning how to read and write seems to be a necessary basis for discovering the complex mappings between spoken and written language.

Spelling and syntax

If we were to ask six- or seven-year-old children to tell us what a verb is, I doubt that many would be able to! And yet, as we saw in chapter 3, they have acquired rules such as those involved in using verb inflexions like '-ed' and '-ing'. They use these spontaneously to mark the fact that they are referring to actions that have been perfected or are in progress, as in 'walked' and 'walking'. So, whilst children may have no explicit knowledge of what a verb is, their systematic use of language shows that they possess implicit knowledge. Their speech is structured in such a way that only words that serve as verbs in the language are used in conjunction with such verb-specific rules.

We have just seen that learning to read and write capitalizes on children's implicit knowledge of the phonological structure of their language. How might we decide if the same holds true of their implicit knowledge of grammatical structure, such as how to use verbs? Bryant, Nunes and Bindman (in press) offer us one means of finding out. In a detailed, three-year study of the ways in which children learn how to spell, they provide us with some important insights into how young children use their knowledge of the structure of spoken language to discover the rules of written English, as we shall see next.

Sound and shape: /d/, /t/ and '-ed', 'd', 't'

Imagine hearing words like 'said', 'slept', 'kissed', 'soft', 'spelt', 'helped' and 'boat'. How different are the /d/ and /t/ sounds involved? They are obviously distinct in their written manifestations (i.e. '-ed', 'd' and 't') but difficult if not impossible to distinguish when heard by the naked ear. How do children come to master the spellings of such words?

When children first start to write, it is often difficult to see any systematic structure, i.e. evidence of rules, in their spelling. Bryant, Nunes and Bindman refer to this as the 'pre-phonological' stage. As children start to discover the correlations between elements of spoken and written language, they enter the second, 'phonological' stage. Working on the not unreasonable assumption that there are totally regular and general rules for mapping speech sound onto written shape, children at this stage produce written tokens such as 'helpt' for 'helped' and 'kist' for 'kissed'. These spellings suggest that children assume, intelligently, that writing down words which contain the same sound patterns (/d/ and /t/) involves using a common written token (e.g. 't').

Later, in Stage 3, children discover that the sound in words like 'walked' is written as 'ed'. Now it is quite common for them to over-generalize the sound-writing correspondence rule to create written patterns such as 'speled' for 'spelt', 'sleped' for 'slept' and 'sofed' for 'soft'. As we find much earlier in development when children are learning how to talk, words that were initially produced correctly are later spelt non-conventionally. This happens because children over-generalize a new rule that they have discovered. The spellings that children produce at Stage 3 include an extension of the rule 'If you hear "d/t," then write "ed" ', both to irregular verb forms (e.g. 'sleped' for 'slept') and to non-verbs (e.g. 'sofed' for 'soft').

Stage 4 is theoretically crucial. Here, children stop over-generalizing 'ed' for 't' in relation to non-verbs but still show generalization of the rule 'If you hear "d/t" write "ed"'' to irregular verbs. To explain this result, we have to assume that, by this stage at least, children are making use of some implicit knowledge of the distinction between verbs and non-verbs. Finally, in Stage 5, they begin to clean up their spelling of irregular verbs as their performance converges on the conventions of mature usage.

Stage 4 children have already had experience of reading and writing. In learning a new and more explicit 'code' for language, they may, for the first time, come to some intuitive grasp of the verb/non-verb distinction. Equally plausible, however, is the hypothesis that children bring an existing (albeit tacit) knowledge of such syntactic distinctions to the task of learning how to read and write. How might we decide between these two possibilities?

Bryant, Nunes and Bindman addressed this issue as follows: if children show some knowledge of the syntactic distinction between verbs and non-verbs *before* they master the spelling conventions involved, then it is reasonable to suppose that grammatical awareness provides the foundations for learning to spell, not vice versa. Further, if this linguistic awareness forms an important basis for learning how to spell, and some children, but not others, develop this knowledge early on, then we should be in a position to predict which children will find spelling relatively easy and those who will struggle. Conversely, if learning how to spell tokens such as 'ed' and 't' occurs *before* children show an awareness of syntactic distinctions, then we would expect early success in learning how to spell to predict later developments in children's syntactic awareness.

The 360 children involved in these investigations were aged between six and eight years and each child was followed up for three years. The fact that the design was a longitudinal one (i.e. involved tracking individual children over time) enabled Bryant and his colleagues to explore the long-term relations between children's syntactic knowledge and their spelling and to address these questions.

One set of tasks used to assess the children's knowledge of verb processes was based on the use of 'sentence analogies'. These work as follows. An adult first reads out loud to children a sentence such as 'Tom helps Mary'. This is followed by saying 'Tom helped Mary'. Thus, the tense of the verb is changed from present to past. Children are then given sentences like 'Tom sees Mary' and asked to transform these in the same way (i.e. to 'Tom saw Mary'). Similarly, children who have listened to past tense forms such as 'John threw the ball' followed by 'John throws the ball' are then asked if they can convert 'Jane kicked the ball' to 'Jane kicks the ball' by drawing an analogy with the first pair of transformed utterances.

In learning to read words which rhyme, as we saw earlier, children use their knowledge of rhyming to recognize the similarities, or analogies, between words which have similar features when written. Now, if children have tacit knowledge of verb processes, they may also be able to draw analogies between such pairs of sentences.

Children succeeded in such sentence analogy tasks involving verbs before they achieved Stages 4 or 5 in learning to spell. In other words, they showed an awareness of verb processes in speech *before* learning how to write them down.

Although most children in Bryant's studies achieved Stage 5 on various spelling tasks by age eight, some did not. Those who did not, as we might expect, displayed a poor grasp of the underlying syntactic structure of verb formation in the spoken tasks and, hence, lacked the necessary linguistic awareness to learn the spelling rules.

Putting all this together, then, it suggests that children's awareness of basic sound patterns in the structure of speech and their intuitive knowledge of grammatical categories pre-dates and makes possible their early achievements in writing.

Beyond the sentence

Perera's analysis of the demands of reading and writing suggests that reading involves more than gaining proficiency at the phonological and grammatical levels. One study which illustrates yet further demands which reading makes on young children was undertaken by Oakhill, Yuill and Parkin (1986). They worked with seven- to eight-year-olds who were asked to listen to short stories of the kind illustrated below:

> The car crashed into the bus.
> The bus was near the crossroads.
> The car skidded on the ice.

They were then asked to say if either of the following implications or 'inferences' was compatible with what they had heard:

> The car was near the crossroads.
> The bus skidded on the ice.

Since the car crashed into the bus which, the story leads us to believe, was near the crossroads (when the car crashed into it), then the first inference seems plausible. The second is less so since there was no link between bus and ice in the story.

Two groups of children took part in the study and they were matched for age and for performance on a sight vocabulary test and on the ability to read words aloud. However, they differed in tests of reading comprehension with one group of 'poor readers' having a reading comprehension age of just over seven years whilst the good ones achieved reading ages of around nine years. The children's reading comprehension abilities were mirrored in their ability to draw inferences from spoken narratives. Those who found it difficult to work out which inferences might plausibly be drawn from a story were relatively poor at reading comprehension. Since they were matched on tests of sight vocabulary and word-reading ability, it would seem both that comprehension involves more than decoding skills and that differences in the ability to draw inferences from spoken narrative influence reading comprehension. This latter point is supported by the fact that training which helped to improve skills in drawing inferences also resulted in improved reading comprehension.

Self-regulation and reading comprehension

Perera demonstrates in some detail how the structural complexity of written language varies according to the specific communicative purpose it serves. Who is a text written for and what are its readers intended to gain from it?

There are marked differences in the organization and structure of text written for different purposes. The style and grammatical structure that are relevant to the creation of an *aide-mémoire*, a letter written to a friend, a novel or historical text, or a worksheet outlining a scientific procedure, differ in many features, gross and fine. Similarly, the intellectual demands involved in reading and writing such very different texts vary. How stringent are the requirements made on the writer's ability to envisage and take account of her intended audience in each case? What background knowledge will a reader need to possess in order to make sense of what is written?

Perera suggests that many children find reading and writing difficult in more demanding contexts because they lack the relevant experiences that help them to understand both the reasons *why* different types or 'genres' of writing exist and the way in which these variations in the purpose of the intended communication lead to demands for different styles of writing and, in consequence, entail a knowledge of special linguistic devices. Whereas children may understand some of these purposes (e.g. writing to a friend) and may draw upon their everyday experiences to make sense of the demands involved, they may not have listened to a historical text or episodes of scientific discourse, nor realize why and how people write about such things. Evidence about the effects of home circumstances on children's reading development demonstrates that access to books at home and the experience of being regularly *read to* are positive indicators of likely progress (Clark, 1976). Perhaps the fact that we do not typically read more *academic* texts to children means that they do not develop any intuitive sense of what such things *sound* like. Perhaps if they did, processes of self-instruction, working towards a goal that is intuitively recognizable, might be set in motion. I don't think we know.

A somewhat similar line of thought has motivated recent attempts to help children with reading and writing problems in the United States (Palincsar and Brown, 1984). This work, motivated by Vygotsky's theory of development and by his writings on literacy, started from the assumption that some children fail to advance beyond the initial stages of reading because they do not know how to 'interact' with text – i.e. they do not become actively engaged in attempts to *interpret* what they read. Briefly, the intervention techniques used involved bringing into the open, making public and *audible,* ways of interacting with text that skilled readers usually undertake automatically and soundlessly. So, for instance, the teacher discussed a text with a child, asking aloud the sorts of questions a sentence or paragraph might provoke. The teacher might speculate aloud about what is likely to come later in the text or puzzle over an ambiguity and ask how it might be resolved. The child would later be encouraged to play the 'teacher's role' and to work alongside and discuss texts with other children. Children taught in this way made marked progress over a handful of formal teaching sessions. They were in the seventh grade (this means they were aged around twelve to thirteen years) and were described by their teachers as having severe problems of reading comprehension.

At the beginning of the study, the children involved were found, on tests of reading comprehension, to be in the bottom 7 per cent of their year. After the study, their success rate on independent tests of comprehension rose from 10 per cent to 85 per cent success, near average for their grade level. How far and to what extent such methods might work for all children with reading problems we do not know. It is important to note that these children were described by the researchers as having 'decoding skills' (or 'word-attack' skills) that were normal for their grade. Whether the same teaching techniques would work for children with problems of decoding we must doubt. However, it is worth noting that even though the children were able to decode, their teachers persisted, before the study, in attempts to teach these skills. The teachers were not attempting to work on the *real* problems facing the child. Their implicit theory of what literacy entails, and hence their views on the nature of reading problems, presumably did not extend to the processes we have been discussing in this chapter.

The argument underlying these studies is that some children who find difficulty in learning how to 'interact' with text can learn how to do so if these normally unobservable processes are made an *explicit* part of what is taught. Following Vygotsky, the argument is that the children in this study progressively 'internalized' self-regulatory activities until these became an automatic part of their own reading. This is why their own performance, both on tests and in class, improved.

In more recent and extensive investigations, Brown, Ferrara, Campione and their colleagues have extended this approach (termed 'reciprocal teaching') to classroom intervention studies involving large numbers of children across the age range (e.g. Brown and Campione, 1990). They report significant effects not only on children's reading comprehension but also on levels of academic achievement across the curriculum.

There are now many educators and researchers, including those involved in teaching both reading and mathematics, who are currently emphasizing the need for teachers to lay greater stress on the activities involved in skilled self-regulation, or 'metacognitive' understanding. If heeded, the demands such pleas make on teachers are formidable. I will explore some of the justifications for making such demands, and the implications they have for the process of education, in the remaining chapters.

Conclusions

Literacy and Logic

Some anthropologists and psychologists have looked to the achievement of literacy within cultures and individuals to explain stage-like changes in logical reasoning. Looked at in one way, they would seem to be offering a solution to a problem that does not exist. We have looked at evidence in this chapter which suggests that Piaget's account of formal reasoning has not withstood the test of time and experiment. If theorists such as Johnson-Laird and Halford are correct, then psychologic fails to provide a useful framework for explaining mature reasoning on 'logical' problems and, hence, cannot be a suitable vehicle for explaining what it is that children are developing towards. Thus, we need no theory to explain how literacy and logic might be related in either culture or development.

However, before trying to close the door on this issue, we need to reconsider (at least) two questions. Big questions such as the role of logic in human cognition, like bad pennies, have a habit of turning up when we think we are rid of them, as history shows. First, there are two different aspects of Piagetian theory that need to be distinguished. He argued *both* that the nature of children's concepts changes with age *and* that we should use logic as a framework for understanding those changes. Even if we reject the utility of his account of logic, we still need to explore the value of the idea that the nature of concepts and conceptual structures undergoes transformation with age and experience. Both Halford and Case, for example, maintain that the complexity of such structures does change with age and leads to developmental discontinuities in cognitive functioning.

Models of the mind, like Johnson-Laird's, suggest that reasoning about certain classes of logical problems prove difficult because, to solve them, we need to construct and evaluate a number of different mental models. Such demands tax, and may over-load, our cognitive capacities. Historical and theoretical analyses of scientific discovery provide a number of examples which demonstrate how the use of cultural inventions such as diagrams and systems of signs (like written numbers) made possible new discoveries and supported new forms of reasoning (e.g. Cheng and Simon, 1995). The mental models that Johnson-Laird and others propose that we use in reasoning about 'logical' problems place a considerable load on cognitive processes. It is still conceivable that, historically, the use of artefacts such as pencil, paper, diagrams and written language was necessary for the discovery and formulation of both complex mental models and the rules of logic themselves. Such artefacts may or may not change *how* people think but they certainly change *what* can be thought *about*. Consequently, the general claim that cultural inventions, such as new systems for representing and modelling the world, can lead to changes and transformations in cognition (stage-like or not) is still open for debate.

These issues form a major theme of the next chapter.

Literacy and development

Learning to read and write makes many demands on children, some of which we have explored in this chapter. The evidence suggests that many (though by no means all) come to schooling possessed of the linguistic awareness needed to forge connections between spoken and written language. Their implicit knowledge of the phonological and grammatical structures in their spoken language is, in most cases, enough to enable them to learn the foundations of reading and writing. The fact that children are able to draw 'inferences' from spoken narrative (to go 'beyond the information given') also enables them to construct models of the situations depicted in stories in which what is said is elaborated to make connections not explicitly mentioned. In the previous chapter, we looked briefly at the ways in which children are able to imagine why people act in the way that they do on the basis of their emerging ability to understand and explain relations between other people's mental states and beliefs on the one hand, and their likely courses of action on the other. Here too, knowledge constructed in the course of coming to understand and explain their everyday experiences provides the foundations for the interpretative 'scripts' or frameworks that can later be exploited in 'reading for meaning' (Feldman, 1992).

If we interpret Vygotsky's theory as implying that it is only by learning a written representation of their language that children (and cultures) first come to develop intuitions about the structure of their speech and syntax, then we must reject it. However, I have tried to argue that such intuitions are further articulated and elaborated through the processes of learning to read and write, citing evidence which suggests that knowledge of the structure, content and use of language are extended with mastery of the printed word.

Some children soon fall behind others in their peer group in learning how to read and write. Given the several demands that we know children face in becoming literate, we might expect that their problems could have one or more origins (see also Clay, 1985, 1993; Clay and Cazden, 1990). Some display little or no awareness of the phonological structure of their speech; others perform poorly on tasks which demand a grasp of fundamental grammatical distinctions in language. Yet others, who keep pace with their peers in discovering how to connect spoken and written tokens, find reading comprehension difficult because they, unlike others of the same age, cannot or do not draw the intended 'inferences' from written text or fail to 'regulate' their interactions with written texts successfully. In each case, however, we have found some grounds for optimism that many of these children do have the potential, given appropriate experience, to overcome such problems. Why they experience problems in the first place is difficult to say. I will be considering some possible explanations in the final chapter.

8

The mathematical mind

Progress in our knowledge of children's mathematical development has been substantial over recent years, with major contributions and insights arising out of psychological, educational and cross-cultural investigation. A combination of experimental, survey and observational studies has both enriched our knowledge of the nature of mathematical understanding and served to inform and challenge theories about how children think and learn in various mathematical domains.

Research into children's mathematics learning also provides the most appropriate single context within which to explore the strengths and weaknesses of Piaget's theory in some detail. His view that logic underpins mathematical development, and related claims about stages of development, will come under close scrutiny.

Cross-cultural studies of children's mathematical abilities, which we will also consider in some detail, reveal both similarities and important culture-related differences in the educational experience and mathematical achievements of children. These help us to explore and evaluate claims from social-constructivism about the formative influence on development of culture, systems of signs, and instruction.

Investigations of mathematics learning in and out of school have been used to challenge contemporary cognitive theories and to question the explanatory value of theoretical concepts such as 'decontextualization' and 'abstraction'. Such studies, as we shall see, also raise issues about the value and relevance of mathematics instruction in school.

In the second part of the chapter, some of the common misconceptions that children entertain about mathematics are presented and examined in the light of theories of intellectual development. We also discuss how and why many children seem to make slow progress in learning mathematics and leave school barely numerate, and consider some of the pedagogical implications of theory and research.

So, regard this chapter not simply as an introduction to the psychology of children's maths learning but also as an arena in which we can compare, contrast and criticize different theoretical perspectives on human development.

PART 1: Theory and research into mathematics learning

In the preceding three chapters, we have been considering a range of issues revolving around the development of language and communication. But language is only one of the systems of symbols that provide tools for thought. Piaget, as we know, considers action and the operations that are constructed through it, not language, as central to the development of intelligence. Vygotsky adopts a somewhat different stance: as we saw in chapter 1, he argues that the developmental origins of language and thought are separate. Although he agrees with Piaget's stress on the importance of activity as the basis for practical intelligence, he argues that, around the third year of life, language intersects with non-verbal thought to form the foundations for the development of verbal reasoning and self-regulation. From this time on, language starts to play a fundamental, formative role in intellectual development. However, non-verbal thinking remains. Not all symbolic activity requires language. Art, arithmetic, skill in sport and many other activities may proceed adaptively and intelligently without the involvement of verbal thought. Consider, for example, Einstein's views on the relations between language and creativity revealed in the following quotation. His distrust of premature attempts to *verbalize* new thoughts is echoed in the writings of many creative individuals (e.g. Ghiselin, 1952):

> The words or the language, as they are written or spoken, do not seem to play any role in my mechanism of thought . . . in thought are certain signs and more or less clear images which can be 'voluntarily' reproduced

and combined ... the elements are, in my case, visual and some of muscular type ... conventional signs and words have to be sought for laboriously only in a secondary stage.

The fact that some forms of activity, including some ways of thinking, do not implicate language does not necessarily imply that they are not influenced by communication and teaching, however. In considering the relation between *communication* and the development of knowledge, we have to discuss more than the issue of speech and its role in thinking. For example, some deaf children with a very limited command of spoken and written language perform as well as the best of their hearing peers on tests of mathematical ability (provided that the tests used are not couched in complex written language). Even so, the average deaf child leaves school in the UK at sixteen performing in mathematics at a level typical of twelve-year-old hearing children (Wood et al., 1984). Although there is evidence that deaf children do not seem to require 'inner speech' or verbal reasoning to do very well in mathematics, the vast majority lag well behind their hearing peers. They find learning more difficult because the process of *communication* with their teachers is difficult. Their acquisition of *knowledge* is consequently impeded (Wood, 1986). However, even with hearing children there is reason to suppose that communications with *their* teachers also generate considerable though less severe problems in lessons on mathematics, as we shall see.

Statements of discontent with the standards achieved in mathematics have been voiced in many tongues. The following quotation, from a Dutch scholar (Wolters, 1986), echoes sentiments expressed by people in many other countries:

> At the present time there is no teacher who can actually say that all is well with the teaching of arithmetic.
>   There are far too many children who dislike arithmetic or worse, children who think it is a 'stupid' school subject. With relatively few exceptions, this situation is quite general and has to be taken for granted.

Mathematics, for many, is difficult to learn and hard to teach. Perhaps one of the reasons for the popularity of Piaget's views on intellectual development was the reassurance it seemed to offer in identifying children's 'natural' capacities to construct the fundamental conceptual basis for mathematical thinking. This view, as we shall see, has received a good deal of support from recent research. The objection that instruction too often involves attention to procedures and a neglect of conceptual understanding can be seen as a criticism of many approaches to the teaching of mathematics. But it also inspires some hope that better methods can be invented. Piaget's emphasis on the importance of relevant activity and self-directed problem-solving as the proper developmental basis for more abstract conceptual understanding is shared by many students of child development, educational theorists and teachers. Where agreement ends, and argument begins, is on the importance of instruction, both informal and formal, at home and in school, in helping children to make mathematical *sense* of their experiences. How active should teachers be, for example, in aiding a child in his problem-solving and his conceptual constructions? Very active, as we shall see.

Bruner (1966a, 1966b, 1971) argues that instruction is a necessary requirement if a child's spontaneous activities are to be transformed into symbolic, rational thinking. He shares Piaget's view that action is the starting place for the formation of abstract, symbolic thinking (like that involved in solving mathematical equations, for example) but does not agree with the notion that the child is *unable* to grasp the conceptual relations between practical activity and more abstract levels of thinking before a particular stage is reached. Rejecting Piaget's emphasis on logical operations and, with this, the view that the evolution of symbolic thinking is constrained by stages of development, Bruner offers a different perspective on both the process of coming to *know* and the nature of learning. He distinguishes between three 'modes' in which knowledge is expressed or 'represented'. He labels his three modes of representation 'enactive', 'iconic' and 'symbolic'. Enactive representation is similar to Piaget's notion of practical intelligence. For example, a child who can group sets of objects according to one or more criteria, say by size, colour or shape, is displaying *enactively* a level of understanding of classification. If children can imagine or draw pictures that *depict* the outcome of sets of actions, then they are using *iconic* representations. Basically, the defining characteristic of this form of 'knowledge representation' is that the representation created must bear a *one-to-one* correspondence with the event or activity that it depicts. I will give some concrete examples later.

Numbers themselves, verbal and written symbols, do not bear a *one-to-one* relationship with the entities they depict. Similarly, symbols like '+' '×' and '−' do not, in themselves, bear any *perceptual* resemblance to the operations to which they refer. And, like function words in language, they possess several different meanings as mathematical symbols, depending upon the sort of problem involved (e.g. dividing whole numbers or dividing fractions) (Skemp, 1971). Like Piaget, Bruner conceptualizes the development of knowledge in terms of growing 'abstraction' and arbitrariness in the symbolic content of thought, but he does not share Piaget's view that different modes of representation only become available to children at specific stages. So, for instance, whereas Piagetian theory implies that children will only be able to perform tasks involving the use of abstract hypothetical propositions or algebraic notation when they reach the stage of formal operations, Bruner argues that much younger children can, given appropriate instruction, learn how to both perform and understand such intellectual activities.

The issue of logic and its role in explanations of children's mathematical understanding has been a focus of much international research over the past fifteen years or so and will figure prominently in this chapter. We will see that much of what Piaget had to say, particularly in relation to the logical relations that underpin mathematics learning, has received support from research. However, it has also become clear that, by largely ignoring the role played by cultural inventions such as written symbol systems, his theory is silent about important determinants of mathematical knowledge. In this respect, Vygotsky's socio-historical account provides an important explanatory dimension in understanding how symbol systems and cultural practices play a vital role in mathematics learning.

In the first sections of the chapter, I will outline some of the major achievements of recent research into the young child's understanding of the foundations of mathematics.

Counting and one-to-one correspondence

In chapter 3, I mentioned studies by Donaldson and her colleagues which challenged Piaget's theory of stages and demonstrated how a child's ability to solve problems was influenced by factors such as task familiarity, the language used and the manner in which the experimenter introduced and explained the problem. Particularly relevant here is the controversy over the role of one-to-one correspondence (see figure 3.1) in the child's understanding of number, which I only touched upon in that chapter.

In relation to the child's development of early number concepts, there are two main issues raised by Piaget's theory. The first concerns the age at which children master the concept of one-to-one correspondence and the second is about the role played by this concept in the development of number understanding. There is still considerable debate about the first question (age of onset). Thus, there is some evidence that babies are able to differentiate sets of one, two and possibly three objects from each other. This had led some theorists (e.g. Gelman and Meck, 1983) to suggest that knowledge of one-to-one correspondence has its roots in innate mechanisms. However, the nature of these mechanisms and the exact role that they play in development of number concepts remains unclear and controversial (see Nunes and Bryant, 1996, for a recent treatment of this issue).

More positively, there is now extensive evidence to show that the child's ability to master Piaget's tests of one-to-one correspondence do lay down some of the necessary (i.e. logical) foundations for counting, adding and subtracting (Fuson, 1992). Let me try to illustrate the outcome of many investigations with a thought experiment. Imagine a situation in which, alternately, you are given a red and then a green ball to place in a bag. You are given many balls and lose count of how many of each you have received. Losing count (or not counting at all) does not matter provided that you know (a) that for every red ball you were also given a green one and (b) that no balls have been added or taken away from the bag. Young children who cannot count will accept that such 'equal sharing' (i.e. a one-to-one correspondence between elements in each of two sets) coupled with the fact that nothing is added or taken away justifies the conclusion that two sets are the same. They come to this realization *before* they learn that they can use numbers and counting to compare sets. Thus, Piaget's view on the developmental primacy and necessity of one-to-one correspondence in learning to count has been vindicated. However, as we shall see in the next section, learning to count and compare sets of objects is only the first step in a surprisingly long journey in the child's mastery of counting, adding and subtracting.

Counting: out, on, up and down!

A five-year-old child is asked to add 5 and 2. Eventually, of course, she will come to 'know' that the answer is 7, recalling it from memory. However, as Piaget argued, the developmental pathway stretching from learning and reciting the names for numbers (sometimes called 'number poems') through to recalling the answers to simple addition sums is a long one and involves more than simply 'practising' or learning the 'fact', say, that $5 + 2 = 7$.

Initially, our five-year-old may solve such addition problems by using tangible materials, such as sets of blocks or her fingers, to provide a concrete 'model' of the problem which she can use to count. Thus, she counts up to 5 on her left hand as she says, 'One, two, three, four, five'. She then looks at her right hand and, counting from the little finger, says, 'One, two'. Next, she touches the two outstretched fingers of her right hand against first the thumb and then the fingers of her left, saying again, 'One, two, three, four, five', and she then counts 'six, seven' as she touches each of the two outstretched fingers of her right hand. She then announces her answer: 'Seven!'.

What can we infer from this, quite complex, performance? Well, the child – let's call her Laura – seems able to count up from at least 1 to 7. By uttering each count name as she first extends her fingers and then by counting them all, Laura also shows some sense of one-to-one correspondence between count names and the fingers which she uses to 'model' the act of counting. She does not miss out any number, nor does she use the same number twice in sequence. She is showing some number sense. However, note the fact that she had first to count out each number (5 and 2) and then proceeded to *count out* all of the set of 7.

Contrast Laura's performance with that of another child, Mary. She, given the same problem, puts up two fingers of her right hand and simply says 'six, seven'. This child *counts on* from one number. Mary's performance suggests that she has a more advanced sense of number than Laura. Technically, she displays some grasp of the *cardinal* nature of number. A number can be used both to refer to an element in the set of fingers counted (the *ordinal* use of a number name) and, at the same time, to refer to the *set* of objects counted (the *cardinal* use of a number name). Put another way, the ordinal use of count names resembles the use of numbers as adjectives (e.g. one finger, two fingers . . . etc.) and the cardinal use is akin to a noun (a name for the set of objects counted). Because Mary 'counts on' in this way, she is showing some understanding of the fact that a number, like 5, is not simply a word that is said as part of a series (1,2,3,4,5) but can also represent a *set* of five things (much as you might look at a 5p coin and know that it is equivalent to five single pennies). I will come back to the significance of this later.

Suppose we ask Mary to add together 3 and 6. She extends fingers in turn and counts 'four, five, six, seven, eight, nine'. We pose her several other problems of a similar kind and discover that she often counts on from the first number given to perform the addition, whether or not this is the smaller of the two numbers in the sum. So, given 5 plus 3 she counts on from 5. Asked to add 4 and 7, she counts on from 4, and so on. Contrast her performance with that of six-year-old Sam who, no matter in what order any two numbers are given to him, always counts on from the larger of the two. Thus, asked to add 4 and 7 he counts out 'eight, nine, ten, eleven'. Sam has developed what has been termed the 'MIN' strategy.

Sam's performance suggests that he has grasped two further things about numbers and counting. First, counting on from the larger number requires less computational *effort*. In recognizing this fact, however, he is also indicating that he can co-ordinate his thinking about the relative sizes of two sets (i.e. a set of 4 and a set of 7) in order to recognize which is the larger. Hence, he is giving evidence of having mentally constructed the beginnings of a 'number line' along which sets of different sizes are structurally related. None of this needs to be 'conscious' knowledge, of course. In Vergnaud's (1982) terms, such knowledge in practice is an example of 'theorems-in-action'.

The developmental changes in children's grasp of number concepts illustrated by these three imaginary case studies are quite general ones and the counting strategies illustrated (along with others) have been found in many studies. Theoretical debates about how we should interpret such developmental changes have proved long and complex. One possibility is that children pass through a series of clear-cut stages as they construct their understanding of number. This view, however, has been seriously undermined by recent research undertaken, amongst others, by Siegler and his colleagues (e.g. Siegler and Jenkins, 1989).

Prior to Siegler's studies, many investigators had attempted to unravel the early stages of mathematical development by testing large numbers of children at different ages to discover the average age at which the different strategies emerged. Siegler has challenged this approach to theory development. Large-scale studies of children at different ages (so-called cross-sectional designs) can provide a general overview of the nature and timing of changes in children's thinking. But using average scores based on grouped performance measures can also lead to false inferences about how individual children change over time. Siegler's group undertook longitudinal investigations of small groups of children in which each child was observed on a regular basis over a relatively long time period (hence the term 'longitudinal'). Interviews with children began before any evidence of the MIN strategy was found in their counting.

Children were presented with sets of problems similar to those illustrated above. Most were addition sums that could be solved by counting using the fingers of two hands to create models of the problems but, occasionally, the child was presented with 'challenge' problems, such as 21 + 2, which are hard to solve by counting out. Children were aged about five at the start of the study. A number of general findings emerged from the interviews.

First, it was never the case that a child at any age would use only one strategy to solve addition problems. The same child might even use a different method on the same problem on different occasions. One striking thing about children's use of strategies was that all were usually successful with addition problems involving small numbers (i.e. less than 10). Typically, children were 80–90 per cent correct whatever method they used. Why, then, do they bother to develop new strategies?

Few children managed to solve the challenge problems; the numbers involved were usually too large to handle using fingers. They were included in the investigation to see if, as 'conflict' theories of conceptual change predict, these were the problems on which children developed new strategies and exhibited their first use of the MIN strategy. This was not the case. All the children studied first adopted the MIN approach on problems that they could *already* solve using one or more other methods. This, according to Siegler, implies that learning is *success* driven rather than motivated by cognitive conflict. In this regard, his account agrees with Karmiloff-Smith's theory of representational re-description (chapter 5) and the role of success and *pattern* finding in promoting developmental change.

When children discovered MIN, it might have been expected that they would immediately drop their other, laborious strategies in favour of the more efficient method. This was not the case. Rather, children continued to use several strategies, MIN included, for some time. What, then, motivated them to eventually drop their early, counting methods? Siegler suggests that the answer to this question may lie with children's experience with the challenge problems. Whilst there was no evidence that the difficult, challenge problems 'caused' the children to invent MIN, they did play an important role in the *generalization* or *transfer* of the strategy to new problems. When MIN was first used successfully by a child to solve a challenge problem, it soon came to dominate their addition activity.

Although we now have a detailed picture of the ways in which children develop different strategies for counting sets, the precise nature of processes which lead them to develop and use new strategies are still a subject of debate, and, as yet, there is no generally accepted explanatory model. Some reasons for this will be explored later.

Since learning arithmetic involves constructing a system of understanding, rather than mere rote learning of number 'facts', one would expect to find parallels and similarities between children's abilities in mathematically related activities such as addition and subtraction. Work by Siegler and others supports this expectation.

As with addition, children develop more than one method for handling subtraction problems. For example, asked to 'take' 5 away from 12, a child might first use fingers to model 'counting down' 5 steps from 12, saying '11, 10, 9, 8, 7', then check that 5 fingers have been flexed (i.e. taken away), finally 'reading off' the answer 7. Alternatively, they might 'count up' on their fingers from 5, to 12 'six, seven, eight, nine, ten, eleven, twelve', and then re-count the number of fingers to find the answer to the sum. As with the development of 'number bonds' for simple addition problems, it takes both time and effort before children simply 'recall' that 12 take away 5 equals 7.

In learning how to take away, children also face some special problems. First, the counting down strategy rests on backwards counting which, for most children, is less likely to be a practised activity than counting up. Unlike simple addition problems in which both numbers in the sum can be modelled directly on the fingers, in counting down subtraction, the answer (e.g. 7 in the problem just mentioned) is not named in the statement of the problem. With counting up, however, the count stops once the larger of the two numbers (i.e. 12) in the problem is reached. Thus, the child who counts down has to remember how many fingers to count before they 'read off' their answer. In counting up, the child may simply wait until they hear themselves say 'twelve' and then stop to re-count the fingers used. The plausibility of such accounts for the difficulty of counting down and the special problems that this creates for children learning subtraction receives some support from classroom experiments. When children were encouraged and supported in using counting up strategies, they improved their performance on simple whole-number subtraction problems (Fuson, 1992).

With both counting up and counting down, however, there are problems not experienced in simple addition counting. Whether the child counts down from 12 or up from 5, neither saying 12 nor 5 should accompany flexing a finger. Should a count in either direction start from the number given in the problem, the child's answer will be out by one – a common finding (Fuson, 1992).

Cardinal knowledge

I have already tried to illustrate the distinction between ordinal and cardinal concepts of number and suggested that the achievement of some grasp of cardinal number represents an important watershed in children's number understanding. Before moving on to discuss further developments in number concepts, I will explore some of the reasons why this is the case.

Consider the humble number 11. Imagine giving a pile of pennies to a group of five-year-olds and asking them to count out a set of 11. Most children of this age are likely to succeed. Then give them a few 10 pence pieces and a few (less than 11) penny pieces. Again, we ask our five-year-olds to make 11 pence. With children aged five to six, only about a third will be able to count to 11 by using a 10p and 1p piece (Nunes and Bryant,1996).

To solve the first task, the children need only knowledge of one-to-one correspondence and the ability to count out sets up to 11. They do not need to be able to count on. To solve the second addition problem, they also need to have some grasp of cardinal number because they have to be able to count on from 10. We now then ask the same group of children to solve the following problem. They are shown a closed wallet in which they are told there are 7 pennies which they cannot see. They are also shown a set of 8 pennies and asked how many pennies there are in total. Some children give the answer 8 or 9: They only count the pennies that they can see, or get to 9 by counting the wallet as one. Others quickly count out 1 to 7, perhaps tapping the wallet as they do so, and then proceed to add on the 8 pennies that they can see. Here, the child counts out the total set. A third group simply count on by counting just the pennies that they can see starting from number 8. Children who count out the whole set or who count only what they can see are unlikely to solve the problem of adding 10p and 1p. However, those children who could solve the 'wallet' problem by simply counting on are likely to be able to do so.

Why is this significant? Well, for one thing, it shows that if a child can't count on and, by implication, does not yet have any grasp of cardinal number, they also cannot begin to appreciate the fact that numbers are organized on a base – in our case, a base of 10. Put another way, the child has to grasp the idea that a count number refers to a set, not just to a thing, before they can start to add things with different denominations. If the child sees a 10 pence piece simply as an object to be counted rather than a sign for a set of 10 elements (which, so-to-speak, are 'hidden'), then they will not be able to appreciate the way in which our number system is ordered around a base. I will elaborate on this point later when we look at the base system in more detail.

When children achieve a firm, intuitive grasp of the cardinal nature of numbers, then they have acquired a new number meaning. They 'knew' the same numbers when they used them as ordinals but this knowledge is transformed when they acquire their cardinal meanings.

Derived number understanding

The achievement of a grasp of cardinality thus marks an important landmark in children's number understanding. But their journey into the realms of addition and subtraction is still far from completion, even in learning about small, whole numbers. When children intuitively grasp the idea that a given cardinal number, say 7, can be assembled or disassembled into various combinations (i.e. $1 + 6, 2 + 5, 3 + 4$ etc.), then they develop some sense of what has been termed the 'additive composition' of small numbers. They realize that the same cardinal number can be formed in different ways and still be the 'same' number. Again, the nature of number meanings is further extended and integrated as they make new discoveries.

Armed with this knowledge, the flexibility and generativity of children's addition and subtraction achieves new heights. For instance, asked to add 7 and 5, a child might transform the problem into $6 + 6 = 12$. In so doing, they are showing some intuitive appreciation of the fact that taking 1 away from 7 is offset, or compensated for, by adding 1 to the 5. The answer given by both sums is the same, 12. Here again, the overall total set is conserved despite the fact that it was derived in different ways. It can be additively composed of either $6 + 6$ or $7 + 5$.

In saying that children exhibit some intuitive grasp of concepts like additive composition, it is not being claimed that they have an explicit or self-conscious understanding of what they know. Vergnaud, whose work has done much to shape recent theory and research into mathematics learning, uses the expression 'theorems-in-action' to refer to such knowledge. This concept is somewhat akin to Bruner's notion of enactive knowledge but it also incorporates Piaget's insight that such knowledge-in-action is also implicitly constrained by logical relations. I will say more about this rather complex concept later.

Addition and subtraction as models for situations

In an overview, analysis and critique of research into children's understanding of addition and subtraction, Fuson points out that the vast majority of research, like Siegler's, has only examined children's knowledge in a limited range of mathematical situations to which addition and subtraction are relevant. Thus, our current theories are limited in scope. In fact, Fuson identifies twenty-two different types of addition and subtraction word problems for whole numbers. I will not try to exemplify all of these here. Rather, I will give a few examples to illustrate some of the main theoretical and educational implications that Fuson draws from her analysis.

In the problems used by Siegler and his colleagues, children are asked either to add one number to another or to take one away from another. In each case, both numbers that need to be used in the sum are stated in the problem. It is possible to construct problems in which this is not the case. For example, in 'Bob got 2 cookies. Now he has 5 cookies. How many cookies did Bob have in the beginning?' one of the 'addends' (i.e. 3) is missing. Contrast this with 'Bob had 3 cookies. He got 2 more cookies. How many cookies does he now have?' In the second problem, akin to Siegler's, both numbers (addends) are given in the statement of the problem. But in the first problem, the 'start' is missing: i.e. we do not know how many cookies Bob had to start with. Such problems are far more difficult for young children. Why?

Well, when both addends are known, together with the operation to be performed (i.e. +), then the child can use fingers or manipulables to model the problem situation being described directly. With the missing start problem, how is the child to set up a model of the situation? The sentence 'Bob got 2 cookies' suggests addition, but to what? One strategy the child might use is to count out 5 objects, count out and throw away 2 and then count the remainder. This model is quite different in that it requires more 'anticipation' (Nunes and Bryant, 1996) or 'operations of thought' (Vergnaud, 1982) in its construction than the problem in which both addends (3 and 2) are given. Thus, problems which involve changes in quantity by adding or taking away elements from a set come in different types – types which demand the construction of different physical or mental models by the child.

In addition to 'change' problems, there are others which demand addition and subtraction. Another class, for instance, involves the comparison of two sets: hence, *compare* problems. An example, from

Fuson: is 'Janice has 8 sticks of gum. Tom has 2 sticks of gum. Tom has how many sticks less than Janice?' A child might solve such a problem by setting out (physically or mentally) 8 tokens to represent Janice's gum. She might then line up 2 tokens in this set to put them into correspondence with two other tokens representing Tom's supply. Then, by counting up those in the 'Janice' set which have no counter-parts in Tom's set, she can get the answer.

I am not suggesting this is the preferred or only model that children might use in such circumstances. Nunes and Bryant, and Fuson, provide other examples. The point I am trying to illustrate is that, like the 'missing start' problem, this compare problem involves different kinds of models from those demanded by Siegler-type tasks. Finally, consider some other problems that children find particularly difficult:

Jim has 5 marbles. He has 8 fewer marbles than Connie. How many marbles does Connie have?

Maxine has 9 sweaters. She has 5 sweaters more than Sue. How many sweaters does Sue have?

There is ample evidence to show that many children, even quite late in their schooling, can be deceived by such problems, giving an answer of 3 to the first and 14 to the second. Words like 'fewer' suggest a take-away-from solution and 'more than' suggests an add-to problem. If the child does not or cannot interpret the situation being described (to 'anticipate' in Nunes and Bryant's terms) to infer the appropriate kind of model to use in solving such problems, then he is likely to fall back on a 'surface structure' reading of the problem and be misled by such linguistic expressions. This phenomenon is common in children's mathematical performance. Sowder (1988, cited in Greer, 1992) characterizes the way in which many children approach such word problems as follows : 'Look at the numbers: they will tell you which operation to use. Try all the operations and choose the most reasonable answer. Look for key words or phrases to tell you which operation to use' (p. 285). Sowder's commentary applies not only to young children learning to solve addition and subtraction problems but is a general observation about the kinds of strategies used by many children in attempting to solve mathematical word problems, as we shall see.

Pause for reflection and review

In my view, one of the most important achievements of recent research into the psychology of mathematics learning is the detailed knowledge that has been gained about the relations between mathematical symbols such as + and − and the variety of real-world situations in which they function. Although I have only explored a small part of the taxonomy that Fuson has elaborated, and this only covers addition and subtraction involving whole numbers, I hope to have communicated some sense of the importance of the style of analysis she and others offer. Such analyses, which are deeply rooted in research on children's mathematical understanding, have provided new frameworks in which we can examine what children know and have to learn in order to master the foundations of arithmetic. As we shall see later, they also offer a means of evaluating and developing both curricula and methods of teaching in maths.

The analysis of mathematical sign systems, coupled with psychological analyses of the cognitive processes that are needed to learn and use them, has also helped to etch out at least some of the details of the interplay between conceptual development and learning in children's mathematical understanding. In so doing, research has explored the importance of the Piagetian emphasis on a child's developing understanding of logical relations and on important changes or discontinuities in development, although debates about the nature and origins of children's grasp of such relations remain. Piaget's theory is, however, insensitive both to the importance of content and meaning in children's mathematical capability and to the central role played by the systems of signs and symbols made available to them by their culture. As Nunes and Bryant observe, his theory assumes that the grasp of logical relations is all that is needed to explain the child's development of mathematical understanding. Whilst some contemporary theorists, like Nunes and Bryant, accept Piaget's stress on logical relations, they also integrate this within a framework which acknowledges the part played by content and culture in children's learning. In so doing, such theories dispense with the concept of stages of development whilst maintaining the idea that development involves conceptual change. I will explore these complex notions further in the following sections.

In the next section, we consider theory and research concerning children's understanding and learning in multiplication and division. It offers a brief and selective overview designed to explore further the interplay between conceptual development and learning in mathematical understanding. It is not intended to be comprehensive but illustrative of some general points. As with addition and subtraction, research into multiplication and division has provided some important insights into the nature of a whole variety of mental and physical models that make use of the same mathematical symbols. Here too, if children cannot learn how to recognize which models are appropriate to different kinds of mathematical situations, then they cannot be expected to use appropriate strategies and procedures. Acquiring skill and expertise in executing procedures without also developing a sense of the nature of the kinds of logical relations involved in different kinds of problems will lead the child to the kinds of surface structure strategies described by Sowder.

Although there is less agreement about the different kinds of situation in which the operations of × and ÷ serve as models than there is in relation to simple addition and subtraction, enough common ground can be found to establish the importance of understanding the mappings between concepts, situations and models in another field of mathematics. There is also some degree of consensus about major developmental changes that (sometimes) occur in children's conceptual knowledge of number which I will also try to illustrate.

Multiplication and division: some beginnings

According to Piaget, whilst addition has its roots in the understanding of one-to-one correspondence, early concepts of multiplication stem from a grasp of *one-to-many* correspondence. He argued that children as young as five years have some grasp of relations between two sets such as one-to-two and one-to-three. Although there has been remarkably little further empirical study beyond Piaget's work on this topic, what has been undertaken supports his claims (see Nunes and Bryant, 1996, for a review).

For example, Frydman (1990), working with four- and five-year-olds, asked children to give two dolls the same number of pretend sweets. These were either single units or double ones (e.g. akin to single and double squares of a chocolate bar). They were told that one doll preferred her sweets in two-unit pieces whilst the other liked hers in single units. Thus, to achieve fair shares, the child must, in turn, give one double to one doll and two singles to the other. Provided that the relation between the single and double units is made clear by using colour cues, young children do well with this task. Thus, where a double sweet is made up of one blue and one yellow unit and the singles are either blue or yellow, even four-year-olds, with a little training, can master such simple 1:2 ratio problems.

But why is this significant? Well, for reasons which parallel those given in relation to the importance of an understanding of one-to-one correspondence in the development of counting, adding and subtracting. Young children are able to grasp simple one-to-many correspondence *before* they learn how to use counting to do such tasks. This implies that the appreciation of the logic of correspondence pre-dates the acquisition of numbers. In Piagetian terms, this grasp of logical relations is what makes possible and underpins the acquisition of ideas such as 'two for one' and, hence, early concepts of multiplication and ratio.

Children grow up in a world full of examples of one-to-many relations (or ratios). Most dogs have four legs, as do the vast majority of cats. Most cars have four wheels and functional motor bikes and bicycles have two. A ratio expresses the numerical relation between two sets: e.g. 1:4 states the ratio between your typical set of dogs and legs and between cars and their wheels. Children also encounter conventional relations: e.g. (at the time of going to press) the cost of a litre of petrol is around 56p and chickens weigh in at around £2.50 a kilo. In these latter cases, the numbers express a relation between two continuous quantities, i.e. weight and price or volume and price, to give numbers expressing price per kilo and price per litre. Although the same mathematical operations can be applied to these two types of measures (i.e. ratios between sets and cost per unit), they involve, as we shall see, quite different number meanings.

When multiplying sets, say of dogs and legs, it is possible to solve many problems by repeated addition. So, if we have 4 dogs, then we have a set of 4 + 4 + 4 + 4 legs. Similarly, to find the cost of 2 kilos of chicken we may add £2.50 to £2.50. Of course, a repeated addition strategy proves cumbersome and error-prone once we start dealing with large numbers.

A ratio, such as 1:4, expresses an *invariant* relation which holds between two sets. When a child solves ratio problems by repeated addition, they can, do so without focusing on, understanding or using this invariant. For example, they can add up each set 4 times (1+1+1+1 and 4 + 4 + 4 + 4) without any attention to, or grasp of, the fact that the relation between the two sets is always the same, as in (1:4, 2:8, 3:12, 4:16 etc.). As the sets are multiplied or 'replicated', the numbers change but the ratio between them remains the same. Thus, 'times by 5', for instance, refers to the number of times (!) the ratio is replicated or repeated. If a child only focuses on the result of a single repeated addition solution, then she will not grasp this invariant which rests on the patterns in the numbers produced by successive replications over the set.

As Nunes and Bryant (1996) conclude, 'there is much more to understanding multiplication and division than computing sums. The child must learn about and understand *an entirely new set of number meanings and a new set of invariances* all of which are related to multiplication and division but *not* to addition and subtraction' (p. 199, italics mine).

Sharing, splitting and dividing

Consider the following word problems:

> Mary has invited 5 friends to her birthday party. She wants to give each friend 3 cakes. How many cakes does she need?

> Mary has 15 cakes. She wants to give each friend coming to her party 3 cakes each. How many friends can she invite?

Children find the second kind of problem more difficult than the first. They may eventually recall the fact that $15/3 = 5$ from memory, but what do they do before this fact is known? And why, before such facts are known, is the second problem harder than the first one?

One could argue that division is harder than multiplication and that is why the second problem is more difficult, but that doesn't get us very far. If, as we found in relation to addition and subtraction, such problems are rooted in different types of situation and demand different underlying models for their solution, then the reason why such word problems differ may become clearer. This, in fact, is what Nunes and Bryant propose.

Let us first attempt to analyse what an understanding of such problems might entail. Start with a thought experiment: imagine the following situation. A set of objects (say 20 sweets) is first shared out between 2 children. The same set size is then shared out between 4 children, and then 5. Clearly, the number of sweets received by each child varies as the number of children increases; the quota received by

2 children is larger than that received by 4. Here, 'division makes smaller' in the sense that, when a given number is divided by n, the size of the resulting share (quota) decreases as the size of n increases. Of course, whilst the size of each quota gets smaller, the *number* of quotas gets larger. There is obviously a systematic relation – an invariant. For any given size of set, the more times it is split into shares, the smaller each share becomes. To grasp these relations, children need to come to understand the way in which three quantities – initial set, number of splits and size of quota – relate to each other. Let us attempt to unpack what they need to learn in a little more detail.

Children need to know that a set of the same size, shared equally between the same number of recipients, leads to equal quotas. With small numbers, it is not necessary to count out sets. If one understands the logical relation that equal shares mean that each gets the same, then, for simple problems, counting is not needed. Most five-year-olds grasp this fact in situations where numbers are small but this early understanding is qualitative; it is not based on numbers.

Children also need to recognize that, for a given set size, as the number of recipients increases, the size of each share or quota gets less. Most five- and six-year-olds assume that if the same numbers of sweets are to be shared between three or four beneficiaries, they all get the same! They do not seem to relate the size of the set to be shared out to the number of individuals who are to receive shares. Current evidence suggests that this insight is, however, achieved by most seven-year-olds (again, under certain conditions). Interestingly, mistakes made by seven-year-olds differ from those made by younger children. The seven-year-old, if incorrect, is likely to say that if there are *more* recipients, then each will get more! This suggests that they recognize the need to co-ordinate the total number of sweets available with the number of recipients in order to work out the size of each share, but haven't yet figured out the nature of the relation between them. Most of their peers, however, appear to have solved this problem. So, they know that as the number of shares or splits increases, then the size of the resulting quotas gets smaller.

But do they recognize the fact that if the size of each quota is decided first and the size of the set to be shared remains constant, then the number of possible recipients gets less as the size of the fixed quota increases? For example, when do children grasp the fact that if, say, they want to give every child who comes to their party 4 sweets, they will be able to invite fewer friends than if they decide to give each child who comes only 3 sweets (the number of sweets available being held constant)?

To a mature mind, an understanding that more splits mean smaller quotas might seem, necessarily, to entail a grasp of the principle that larger quotas mean fewer beneficiaries. However, this does not hold for young children. What evidence we have suggests that the two mathematical insights are rooted in different kinds of models of situations.

A recent study by Correa (1995, cited in Nunes and Bryant 1996) illustrates this point. Children were asked to undertake two tasks. In one, they were told that a number of rabbits were to be invited to a party and that they were to receive equal shares of a set of sweets. The children were given blocks (as tokens of sweets) to help them to model the situation. Six-year-olds typically solved such problems by letting different locations on a table 'stand for' each rabbit and then sharing blocks out on a one-to-one basis until they ran out. They could then count out the number of blocks in a set to work out the size of each quota.

When asked how many rabbits they could invite to a party when share size was fixed (e.g. each rabbit was to receive 3 sweets), they counted out a share and put it on the table, and then counted out another share, and so on, until they ran out of blocks. Some then counted out the *number* of shares or quotas as requested. Others counted out the *size* of a quota, illustrating a similar difficulty to that of seven-year-olds faced with harder tasks. Such children modelled the situation correctly, but failed to figure out (or remember) *what* needed to be counted. However, whilst younger children, aged five, were sometimes able to solve the problem of working out how many sweets each rabbit would receive in the first situation (with small numbers of imaginary rabbits), they could not produce a model for the second type of problem in which share size was fixed ahead of time.

Thus, the strategies used for the first type of problem (in which a set is partitioned into shares – called 'partitive') is mastered at an earlier age than one in which both the total to be split and the size of each share are decided ahead of time and the task is to work out how many shares or quotas can be made (called 'quotitive' problems).

The relative difficulties that children have with word problems of the type illustrated at the start of this section thus echo the order in which an understanding of similar problems occurs in practical problem-solving earlier in development. The research reviewed by Nunes and Bryant leads them to conclude that young children do develop a conceptual grasp of both types of situation before they meet such problems in school, typically in the form of word problems. They argue that the 'difference in the manipulations of objects is indicative of a parallel difference in the operations of thought' that are needed to connect tasks with the logical relations that the child understands. So, what later occurs on the 'mental plane' reflects the structure of earlier activity in the practical world.

Dividing and division: parts and wholes

Consider the following problems:

> If you have 2 pizzas of the same size and 1 is shared between 6 people and the other between 8, which group will have larger pieces?

> Which fraction is larger, 1/6 or 1/8?

Children who can work out the first problem without difficulty often fail the second one. In fact, as we shall see, fractions and decimal numbers between 0 and 1 create tremendous problems for many children. The fact that children can answer the first problem shows that they have some intuitive grasp of the fact that as a given 'whole' is divided into 'parts', the size of the parts so formed decreases as the number of parts increases. This is similar to the invariant which holds when sets of objects are shared out. However, as we shall see, the two invariants are rooted in different situations, activities and models. So, why do children have problems with fractions?

A common strategy for introducing fractions in schools is illustrated in figure 8.1.

Children are asked to work out what fraction of the whole the shaded areas represent. They typically solve such problems by counting. First, they count the number of shaded segments. Then they count the total number of segments and use the convention of putting a / mark between them to derive an answer of 2/6 or whatever. Suppose that they employ the strategy with all of the problems shown. What is the nature of the invariant which governs this class of problems? The relation between the *parts* and the *whole*. So, 3/8 means 3 parts of a whole which has been divided or split into 8 parts. Is this what children understand when they read or write 3/8? A great deal of evidence suggests that many do not. They do not see such marks and symbols for division at all. Many fail to make a connection between their intuitive knowledge, such as that revealed by the pizza example, and the mathematical marks used to

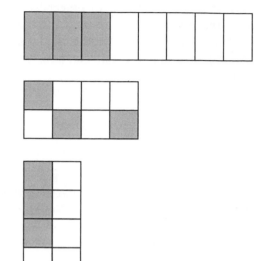

Figure 8.1   Illustration of materials used in teaching and learning fractions

express fractions. The same generalization extends to children's understanding of decimals between 0 and 1 (Greer, 1992). Why might this be the case?

Imagine sharing out a small, medium and large pizza to three different groups of 6 people. Each pizza is divided into 6 parts, so each person gets 1/6th of a pizza. But, of course, they do not each get the same *amount* to eat. They each get to eat the same fraction of a pizza, but the quantity varies. The size of the piece received depends upon two factors, the size of the whole to be divided and the number of parts created by dividing it up.

The number of pieces into which a whole is divided can be counted, as can any subset of them. They are, so to speak, 'amounts of stuff'; they are called *extensive* quantities. However, the relation between them (e.g. a fraction) is *not* an amount of stuff. It is insensitive to the actual size of either the whole or its parts, being a conceptual relation between them. Such conceptual or abstract relations are sometimes referred to as *intensive* quantities. Where the extensive aspect of quantity is concerned with the relations between numbers and what they refer to in a given situation, the intensive aspect refers to conceptual relations *between* the numbers themselves. I will provide more examples of the distinction between intensive and extensive aspects of number meaning later. These, hopefully, will help to illustrate further this rather difficult distinction.

Schoenfeld (1992) argues that mathematics is the science of patterns and pattern finding. In relation to fractions, one pattern, as we have seen, is an *invariant* that has to do with relations between values put on two variables (parts and wholes). This invariant has roots in situations like dividing continuous quantities, such as circles, into parts.

If a child is unaware of the invariant which holds over perceptual changes in appearance (e.g. the actual size of parts and wholes), then they will not discover such patterns nor grasp the new number concepts to which they give rise. However, when children are supported in learning, explicitly, the mappings between their intuitive knowledge of part–whole relations on the one hand, and the system of signs used to model these relations in mathematics on the other, their understanding can be advanced. For example, by alternating between signs and operations that they can grasp (e.g. dividing pizzas) and the manipulation of the relevant system of mathematical signs (the 'language' of fractions), they can be helped to make connections between their everyday knowledge and symbolic representations (Mack, 1993, cited in Nunes and Bryant, 1996, p. 229). I will return to the issue of bridging everyday understanding and systems of mathematical signs later.

New kinds of numbers

The distinction between extensive and intensive aspects of number is an important one in our understanding of the concepts that children have to grasp if they are to advance in mathematics. The distinction is also important in understanding how and why multiplication and division, though employing the same symbols for different types of problem (e.g. the use of × for multiplying with both whole numbers and fractions or decimals), demand different procedures because the mathematical situations in which they serve vary. I will give a few more examples to illustrate these important points further.

Imagine asking a group of ten-year-olds to decide whether a given amount of orange concentrate will produce a stronger or weaker drink when mixed with two different amounts of water (say 2 cups versus 3 cups). They will probably have no difficulty in deciding that adding more water makes for a weaker mixture. Next, imagine setting the following problems (adapted from a study by Noelting, 1980):

Problem 1: If we mix the following amounts of orange concentrate and water, will the two mixtures taste the same or will one taste stronger (more concentrated):

4 cups of orange concentrate mixed with 2 cups of water

2 cups of orange concentrate mixed with 1 cup of water

Problem 2: If we mix the following amounts of orange concentrate and water, will the two mixtures taste the same or will one taste stronger (more concentrated):

3 cups of orange concentrate mixed with 2 cups of water

4 cups of orange concentrate mixed with 3 cups of water

Where, as in first problem, children can work out the answer by simply adding or multiplying the numbers involved (i.e. they appreciate that doubling 2 to 4 cups of orange concentrate is equivalent to doubling 1 to 2 cups of water) then the chances of success are high. However, a majority of school-leavers are likely to get the second problem wrong. Why?

It is not simply because the numbers in the second example are larger. Of course, harder numbers do influence a problem's difficulty, but the real source of the difficulty that children face with such 'two-variable' situations, which cannot be solved by simply adding or multiplying both sets of terms in the problem, are largely conceptual, not computational.

Before I elaborate on this point, consider another example:

If coffee is priced at £2.50 per 100 grams and a pile of coffee weighs 250 grams, what is the cost of the coffee pile?

There are two kinds of numbers being used here – numbers with different mathematical properties. Thus, the amount of coffee is another example of an 'extensive' quantity. It refers to an actual amount of stuff. Similarly, the price of that given amount is extensive – it refers to the cost of a particular, visible pile of stuff. The third number – price per unit of weight – is different: it is an intensive quantity. Like a fraction, it expresses an *invariant relation* between two things, each of which can vary.

The difference between the two aspects of number concepts, intensive and extensive, can be illustrated further by considering the kinds of mathematical models that each can and cannot enter into. For example, if one doubles the amount of coffee, then the pile made is 2 times the original. The cost of the new pile is also twice the original. Both refer to changes in extensive quantity. But the price per unit cost is the same. Multiply *this* number by 2 (i.e. assimilate it to the same mathematical model as that used for extensive quantity) and you make an error. The error has nothing to do with the accuracy or otherwise of your knowledge of the two times table. Rather, it stems from a misconception of the *kind* of number you are dealing with and of the type of mathematical model that relates to the situations described.

Look at the two number types from a different point of view. When you split the amount of coffee into 2 piles, the amount in each pile is halved (this change, of course, is offset by the fact that you now have 2 piles; the quantity of coffee is *conserved* over division). The logical relations between the initial amount found in one pile and the two amounts formed by splitting into 2 piles are of a specific kind. The 2 *parts* made by splitting add up to the whole from which those parts were made. What effect does the act of splitting the pile have on the cost per unit weight? None whatsoever. The unit cost of the pile and of any of its parts, no matter how often they are split up, remains a constant or invariant.

Numbers like cost per unit are of a special kind: they have different part–whole relations from those exhibited by numbers or measures which can be used to model operations with extensive quantities. And their understanding demands more than mere practice with sums. They require some serious thinking about the relations between situations, number concepts, mathematical models and procedures.

At the risk of labouring the point, let me provide one more example before returning to the general idea I am trying to put over. Imagine two containers of liquid. One container holds 2 litres and the other 1. Each is filled with water at the same temperature (30°C). What happens to that temperature when the contents of the two containers are added? Children often suppose that the temperature of the combined liquids is higher. But temperature is not an extensive quantity. Values for temperature cannot be assimilated to the same models as those for amount-like quantities. If, faced with such a problem, a child does what Sowder argues they typically do, what would we predict should happen? Well, triggered into action by words like 'added' and stimulated to 'compute' by the presence of numbers such as 2,1 and 30, they will probably derive an answer such as 90 or 60. Children go from a surface textual description to the execution of (over-generalized) procedures without making any attempt to reason about the kind of number meanings and models that are relevant to the situation being described.

The examples I have given illustrate how different kinds of number concepts, which demand computation using appropriate mathematical models, are necessary for understanding concepts in chemistry (e.g. concentration), physics (e.g. temperature) and economics (e.g. price rates). One could cite many more examples (see Greer, 1992). Although it is relatively easy to show how maths intersects with science, it is not yet clear how learning in maths and science interact. For example, it is possible that developments in children's grasp of scientific phenomena provide them with entry to intensive number concepts which, in turn, helps them to extend their concepts of number in maths. However, this is conjecture. The interplay between the content of mathematical problem-solving and the development of mathematical models involving intensive number concepts is still poorly understood.

For our present purposes, however, the aim has been to illustrate some of the fundamental conceptual problems that face children in learning how to perform what, on the surface, might seem to be simple calculations to solve problems involving multiplication and division.

Understanding written numbers: base, place and space

In a later section, I will provide an overview of some of the literature on children's performance in written tests of mathematics in an attempt to demonstrate how the theoretical analyses we have just been considering help us to understand their performance and achievement. Before doing so, however, it is necessary to look more deeply into one other important source of discontinuities in children's learning of maths – discontinuities which have their origins in differences between spoken and written mathematical sign systems.

One of the themes that permeates this chapter concerns the role played by the systems of signs that children have access to in modelling and manipulating mathematical situations. We have looked, for example, at how some use their fingers or sets of blocks and we have considered the use and meaning of mathematical symbols such as +, –. To understand children's achievements in maths and the challenges that they face in learning and understanding the subject, analyses of the nature and role of such systems of signs has proved crucial.

Our system of counting, both spoken and written, rests on a base of 10. This is so familiar to us that it seems 'natural' and automatic. It is neither. It may well have its roots in the fact that most of us possess ten fingers but it is by no means the case that it is either historically or cross-culturally universal.

Not all societies adopt 10 as the base for their numerical calculations. Saxe (1981) for example, cites a system used by the Oksapmin of Papua New Guinea which is based, not simply on counting fingers, but on many body parts (such as elbows) which are used according to a convention governing the sequence for counting (i.e. to provide a model) which goes from 1 to 27. When exposed to an imported currency system (based on 20 shillings to the pound), the Oksapmin adapted their system to create a base 20 counting system which utilized only the first 20 elements of their original one.

Historical studies of the construction and development of mathematical systems serve both to illustrate the diversity of methods for recording and manipulating number and to show how different systems make mathematical discovery more or less likely. Consider, for example, the Roman number system. As Nunes (1992) points out, there are distinct rules in this system which dictate how such numerical values can and cannot be combined. However, unlike the base 10 place-value system which we use today (which has its roots in Hindu/Arabic mathematics), one cannot readily *compute* with the Roman system. Lacking a counting aid such as an abacus, how would one multiply LXXV with MXXIV or subtract CXV from MMXI?

Within the *written* base 10 system, relative *spatial* position in a visible code is used to represent the relative values of numbers. This system has made it possible for generations of mathematicians to develop rules (or algorithms, as they are often called) for manipulating such representations in ways that, amongst other things, model the results of counting, adding, subtracting and so on. In Bruner's (1966a) terms, the written symbol system serves as a 'cultural amplifier' enabling the investigation, discovery and solution of problems that cannot be handled within the limits of unaided human cognition. For instance, attempting to reason about very large numbers without such cultural artefacts as systems of written signs soon outstrips the limitations of working memory.

When children learn to write and read numbers, together with the procedures for performing arithmetical operations on them, their mathematical powers are amplified. They are able to write and calculate numbers that they may never have encountered before – i.e. the system is generative – and to express and calculate with numbers that are too large to handle mentally. It is quite likely that you will never have seen the number 1,348,227.3 before but, knowing the rules of written number representation, you can read it. But there are costs involved. The translation of oral mathematical expressions such as 'one hundred and three' into written tokens is not straightforward. For instance, children who are learning how to write such numbers may write '1003' on the assumption that the symbol for 'one hundred' is '100' (rather akin to C in the Roman system). Given that the symbol for 'three' is '3', then 'one hundred and three' becomes '1003'. In learning that this is not the case – that '1003' is 'one thousand and three' and '103' is 'one hundred and three' – the child must come to recognize that, unlike spoken numbers, where, for instance, numbers of the order of 'thousand' have a very different sound from those of the order of 'hundred', what differentiates them in written form is relative spatial position in a horizontal array of written tokens: i.e. 1000 plus needs four columns whilst 100 needs three.

Further, in saying 'one hundred and three', there is no explicit sign for the zero that has to be used in the written form '103' to signal the fact that the 'tens' column is empty. Thus, written and spoken forms differ both in the way they handle zero cases and the manner in which they express base values.

In learning how to calculate using written numbers, children have, so to speak, to 'keep in mind' the fact that the relative spatial position of numbers involved in a calculation dictates their order of magnitude. Thus, a child may know that $3 + 6 = 9$ but, in multi-digit numbers, they also need to recognize the fact that the same act of addition has different values in contexts where they represent 9 units or 9 tens:

$$
\begin{array}{ll}
23 & 230 \\
+16 \text{ (nine)} & +160 \text{ (nine-ty)}
\end{array}
$$

Similarly, they need to understand how, in problems like those below, acts of addition which lead to values greater than 9 have implications for numbers in columns to the left: i.e. that

$$
\begin{array}{l}
23 \\
+18 \\
\hline
=41 \quad \text{and not } 311 \text{ or } 411
\end{array}
$$

Errors such as '311' in the example given are common in children's early attempts at large whole-number addition, illustrating the difficulties they have in learning how to keep hold of place value when doing written arithmetic.

Do children find learning how to do such sums in written arithmetic hard because they lack any conceptual grasp of base 10 before they learn how to read and write numbers? Luria, a colleague of Vygotsky, suggested that this is the case. He hypothesized that it is only by learning the conventions of a written number system that knowledge of base structure can be discovered. Put another way, the invention of written numbers within a culture may have been a necessary pre-condition for the discovery of the value and power of a base system in arithmetic. This seems unlikely to be the case, however (though note, in passing, how the introduction of currency to the Oksapmin did lead them to adopt a new base system). Whilst it seems reasonable to accept the idea that written number systems provide a powerful means for extending or 'amplifying' mathematical knowledge, it seems that an (intuitive) grasp of the base pre-dates the development of written numbers. Why do we have reason to believe this?

Recall that in an earlier section we met examples from work by Nunes, Bryant and their colleagues which showed that some five- to six-year-olds were able to solve problems in which they had to add together tokens such as 10 pence pieces and 1 pence pieces. The fact that young children are able to handle problems such as 11p = 10p + 1p and 21p = 20p + 1p implies that they have some intuitive grasp (or 'theorems-in-action') of the fact that the use of numbers is organized on a base of 10. More graphic illustrations of 'non-literary' reasoning about base 10 come from studies of children and adults who have not learned how to read and write numbers. Nunes, for example, reports that people who have not been exposed to written numbers can calculate with currency involving amounts with units, tens, hundreds and so on in ways that demonstrate an understanding of the base 10 system.

Such examples illustrate a number of general points. First, it is clear that individuals who are skilled in oral mathematics display an intuitive or practical knowledge of number base; I will come back to this later. Consequently, the problems of learning to use a written number system cannot be due to a total lack of knowledge about the decimal (base 10) system nor of skills in handling problems which demand operations using the base system. Rather, the discontinuities imply that the problem of learning how to read, write and operate upon written numbers is non-trivial (more about this later, too), even when the learner possesses some relevant knowledge and skills in oral computation.

Other sources of evidence which illustrate some of the specific problems that children face in learning basic mathematical literacy have also arisen out of recent cross-cultural and cross-linguistic investigations of mathematics learning.

Language variation: reading, writing and using numbers

One of the problems that English-speaking children face in learning how to map spoken numbers onto written ones stems from irregularities in the English oral number system. Children learn to say and use spoken numbers such as 'eleven', 'twelve' and the rest of the 'teens' before they learn to read and write them. The 'decimal relation' between the teens and the numbers 1 to 9 is far from transparent. For children in Asian cultures, however, like China, Japan and Taiwan, the decimal relations between these numbers in their spoken form is much more obvious. The teens in these languages are expressed in terms equivalent to 'ten one', 'ten two' and so forth. Similarly, numbers like 52 are spoke of as 'five ten two' again highlighting the fact that the use of the five in this number refers to 'tens'.

One implication of such variations in spoken number systems is that it may be easier for children who are exposed to the more regular or obvious base relations to master the mappings between oral numbers and the written base system. There is evidence that this is indeed the case (e.g. Fuson, 1992). School children in Japan, for example, are exposed to sums involving two or more digit numbers (e.g. 11 + 3) earlier than those in American schools. Experimental comparisons of number competence amongst children from such different language groups also shows that children who are exposed to the more regular systems master oral addition involving the teens earlier in development.

For example, comparisons of young Chinese-speaking and English-speaking children reveal that Chinese pre-schoolers find the task of constructing amounts such as 11 from 10 and 1 unit denominations easier than English-speaking ones. They also find such sums easier than children from other language groups, such as Portuguese, which, like English, does not make the 'teens' so explicit.

Thus, before they start to learn the written number system, children from some cultures achieve greater competence in two-digit addition than those from cultures where irregularities exist. Since such problems also recur with numbers such as 'one hundred and twelve' and 'one thousand and eleven', such irregularities may well produce a significant handicap for children exposed to an 'irregular' oral number system. It also seems plausible to suppose that the task of writing, reading and calculating with written numbers will also be easier for children who read symbols such as 13 as 'ten three' rather than 'thirteen' and 53 as 'five ten three' rather than 'fifty three' because the structure of their oral language provides *reminders* of the fact that the written '1' and '5' refer to the 'tens' column.

Such cross-cultural differences in the structure of the signs in oral number systems impact both on children's pre-school experience with counting, adding and taking away and upon the ease with which they learn some aspects of arithmetic. We will consider how such differences may impact on school achievement in maths later.

Mathematics in school and community

There are now a number of studies which have investigated people's use of 'everyday mathematics' in situations such as shopping (e.g. Lave, 1988), working (e.g Scribner, 1986) and recreational activities (e.g. Nunes and Bryant, 1996). Particularly graphic are studies of the mathematical competence of young Brazilian street vendors undertaken by Nunes and her colleagues (e.g. Nunes, Schlieman and Carraher, 1993). Children were observed and interviewed at work in the streets as they plied their trade. They were asked to explain how they calculated the costs of various items in the street context and later asked to solve the 'same' problems using pencil and paper. An example helps to illustrate some of the main findings of this study.

> *Interviewer*: I'm going to take 4 coconuts (at Cr$35.00 each).
> How much is that?
> *Child*: Three will be 105, plus 30, that's 135 ... 1 coconut is 35 ... that is ... 140.

In a later interview, the child was asked to work out the sum 35×4 by writing the problem down. Explaining what he was doing, he said '4 times 5, 20, carry the 2; 2 plus 3 is 5, times 4 is 20'. He then gave an answer of 200.

Thus, on mathematically 'identical' problems, the child performs quite differently in reasoning with words versus written tokens. In the market version, he appears to de-compose the problem first and to retrieve from memory the cost of 3 times 35. He then adds 3 tens and, finally, remembers to add on the remaining 5 units to reach his answer. In the written form, when he carries the 2, he adds it to the 3 in the tens column to produce an erroneous step of 5 times 4.

Nunes and Bryant (1996) argue that in trying to grasp the deeper significance of the children's competence with 'practical' arithmetic and more 'abstract' school maths, we need to pay attention to two aspects of their activities. First, we must consider the systems of signs that they use. In the streets where, as we have seen, they use oral mathematics,

> Representation of the numbers . . . allows them to think of the values that they are working with at the same time. When tens and hundreds are added, for example, *they are spoken of as tens and hundreds.* In contrast, in written arithmetic we set the meaning of the numbers aside during calculation. We operate with digits and speak about them as if they were all units, following the same rules as we move from units to tens and hundreds. This approach seems to detach the children from the meaning of what they are trying to calculate and thereby makes it easier for bugs (i.e. faulty procedures) to appear in their solutions. (p.106)

The second aspect of the children's reasoning in street and school maths concerns the underlying mathematical principles which under-pin and constrain their activity. Nunes and Bryant argue that: 'The moves that can be carried out with one system of signs may not be carried out with another even if the logical principles implicitly used when operating with each system are the same.' Thus, whilst the street vendors know and use logical-mathematical relations in their oral calculations, they do not extend these to the way in which they attempt to solve school-type pencil-and-paper word problems.

Nunes and her colleagues argue, then, that practical mathematical problem-solving displays the same underlying logic as that needed to solve school-type tasks. Looked at in one way, this conclusion may seem in harmony with Piaget's theory which holds that practical problem-solving with concrete tasks is governed by the same logic as that which constrains symbolic problem-solving. On his account, more abstract, symbolic logic is constructed out of intuitions derived from such practical activities. By a similar argument, concepts such as 'de-contextualization', 'disembedding' and 'representational re-descrip-tion' might lead us to conclude that maths problem-solving involving computations on abstract symbols is rooted in and *abstracted* from such practical activities. Viewed in this way, school maths might be seen as perfecting more abstract, 'timeless' and less situation-specific methods for solving general classes of maths problems.

This general view, whilst deeply embedded in much psychological and educational thinking, has come in for critical scrutiny and even rejection by theorists who advocate a 'situated action' perspective on knowledge generally and mathematical competence in particular. However, if one accepts Nunes and Bryant's interpretation, then there are conceptual similarities in the knowledge used in different situations. Where they disagree with Piaget (and others) is in the nature of the relations between practical and 'theoretical' mathematical knowledge. The latter is not 'abstracted' from the former. Both represent the application of the same logical relations to tasks which involve different systems of signs. Thus, what differs is not the 'stage' at which practical and theoretical maths can be undertaken but the systems of signs that the child is able to use in order to exploit her conceptual knowledge of mathematical relations in the two different contexts. This is a hard distinction to grasp, but rather crucial theoretically (and, as we shall see, educationally).

PART 2: Theory and practice

Children's achievements and problems in mathematics

So far in this chapter, I have been concentrating mainly on theoretical and experimental investigations of mathematics. In the following sections, I try to sketch out a somewhat broader view of children's mathematical achievements and problems as revealed by the results of large-scale, pencil-and-paper tests.

There now exist a number of large-scale investigations which attempt to chart the progress of children in mathematics. Some, which I will consider later, involve comparisons of performance across cultures and have generated somewhat controversial international 'league tables' (see Robitaille and Travers, 1992, for a review of such work – and its problems).

Here, however, I will concentrate mainly on a large UK study. An attractive feature of the design of this study is that the research team augmented pencil-and-paper tests with in-depth interviews of children to try to get some sense of how they tackled test items.

The investigation included two large-scale surveys of mathematical achievement in England and Wales. The main findings of one, undertaken by the Assessment of Performance Unit, are published in six volumes. These list both achievement levels and common errors made by children aged from eleven to fifteen on a large number of different mathematical tasks (Department of Education and Science, 1980–2). The second study, which I will draw on more heavily here, was undertaken by a research team working on 'Concepts in Secondary Mathematics and Science' (CSMS) at Chelsea College, London (see Hart, 1981, for an overview). These surveys enable us both to assess the things that children learn or have failed to learn up to eleven years of age and to anticipate what they are likely to learn before they leave school.

Mathematical abilities and mathematical misconceptions

In the CSMS study, Hart and her colleagues examined the mathematical achievements of, and the errors made by, some 10,000 children aged from top junior (eleven years of age) to fifteen-year-old secondary school pupils. The tests used were specially developed by the team. They covered a range of topics including measurement, number operations, place value, decimals and fractions.

The tests provided a measure of children's levels of performance in the ten mathematical domains studied and revealed many common weaknesses and widespread, persistent problems. As I have already said, testing was followed up with more intensive interviews with individual children who were asked to talk about their techniques for solving various problems. These interviews provided insights into the nature of children's understanding and misconceptions and provided a basis for inferences about how and why they find specific aspects of arithmetic and mathematics difficult.

One of the general conclusions to emerge from the study is gloomy but typical. 'The overwhelming impression obtained is that mathematics is a *very difficult* subject for most children.' The investigators also note that the introduction of 'modern mathematics', motivated by a desire to engender greater *conceptual* understanding in children about the 'foundations' of mathematics, has not succeeded. 'It was hoped that a child faced with a new mathematical system might ask "What are the elements; which operations combine those elements; are the commutative, associative and distributive laws applicable etc.?" This aim does *not* appear to have been fulfilled.'

The CSMS group developed some rather complex statistical procedures to identify four main stages in children's mathematical achievement. These stages represent different groupings of mathematical tasks and operations that tend to 'go together' in performance. They are not stages in the Piagetian sense; so we cannot say, for example, that children at CSMS Stage 1 lack certain operations of mind possessed by children at higher stages. The groupings of the things that children can and cannot do at different ages and levels of achievement 'emerged' from the data. Consequently, it is not possible for me to give a simple, general picture of what the stages are. Instead I will try to illustrate some of the things that children can and cannot do at different levels of performance.

The first two stages, in which approximately *half* the children remained throughout their years of secondary schooling, were characterized as involving knowledge of a 'form of social arithmetic or mathematical literacy'. Children, about half of whom were 'arrested' at these stages, were able to perform most of the 'basic' operations (i.e. +, −, ÷, ×) but only on small (1 to 12) whole numbers.

Thus, the problems with written numbers, place value and calculations involving large numbers discussed earlier are not solved by many children. Even at this level, many still find multiplication difficult (more so than division, which, as the team point out, goes against the received wisdom). These children often 'avoid' multiplication and substitute addition. So, for instance, asked to multiply 5×3, they add 5 to itself 3 times. This strategy may be effective with small numbers, but once large integers are introduced or the problem involves fractions or decimals, the procedure breaks down. Thus, despite the fact that research has demonstrated that young children enter school with some conceptual grasp of multiplication and division, for children at Stages 1 and 2, this has not been developed far with written arithmetic.

Some children, faced with a fraction, may resort to the simple expedient of adding together all numbers at the top and then adding together the numbers at the bottom, so $3/4 \times 4/5$ yields the 'solution' $7/9$. More generally, the strategies displayed by children at these stages imply that they have neither developed the new number meanings discussed by Nunes, Bryant and others nor grasped what we have termed intensive concepts of number.

About half of the children in the sample displayed, at best, only a tenuous and extremely limited basic understanding of the number

The signpost shows that it is 29 miles west to Grange and 58 miles east to Barton

How do you work out how many miles it is from Grange to Barton?

$$29 + 58 \qquad 58 \div 29 \qquad 58 - 29 \qquad 29 \times 2$$
$$29 \div 58 \qquad 58 + 29 \qquad 58 \times 29 \qquad 87 - 29$$

Figure 8.2   The 'signpost' problem

system. They did not realize, for instance, that between 1.4 and 2.3, as between any two numbers, there are a theoretically *infinite* number of other numbers. Only children who reach the fourth stage, some 30 per cent of the fifteen-year-olds and a mere 2 per cent of those aged thirteen, display this level of sophistication. Similarly, children in the early stages find it difficult to handle any degree of abstraction and many do not even *recognize* which operations they should perform on a verbally stated problem. For example, one type of problem used shows a signpost displaying the names and distances of two towns that lie in 'opposite' directions. The children are asked to say how far apart the two towns are and shown eight possible solutions to the problem (figure 8.2). They are asked to *identify* the operation that would yield a correct answer. The child in the following sample interview was trying to solve a problem of the type illustrated in figure 8.2, but different distances (18 and 23 miles) were involved.

Tracey (age 11)   Does it mean that is, er, 18 kilometres to Grange and 23 kilometres to, er, Barton, does that mean that it's from the same place?

Interviewer   That's right: from this signpost here. It's 18 miles that way to Grange and 23 miles that way to Barton.

Tracey   Take 18 away from 23... 5.

The problems that children face when they have not only to do 'sums' but to determine what *type* of mathematics a verbally stated problem involves are well documented (Bell, Costello and Kuchemann, 1983). The CSMS data show that, for 'a significant proportion of secondary-aged children, it is not simply the case that they are unable to *generate* a solution. They cannot even *recognize* one.'

For many children, progress in mathematics appears to be a very slow affair. For instance, about 40 per cent of children in the first year of secondary school were unable to solve the problem:

$$2312$$
$$- \ 547$$

About the same proportion of children in the fourth year also failed such items. Although there were some signs of progress, for around 50 per cent of children this was extremely limited. Evidence, amongst this group, of any real increase in the *understanding* of the foundations of school mathematics and the nature of number was conspicuous by its rarity.

Mathematical discourse and everyday language

Verbally stated questions not only demand an ability to work out the nature of the problem. Children have to understand what the *words* used mean in mathematical terms! Consider, for example, humble words like 'share', 'bigger' and 'straight'. A problem like '10 sweets are *shared* between two boys so that one has 4 more than the other. How many does each get?' provoked, from one child interviewed, the protest, 'That's wrong, if you *share* they each have 5, so one can't have 4 more.' Similarly, in graphical problems, 'straight' for many children means only a line that is perpendicular to the edge of a page, so a slanting line, by their definition, can't be 'straight'. Terms used in mathematics are often 'parasitic' upon words used in everyday discourse. But they have special and technical mathematical meanings which, if not *negotiated* with children in activity and discourse, cause problems. For example, prepositions like 'into' and 'by' should invoke specific procedures when they are implicated in maths problems like '391 *into* 17' and '17 divided *by* 391'. Confusion over the meanings of such terms was common in the CSMS data. Children tend to use these prepositions, for example, as though they have the same meaning as 'shared between'. They did not appreciate the very different *interpretations* of problems that these little words should imply. The 'pluri-functional' nature of many linguistic terms has been discussed in earlier chapters. When used technically, as they are in mathematics and other disciplines, the meanings of many common words expand even more.

Unless the connections between situations, systems of signs, models and procedures are firm in children's understanding, they will, quite naturally, fall back on everyday, plausible interpretations of problems which implicate them. Consider how many more times they hear and use such words in everyday discourse, and it is not surprising that they should need considerable experience of their 'concrete' meanings in mathematics to learn and memorize what procedures they should evoke.

A final example of the important relations between everyday language and mathematical discourse would be amusing, if its implications for the (secondary school) child involved were not so serious:

Interviewer	Do you know what volume means?
Child	Yes.
I.	Could you explain to me what it means?
C.	Yes, it's what is on the knob of the television set.

Instruction, interview and dialogue

There are several examples given in the CSMS publication of children discovering how to solve a problem that, initially, they got wrong. The reasons for their errors were numerous, but the simple expedient of discussing how they were thinking about and trying to solve a problem sometimes cleared up the source of their difficulty. Such incidents illustrate the fact that children sometimes possess the competence to solve problems but do not appear to recognize the relevance of what they know when they tackle word problems.

For example, in the following excerpt, the interviewer simply *reminds* a child of a critical 'step' in the problem that she has 'overlooked'. The child is trying to subtract 28 from 51 (another preposition, notice)

| *Maria* | Do you take the top from the bottom? [Tries, and takes 1 from 8, writing 7 in the answer]. Can't take 5 from 2 – have to take one of these [indicates 1 in 51]. |
| *Interviewer* | Explain what you did there. |

M	Crossed out the 1 [of 51] and put nought [in its place] and put the 1 on there (i.e. to the left of 5 to make 15).
I	What was that to do? Why did you do that?
M	I put 1 on the tens.
I	OK. Right, now what are you going to do?
M	That's wrong.
I	Why is it wrong?
M	I'm supposed to take 15 from 2 and not 2 from 15.
I	Can we do it the other way? Can we do it this time so that we take the bottom one from the top one?
M	Is that how we're supposed to do it?
I	That's how you usually do it, yes.

Maria then went on to solve the problem and explained how 'borrowing' of the ten works.

Another child, tackling one of the 'signpost' problems referred to above, was helped to understand the problem by being invited to think about it (represent it to herself) by 'imagining' herself at a crossroad. When this did not work, the interviewer re-formulated the problem in 'simpler' terms. By inviting the child to 're-view' the problem in a simplified, more context-dependent, immediate and 'concrete' form, she was led to recognize the *type* of problem she was dealing with and thence to formulate the correct answer to the original, more difficult problem. Note, too, how the child decides, even before she attempts the problem, that she is likely to fail.

Hilary	Oh no, I'm no good at these... you times those two together don't you?... No, you can't . . . [long pause]
Interviewer	Imagine standing there and you're looking up at the signpost, OK? Now that way it's 18 kilometres to Grange and that way it's 23 to Barton: we want to know the distance between the two.
H	23.
I	23?
H	[Long pause . . . I'm not very good at doing kilometres . . .
I	Let's try something else. We're sitting right here, right? Say someone said it was 3 paces to the window and it was 5 paces to the window that way . . .
H	You'd add them.

I	How far from one window to the other?
H	[Long pause] . . . 8.
I	Yes, what are you doing?
H	Adding them!

Asking a child to *approximate*, to think of the problem in general terms before tackling its procedural complexities, provides, as in the following example, a sense of the solution and leads on to effective problem-solving. The child is trying to multiply 5.13 by 10:

Billy	You can't put a nought on the end of there as it's a decimal . . . [long pause]
Interviewer	How big, roughly?
Billy	50 . . . 51.3

Children have to *regulate* their own thinking in mathematics, as in any other effective problem-solving situation. They have to learn that 'appearances' may be deceptive and that the first answer that happens to 'pop into their head', or the initial conceptualization of the problem's *nature* that comes to mind, may not necessarily be appropriate. Overcoming impulsive first thoughts and *re-viewing* one's initial attempt at solution does not come easily or readily to some children. In the following example, a child (aged 13) had already decided that 8 multiplied by 0.4 yields a larger number than 8 divided by 0.4 (illustrating, in passing, another of children's misconceptions, that 'multiplication makes it bigger'). The child was shown these three pairs of sums and asked to 'ring the one which gives the BIGGER answer':

$$\text{(a) } 8 \ \times 4 \quad \text{or} \quad 8 \ \div 4$$
$$\text{(b) } 8 \ \times 0.4 \quad \text{or} \quad 8 \ \div 0.4$$
$$\text{(c) } 0.8 \times 0.4 \quad \text{or} \quad 0.8 \div 0.4.$$

Left to her own devices, the child placed rings around all the multiplications. She was asked some time later:

Interviewer	Why did you choose the others first time?
Fung Mei	'Cos they're times and it always seems more than divide.
I	Why isn't that true here?
F	They've got decimals – in 8×0.4 you times by a little, in $8 \div 0.4$ you share between a little so each

I	person gets more.
	What if I asked you which was biggest, 0.8 × 1.2 or 0.8 ÷1.2?
F	That one (0.8 × 1.2).
I	It's got a decimal, though.
F	'Cos it's got a whole number as well it makes it bigger.

This child clearly has some sophisticated notions about decimals, division and multiplication. Her only 'error' was not to *think carefully* enough about the problems.

Learning and teaching mathematics: Why is it all so hard?

The account of young children's early understanding of the foundations of number that I gave earlier portrays an essentially positive and optimistic picture of their abilities and readiness for school learning. As Nunes and Bryant observe, 'take any mathematical concept taught in primary school, and you will find that children have some understanding of this concept before they are taught about it formally'. Yet, when we contrast this optimism with the gloomy conclusions of those who have surveyed children's eventual achievements in school mathematics, we find that this early promise is not fulfilled for many.

Such observations are neither new nor recent. For many years, there have been widespread misgivings about mathematics education. In this section, I will attempt to summarize just some of the reasons that have been put forward in attempts to explain (and to ameliorate) this state of affairs in relation to the research we have just been exploring.

Nunes and Bryant point out that whilst children 'show an impressive understanding of simple relations', they 'seem to be quickly thrown off their balance when numerical values are introduced'. Learning is not guaranteed by knowledge of the logical relations alone. As we have seen, whilst Piaget's emphasis on the role of logical relations in maths learning has received support in recent research, his neglect of the role of mathematical symbol systems, such as the written number system, means that his theory is silent about many of the learning tasks which children have to master in order to develop their mathematical competence. And, as I have also tried to illustrate, entry into these systems of signs is neither fast nor easy.

If one accepts Nunes and Bryant's stress on the importance of logical relations in maths learning, one also accepts that there are discontinuities in children's conceptual development which occur at least through to age 15 years (Vergnaud argues to age 18). This, in turn, implies that children will only be able to master mathematical concepts and procedures when they have developed the prerequisite conceptual understanding. Nunes and Bryant argue, for example, that understanding and use of the base 10 system in written arithmetic can only be perfected when the child has developed his or her conceptualization of additive composition. Although, as I have attempted to illustrate, young children show some intuitive knowledge of additive composition in relation to small numbers, the development of that understanding to grasp the hierarchical relations between tens, hundreds, thousands and so forth in written maths comes much later (if at all). Further, as we have also seen, even when children show some intuitive grasp of larger numbers in oral arithmetic, the task of extending this competence to calculations involving written numbers is far from trivial. In short, we should underestimate neither the conceptual demands nor the learning tasks that face teacher and child as, within the space of a few years, they attempt to teach and learn ideas that have taken mathematicians many centuries to discover. Is it simply the case, then, that school maths is too hard for many children? Or does the answer lie, in part at least, with curricula and teaching methods?

Aspects of the curriculum

Fuson argues that one reason why schools fail to develop the early mathematical competence of children rests on the poverty of the mathematics curriculum. Recall that she identified a wide range of different problem types in whole-number addition and subtraction, together with examples of the kinds of real-world situations which these serve to model. Analysis of textbooks widely used in North American schools reveals the fact that only a few of the different types of problem are ever used as examples. Despite the fact that young children have been shown to possess the necessary intuitive understanding to master addition and subtraction, the implication is that only part of this understanding is actually exploited or developed by the diet of problems offered in the curriculum. The danger here is not simply that children are unlikely to encounter early in schooling those tasks which help to develop their conceptual understanding: they can also be led into error when they attempt to generalize the procedures that they *have* learned over a restricted range of problems to tackle other problem types encountered later. If young children do not experience the appropriate mathematical situations, how are they ever to 'see' those situations when they are encoded in written symbols?

Fuson, and many other contemporary students of maths education, also argues that too little time is spent on the use of concrete materials, 'manipulables', to help children to bridge the gap between their early conceptual understanding and mathematical symbol systems. In her writings, she deliberately talks of symbols such as + and – as 'marks' to underline the fact that, from a learner's perspective, they cannot be assumed to possess mathematical meaning. Only when the meaning of these terms is 'grounded out' in practical activities and models can the processes involved in mapping their symbolic meaning onto the child's conceptual understanding take place. Too little time given over to this process of negotiated meaning results in the kinds of 'surface structure' strategies that I have illustrated in earlier sections. Nunes and Bryant also provide examples from a range of mathematical domains to illustrate ways in which effective use can be made of practical activities with appropriate materials to help bridge the gap between concepts, situations, invariants and procedures.

Such calls for greater attention to practical activity are not recent, nor are they restricted to the early years of schooling. Greer also argues that attempts to teach more advanced mathematical concepts in relation to multiplication and division (e.g. involving intensive number concepts) are often hampered by the fact that little or no attempt is made to map concepts and procedures into the kinds of real-world situations which they serve to model. If children are only taught rules and procedures, they arrive at a conceptualization of what maths *is* that actively inhibits their learning. Greer argues, for example, that the belief held by many children (and some teachers) that 'multiplication makes bigger' and 'division makes smaller' can be traced back to the limited range of situations that children experience in learning the maths. If tasks are not experienced which enable the learner to map mathematical symbols onto situations in which such beliefs do not hold, and which implicate number concepts that have not yet been developed, then it is difficult to see how children could come to doubt the validity of their beliefs and easy to see why they make the 'errors' that they do. All they have to fall back on when they encounter the more difficult maths are rules for manipulating the surface structure of word problems. They cannot 'see' the mathematical model in the formulation of the problems.

In addition to calls for greater attention to the mappings between practical situations, mathematical concepts and procedures, there are related demands for less use of 'word puzzle problems' as a primary vehicle for instruction. It is argued that the extensive use of such problems encourages both teachers and children to treat maths as a task of recalling and applying rules, not as a process of trying to understand situations mathematically, nor one of looking for patterns, regularities and invariances. Such complaints are reminiscent of some of Bruner's early writings in which he argued for less attention to the 'syntax' of disciplines (i.e. systems of rules and procedures) and more concern with the process of finding out how to turn practical situations into mathematical problems.

Another common, general criticism is of an over-reliance on the use of word problems. In an attempt to make maths seem more 'relevant' to everyday life, word problems have been created for maths curricula which seek to capture 'real world' situations to serve as models for mathematical applications. For instance, the 'orange juice' problem that I used to provide an example of intensive number concepts is illustrative of this trend, which was popular in maths textbooks (and research) in the 1970s and 1980s.

As Nunes and Bryant point out, however, problems like the orange juice example (and one could cite many more) do not really tap into everyday cultural activities which are 'framed' as involving computation or calculation. If a child wishes to work out the effects of different amounts of water on the concentration strength of a mixture, their most likely (and sensible) strategy would be to taste it and vary amounts until it tastes good. It is not immediately apparent that one might, let alone should, use mathematics to solve such problems. Thus, the activities and practices brought to mind by such problems are likely to be at variance with mathematical reasoning. As research has shown, attempts to teach are more effective when everyday situations which are seen as demanding computation are used, involving e.g. price or speed (Kaput and Maxwell-West, 1994).

As we have seen in several earlier chapters, problem content, viewed in relation to everyday cultural practices and common sense, has a profound effect on how people think. In chapter 3, I outlined research by Donaldson and her colleagues which demonstrates how the nature of the tasks used to assess children's reasoning exerts a profound effect on how they think. Similarly, in the preceding chapter, we saw how some problems framed as 'logical' ones are assimilated to everyday knowledge and reasoned about in terms of their plausibility. They are evaluated not against rules of formal logic but against conventions of everyday conduct involving issues such as rights and permission. In maths, too, the representations used in word problems may activate pragmatic reasoning schemes based on common cultural practices.

Thus, another reason why children may fail to 'see' a word problem as an invitation to reason mathematically is that, in their everyday experience, numerical computation is not associated with the problem content used. Of course, it can be argued that, eventually, the child must come to understand that tasks and problems which do not 'look' mathematical can, in fact, be modelled in mathematical terms. However, it seems reasonable to suppose that teaching will be more effective if it starts out with situations about which children are likely to think spontaneously in numerical and computational terms.

Language, instruction and self-regulation

Many specific problems that children experience with word problems are well documented in research. I used examples taken from the CSMS survey to illustrate a variety of these.

Viewed in one way, such examples illustrate how the meaning of natural language terms can create negative transfer from the everyday uses of verbal expressions into mathematical problem-solving. However, they can also be seen as symptomatic of the fact that the child is not trying, so to speak, to get 'beneath' a surface description of a problem in an attempt to determine what kind of mathematical situation or what invariants are implicated in it. Viewed in this way, their linguistic problems are symptomatic of the fact that they are attempting to recall learned rules triggered by surface content, rather than seeking to model the situation being depicted mathematically.

Earlier, I gave examples from the interviews undertaken by the CSMS team to illustrate two main arguments. First, they provide examples of situations in which children are shown to *think* mathematically about problems on which they initially err. Such cases illustrate the fact that children may know how to solve a problem, in the sense that they have the resources to solve it, but do not make use of those resources spontaneously. They fail to regulate their own activities effectively. The second argument that the interviews illustrate is that even minimal prompts from another person, when these are contingent upon the child's activity, can motivate children to think and succeed where, left to their own devices, they act impulsively and, in so doing, fail to mobilize their resources to tackle problems that they are capable of solving. Thus, regulation by another can occasion success when, left alone, a child fails.

Both Fuson (1992) and Schoenfeld (1992) argue that at least part of the reason for such impulsive and non-reflective approaches to problem-solving in mathematics can be attributed to teaching practices. Fuson, for example, argues that a stress on speed in solving problems and the common North American practice of solving several problems of the same type in rapid succession lead pupils to view 'doing' maths as a case of recalling and applying rules without reflection. As we saw in chapter 4, one difference between expert and novice problem-solvers is the tendency of the former, but not the latter, to explain their own activities to themselves as they attempt to work through problems. In a sense, they 'interview' themselves. On a Vygotskian account, of course, such self-explanations are a form of self-regulation which has its origins in discourse and social interaction. Fuson's argument is that teaching strategies common in North American schools lead learners to a conceptualization of what doing maths *means* and ways of regulating problem-solving activities which are directly at variance with such practices of reasoning.

Cross-cultural comparisons between maths teaching methods often employed in Western countries and those more likely to be encountered in Asian and Russian classrooms help to illustrate alternative approaches to mathematics instruction. In Japanese schools, for example, the use of purpose-designed practical materials for modelling mathematical situations is reported to be common. This contrasts with surveys of the use of manipulables in some Western countries. The CSMS team, for example, report on the results of a survey in which teachers of ten-year-olds were asked how often they used apparatus in teaching mathematics. None of the schools surveyed used equipment every day. About half employed it once or twice a week.

In Russian textbooks, it is common practice to 'mix' different kinds of mathematical problems so that the learner is not confronted with long sequences of problems which can be solved by the repetitive application of the same procedure or strategy. This approach to instruction, it is argued, helps to militate against the mechanical and rapid application of rote-learned rules. It is also less likely to lead the learner to view mathematics itself as a task of mere rule recall and application. There are certainly many examples to be found in early psychological literature on problem-solving which lend credibility to this claim. These demonstrate that the repetitive practice of a strategy eventually 'blinds' the thinker to alternative (and better) approaches. As a strategy becomes practised and automated, the thinker's ability to 'see' new and more elegant solutions is diminished.

Japanese school children are not only exposed to frequent use of materials to help them to model and solve problems, but they are also encouraged to look at problems in several ways and to consider and evaluate alternative solution strategies. This, I suggest, builds upon and develops children's natural tendency to use multiple methods. I gave examples in earlier sections of investigations which have shown how young children spontaneously employ multiple strategies when they start to count, add and subtract. There are also many examples in the literature which illustrate how children sometimes invent their own procedures for solving maths problems. Indeed, some invent methods of solution more elegant than those suggested by the teacher (Resnick, 1976). There is usually more than one way to skin the mathematical cat!

Having the means to solve a problem in more than one way confers several possible benefits. For one, having two or more methods, each of which delivers the same answer, offers a powerful means for discovering what is invariant in a situation. Contradiction between the results of two methods is also potentially useful as a way of stimulating thought, reflection and, perhaps, the detection and explanation of errors. The *same* strategy, executed twice, may deliver the same answer but still be incorrect if the procedures used are faulty. Similarly, if the same method yields different results, there is no other means for assessing on which occasion, if any, the strategy was applied correctly.

Getting the same answer by more than one means inspires confidence in the validity of each strategy employed. Comparing and contrasting strategies on the basis of factors such as ease of execution, elegance and generality also helps to promote mathematical reflection and to provide a means of inhibiting the blind application of rules to the surface structure of problems. In Japanese classrooms, it is reported to be common practice for small groups of children to work together in solving problems and then to come back to whole-class teaching in which each group presents its own solution and offers a critique of others. On a Vygotskian account, this helps to bring mathematical reflection and the processes of self-regulation and evaluation onto the 'social plane', thus affording opportunities for children to learn how to regulate their own activities.

Maths and culture

A general thrust behind the thesis advanced by both Fuson and Schoenfeld, and by Nunes and Bryant, is that methods of instruction and curriculum design influence not only the specific strategies that children attempt to learn in mathematics but also their conceptualization about what mathematics *is* and what doing mathematics means. In her studies of 'darts mathematics', for example, Nunes found that expert darts players rejected the idea that they were doing 'real' mathematics, even though their procedures were successful, generative and consistent with the dictates of mathematical logic. In the investigations of Brazilian street mathematicians, she also found that the children's teachers would sometimes dismiss their pupils' competence as not 'real' mathematics. Thus, cultural attitudes towards mathematics may serve to rule out what many educators have been searching for: a means for making maths meaningful and relevant and a way of rooting it firmly in children's conceptual understanding.

I have already referred to the international 'league tables' which put many Western countries low on the list of mathematical achievement and many Asian countries high up. In this chapter, we have looked at some cross-cultural investigations which may tempt us into an explanation for this fact. Differences in language, in the use of materials for mathematics instruction and in teaching methods might each or all be recruited to explain why Western children are disadvantaged in learning maths. However, it would be unwise to take such putative explanations too seriously on the basis of our current knowledge. There are many other potential factors involved (such as cultural variations in the amount of time given over to maths teaching and learning). Not the least of these, cultural attitudes towards mathematics provide us with a bridge into the final chapter.

Surveys of attitudes towards mathematics and what it takes to learn maths have revealed some marked cross-cultural differences in the way in which maths and its learning are viewed. For example, a Japanese person is more likely to attribute poor mathematical achievement to a lack of effort and to see a remedy in further work. A North American, on the other hand, is more likely to see poor performance as due to a lack of ability and give up. I will return to this observation later.

Concluding comments

The overview of children's mathematical understanding just presented has confronted us with a whole raft of theoretical and practical issues which are at the heart of developmental psychology and its potential applications.

First, I have tried to show that there is a considerable case to be made for Piaget's emphasis on the role of logical relations in the development of mathematical understanding. For example, we have considered evidence supporting his prediction that knowledge of both one-to-one and one-to-many correspondence pre-date and make possible the acquisition and use of numbers in the service of arithmetical procedures such as counting, adding and multiplying. This adds weight to his general claim about the central role of logical relations in the development of number concepts. Further, analyses such as those offered by Nunes and Bryant, which support the idea that an understanding of common logical relations is implicated in both everyday and school-based mathematical activities, also lend empirical weight to the claim that necessary or logical knowledge forms the basis for valid mathematical reasoning.

However, an acceptance of the role of logical *relations* need not imply agreement with Piaget's more general theory about the nature and role of formal reasoning and logical *operations* in cognitive development. Crudely, we can buy into the idea that logical relations are necessary for rational thinking without also purchasing the notion that all rational thought, including mathematical reasoning, is constrained by the rules and operations of a formal logic.

Let me try to elucidate. In both this and preceding chapters, we have met with examples where the ability of both children and adults to understand, handle and comprehend tasks and reason through problems relates to task content and context. The ability to perform a given 'logical' task, draw a particular kind of inference, 'read minds' or solve a problem in arithmetic may vary, even across tasks which would seem to possess similar logical structures and demand the same mental abilities. We have considered Piagetian tasks which suggest that young children are egocentric, and contrasted performance on these with success on other problems which appeared to exhibit a similar logical structure. Performance on formal, 'logical' problems, in which task content and procedures of reasoning are rather arbitrary and strange with respect to everyday activities, has been contrasted with that on tasks which activate knowledge, processes of communicating and thinking more closely related to everyday social practices. In this chapter, mathematical practices associated with familiar and personally significant tasks have been juxtaposed with those arising out of school-based mathematical problem-solving. Although, in some of the examples considered, the 'same' mathematical concepts and operations seemed to be involved across such diverse situations, we found differences in performance which split along the lines of social context, personal significance and the systems of signs (e.g. oral versus written) exploited in the activity of problem-solving.

One can look at such discontinuities in at least two different ways. It can be argued that performance on abstract, relatively artificial tasks provides the 'purest' measure of an individual's most advanced stage or level of functioning. Performance in uncontrolled, socially familiar situations may be influenced and made possible by learned practices, procedures and cues which do not demand the mental abilities revealed in well-designed, experimental situations. Similarly, it can be argued that the mental processes involved in solving practical, everyday mathematical problems are situation-specific and lack the power and generality of the mathematical concepts, procedures and context-independent laws which govern 'pure' mathematical reasoning.

On this kind of perspective, knowledge and understanding become increasingly abstract and reliant on logical form (more 'structure-dependent') with development. Cognitive development involves the progressive abstraction, construction and realization of increasingly abstract and context-independent mental structures and operations. Practical commerce with nature, and the need to co-ordinate thought and action with beings whose understanding is also constrained by the logic of nature, will ultimately drive both individuals and the species towards modes of thinking which embody logical operations. Thus viewed, logical relations provide the constraints out of which universal logical operations will eventually be constructed.

This general view (Piaget's theory provides but one example) leads to a 'vertical' analogy for conceptualizing the development of cognition in which more advanced forms of reasoning are abstracted from lower-order ways of thinking.

Looked at from a different perspective, one can accept the importance of logical relations but adopt a more 'horizontal' analogy for mind and its development. On this kind of view, the process of learning to reason about different kinds of situation does not involve abstraction and 'vertical' growth but the 'horizontal' extension of logical relations to different systems of thinking. Nunes and Bryant's interpretation of 'everyday' and 'school' mathematics provides a good illustration of this alternative view. They argued, recall, that the practices which Brazilian street vendors employ in their everyday economic activities are constrained by the same logical relations as those governing 'schooled' mathematical reasoning. However, the physical and mental processes which mediate the two forms of reasoning differ. For one thing, street mathematics is reliant on oral practices, while school maths is more dependent on methods developed to manipulate and solve written representations of problems. The two types of reasoning differ because the physical and mental operations they exploit are developed out of, and adapted for use with, different systems of signs. But it is not the case that the procedures and operations designed for the manipulation of written forms of representation are simply 'abstracted' from more context-specific, concrete or lower-order oral representations. Rather, each offers a special system of operations designed to work with the representations they provide. The practical and mental operations that they demand and support cannot be viewed as a hierarchy. Rather, they are distinct mental technologies (each of which honours the constraints of logical relations).

Such an emphasis on the *formative* role of systems of signs in the way in which physical and mental processes develop and work is, of course, compatible with the historical, social constructivist views advanced by theorists such as Vygotsky, Luria and Bruner. Thinking about the special properties of cultural tools and sign systems, in relation to the logical relations which constrain their operation and use, offers one way in which we might, if we so choose, try to integrate theory and evidence from both constructivist and socio-historical schools of thought.

9

Education and educability

As we have seen throughout this book, research into the psychology of infants and young children portrays an essentially up-beat picture of their abilities. In relation to areas such as language acquisition, the development of social awareness and an understanding of other people's minds, and in the early development of a conceptual understanding of the foundations of mathematics, research paints a basically positive picture both of what children know and of their ability to learn as they first enter the school gates. Why, then, do so many seem to fare poorly in school, come to dislike learning in the classroom and leave school with such a poor grasp of skills in communication, literacy and numeracy? This question has been asked many times over the years and, in this final chapter, I will consider some possible answers, both theoretical and practical. Be warned, however, that my treatment of these issues will be limited to a consideration of the developmental theories we have been examining throughout this book.

One possibility is that individual differences in school achievement and the ability to learn in the later stages of schooling are simply determined by genetic variations in ability. Another explanation might lie in individual differences in levels of interest, attention, motivation and effort. Alternatively, the gap between the values, attitudes and practices of home life and those demanded by schooling may be too wide for some children to bridge easily. Or, as situated action theorists might argue, given the discrepancies between what some children can do and learn in and out of school, the reason for disillusionment with schooling is that it has no relevance, and hence no value, to children's everyday life outside the classroom.

A second theme taken up in this chapter concerns the relations between theory, research and educational practice in connection with the issue of how and why it is so hard to derive, in classrooms, the learning benefits often promised by research. Why, for example, do so many children continue to have problems in learning to read or to communicate when research claims to have discovered some of the solutions to their problems? Again, why is there a divide between the images of childhood derived from different situations?

Theories of psychology and practices of education

Throughout this book, I have been exploring and emphasizing the importance of social interaction, communication and instruction in the intellectual development of children. I have also underlined the central role played by systems of signs in structuring and extending the child's communicative and cognitive abilities. Such an approach, which stresses the external or 'exogenous' influences on human development, is in a continual state of tension, if not open opposition, with those theories which emphasize the internal or 'endogenous' control of cognitive development. Such disagreements of theoretical emphasis lead to very different views about the nature of education and educability.

Both neo-Piagetian and neo-nativist theories are more likely to attribute to nature what socio-cultural theories claim as products of the process of social construction. Whilst both the neo-Piagetian and neo-nativist approaches are motivated by a search for universal and timeless truths about individual minds, the more socio-culturally oriented approaches are more concerned with the culturally and sub-culturally specific aspects of human psychology, with the historical relativity of the influences which constrain cultural practices, and with trying to understand the processes which lead both to individual differences within cultures and to general patterns of similarity and difference across them. They seek universals and peculiarities in the way in which cultures perpetuate themselves and induct the young into their ways of life. Where the modularity theorist might be tempted first to explain individual differences in school achievement in terms of factors like differential rates of maturation and genetically mediated natural variations in ability, the socio-culturalist is likely to try to account for such differences by appealing to variations in social practices, values and access to sources of power and knowledge within the culture. Thus, the weight that different theories are likely to place on educational practices as a source of variations in educational achievement differs considerably.

But there are also important differences within each general theoretical approach. For example, modern constructivist theories vary in the degree of importance that they attribute to the role of socio-cultural factors and systems of signs in influencing the course of cognitive development. Case, for example, argues that both evidence derived from socio-cultural research and that demonstrating the modular structure of mind must, and can, be accommodated within his theoretical framework. His position, though still mainly a constructivist one, is thus far removed from that of Piaget. However, by maintaining the view that the basic processes which support all learning and performance change with age, his theory still remains distinct from the approach taken, for example, by modularity theorists.

As I have tried to illustrate throughout this book, different psychological theories of how children think and learn adopt very different stances in relation to issues such as the links between processes of maturation, development and learning and they disagree about such things as the role of logic in cognition and the relations between language and thinking. Yet, they all agree that we need a theory to explain the workings of the mind. The drive to develop such theories has led, in the hands of different theorists, to the formulation of concepts such as mental operations, models and modules, rules of the mind, inner speech and inner dialogue. They appeal to different psychological processes of 'abstraction' variously termed internalization, appropriation, reflective abstraction, de-contextualization, disembedding, representational re-description, interiorization, and so forth. They are all theories about the same sorts of things: the presumed contents and processes of cognition. We certainly do not lack a vocabulary of mental terms. Perhaps, as the early behaviourists might have argued, this proliferation of terminology for describing cognition is itself a sign that we will never make a science of mental life out of anything but the study of behaviour.

One reading of situated action theory is that the 'reification' of mind signalled by such terms does indeed leave too much in the head and too little in the situations in which human beings act out their lives. Physical and social environments are not simply 'places' in which people act: they remain an integral part of their knowledge and action. In chapter 8, recall, I outlined research into the mathematical practices of Brazilian children which compared their performances in 'street' and 'school' mathematics. To a mathematical eye, the tasks they were asked to undertake in both situations appear identical: they demand facility with the same numbers and mathematical operations. The children's 'failure to generalize' what they knew from one context to another, on a situated account, reveals the fallacy of the assumption that the same or similar 'cognitive processes' are involved. The two activities, street and school maths, embody different purposes, practices, people and places. Each of these situational dimensions is an integral part of what is learned. The notion that such different cultural activities involve the 'same' tasks or require the 'same' mental operations is a myth – a myth created by those who wish to draw parallels between performance in such different situations simply for their own theoretical purposes. Street vendors, of course, share neither those purposes nor the proposed mental connections that they construct. Maybe, like radical behaviourism, situated action theory demands a rejection of mind.

Such a radical reading of situated action theory also implies that schools and teachers can do little to prepare children for everyday life in the wider culture. Yet, as we saw in the last chapter, others interpret the same body of evidence less radically. For example, studies of the mathematical performance of children in school and on the streets show that their activities differ in terms of the *systems of signs* used in the two contexts. Thus, the notion that they demand the 'same' cognitive processes is invalid because the two forms of mathematical reasoning (not simply the situations in which that reasoning takes place) are different. Nonetheless, Nunes and Bryant (1996) argue, whilst their reasoning involves the use of different signs, both street and school maths demand a similar conceptual grasp of the basic logical relations which underpin mathematical thinking. This view acknowledges that practices vary across different situations and leads to a very different account of the relations between 'everyday' mathematical reasoning and school maths from that entertained in traditional cognitive and educational theory, but it has powerful implications for the way in which the teaching of mathematics in school might be improved, as we saw in the previous chapter.

One intelligence or many?

As I have said several times, modular theories of mind differ from positions such as that taken by Piaget and modern learning theories in that they reject the view that cognition and cognitive development are single, unitary processes. For the best part of a hundred years, similar arguments have been heard in the field of mental testing. Here too, arguments about how we should conceptualize human intelligence – as a single or multiple affair – are still taking place. Since this furthers our consideration of the relations between ability and education, we consider a very brief account of these issues here.

Ever since IQ tests were developed at the turn of this century, arguments about how they should be analysed and interpreted have continued unabated. Some believe that they measure a single, underlying general intelligence, 'g', others that they reveal up to 120 different abilities or 'vectors of the mind'. Historically, such arguments have centred on methodological issues concerning the appropriate statistical techniques to be used in analysing test scores, and on the interpretation of evidence which shows correlations between differences in the general speed of mental processing and IQ test performance (Eysenck, 1987). As we have seen, the role of speed of processing and the interpretation of changes in processing speed with age and expertise have also surfaced in relation to contemporary developmental theory. In principle, the two literatures might be expected, jointly, to enable such questions to be resolved. In practice, both traditions have been split by similar differences of interpretation.

Piaget, who worked as an assistant to Binet, the developer of the first intelligence tests, became interested in the common patterns of correct responses and errors made by children with similar 'mental ages' on Binet's tests. This, in company with his interest in evolution and biology, set him on the path to the formulation of his theory of stages. This, as we have seen, argues for a single, monolithic structure of mind, which undergoes wholesale transformation with age. In cognitive psychology, modern learning theories, such as that formulated by Newell (1991), also view the mind as a general purpose problem-solving system. For them, however, differentiation of performance comes about through practice, problem-solving and expertise, not changes in stages of development (although Newell was prepared to be persuaded!). Time on task and an interest in solving problems are the major determinants of achievement. This approach, though it does not necessarily rule out ability as a source of variations in achievement, places greater stress on the role of interest and experience.

An alternative perspective, which we have also explored in this book, holds that the mind exhibits 'multiple intelligences' and that children develop more domain-specific or module-based 'theories' in different areas of functioning such as language, number, spatial concepts and so forth. Gardner's (1983) theory of intelligence, for instance, posits at least seven distinct 'frames of mind'. Cultures, he argues, place different values on these abilities. For example, Western cultures value most the importance of logical and mathematical abilities, whereas others, such as the Balinese, place greater stress on kinaesthetic intelligence which is developed to high levels of performance in dance. Thus, different societies selectively develop the latent talents of their children in ways that reflect their collective values. In this sense, the concept of intelligence is culturally relative. However, variations in levels of achievement within any given ability are largely due to genetic factors.

On this account, exceptional children exhibit outstanding achievement because they are endowed with a high level of native ability in one intelligence or frame of mind. Unlike learning-theory accounts of individual differences, the modular view argues that not only practice and expertise but also the 'quality' of functioning of those parts of the brain and nervous system which serve different intelligences determine achievement. One implication of theories of multiple intelligences is that if we want more of our children to achieve their full potential, we should diagnose and build upon their strengths and enlarge our view of what it means to be intelligent. Thus, differentiation on the basis of ability is the best way to proceed in educating children.

As I have suggested in several chapters, there are now several attempts taking place to achieve a coherent theoretical synthesis of these positions in relation both to theories of intelligence (e.g. Sternberg, 1985) and to developmental theory (e.g. Case, 1991). There seems to be a general movement, then, which seeks to acknowledge the fact that minds do exhibit a modular structure (as many studies of infancy show) but that later development also involves more general, cross-modular integration and exploits the cognitive practices and sign systems made available by the culture in which development takes place. The extent to which such efforts towards a grand synthesis will succeed remains to be seen. To the extent that it can, we will be better placed to resolve competing explanations for differences in ability, experience and attainment.

Socio-cultural theories are more concerned with exploring variations in children's life circumstances as a way of understanding both universals and differences in development within and across cultures. There is no reason, in principle, why such approaches should be incompatible with either a modular view of mind or theories about genetically determined differences in ability. In practice, however, the advocates of the different theoretical traditions have tended either to disagree or to ignore each other. As Case points out, the fact that each tradition has focused on different phenomena and used different methodologies makes it extremely difficult to locate areas of common ground where it would be possible either to adjudicate between different explanations or, as he does, to attempt a theoretical synthesis of the different perspectives.

Effort and ability

Throughout this book, I have been concerned with processes of learning and development and with issues about the importance of communication and instruction in fostering or impeding these. Tests of general ability, however interpreted, which provide predictions about the likely future achievements of different groups of children, can be used to contribute to discussions of these processes and issues in a number of ways. For example, several investigations and classroom experiments that I have discussed in this book have employed formal tests of 'general academic ability' to address questions like 'How does the performance of a child with a high test score differ from that of a child with a low one?' or 'How might such differences be implicated in the relative difficulty a given child experiences in learning how to read or to solve specific types of learning problem?' Where we find, for example, that children with high scores are more expert in processes of self-regulation and self-explanation, we can go on to ask if other children can be taught how to develop these abilities. Such comparisons prove useful to the extent that they provide insights into the sorts of classroom activities we might use to help children become more effective in learning and self-instruction. The work of Brown, Ferrara and their colleagues, discussed in several chapters, illustrates this approach to curriculum development.

In each chapter, we have considered different abilities that underlie the capacity to learn in school. Problems in one or in any combination of these abilities will create learning problems for a child. They include a desire and ability to attend, concentrate and memorize; knowing how to apportion one's time and resources in order to study and learn; understanding what people mean by what they say and do; the confidence and expertise to present and explain oneself and knowing how to make what one has to say or write accessible to one's audience; the ability to evaluate and redirect one's efforts, to self-correct and self-instruct; and knowing how to make one's attentions and actions contingent upon the requests, demands and needs of others. Difficulties in gaining competence in any of these activities will generate problems for a child. To the extent that we are able to help a child to gain and perfect such abilities, that child is educable.

What I propose to do in these final pages is to re-examine, briefly, some aspects of the processes involved in learning how to think and learn in school that we have considered at greater length in the preceding chapters. I do not intend to present a summary. Rather, I will apply some of the ideas, findings and questions we have already discussed to consider what, if anything, we know about the nature and origins of individual differences in children's powers in these areas. I will also attempt to mention, albeit briefly, factors which contribute to a child's likely experiences in school which lie outside the remit of the theories of learning and development that we have been considering but which need to be integrated into our thinking about education and educability.

Attending and concentrating

Picture a classroom in which all but one or two children are concentrating on the task at hand. Then imagine another in which the majority of children seem restless, talkative, fidgety and inattentive to the lesson. If, observed over time, the same handful of children in the first class seem inattentive and easily distracted, then one would be led to ask what it is about those children that renders their concentration so poor. If the state of affairs persists in the second imaginary class, one might be led to ask questions about the teacher and what is being taught.

We may be tempted to conclude that evidence of consistent inattention is proof of the fact that some pupils lack 'powers' of attention and concentration. However, I have argued several times in different chapters that the ability to attend and concentrate is not simply a natural capacity that children 'possess' to a greater or lesser extent. When we examined what was involved in the development of powers of concentration, for example, we found that it implicates a number of processes of self-regulation, some aspects of which have to be learned. Further, what can be perceived and memorized depends upon a learner's existing conceptual understanding and task-specific knowledge. Where the gap between a child's current level of understanding and that demanded by what is being taught is too great, then we cannot expect to find the child concentrating on what is being said and done.

For example, if, as Hart and her colleagues suggest, around half of children in secondary mathematics classes are unlikely to have sufficient grasp of the subject to understand what the teacher does and says in group lessons, then, as they advocate, we should seek explanations in terms of what is being taught and how, rather than attribute blame to 'inattentive children'.

But common observation suggests that children differ in the extent to which they can learn such things as strategies which help them to buffer themselves from distraction, and to develop the ability to study. There are several lines of evidence which suggest that *some* (and I emphasize the word) children do face problems of adjustment to school because they are temperamentally ill-suited to sitting still and concentrating. The relationships between such 'inborn' temperamental characteristics and social experiences in the formation of personality are complex and controversial. A detailed consideration of the issues involved lies outside our immediate concerns. However, I think it is useful to look at some of the studies in this field since they illustrate that, for some children, learning *how* to pay attention and concentrate is difficult because of their temperaments. For a tiny minority of children, I think we must conclude that their problems of attention and concentration are not of their own, or anyone else's, making. Some of the evidence for this argument comes from what looks like an unlikely source – the study of anatomy.

Most of us are born with two or three 'minor physical abnormalities' (MPAs). For instance, one of our toes may be too long relative to the others, we may have no ear lobes or a slight palatal defect. Children with an unusually large number of such minor physical characteristics may display learning problems in school (Bell and Waldrop, 1982). For example, boys with five or more minor abnormalities are likely to appear restless, fidgety and inattentive in comparison to children with fewer than five, whereas girls with five or more are more often passive, shy and withdrawn.

Most of these minor defects are invisible to the non-clinical eye and careful inspection is needed to discover them. So it seems highly unlikely that other people's responses to the child cause such learning problems. Identifying precise causes is difficult. However, there is evidence of association between minor physical abnormalities at birth and both maternal *diet* during pregnancy, such as a high intake of refined foods, and maternal infection at crucial periods in the development of the foetus. Such evidence suggests that the causes of MPAs lie in damage to foetal chromosomes during gestation. Thus, social factors, like maternal diet, and socially related experiences, such as the probability of exposure to infection during pregnancy, are known to affect the developing foetus (Bell and Waldrop, 1982). Children's bodies and aspects of their mental adjustment, like levels of activity and proneness to distraction, are in turn affected by impaired biological processes. The divide between social and biological influences on development and that between physical and mental characteristics of an individual are not clear-cut. Similarly, malnutrition is a pretty good prescription for producing apathy in normally alert, active and attentive children. The correlation between poverty and school achievement has been long recognized. We have been considering mainly cognitive and linguistic accounts of development in this book, but it is important to note that such considerations rest on the tacit assumption that a child's basic needs are being met. In some cultures (and in some households in our own culture), this assumption is unwarranted.

There are other lines of evidence that point directly to the effects of a child's life experiences on his ability to concentrate in class. For example, children from abusing homes are sometimes (though by no means invariably) overactive, easily distracted and disruptive in school (Kempe and Kempe, 1978). Similarly, the study of children with histories of local authority, institutional care and adoption reveal differences in school behaviour, including fidgeting, restlessness and an inability to concentrate (Tizard and Hodges, 1978). Children who, in their first years of life, experience long periods of time being cared for outside their family may, when they are returned to the family, exhibit problems of concentration and attention. Interestingly, many of these problems are more evident at school (where children are in groups and usually have to make what they say and do contingent upon the teacher's demands) than they are at home.

If a particular child is characteristically restless and inattentive in class, and there is any reason to suspect poor diet or chronic stress and upset (or, sadly, these days, drugs) as causes for his or her problem, then, clearly, more than educational intervention is called for. I do not think we know to what extent differences in children's powers of concentration are attributable to such factors. However, where a large proportion of children find concentration heavy going and the classroom admonition 'pay attention!' is heard frequently, it is probably a sign that the match between what children understand and what they are being required to attend to is too great for them to bridge.

Effort, ability and motivation: the social dimension

In an earlier chapter, I outlined studies of children's developing 'theories of mind'. By the time they enter school, children are aware of the fact that other people hold beliefs about the world and that they act on the basis of such beliefs. Young children are not behaviourists! Amongst those beliefs, one set is of particular importance to the child: the beliefs that affect how others view them. Developmental studies of children's concepts of friendship, in line with common experience, demonstrate the crucial import, even for the young school child, of what they think their peers believe about them. The child's view of himself as a social being, as an object of other people's regard, can be a crucial determinant of his motivations. And if you accept this, then you also buy into the notion that motivation and de-motivation for learning are not simply manifestations of individual cognition but a consequence of a complex interaction between the personal and the social.

The issue of 'motivation' and 'de-motivation' of children has received much, often wise, thought (e.g. Holt, 1967) and I do not intend to consider the issue at length here. However, research into the development of motivation and its relation to *effort* and performance has shed some new light on the issue. Heckhausen, a German psychologist, has undertaken a series of studies to investigate changes in children's motivation with age and cognitive development (e.g. Heckhausen, 1982). Briefly, he argues that up to the age of around eleven years (another shift coming up!) children do not entertain a very clear distinction between *effort* and *ability*. The young child, in his view, perceives as equal all who manage to achieve the same goals. The fact that some children do things faster than others does not seem to overly concern them. However, around age eleven, things begin to change. The child now appreciates the fact that two people who put in different amounts of *time* and *effort* to achieve the same ends must differ in some way. The concept that emerges to co-ordinate the concepts of effort and achievement is *ability*.

Some children, when this realization dawns upon them, are in a cleft stick. If they work hard to achieve what others seem to find easy, then they betray their *low ability*. Since ability is at a premium (at least, in some cultures) the child may experience a desire not to try, to run away, drop out, show a lack of interest and decide that schooling is 'silly' and a waste of time. In this view, the relation between ability and performance is mediated not simply by the genes but by *self-perception* and a desire to avoid betraying signs of incompetence. One suspects, given the results of David Hargreaves' (1967) study of child 'cultures' in the secondary school, that such children will soon find others who share their views on schooling.

Dweck and her colleagues (1978) have also looked beyond innate differences in aptitude to explain achievement in studies of the different experiences of boys and girls in the classroom. They provide many insights into the complex social dynamics in lessons, but two of their observations are of interest to us here. They examined the 'feedback' given to boys and girls by their teachers in mathematics lessons. There were some marked differences. Boys, for example, more often received negative feedback. But this did not often reflect on their intellectual abilities. There was, so to speak, a 'hidden message', which was that if they were not doing well, the reason was not due to mathematical incompetence but to other factors, such as inattentiveness. When the boys received praise, or positive feedback, this was likely to focus upon intellectual competence, signalling that they were good at maths. Girls received infrequent negative feedback from their teachers, but when it did occur, it was very likely to reflect upon their ability in maths. So for boys, criticism is common and by no means a special event, and it does not reflect upon their competence. However, if feedback is positive (and this is a special event for boys), it usually reflects well on their mathematical ability. Because negative feedback is rare for girls, when a girl *does* receive it, it forms a notable event and is likely to convey the idea, to both herself and her peers, that she is not very good at the subject.

One implication of these observations is that, perhaps unwittingly, teachers create a very different climate in the mathematics classroom for girls and boys. This acts to make 'error' a more serious affair for girls and to induce in some a sense of mathematical incompetence. Another important finding is that boys who were subjected to a similar pattern of feedback to that met by girls also felt that they lacked ability in maths, supporting the notion that teachers may contribute to their pupils' sense of competence (or otherwise). Thus, the image that a child develops about both herself and her sense of how others regard her is constructed, at least in part, in the course of classroom interaction.

In the last chapter, I referred to cross-cultural investigations of achievements in, and attitudes towards, mathematics. One finding is that in Asian cultures, like Japan, which fare well in international comparisons of achievement, cultural attitudes towards effort and achievement appear to differ from those held in Western cultures. Poor attainment is attributed to a lack of effort, not a shortage of ability. Conversely, in the West, failure is more likely to be attributed to a lack of ability rather than a shortfall in effort.

If one accepts Gardner's claim that Western cultures view intelligence largely in terms of achievements in logico-mathematical domains, then they may have painted themselves into an educational corner. If, through an emphasis on ability over effort, we implicitly force many children into feelings of incompetence in subjects, like maths and science, which are held in high cultural regard, then we are likely to defeat our own aims with many of our children. These, sensing that they are 'below average', can only succeed through effort and, in so doing, display a lack of ability in areas which are culturally valued. Both they and the system are in a no-win situation. Paradoxically, then, the low esteem in which they hold learning and the anti-intellectual stance which many children appear to adopt as they leave school may be due to their sense of failure in what they know, deep down, are the things that our system tells them 'really matter'.

All this is pure speculation, of course. However, the view that we should try to encourage in our schools the development of a culture which acknowledges effort, rather than ability alone, is being advocated by some who have spent a professional lifetime in the study of how children think, learn and can be taught (Resnick and Nelson-Le Gall, in press). However, if the observations by Dweck and her colleagues are sound, and the critique of Western approaches to teaching which encourage speed at the cost of reflection are accepted (see chapter 8), then we face a task of massive changes in attitudes and practice if such a vision is to be achieved.

Theory to practice: a hard road?

In several chapters, I have discussed classroom intervention studies in which, working with individuals or small groups of children, success has been achieved in the teaching of reading, writing, communication skills and mathematics to children who were struggling to learn. Where the effects obtained from such studies were great and suitable controls were used to ensure that success could be attributed to the teaching strategies used, rather than to factors like extra time on task or just the additional attention of an adult, then we can be confident that our knowledge, both of the nature of the children's learning problems and of the experiences needed to overcome or ameliorate these, has been expanded. The question then arises as to how we get such knowledge into practice. And this question is not an easy one to answer.

This has not been a book about teaching methods, curriculum development or classroom management. This is not because I think these issues are unimportant – far from it. Rather, it is simply that I do not profess to know much about such things. However, in concluding this book, I think it is important to acknowledge some of the difficult conceptual and practical problems that we face in trying to derive benefits from theory and research by seeking their exploitation in the classroom.

Intervention programmes, such as the Reading Recovery approach developed by Marie Clay and her colleagues (e.g. Clay and Cazden, 1990; Hobsbaum, Peters and Sylva, 1996), make significant demands on teaching time and teachers' knowledge and skills. Teachers have to learn how to assess 'gradients of difficulty' in the reading and writing tasks they set for children to ensure that learners are faced with sufficient challenge to promote progress without being overwhelmed by too many new demands. In Vygotskian terms, they need to locate and work at the upper bounds of a child's zone of proximal development. The teacher must then be capable of scaffolding the child's activities to ensure that they meet the challenges set and do as much as they can for themselves but without being left to struggle alone when demands exceed their current abilities. Teachers must also be ready to 'fade' their support for aspects of the tasks that the child is ready to perform alone and then stand ready to help them as they are moved on into new terrains of learning. As I said in chapter 4, even on simple tasks, successful scaffolding of the learning process and the maintenance of contingent instruction call for considerable knowledge, skill and vigilance on the part of the tutor. Learning how to operate a Reading Recovery programme entails considerable teacher training. This is one reason why there is no simple prescription for putting knowledge of the teaching and learning processes into action in the classroom. The same argument can be extended to the other intervention programmes outlined in earlier chapters.

The 'gap' between what is promised by research and what happens in the majority of classrooms is also illustrated by investigations into the effects of peer interaction on learning. There is now an extensive body of evidence which shows that getting children to work collaboratively in pairs and small groups can help them to develop their skills and conceptual understanding (Wood and O'Malley, 1996). For example, interactions between small groups of children, without direct aid from a teacher, can lead to advances in their understanding of phenomena such as why and how things float or sink and of the factors which influence the motion of objects (Howe, Tolmie and Rodgers, 1990). This work provides us with some important insights into the conditions which need to be fulfilled if children are to benefit maximally from such group work.

First, the children involved should, collectively, know or believe different things about the phenomena being investigated and they must also come up with different predictions about what will happen in the practical task situations set. In this way, both the likelihood that they will voice different ideas about what is likely to happen when they undertake experiments and the chances that they will help each other to consider and co-ordinate different explanations are maximized. The chances are that they will then revise their ideas about the phenomena being investigated and develop more elaborate explanations.

This means that, to create the effective conditions for group work, the researchers had to (a) diagnose what individual children knew and were likely to expect to happen in the phenomena to be investigated, (b) select groups to ensure that children were likely to encounter competing ideas and predictions from each other, and (c) identify and create task situations likely to provoke the children into discussing different possible outcomes and explanations. To achieve such group situations in the classroom entails considerable demands on a teacher's knowledge of both the subject matter and the children's current knowledge and expectations.

Despite the fact that such research shows that children have the potential ability to work successfully in groups and can learn from each other, when we look at the findings of observation studies that have examined how children behave in group work in the classroom, we see that this potential is seldom realized (Bennett et al., 1984; Galton and Williamson, 1992). Most attempts to get children to work in teams do not generate the outcomes one might expect from research. In part, this may be due to the way in which children are selected for group work and the nature of the tasks set. However, Galton, a researcher of long standing in this area, suggests that major reasons for lack of success are that children are not schooled in the attitudes and skills needed to sustain effective collaboration and that they receive 'mixed messages' from teachers. Typically told to work quietly, alone and at speed, they find it hard, Galton suggests, to accept that talking, arguing and discussing things in groups is really acceptable in class. Other investigations into the conditions for effective group work also suggest that the 'ground rules' for acceptable behaviour in groups and the processes involved need to be made explicit to children. Discussion about the nature of effective discussion, for example, can help them to appreciate both the intended goals of group work and the communicative practices involved.

Cross-cultural comparisons of classroom practices provide some possible insights into how effective group work in the classroom might be achieved. Some observations of Japanese classrooms, for example, show that teachers often set problems to small groups of children. In maths lessons, groups are encouraged to find their own ways of solving a problem. They are then invited, in whole-class settings, to illustrate and explain their solutions to the others. This provides opportunities for discussing any differences in solution strategies and any slips or mistakes revealed. In this way, children have an opportunity to discover that most problems can be solved in different ways and this invites them to consider factors such as the relative elegance of the methods used. This helps to make explicit and public the conceptions, strategies and procedures implicated in different ways of construing problems. However, as I cautioned in chapter 8, it is unwise to conclude from such observations that differences in teaching practice necessarily cause cross-cultural variations in school achievement. Many other factors, such as differences in language and in cultural values and attitudes towards learning, may also play a part.

When researchers enter a classroom they can, so to speak, negotiate their own contracts with pupils. Children are likely to know that something out of the ordinary is taking place and may accept new ways of trying to learn and keep on task more readily than they would in the normal classroom setting. Thus, the 'culture' of classroom life and that which governs experimental investigations – even when these take place in schools – are likely to differ. If one culture supports different ways of acting and learning from another, then we should not be surprised to find that it is hard to 'apply' the findings of research to everyday classroom practice.

Theory, technology and teaching

In the previous chapter, I outlined Fuson's analysis of the variety of situations to which an understanding of addition and subtraction with whole numbers applies. I also mentioned her critique of the maths curriculum as presented in North American textbooks. She argues that the mathematical content of these is too narrowly conceived and that the way in which problems are presented and sequenced is far from ideal. Her analysis of the conceptual foundations of such mathematical knowledge and of the way in which curricula might be re-designed to be more in tune with what children need to learn and how they might be taught suggests another route for the application and exploitation of theory and research. Technologies like textbooks provide vehicles for transporting research findings into the classroom. If these are revised on the basis of research findings, as Fuson implies, then they provide one means for carrying the lessons of research into schools.

In recent years, we have been experiencing the impact of information technology in schools. With the promise of universal access for schools to electronic networks, the possible effects that the information revolution might have on the future of education can only be guessed at. I will not attempt to second-guess the future here, however. Rather, I want to use this final section to explore the impact that the theories of learning and development that we have been considering in this book have already had on the design of educational technology, in an attempt to assess the extent to which, like textbook technology, they have provided, or might provide, a new route for the exploitation of theory and research in practice.

Skinner, as I mentioned in chapter 4, foresaw much promise in the application of learning theory to the design of 'teaching machines'. He believed that, programmed to teach according to strict principles of shaping and reinforcement, such machines would free children from the irrationalities of human teaching and help to perfect a scientifically based technology of teaching. Although some Skinnerian teaching machines were built and used in schools, they never took off, for reasons I will discuss later.

Another attempt to free children from the dictates of teachers came from a very different theoretical quarter. This approach, developed by Seymour Papert (1980, 1994) and his colleagues, drew its inspiration from Piaget's theory and aimed to provide children with new tools to help them to construct their own knowledge and, whilst so doing, to discover and exploit their own powers of learning. Where Skinner set out to program machines to teach children, Papert, by getting children to program machines for themselves, endeavoured to help them to teach themselves using the LOGO programming environment. Although evaluations of LOGO have produced some evidence that it can support learning of specific mathematical concepts, the larger benefits hoped for in terms of global effects on children's conceptual understanding and general problem-solving skills have not been forthcoming. Papert argues that such lack of success stems not from any theoretical or technical inadequacies of LOGO but from the fact that teachers have not been able or willing to provide a learning culture within which children can develop their potential. Another possibility, of course, is that the theory itself stands in need of revision and that children require more support in order to develop their conceptual understanding. As we have already seen, many neo-Piagetian theorists have acknowledged the need to incorporate elements of the socio-cultural perspective in order to carry the constructivist agenda further. In relation to learning within the LOGO environment, there are also those who argue that children need more guidance and support in the use of LOGO if they are to explore and benefit from the learning opportunities it opens up (Hoyles and Sutherland, 1989).

In chapter 4, I gave a very brief account of Anderson's Intelligent Tutoring Systems and referred to evidence that they can speed up rates of achievement in areas like the learning of geometry and programming languages. Some reactions to Anderson's achievements echo those which greeted Skinner's teaching machines. Anderson's tutors respond to a learner's interactions on an act-by-act basis: they monitor each learner action and evaluate performance at this 'micro-level'. Whilst Anderson defines procedural learning in terms of the acquisition of new production rules, Skinner defines it in terms of the shaping and reinforcement of S–R connections, both focus on local behaviour. Skinner's teaching machines were designed to present learning sequences in steps so small that a learner should never make an error. Anderson's tutors, whilst designed to minimize the chances of overloading the learner, are not designed to achieve error-free performance. But, as we saw in chapter 4, his tutors are designed to correct errors immediately. On both theoretical accounts, there is no benefit attributed to errors in learning.

In the preceding chapter, I explored research into mathematics instruction which is highly critical of attempts to teach procedures at the expense of conceptual understanding. Such criticisms, as I pointed out, are not new, and both Piaget and Bruner, amongst others, were critical of drill and practice approaches to instruction. More recently, Schoenfeld (1988) has argued that 'good teaching leads to bad results' when it only helps learners to perfect the application of procedures to problems. This results in learning outcomes which do not support either understanding or generalization, for reasons that were explored in chapter 8.

Another criticism levelled against such teaching methods by Schoenfeld and others is that they do not foster (and may inhibit) the development of strategies for regulating one's own problem-solving. For example, the detection, interpretation and remediation of one's own errors is an important part of acquiring and making intelligent use of knowledge. If the responsibility for such activities is controlled by an external agent (teacher or machine), then the opportunities for developing effective self-regulatory strategies is minimized and a view of learning as the mere acquisition of procedures reinforced. These are precisely the arguments levelled against early behaviourist theories of instruction.

In recent years, several attempts have been made to apply notions like scaffolding and cognitive apprenticeship to the design of computer-based learning environments. One approach, developed by Katz and Lesgold (1993), and others, seeks to promote learning through 'authentic' problem-solving. The system presents learners with a simulation of the learning task and they are able to 'run' the simulation to see what happens when they take specific actions. One application of this approach (a system termed 'Sherlock' in deference to Dr Watson's colleague) is designed to teach trainee electronics technicians how to diagnose and rectify errors in aircraft engines. The problems set resemble those found in the 'real world' and are initially 'out of reach' for the learner in the sense that they cannot, initially, solve problems without help. The amount of help provided by the computer 'coach' is determined by the learner's level of skill. Initially, any help given is likely to take the form of a 'walk through' as the computer demonstrates a solution. When a similar problem is next encountered, however, the computer is programmed to offer less help: it tries continually to 'fade'. If the help provided is not understood, however, then more help is given on request. Thus, such tutoring systems are designed to support learning of complex skills in a simulated environment, offering help in a way that is contingent upon the learner's developing competence. After around twenty hours on the system, trainees function on the job as well as those with four years of practical experience.

Although this example is taken from a training context rather than an educational one, attempts are currently underway to create similar systems for teaching school subjects such as biology.

Concluding comment

It is estimated that around 25 per cent of school districts in the USA now make use of extensive computer-based teaching systems, generically called Integrated Learning Systems (Underwood, 1997). I have ended this chapter with a brief consideration of educational technology to underline the fact that these systems have their roots in assumptions about theories of how children learn. If we question these assumptions, then we have reason to expect limits on the systems derived from them.

The technical achievements represented by the creation of such computer-based learning environments are impressive. However, it is important not to be too impressed. Once such systems achieve even a moderate degree of complexity, they are liable to become unpredictable and, hence, potentially fascinating. Even systems which are programmed to follow a few simple rules can appear more 'intelligent', flexible and adaptive than they really are and we have known for a long time that people are often quite prepared to attribute them with powers that far exceed their true capabilities. Amongst the current limitations of such systems are their lack of flexibility in supporting different learning strategies and their weak powers of explanation. Most systems are also designed to function with a single end user in mind working on a stand-alone machine. If there are intellectual benefits to be gained from communication and interaction with peers, for example, then current systems are not designed to support such activities (though some attempts to create shared learning environments are underway).

More generally, however, it is important to recognize the theoretical assumptions about the nature of human learning and development which have inspired the design of such systems. Any limitations of the theory will be inherited by the system. Thus, one reason for concluding with a discussion of the application of theory to computer-based learning is to highlight the fact that, in trying to assess their likely worth and potential, all of the conceptual and empirical ideas we have been exploring in this book are relevant. If we are to be intelligent users of such systems in education, and not simply dupes to a hard sales pitch, then we must measure their promise against our general knowledge of how children think and learn.

BIBLIOGRAPHY

Anderson, J. R. (1993). *Rules of the mind.* Hillsdale, N.J.: Lawrence Erlbaum Associates.

Bartlett, F. C. (1932). *Remembering: a study in experimental and social psychology.* Cambridge: Cambridge University Press.

—— (1958). *Thinking.* New York: Basic Books.

Beer, S. (1977). Cybernetics. In A. A. Bullock & O. Stallybrass (eds), *The Fontana dictionary of modern thought.* London: Fontana/Collins.

Bell, A. W., Costello, J. & Kuchemann, D. (1983). *A review of research in mathematical education. Part A: research on learning and teaching.* Windsor, Berks: NFER Nelson.

Bell, R. Q. & Waldrop, M. F. (1982). Temperament and minor physical abnormalities. In R. Porter & G. Collins (eds), *Temperamental differences in infants and young children.* London: Pitman.

Bennett, N., Desforges, C., Cockburn, A. & Wilkinson, B. (1984). *The quality of pupil learning experiences.* London: Lawrence Erlbaum.

Bereiter, C. & Englemann, S. (1966). *Teaching disadvantaged children in the pre-school.* Englewood Cliffs, N.J.: Prentice Hall.

Bernstein, B. (1960). Language and social class. *British Journal of Sociology,* 11, 271–6.

—— (1961). Social class and linguistic development: a theory of social learning. In A. H. Halsey, J. Floud & L. A. Anderson (eds), *Education, economy and society.* Glencoe, Ill.: Free Press.

—— (1970). A sociolinguistic approach to socialization with some references to educability. In D. Williams (ed.), *Language and poverty.* Chicago, Ill.: Markham.

Blank, M., Rose, S. A. & Berlin, L. J. (1978). *The Language of learning: the pre-school years.* New York: Grune and Stratton.

Boden, M. (1979). *Piaget.* London: Fontana Paperbacks.

Brown, A. L. & Campione, J. C. (1990). Communities of learning and thinking, or a context by any other name. In D. Kuhn (ed.), *Developmental perspectives on teaching and learning thinking skills*. Contributions to Human Development, Vol. 21. Basle: Karger.

Brown, A. L. & Ferrara, R. A. (1985). Diagnosing zones of proximal development in culture, communication and cognition. In J. V. Wertsch (ed.), *Vygotskian perspectives*. Cambridge: Cambridge University Press.

Brown, G., Anderson, A., Shillcock, R. & Yule, G. (1984). *Teaching talk: strategies for production and assessment*. London, New York, New Rochelle, Melbourne, Sydney: Cambridge University Press.

Bruner, J. S. (1957). Going beyond the information given. In J.M. Anglin (ed.), *Beyond the information given*. New York: W. W. Norton.

—— (1966a). *The process of education*. Cambridge, Mass.: Harvard University Press.

—— (1966b). *Toward a theory of instruction*. New York: W.W. Norton.

—— (1968). *Processes of cognitive growth: infancy*. USA: Clark University Press.

—— (1971). *The relevance of education*. New York: W.W. Norton.

—— (1983). *Child's talk: learning to use language*. Oxford: Oxford University Press.

——(1990) *Acts of meaning*. Cambridge, Mass.: Harvard University Press.

Bruner, J. S. & Kenney, H. J. (1965). Representation and mathematics learning. *Monographs of the Society for Research in Child Development*, 30 (1), 50–9.

Bruner, J. S., Goodnow, J. J. & Austin, G. A. (1956). *A study of thinking*. New York: John Wiley.

Bruner, J. S., Olver, R. R. & Greenfield, P.M. (1966). *Studies in cognitive growth*. New York: John Wiley.

Bryant, P. (1974). *Perception and understanding in young children: an experimental approach*. London: Methuen.

Bryant, P. & Bradley, L. (1985). *Children's reading problems*. Oxford: Blackwell.

Bryant, P., Nunes, T. & Bindman, M. (in press). Children's understanding of the connection between grammar and spelling. In B. Blachman (ed.), *Linguistic underpinnings of language*. Hillsdale, N.J.: Lawrence Erlbaum.

Bryant, P.E., MacLean, M., Bradley, L. & Crossland, J. (1990). Rhyme and alliteration, phoneme detection and learning to read. *Developmental Psychology*, 26, 429–38.

Butterworth, G. & Cochran, E. (1980). What minds have in common in space: a perceptual mechanism for joint reference in infancy. *International Journal of Behavioral Development*, 3, 253–72.

Carew, J. V. (1980). Experience and the development of intelligence in young children at home and in day care. *Monographs of the Society for Research in Child Development*, 45 (6–7)Serial No. 187.

Carey, S. (1986). *Conceptual change in childhood.* Cambridge, Mass.: MIT Press.

——(1990). Cognitive development. In D.N. Osherson & E.E. Smith (eds), *An invitation to cognitive science.Vol 3: Thinking.* Cambridge, Mass.: MIT Press.

Case, R. (1985). *Intellectual development: birth to adulthood.* New York: Academic Press.

——(1991). *The mind's staircase: exploring the conceptual underpinnings of children's thought and conceptual knowledge.* Hillsdale, N.J.: Lawrence Erlbaum.

Castle, E.B. (1970). *The teacher.* London: Oxford University Press.

Chase, W. G. & Simon, H. A. (1973). Perception in chess. *Cognitive Pyschology,* 4, 55–81.

Cheng, P. W. & Holyoak, K. J. (1985). Pragmatic reasoning schemas. *Cognitive Psychology,* 17, 391–416.

Cheng, P. C.-H. & Simon, H.A. (1995). Scientific discovery and creative reasoning with diagrams. In S. Smith, T. Ward & R. Finke (eds), *The creative cognition approach.* Cambridge, Mass.: MIT Press.

Chi, M.T.H. (1976). Short-term memory limitations in children: capacity or processing deficits? *Memory and Cognition,* 4, 559–72.

Chi, M. T. H., Glaser, R. & Farr, M. J. (1988). *The nature of expertise.* Hillsdale, N.J.: Lawrence Erlbaum.

Chi, M. T. H., Glaser, R. & Rees, E. (1982). Expertise in problem solving. In L. Sternberg (ed.), *Advances in the psychology of human intelligence.* Hillsdale, N.J.: Lawrence Erlbaum.

Chomsky, N. (1957). *Syntactic structures.* The Hague: Mouton.

——(1959). Review of B F. Skinner, 'Verbal behavior'. *Language,* 35, 26–58.

——(1965). *Aspects of the theory of syntax.* Cambridge, Mass.: MIT Press.

——(1980). *Rules and representations.* Oxford: Blackwell.

Clark, E. V. (1978). From gesture to word: on the natural history of deixis in language. In J. S. Bruner & A. Garton (eds), *Human growth and development.* Oxford: Oxford University Press.

Clark, M. (1976). *Young fluent readers.* London: Heinemann.

Clay, M. M. (1985). *The early detection of reading difficulties.* Auckland, NZ: Heinemann.

——(1993). *Reading recovery: a guidebook for teachers in training.* Auckland, NZ: Heinemann.

Clay, M. M. & Cazden, C. B. (1990). A Vygotskian interpretation of reading recovery. In L. Moll (ed.), *Vygotsky and education.* Cambridge: Cambridge University Press.

Cole, M. & Scribner, S. (1974). *Culture and thought. A psychological introduction.* New York: John Wiley.

Cole, M., Gay, J., Glick, J. A. & Sharp, D.W. (1971). *The cultural context of learning and thinking: an exploration in experimental anthropology.* London: Tavistock Publications in association with Methuen.

Condon, W.S. (1980). The relation of interactional synchrony to cognitive and emotional processes. In M. R. Key (ed.), *The relationship of verbal and nonverbal communication*. The Hague: Mouton.

Crystal, D. (1976). *Child language, learning and linguistics: an overview for the teaching and therapeutic professions* (paperback ed). London: Edward Arnold.

Cunningham, A. E. (1990). Explicit versus implicit instruction in phonemic awareness. *Journal of Experimental Child Psychology*, 50, 429–44.

De Groot, A. D. Van (1965). *Thought and choice in chess*. The Hague: Mouton.

DeLoache, J. S. (1984). What's this? Maternal questions in joint picturebook reading with toddlers. *Quarterly Newsletter of the Laboratory of Comparative Human Cognition*, 6, 87–95.

Department of Education and Science (1975). *A Language for Life* (The Bullock Report). London: HMSO.

—— (1980–2). *Mathematical development*. Primary Survey Reports, nos. 1–3, and Secondary Survey Reports nos. 1–3. London: HMSO.

Dienes, Z. P. (1960). *Building up mathematics*. London: Hutchinson.

Dienes, Z. P. & Jeeves, M. A. (1970). *The effects of structural relations of transfer*. London: Routledge and Kegan Paul.

Doise, W. & Mugny, G. (1984). *The social development of the intellect* (trans. A. St James-Emler, N. Emler, D. Mackie,). Oxford: Pergamon Press.

Donaldson, M. (1978). *Children's minds* (paperback edn). Fontana/Collins.

Dunn, J. (1996) The Emanuel Miller memorial lecture 1995. Children's relationships: bridging the divide between cognitive and social development. *Journal of Child Psychology and Psychiatry*, 37 (5), 507–18.

Dunn J. & Kendrick, C. (1982). *Siblings: love, envy and understanding*. London: Grant McKintyre.

Dweck, C. S., Davidson, W., Nelson, S. & Enna, B. (1978). Sex differences in learned helplessness II: the contingencies of evaluative feedback in the classroom and III: an experimental analysis. *Developmental Psychology*, 14, 268–76.

Elkind, D. (1974). *Children and adolescents: interpretive essays on Jean Piaget*. Oxford: Oxford University Press.

Eysenck, H. J. (1987). A general systems approach to the measurement of intelligence and personality. In S.H. Irvine & S.E. Newstead (eds), *Intelligence and cognition: contemporary frames of reference*. Lancaster: Martinus Nijhoff Publishers.

Feldman, C. F. (1992). The new theory of theory of mind. *Human Development*, 35, 107–17.

Fischer, K. W. (1980). A theory of cognitive development: the control and construction of hierarchies of skills. *Psychological Review*, 87, 477–531.

Fodor, J. (1982). *The modularity of mind*. Cambridge, Mass.: MIT Press.

Frazier, L. & Rayner, K. (1982). Making and correcting errors during sentence comprehension. *Cognitive Psychology*, 14, 178–210.

Frydman, O. (1990). The role of correspondence in the development of number based strategies in young children. D. Phil. thesis, University of Oxford. Cited in Nunes and Bryant (1996).

Fuson K. C. (1992). Research into whole number addition and subtraction. In D. A. Grouws (ed.), *Handbook of research on mathematics teaching and learning*. New York: Macmillan.

Galton, M. & Williamson, J. (1992). *Group work in the classroom*. London: Routledge.

Gardner, H. (1983). *Frames of mind: the theory of multiple intelligences*. New York: Basic Books.

Gelman R. & Meck, E. (1983). Preschoolers counting: principles before skill. *Cognition*, 13, 343–60.

Gentner, D. & Stevens, A. L. (1983). *Mental models*. Hillsdale, N.J.: Lawrence Erlbaum.

Ghiselin, B. (ed.) (1952) *The Creative Process*. Berkeley, Calif.: University of California Press.

Gibson, J. J. (1950). *The perception of the visual world*. Boston, Mass.: Houghton and Mifflin.

Glachen, M. & Light, P. (1982). Peer interaction and learning: can two wrongs make a right? In G. Butterworth & P. Light (eds), *Social cognition*. Brighton: The Harvester Press.

Gleitman, L. R. & Wanner, E. (1982). Language acquisition: the state of the state of the art. In E. Wanner & L. R. Gleitman (eds), *Language acquisition: the state of the art*. Cambridge: Cambridge University Press.

Goody, E. N. (ed.) (1978). *Questions and politeness: strategies in social interaction*. London, New York, Melbourne: Cambridge University Press.

Goswami, U. & Bryant, P. (1990). *Phonological skills and learning to read*. London, Lawrence Erlbaum.

Greer B. (1992). Multiplication and division as models of situations. *Handbook of research on mathematics teaching and learning*. New York: Macmillan.

Halford, G. S. (1992). *Children's understanding: the development of mental models*. Hillsdale, N.J.: Lawrence Erlbaum.

Halliday, M. A. K. (1975). *Learning how to mean: explorations in the development of language* (paperback edn). London: Edward Arnold.

Halliday, M. A. K. & Hasan, R. (1976). *Cohesion in English*. London: Longman.

Hargreaves, D. (1967). *Social relations in a secondary school*. London: Routledge and Kegan Paul.

Harris, P. L. (1989). *Children and emotion: the development of psychological understanding*. Oxford: Blackwell.

Hart, K. M. (1981). *Children's understanding of mathematics, 11–16*. London: John Murray.

Heckhausen, H. (1982). The development of achievement motivation. In *Review of Child Development Research* (ed. W.W. Hartup), 6, 600–68.

Hewison, J. & Tizard, J. (1980). Parental involvement in reading attainment. *British Journal of Educational Psychology*, 50, 209–15.

Hickman, M. E. (1985). The implications of discourse skills in Vygotsky's development theory. In J. V. Wertsch (ed.), *Culture, communication and cognition: Vygotskian perspectives*. Cambridge: Cambridge University Press.

Hilgard, E. R. (ed.) (1964). *Theories of learning and instruction*. Chicago, Ill.: University of Chicago Press.

Hobsbaum, A., Peters, S. & Sylva, K. (1996). Scaffolding in reading recovery. *Oxford Review of Education*, 22 (1), 17–35

Holt, J. (1967). *How children fail*. New York: Pitman.

Howe, C., Tolmie, A. & Rodgers, C. (1990). Physics in the primary school: peer interaction and the understanding of floating and sinking. *European Journal of Psychology of Education*, 5 (4), 459–75.

Hoyles, C. & Sutherland, R. (1989). *Logo mathematics in the classroom*. London: Routledge.

Hulme, C. & Snowling, M. (1994). *Reading development and dyslexia*. London: Whurr Publishers.

Hundeide, K. (1985). The tacit background of children's judgements. In J.V. Wertsch (ed.), *Culture, communication and cognition: Vygotskian perspectives*. Cambridge: Cambridge University Press.

Isaacs, S. (1936). *Intellectual growth in young children*. London: Routledge.

Johnson-Laird, P. N. (1983). *Mental models*. Cambridge: Cambridge University Press.

Kail, R. (1979). *The development of memory in children*. San Francisco, Calif.: Freeman.

—— (1990). *The development of memory in children* (2nd edn). New York: W.H. Freeman.

Kaplan, E. J. (1969). *The acquisition and development of language*. Englewood Cliffs, N.J.: Prentice Hall. Cited in Menyuk (1971).

Kaput, J. & Maxwell-West, M. (1994). Missing-value proportional reasoning problems: factors affecting informal reasoning patterns. In G. Harel & J. Confrey (eds), *The development of multiplicative reasoning in the learning of mathematics*. Albany, NY: State University of New York Press.

Karmiloff-Smith, A. (1979). *A functional approach to child language: a study of determiners and reference*. London, New York, Melbourne: Cambridge University Press.

—— (1992). *Beyond modularity: a developmental perspective on cognitive science*. Cambridge, Mass.: MIT Press

Katz, S. & Lesgold, A. (1993). The role of the tutor in computer-based collaborative learning situations. In S. P. Lajoie and S. J. Derry (eds), *Computers as cognitive tools*. Hillsdale, N.J.: Lawrence Erlbaum.

Kempe, R. S. & Kempe, C.H. (1978). *Child abuse*. London: Fontana/Open Books.

Kempton, W. (1980). The rhythmic basis of interactional micro-synchrony. In M. Ritchie-Key (ed.), *The relationship of verbal and nonverbal communication*. The Hague: Mouton.

Keough, B. K. (1982). Children's temperament and teachers' decisions. In R. Porter & G. M. Collins (eds), *Temperamental differences in infants and young children*. London: Pitman.

Kochman, T. (1981). Classroom modalities: black and white communicative styles in the classroom. In N. Mercer (ed.), *Language in school and community*. London: Edward Arnold.

Labov, W. (1969). The logic of nonstandard English. In P. G. Giglioli (ed.), *Language and social context*. Harmondsworth: Penguin.

Lave, J. (1988). *Cognition in practice: mind, mathematics and culture in everyday life*. Cambridge: Cambridge University Press.

Light, P. & Gilmour, A. (1983). Conservation or conversation? Contextual facilitation of inappropriate conservation judgements. *Journal of Experimental Child Psychology*, 36, 356–63.

Light, P., Buckingham, N. & Roberts, A. H. (1979). The conservation task as an interactional setting. *British Journal of Educational Psychology*, 49, 304–10.

List, G. (1963). The boundaries of speech and song. *Ethnomusicology*, 7 (1), 1–16.

Lundeberg, I., Frost, J. & Petersen, O. P. (1988). Effects of an extensive program for stimulating phonological awareness in preschool children. *Reading Research Quarterly*, 23, 264–84.

Lunzer, E. A. (1973). Formal reasoning: a re-appraisal. In A. Floyd (ed.), *Cognitive development in the school years*. London: Croom Helm.

McNeill, D. (1970). *The acquisition of language*. Cambridge, Mass.: MIT Press.

Menyuk, P. (1971). *The acquisition and development of language*. Englewood Cliffs, N.J.: Prentice Hall.

Mercer, N. & Edwards, D. (1981). Ground rules for mutual understanding. In N. Mercer (ed.), *Language in school and community*. London: Edward Arnold.

Miller, G. A. (1956). The magical number seven plus or minus two: some limits on our capacity for processing information. *Psychological Review*, 63, 81–97.

Mohr, C. (1965). 'Head Start' plan for pupils begins. *New York Times*, 19 May.

Murphy, C. M. & Wood, D.J. (1982). Learning through media: a comparison of 4- to 8-year-old children's responses to filmed and pictorial instruction. *International Journal of Behavioral Development*, 5 (2), 195–216.

Newell, A. (1991). *Unified theories of cognition*. Cambridge, Mass.: Harvard University Press.

Newman, D., Griffin, P. & Cole, M. (1989). *The construction zone: working for cognitive change in school.* Cambridge: Cambridge University Press.

Newson, J. & Newson, E. (1974). Cultural aspects of child-rearing in an English speaking world. In *The Integration of a child into a social world.* Cambridge: Cambridge University Press.

Noelting, G. (1980). The development of proportional reasoning and the ratio concept. Part 1: Differentiation of stages. *Educational Studies in Mathematics,* 11, 217–53.

Norman K. (ed.) (1992) *Thinking voices: the work of the National Oracy Project.* London: Hodder and Stoughton.

Nunes, T. (1992). Ethnomathematics and everyday cognition. In *Handbook of research on mathematics teaching and learning.* New York: Macmillan.

Nunes, T. & Bryant, P. (1996). *Children doing mathematics.* Oxford, Blackwell.

Nunes, T., Schlieman, A.-L. & Carraher, D. (1993). *Street mathematics and school mathematics.* New York: Cambridge University Press.

Nuthall, G. & Church, J. (1973). Experimental studies of teaching behavior. In G. Chanan (ed.), *Towards a science of teaching.* Slough: NFER.

Oakhill, J., Yuill, N. & Parkin, A. (1986). On the nature of the difference between skilled and less-skilled comprehenders. *Journal of Research in Reading* 9, 80–91.

Olson, D. R. (1977). Oral and written language and the cognitive processes of children. *Journal of Communication,* 27 (3), 10–26.

Opie, I. & Opie, P. (1959). *The lore and language of schoolchildren.* Herts: Granada.

Palincsar, A. S. & Brown, A. L. (1984). *Reciprocal teaching of comprehension fostering and monitoring activities: cognition and instruction.* Hillsdale, N.J.: Lawrence Erlbaum.

Papert, S. (1980). *Mindstorms: children, computers and powerful ideas.* New York: Harvester Press.

—— (1994). *The children's machine.* Hemel Hempstead: Harvester Wheatsheaf.

Pavlov, I. P. & Anrep, G. V. (1927). *Conditioned reflexes.* London: Oxford University Press.

Perera, K. (1984). *Children's writing and reading: analysing classroom language.* London: Blackwell in association with André Deutsch.

Perner, J., Leekam, S. R. & Wimmer, H. (1987). Three-year-olds' difficulty with false belief: the case for a conceptual deficit. *British Journal of Developmental Psychology,* 5, 125–37.

Piaget, J. (1967). *Six psychological studies.* London: London University Press.

—— (1971). *Structuralism.* London: Routledge and Kegan Paul.

Pilling, D. & Pringle, M. K. (1978). *Controversial issues in child development.* London: Paul Elek.

Pine, J. & Martindale, H. (1996). Syntactic categories in the speech of young children: the case of the determiner. *Journal of Child Language,* 23, 369–95.

Pinker, S. (1989). *Learnability and cognition: the acquisition of verb-argument structures*. Cambridge, Mass.: Harvard University Press.

Pratt, M. W., Kerig, P., Cowan, P. A. & Cowan, C. P. (1988). Mothers and fathers teaching three-year-olds: authoritative parenting and adults' use of the zone of proximal development. *Developmental Psychology*, 24 (6) 832–9.

Redfield, D. L. & Rousseau, E. W. (1981). A meta-analysis of experimental research on teacher questioning behavior. *Review of Educational Research*, 51, 237–45.

Resnick, L. B. (1976). *The nature of intelligence*. Hillsdale, N.J.: Lawrence Erlbaum.

Resnick, L. B & Nelson-Le Gall, S. (in press). Socializing intelligence. In L. Smith & P. Tomlinson (eds), *Piaget, Vygotsky and Beyond*. London: Routledge.

Robinson, W. P. (1981). Language development in young children. In D. Fontana (ed.), *Psychology for teachers*. London: British Psychological Society and Macmillan.

—— (1986). Children's understanding of the distinction between messages and meanings: emergence and implications. In M. Richards & P. Light (eds), *Children of social worlds*. London: Polity Press in association with Blackwell.

Robitaille, D. F. & Travers, K. J. (1992). International studies of achievement in mathematics. In D. A. Grouws (ed.), *Handbook of research on mathematics teaching and learning*. New York: Macmillan.

Rogoff, B. (1990). *Apprenticeship in thinking: cognitive development in social context*. Oxford: Oxford University Press.

Rogoff, B., Ellis, S. & Gardner, W. (1984). Adjustment of adult–child instruction according to child's age and task. *Developmental Psychology*, 20,193–9.

Romaine, S. (1984). *The language of children and adolescents: the acquisition of communicative competence*. London: Blackwell.

Rose, S. & Blank, M. (1974). The potency of context in children's cognition. *Child Development*, 45, 499–502.

Rosenthal, R. & Jacobson, L. (1968). *Pygmalion in the classroom*. London: Holt, Rinehart and Winston.

Rowe, M. B. (1974). Wait-time and rewards as instructional variables, their influence on language, logic and fate control. I: Wait time. *Journal of Research in Science Teaching*, 11, 81–94.

Saxe, G. (1981). Body parts as numerals: a developmental analysis of numeration among the Oksapmin in Papua New Guinea. *Child Development*, 52, 306–16

Schoenfeld, A. H. (1988). When good teaching leads to bad results: the disasters of well-taught mathematics courses. *Educational Psychologist*, 23, 145–66.

—— (1992). Learning to think mathematically: problem solving, metacognition and sense making in mathematics. In D. A. Grouws (ed.), *Handbook of research on mathematics teaching and learning*. New York: Macmillan. 3345–70.

Schwartzman, H. B. (1978). *Transformations: the anthropology of children's play*. New York: Plenum Press.

Schwebel, M. & Raph, J. (eds) (1974). *Piaget in the classroom*. London: Routledge and Kegan Paul.

Scribner, S. (1986). Thinking in action: some characteristics of practical thought. In R. J. Sternberg and R. K. Wagner (eds), *Practical intelligence*. Cambridge: Cambridge University Press.

Serpell, R. (1976). *Culture's influence on behaviour*. London: Methuen.

Siegler, R. S. and Jenkins, E. (1989). *How children discover new strategies*. Hillsdale, N.J.: Lawrence Erlbaum.

Sigel, I. E. & McGillicuddy-Delisi, I. (1988) *Parents as teachers of their children in the development of oral and written language: readings in developmental and applied linguistics*. Norwood, N.J.: Ablex.

Skemp, R. R. (1971). *The psychology of learning mathematics*. Harmondsworth: Penguin.

Skinner, B. F. (1938). *The behavior of organisms*. New York: Appleton-Century-Crofts.

—— (1968). *The technology of teaching*. New York: Appleton-Century-Crofts.

Snow, R. E. & Yallow, E. (1982). Education and intelligence. In R.J. Sternberg (ed.), *Handbook of human intelligence*. Cambridge: Cambridge University Press.

Sternberg, R. J. (1985). *Beyond I.Q.: a triarchic theory of human intelligence*. New York: Cambridge University Press.

Swift, J. N. & Gooding, C. T. (1983). Interaction of wait time, feedback and questioning instruction in middle school science teaching. *Journal of Research in Science Teaching*, 20, 721–30.

Tizard, B. & Hodges, J. (1978). The effect of early institutional rearing on the development of eight-year-old children. *Journal of Child Psychology and Psychiatry*, 15, 99–118.

Underwood, G. (1979). Memory systems and the reading process. In M. M. Gruneberg &. P. Morris (eds), *Applications of memory*. London: Academic Press.

Underwood, G. & Batt, V. (1996). *Reading and understanding*. Oxford: Blackwell.

Underwood, J. & Brown, J. (1997) *Integrated learning systems*. Oxford: Heinemann.

VanLehn, K., Jones, R.M. & Chi, M.T.H. (1991). A model of the self-explanation effect. *Journal of the Learning Sciences*, 2 (1), 1–59.

Vergnaud, G. (1982). A classification of cognitive tasks and operations of thought involved in addition and subtraction problems. In T. P. Carpenter,

J. M. Moser & T. A. Romberg (eds), *Addition and subtraction: A cognitive perspective*. Hillsdale, N.J.: Lawrence Erlbaum.

Vurpillot, E. (1976). *The visual world of the child*. London: Allen and Unwin.

Vygotsky, L.S. (1962). *Thought and language*. Cambridge, Mass.: MIT Press.

Walkerdine, V. (1982). From context to text: a psychosemiotic approach to abstract thought. In M. Beveridge (ed.), *Children thinking through language*. London: Edward Arnold.

Wardhaugh, R. (1985). *How conversation works*. Oxford and New York: Blackwell in association with André Deutsch.

Wason, P. C. & Johnson-Laird, P.N. (1972). *Psychology of reasoning (structure and content)*. London: Batsford.

Wells, C. G. (1981). *Learning through interaction: the study of language development*. Cambridge: Cambridge University Press.

Wells, C. G. (1992). The centrality of talk in education. In K. Norman (ed.), *Thinking voices*. London: Hodder & Stoughton.

Wells, C. G. & Raben, B. (1978). *Children learning to read*. Final report to Social Science Research Council No. HR/3797/1.

Wertsch, J. V. (ed.). (1984). *Culture, communication and cognition: Vygotskian perspectives*. Cambridge: Cambridge University Press.

Wiener, M., Shilkret, R. & Devoe, S. (1980). Acquisition of communication competence: is language enough? In M. Ritchie-Key (ed.), *The relationship of verbal and nonverbal communication*. The Hague: Mouton.

Wolters, M. A. D. (1986). Rules in arithmetic: learning the basic facts. In F. Lowenthal & F. Vandamme (eds), *Pragmatics and education*. New York: Plenum Press.

Wood, D. J., (1986) Instruction, learning and deafness. In E. De Corte, J. G. L. C. Lodewijks, R. Parmentier & P. Span (eds), *Learning and instruction*. Leuven: Leuven University Press and Oxford: Pergamon Press.

Wood, D. J., & O'Malley, C. (1996). Collaborative learning between peers: an overview. *Educational Psychology in Practice*, 11 (4), 4–9.

Wood, D. J. & Wood, H. A. (1988). Questioning versus student initiative. In J. T. Dillon (ed.), *Questioning and discussion: a multi-disciplinary study*. Norwood, N.J: Ablex.

Wood, D. J. Bruner, J. S. & Ross, G. (1976). The role of tutoring in problem solving. *Journal of Child Psychology and Psychiatry*, 17 (2), 89–100.

Wood, D. J. McMahon, L. & Cranstoun, Y. (1980) *Working with under fives*. London: Grant McIntyre.

Wood, D. J., Wood, H. A. & Middleton, D. J. (1978). An experimental evaluation of four face-to-face teaching strategies. *International Journal of Behavioral Development*, 1, 131–47.

Wood, D. J., Wood, H.A., Griffiths, A. & Howarth, I. (1986). *Teaching and talking with deaf children*. Chichester: John Wiley.

Wood, H. A., & Wood, D. J. (1983). Questioning the preschool child. *Educational Review*, 35 (15), 149–62.

Wood, H. A., Wood, D.J., Kingsmill, M. C., French, J. R. & Howarth, S.P. (1984). The mathematical achievements of deaf children from different educational environments. *British Journal of Educational Psychology*, 54, 254–64.

INDEX

ability
  and effort 282–3, 286
  and motivation 286–8
abstract thinking 9–10
  and literacy 182
accommodation, in Piaget's theory
  53–4
achievement, differences in school
  276
action
  and learning theory 5
  and self-directed problem-solving
  5
  thought as internalized 21–4
addition (numbers) 230–4, 237–8,
  239, 252–3
adolescents
  change in cognitive abilities
  186–90
  and communication skills 179
  speech and writing 210–13
adult–child tutoring situations
  98–102
adults
  age and experience 93
  and information-processing
  theory 33–4
  and logical problems 193–5
  mental models 70, 71
  reasoning 9, 183, 185

rehearsal and memorizing 76
age
  and cognitive ability 108–9,
  186–7
  and language learning 136–7
  of one-to-one correspondence in
  counting 230
  and production rules 103–4, 109
  and theory of mind tasks 161
algorithms 251
alliteration 215
ambiguity, and language acquisition
  118–20
Anderson, John 102–3, 104–5, 106,
  107, 109, 293
Assessment of Performance Unit
  258
assimilation, in Piaget's theory 53–4
attention 283–5
  children's patterns of 82–9
Austin, G. A. 9

babies see infants
Bartlett, Sir F. 14
Batt, V. 203, 205, 207
Beer, S. 31
behaviourism
  and computer-based tutors 107
  see also S–R (Stimulus–Response)
  theory

Bell, A. W.   261
Bell, R. Q.   284, 285
Bennett, M.   290
Bereiter, C.   115
Berlin, L. J.   63, 174
Bernstein, B.   7–8, 111–14
Bindman, M.   216, 217
birth order of children, and theory of mind   161–2
black children   113–16
Blank, M.   63, 174
Boden, M.   8, 9, 185
body language   145–7, 150
boys, 'feedback' in mathematics lessons   287
Bradley, L.   215
Brown, A. L.   220, 221, 222, 282
Brown, G.   115, 168–9, 171–2, 173, 178, 202
Bruner, J. S.   27, 38, 39, 41, 87, 96, 97, 109, 236
   and the child as problem-solver 168
   and communication   179
   and instruction   108
   on learning and schooling   15–16
   and mathematics learning   228–9, 251, 268, 293
   and Piagetian theory   8–10, 183
   research into adult–child interaction   98–9
   and speech development in infants 148
   on theory of mind performance 162, 166, 167
   and Vygotsky   11
Bryant, P.   94–5, 96, 215, 216, 217
   and mathematics   230, 235, 237, 238, 239, 240, 242, 253, 256, 257, 265, 266, 275
Buckingham, N.   64
Bullock Report (1975)   173, 212
Butterworth, G.   147

Campiogne, J. C.   221, 222
card-turning experiment   192–3, 195

cardinal numbers   235–7
Carew, J. V.   100
Carey, S.   44, 49
Carraher, D.   255
Case, R.   49, 69–70, 165, 222–3, 278, 281, 282
Castle, E. B.   1
Cazden, C. B.   224, 289
centration   54–6, 61, 73
channel capacity   34
Chase, W. G.   35, 200
chat   169
Cheng, P. C.-H.   223
Cheng, P. W.   196, 198
Chi, M. T. H.   44, 92, 93, 107, 108
Chinese-speaking children, and mathematics learning   254–5
Chomsky, Noam   6, 7, 8, 46, 115, 116–23, 127, 140, 141–2, 192
   on ambiguity and paraphrase 118–20
   and the LAD (Language Acquisition Device)   120–1, 123
Church, J.   175
Clark, E. V.   128, 129, 142
Clark, M.   220
class *see* socio-economic class
classes of objects, children's understanding of   60–2
classroom discourse   173–8, 179, 180
classroom practices, cross-cultural comparisons of   291
Clay, M. M.   224, 289
Cochran, E.   147
cognitive apprenticeship   294
cognitive development
   and age   108–9
   and language acquisition   117, 135
   and mathematics learning   274
   and modular theories of mind   279–80
   and socio-cultural theories   278
   see also thought

Cole, M.   80, 177, 194, 195, 196
commas, avoiding ambiguity by
    205–6
communication
    between teachers and children
        139, 173–8, 179, 180
    and birth order   161–2
    in Bruner's theories   10
    and child development   17
    children and Piaget's
        questions   63–5, 69
    developing skills in   173–8
    and electronic communication
        systems   11–12
    games   163–5
    and information-giving   167–72
    and mathematics learning   227
    pragmatic features of   64–5
    problems in children   110, 173,
        178
    and representational competence
        165–7
    synchronization of   176
    verbal and non-verbal   144–50,
        176
    in Vygotsky's theories   11, 37
    see also narratives
commutativity   188
competence, change in
    representational   165–7
computer-based teaching
    systems   102–3, 105–7, 294–5
computers, and the human brain   48
concentration   283–5
    children's powers of   74, 75, 82–9
    and expertise   92
    in traditional societies   81
conceptual development, and
    mathematical understanding
    239–40, 266
conceptual understanding   189–90
concrete operations
    and deaf children   184
    development of   29, 57–9
    and language   62, 159
    and transition to formal

operational thinking   183,
    187–90
conflict, and the concrete operations
    stage   58–9
conservations, in Piaget's theory
    56–7
constructivism   39, 50, 278
contrived encounters   16
conversation *see* talking
Correa   244
Costello, J.   261
counting
    on a base of 10   251, 266
    one-to-one correspondence
        229–30, 235
    out, on, up and down   230–4
Cranstoun, Y.   151
creative thinking   38
'critical periods' for learning   5–6
Crystal, D.   123, 144
CSMS (Concepts in Secondary
    Mathematics and Science)
    study   258–65, 269, 270
culture
    and classroom practices   291
    and human development   17–18,
        40–1, 49, 70
    and intelligence   281–2
    and mathematics   225, 270–2
    and memory   81–2
    and non-verbal
        communication   145
    and number systems   254–5
    and the transmission of
        knowledge   27
Cunningham, A. E.   215
curriculum
    mathematics   266–9
    secondary school   181, 186
cybernetics   31–2

Darwin, C.   46
De Groot, A. D. Van   35
de-centring   56, 159, 202
deaf children
    and literacy   184, 213

and mathematical ability 227
decontextualization
  and literacy 201–2
  and mathematics 225, 256
deictic forms, and language
    learning 129–31, 136
deictic indexical signs 154, 155,
    156
DeLoache, J. S. 100
developmental theory 8
disequilibrium 56
division (numbers) 242–7, 249
Donaldson, M. 68, 183, 196, 229,
    268
Dunn, Judy 161, 162, 166, 167
Dweck, C. S. 287, 288

educability 276
  and questioning children 176
  and social background 138–40
Educational Priority Areas 114
effort
  and ability 282–3, 286
  and individual differences in
    development 47–8
  and motivation 286–8
egocentric, pre-operational children
    as 65–8, 72, 159
egocentric speech 30–1, 154
Einstein, A. 9, 226
elaborated speech codes 111–13
electronic communication systems,
    and communications theory
    11–12
Elkind, D. 27
Ellis, S. 100
embedded figures, perception of
    90–1
emotional dimensions of experience,
    and theory of mind 162
empiricism 46
enactive representation 228
Englemann, S. 115
errors
  and Intelligent Tutoring Systems
    (ITS) 106

and language acquisition 131,
    135
ethnicity *see* black children
evolution, and neo-nativist theories
    of development 46
expertise
  development of 47–8
  and experience 91–3, 96
  and information-processing
    theory 34, 35–7, 44, 73
  local 98
  and problem-solving 105, 107–8
  in reading and writing 208
explanation in learning 108
Eysenck, H. J. 280

false-belief paradigm 160–1, 165
Feldman, C. F. 224
Ferrara, R. A. 221, 282
first-born children, and theory of
    mind 161
Fischer, K. W. 70
five-year-olds
  and counting 230–2, 235
  and memorizing 78–9
  and multiplication 240–1
Fodor, J. 47, 48, 121, 136
formal operational thinking 183,
    191, 197–90
four-year-olds
  communication games 163–5
  and multiplication 240–1
  narratives 155–6, 157
fractions (numbers) 245–7
Frazier, L. 205
French-speaking children, and
    language acquisition 131–4
Frost, J. 215
Frydman, O. 240
Fuson, K. C. 230, 234, 237, 238,
    239, 254, 266, 267, 270, 272,
    291–2

Gagne 97
Galton, M. 290
Gardner, H. 48, 281, 288

Gardner, W. 100
Gelman, R. 230
gender, and 'feedback' in
     mathematics lessons 287
genetic epistemology 32
Gentner, D. 45
gestures 145–6
Ghiselin, B. 226–7
Gibson, J. J. 12
girls, 'feedback' in mathematics
     lessons 287
Glaser, R. 44, 92
Gleitman, L. R. 124, 153
goals
     and information-processing
          theory 13
     and Intelligent Tutoring Systems
          (ITS) 106
     of schools 175
Gooding, C. T. 176
Goodnow, J. J. 9
Goody, E. N. 170
Goswami, U. 215
graphemes 203
Greer, B. 238, 246, 250, 267
Griffin, P. 177
group work 289–91
guided participation 101–2

Halford, G. S. 45, 49, 69–70, 71,
     95, 96, 178, 222–3
     and change in representational
          competence 165–6
     and mental models 198–9
     and processing capacity of
          children 200
Halliday, M. A. K. 154, 180
Hargreaves, D. 287
Harris, P. L. 167
Hart, K. M. 258, 284
Hasan, R. 154
Head Start programme (United
     States) 114–15
Heckhausen, H. 286
Hickman, M. E. 153–5, 159, 168
Hilgard, E. 2, 4, 5, 6, 7, 10

Hobsbawm, A. 289
Hodges, J. 285
Holt, J. 286
Holyoak, K. J. 196
homophones 204
Howe, C. 290
Hoyles, C. 293
Hulme, C. 215
Hundeide, K. 65

iconic representation 228
illiteracy 212–13
individual differences in development
     47–8
infants
     assimilation and accommodation
          53–4
     language acquisition 126–7, 131,
          140–1, 144–5, 147–50
     and neo-nativist theories of
          development 48
     Piaget's observations of 21–2
     verbal and non-verbal
          communication 147–50
informal teaching 16–17
information technology in
     schools 292
information-giving 167–72
     speech 169, 170–2
information-processing theory
     12–14, 32–7, 38
     and adults 33–4
     and children 34, 36–7, 199–200
     and expertise 34, 35–7, 44, 73
     learning and instruction 102–3
     and mental models 45
'inspection' tasks, and memorization
     85–8
institutional context, and language
     116
instruction
     adult–child tutoring situations
          98–102
     effective 97
     and information processing
          102–3

and procedural learning 108
and Vygotsky's theories 10–11,
    26–7, 73, 94, 98
intelligence
    conceptualizing human 280–2
    and instruction 26–7
    and motivation 288
    'multiple intelligences' 280–1
Intelligent Tutoring Systems
    (ITS) 103, 105–7, 293
interest, and individual differences in
    development 47
internalization 165
interpretation, and reading 206
intralinguistic indexical
    relationships 154, 156
IQ tests 280
Isaacs, Susan 59–60

Jacobson, L. 138
Japan
    attitudes to effort and
        achievement 287–8
    classroom practices 291
    mathematics learning 254, 270,
        271
Jenkins, E. 232
Johnson, Lyndon B. 114, 138, 140
Johnson-Laird, P. N. 45, 185, 192,
    198, 222, 223
Jones, R. M. 107

Kail, R. 74
Kaplan, E. J. 148
Kaput, J. 268
Karmiloff-Smith, A. 43–4, 49,
    131–3, 142, 178, 211
    and children's narratives 154,
        155–6, 157–9
    on learning to read 204
    and representational re-description
        136–7, 157–9, 233
Katz, S. 294
Kempe, C. H. 285
Kempe, R. S. 285
Kempton, W. 146

Kendrick, C. 161
Keough, B. K. 74
kinesics (analysis of movement), and
    speech 145–7
knowledge, distinct systems of 43–4
Kuchemann, D. 261

Labov, W. 116, 178
LAD (Language Acquisition Device)
    120–1, 123
language
    in Bruner's theories 10
    Piaget and the importance of
        60–3
    and play on words 214
    spoken and written 181
    and stage of intellectual
        development 6–7
    and thought 8, 25–6, 117, 142,
        159–65
    in Vygotsky's theories 11
language learning 110–43, 276
    ambiguity and paraphrase
        118–20
    and birth order 161
    Chomskian theory 115, 116–23,
        127, 140, 141–2
    'critical period' 6
    and deictic forms 129–31, 136
    discontinuity and change 124–5
    early stages of development
        123–4
    infants 126–7, 131, 140–1,
        144–5, 147–50
    and learning to read and write
        136
    linguistic variations and social
        class 7–8, 110–15, 138
    listening and talking 126–9
    and literacy 125–6
    maturation and 46–7, 122
    meaning and 'structure
        dependency' 122–3
    representational re-description
        136–7, 157–9
    and self-correction 131–6, 152–3,

156–7
and self-regulation   108
and teacher expectations   138–9
see also speech; talking
Lave, J.   255
learning by rote   52
learning difficulties, and MPAs
    (minor physical abnormalities)
    284
'learning how to mean'   180
learning theory
    decline of   4–8
    rise of   2–4
learning to read   136, 180, 181–2,
    200, 202–8
    and phonological awareness
        215–16
    and word play   214–15
Leekam, S. R.   165
Lesgold, A.   294
Light, P.   64
linguistic deprivation   7–8
linguistic variations   7–8, 110–15
List, G.   146
listening
    children as listeners   163, 172
    talking and language learning
        126–9
literacy   181–224
    becoming literate   213–16
    and decontextualization   201–2
    and development   223–4
    and illiteracy   212–13
    and language learning   125–6
    and logic   182–5, 190–5, 222–3
    non-literate cultures   184, 194–5
    and speech   211–12
local expertise   98
logic
    in Bruner's theories   10
    and development   69
    and literacy   182–5, 190–5,
        222–3
    and mathematics learning   268,
        273–4
    and memory   93–6

and mental models   45
and neo-Piagetian theorists   72,
    222–3
Piagetian theory   9, 24, 68–9,
    182–5, 222
and reasoning   195–200
LOGO programming, and teaching
    machines   292–3
Lundeberg, I.   215
Luria   17, 41, 49, 97, 253

McGillicuddy-Delisi, I.   176
Mack   247
McMahon, L.   151
McNeill, D.   120
Martindale, H.   123
mathematic models in
    psychology   12
mathematics   225–75, 276, 293
    abilities and misconceptions
        258–62
    and abstraction   225
    children's achievements and
        problems in   257–8
    and conceptual understanding
        239–40, 266
    concrete and formal operations in
        189
    cross-cultural studies of
        mathematics teaching   225,
        270–2
    CSMS (Concepts in Secondary
        Mathematics and Science)
        study   258–65, 269, 270
    curriculum   266–9
    and decontextualization   225, 256
    and the development of reasoning
        183
    difficulties in teaching and learning
        265–9
    discourse and everyday language
        261–2
    'feedback' in lessons   287
    instruction, interview and dialogue
        262–5
    and science   250

and situated learning 42
in street and school 255–7, 275,
    278–9
theory and research into
    learning 226–57
theory, technology and
    teaching 291–4
see also numbers
maturation
    and culture 49
    and language learning 47–8, 122
    and mental modules 45–9
Maxwell-West, M. 268
meaning, and 'structure
    dependency' 122–3
Meck, E. 230
memory
    and counting 230–1
    development 77–9
    and expertise 91–3
    limitations of children's 70
    and logic 93–6
    rehearsal and organization 74–7,
        81, 82–5
    and schooling 80–2
mental models 49
    adults compared with children
        70, 71
    drawing inferences from 70–1
    and information-processing
        theory 45
    and logical reasoning 197,
        198–200
mental modules, and maturation
    45–9
mental operations, in Piaget's theory
    56–8
Menyuk, P. 148
Middleton, D. J. 99
Miller, George 33, 35
MIN strategy in counting 232, 233
model-building tasks, and
    memorization 87–8
modular theories of mind 43–4,
    47–8, 49, 50, 277, 279–80
    and language learning 136, 137,
        140–1
    and 'multiple intelligences' 280–1
modularity theory 277
Mohr, C. 114
morphemes, and language learning
    124, 200–1
mothers, teaching young children
    99, 100
motivation 286–8
    and development 50
    and individual differences in
        development 47–8
MPAs (minor physical
    abnormalities) 284–5
multiplication (numbers) 240–2,
    247, 248, 249
Murphy, C. M. 87

narratives
    and cognition 159–60
    and conversation 150–3
    development of narrative skills
        153–7
    and information-giving speech
        171–2
    and literacy 211
    and representational re-description
        157–9
    and theory of mind 167
nativist theories of development 46,
    50, 178
'natural line', and 'cultural line' in
    development 38–9
Nelson-Le Gall, S. 288
neo-nativist theories of development
    46, 48, 49, 277
    and perception of human speech
        121
neo-Piagetian theory 2, 43–4, 49,
    178, 277
    and change in representational
        competence 165–6
    see also Halford, G. S.; Karmiloff-
        Smith, A.
neo-Vygotskian perspective, and
    questioning 177

Newell, A.   280
Newman, D.   177
Newson, E.   81–2
Newson, J.   81–2
Noelting, G.   247–8
Norman, K.   143, 173
numbers
    addition   230–4, 237–8, 239,
        252–3
    cardinal   235–7
    counting   229–34
    derived number understanding
        236
    division   242–7, 249
    extensive and intensive aspects of
        247–50, 259
    fractions   245–7
    language variation in reading,
        writing and using   254–5
    multiplication   240–2, 247, 248,
        249
    subtraction   234, 237–8, 239
    understanding written   250–4
    see also mathematics
Nunes, T.   216, 217, 230, 235, 237,
    238, 239, 240, 242, 251, 253,
    255, 256, 257, 265, 266, 272,
    275
Nuthall, G.   175

Oakhill, J.   219
Olson, David   184
O'Malley, C.   289
only children, and theory of mind
    161
operational thinking   25
    transition from pre-operational
        thinking to   94
    transition to formal   183, 197–90
operations, Piaget on mental actions
    and   22–3, 56–9
Opie, I. and P.   214
oracy   143, 173
oral mathematics   255–6, 266

Palinscar, A. S.   220

Papert, Seymour   292–3
paraphrase, and language acquisition
    118–20
parents, questioning children   175–6
Parkin, A.   219
part-whole relations, in mathematics
    245–7
partitive problems   244
passive voice structures   209–10
patterns, and mathematics   247
Pavlov, I.   2–3, 4
perception   88
    and expertise   92
    theories of   89–91
    and thought   24–5
Perera, K.   202, 203, 204, 206, 208,
    209, 211, 212, 219, 220
Perner, Josef   165, 166, 167
Peters, S.   289
Peterson, O. P.   215
phonemes   200, 202–3
phonological awareness, and learning
    to read   215–16
Piaget, J.   1, 2, 5–7, 11, 17, 21–6,
    39, 42, 45, 51–72
    and adolescent thinking   183,
        191–2, 197–90
    assimilation and accommodation
        53–4
    and assisted performance   96
    and Bruner   8–10
    centration, disequilibrium and de-
        centring   54–8, 72
    and the child as problem-solver
        168
    and Chomsky's theory of language
        acquisition   116–17, 118
    conflict, instruction and
        accommodation   58–9
    critique of theory   59–68
    and cybernetics   32
    and intelligence testing   280
    on language and cognition   24–6,
        142, 159
    legacy   68–9
    on logical thinking and

literacy 182–5, 222
and mathematics learning 226,
227–8, 229, 239, 240, 241, 257,
265, 273, 293
and pre-operational thinking
65–8, 72, 73, 94, 99
and procedural approaches to
teaching 109
and readiness for learning 8,
26–7, 37, 108
restructuring 59
stages of development 6–7, 8, 37,
52–3
on talking and thinking 27–31
tests of one-to-one correspondence
230
see also concrete operations; neo-
Piagetian theory
pictures, perception of 88, 89–91
Pilling, D. 139
Pine, J. 123
Pinker, S. 121
plural words, and language
development 131–3, 137
plurality, and totality 133–4
poverty
and educational politics 114–15
and school achievement 285
pragmatic features of communication
64–5
Pratt, M. W. 100
pre-operational children
and assisted performance 99–100
as egocentric 65–8, 72, 159
pre-operational thinking 65–8, 72,
73, 94
and lack of experience 96
pre-school children
and memorizing 77–8
questioning 171
and talking 28–31, 149–50
Pribram 4–5
Pringle, M. K. 139
problem-solving
'authentic' 294
Bruner's study of 9, 168

experts 105, 107–8
and language learning 125
in mathematics 256–7, 270,
274
'seriation' tasks 94–5
procedural knowledge 189–90
productions (situation-action) rules
103–5, 109
pronouns, in children's narratives
152–3, 154, 157, 159
prosody, in written English 205–8
psychological theories, and practices
of education 277–9
punctuation, in written
English 205–8

questions
asked by parents 175–6
asked in school 170–1, 174–7
cultural variations in questioning
children 101
and information-seeking 170
quotitive problems 244

Raph, J. 8, 97, 185
Rayner, K. 205
readiness for learning 8, 26–7, 37,
108
reading
comprehension abilities 219–22
and literacy 186
see also learning to read
Reading Recovery approach 289
reasoning 19–21
and literacy 125, 182, 184
and logic 195–200
and maturation 47
verbal 180, 183–4
receptive language ability 126–7
reciprocal teaching 221–2
Redfield, D. L. 175
Rees, E. 44, 92
'registers' of classroom discourse
173–8
rehearsal, and memorization 75–6,
81, 82–5

reinforcement, and learning theory 2–5, 6
remembering *see* memory
representational competence, change in 165–7
representational re-description, in language learning 136–7, 157–9, 233
Resnick, L. B. 271, 288
restricted speech codes 111–13
restructuring, in Piaget's theory 59
rhyming 215
Roberts, A. H. 64
Robinson, Elizabeth 163–4, 166, 167
Robinson, Peter 141, 163–4, 166, 167
Robitaille, D. F. 257
Rodgers, C. 290
Rogoff, B. 100, 101, 161
Romaine, S. 202, 211
Roman number system 251
Rose, S. A. 63, 174
Rosenbluth, Arturo 31
Rosenthal, R. 138
'Rosenthal effect' 139
Ross, G. 99
Rousseau, E. W. 175
Rowe, M. B. 176

S–R (Stimulus–Response) theory 3, 12, 107, 293
Saxe, G. 251
scaffolding 99–101, 103, 289, 294
Schlieman, A.-L. 255
Schoenfeld, A. H. 247, 270, 272, 293–4
schooling 15–16
and memory 80–2
schools
information technology in 292
'registers' of classroom discourse 173–8
use of language in 170–2
Schwartzman, H. B. 214
Schwebel, M. 8, 97, 185

science, and mathematics 250
Scribner, S. 80, 255
secondary schools, and literacy 181, 186
self-correction 282
and decontextualization 201–2
and information-giving 168
and language learning 131–6, 152–3, 156–7, 179
self-regulation 73, 98, 108, 200–1
and concentration 283
and development 109
and 'inspection' tasks 87
and language 108
in mathematics 264, 270
and reading comprehension 220–2
and writing 208–10
sensory-motor development 22, 30
'seriation' tasks 94–5
Serpell, R. 88
seven-year-olds, narratives 156–7
Sheffield 97
siblings, and theory of mind 161–2, 166
Siegler, R. S. 104, 232, 233, 234, 237
Sigel, I. E. 176
Simon, H. A. 35, 223
singular and plural determinators, and language acquisition 131–3
situated action theory 42–3, 278–9
situated learning 42–3
situation-action (production) rules 103–5, 109
Skemp, R. R. 229
skills, and information-processing theory 13–14
Skinner, B. F. 3–4, 97, 292, 293
Snowling, M. 215
social constructivist theories of development 39, 42, 50, 166
social context, and language 116
social interactions, and child development 16–17

socio-cultural theorists 277
socio-economic class
  and educability 138–40
  and language learning 7–8,
    110–15, 138
Sowder 238, 240
speech
  chat 169
  dramatic effect in 210
  egocentric 30–1, 154
  information-giving 169, 170–2
  and kinesics (analysis of
    movement) 145–7
  and learning to read 202–8
  and literacy 184, 211–12, 213
  'paralinguistic' features of 145,
    148–9, 169
  'prosodic' features of 148, 200–1
  restricted and elaborated codes
    111–13
  and spelling 216–17
  stress in 208, 209–10
  see also language learning;
    narratives; talking
spelling 216–18
spontaneous encounters 16–17
stages of development (Piaget) 6–7,
    8, 37, 52–3
  and talking 28–9
Sternberg, R. J. 281
Stevens, A. L. 45
stress
  and learning to read 207
  in speech 208, 209–10
  in writing 208–9
subtraction (numbers) 234, 237–8,
    239
Sutherland, R. 293
Swift, J. N. 176
Sylva, K. 289
symbolic representation 228–9
syntax 216–18
  and literacy 184–5

talking
  children overhearing

conversations 163
  development of narrative
    skills 153–7
  and language learning 115–16,
    126–9, 138, 140
  learning to talk 6, 7
  in school 170–2
  and thinking 6, 19–21, 27–31
  see also language learning;
    narratives; speech
task induction 100
teachers
  and children-as-learners 18–19
  and children's powers of
    concentration 74
  and classroom discourse 174–8,
    179
  discourse with children 151–3
  expectations and language learning
    138–9
  and intervention programmes
    289–90
  and 'schedules of reinforcement'
    3–4
teaching machines 292–3
ten-year-olds, narratives 155, 157
theorems-in-action 236
thinking
  creative thinking 38
  and learning 18
  and talking 6, 19–21, 27–31
third persons, and theory of mind
    166–7
thought
  as internalized action 21–4
  and language 8, 25–6, 117, 142,
    159–65
  and perception 24–5
three-year-olds, and theory of mind
    160–1
Tizard, B. 285
Tolmie, A. 290
traditional societies
  and memory 80–1
  and schooling 82
training, computer-based 294

transitive inferences, children's ability to make   94–5, 96
Travers, K. J.   257
tutor-assisted learning   102

Underwood, G.   203, 205, 207, 295
United Kingdom
   Educational Priority Areas   114
   illiteracy   212
United States
   children with reading and writing problems   220–2
   computer-based teaching systems   295
   educational politics   113–15
   illiteracy   212
   Project Head Start   114–15

VanLehn, K.   107, 108
verbal and non-verbal communication   144–50
verbs, spelling and syntax   216–18
Vergnaud, G.   232, 236, 237, 266
Vurpillot, E.   85
Vygotsky, L. S.   17, 26–31, 37–9, 40–3, 49, 72
   and communication   179
   and the development of literacy   182
   and instruction   10–11, 26–7, 73, 94, 98
   and internalization   165
   on language and cognition   159–60
   and mathematics learning   226, 271
   'natural line' and 'cultural line' in development   38–9
   and Piagetian theory   96, 183
   and self-regulation   73, 98, 108,

200–1, 208, 220, 221
   and written language   224
   and the zone of proximal development   26–7, 97–102, 289

Waldrop, M. F.   284, 285
Wanner, E.   124, 153
Wardhaugh, R.   169, 177
Wason, P. C.   192, 193, 195
Wells, C. G.   100, 164, 171, 177, 179
Wertsch, J. V.   10, 39
Wiener, N.   31
Williamson, J.   290
Wimmer, H.   165
Wolters, M. A. D.   227
Wood, D. J.   87, 98–9, 151, 174, 184, 227, 289
Wood, H. A.   99, 174, 227
word play   214–15
written language
   in adolescence   210–13
   and decontextualization   201–2
   and learning to read   202–8
   and learning to write   136, 180, 181–2, 200, 201
   planning and self-regulation   208–10
   prosody and punctuation   205–8
   spelling and syntax   216–18
   structural complexity of   220
   and theories of human development   48–9

Yuill, N.   219

zone of proximal development   26–7, 97–102, 289